Shaft of a bronze thymiaterion
(incense burner), Etruscan,
5th century BCE, bronze,
height: 16.7 cm, The Metropolitan
Museum of Art, New York,
Fletcher Fund, 1927.

Censer in the form of a mythical beast, China, early 17th century, porcelain (Jingdezhen ware), 17.8 × 24.8 cm, The Metropolitan Museum of Art, New York, Purchase, Bequests of William Rhinelander Stewart and Matilda E. Frelinghuysen, Gift of R. Thornton Wilson, in memory of Florence Ellsworth Wilson, Purchase by subscription, and Gift of Edgar Worch, 2018.

HOLY SMOKE
CENSERS ACROSS CULTURES

EDITED BY
BEATE FRICKE

HIRMER

Censer with cover, Japan, 1750,
stoneware covered with glaze
(Bizen ware), The Metropolitan
Museum of Art, New York,
gift of Mrs. V. Everit Macy, 1923.

Censer with floral design in red paint on white background, Egypt, ca. 3850–2960 BCE, pottery, The Metropolitan Museum of Art, New York, Rogers Fund, 1907.

Incense burner, Costa Rica or Nicaragua, 7th–12th century, ceramic, 81.3 × 31.8 cm, The Metropolitan Museum of Art, New York, The Michael C. Rockefeller Memorial Collection, Bequest of Nelson A. Rockefeller, 1979.

Bronze bowl from a thymiaterion (incense burner), Etruscan, late 4th century BCE, Bronze, height: 11.3 cm, The Metropolitan Museum of Art, New York, Rogers Fund, 1903.

Figure 1
Peruvian Copal.
Myvision, Adobe Stock,
No. 482694966.

INTRODUCTION:
CENSERS ACROSS CULTURES
Beate Fricke

Figure 1

A chunk of copal [Figure 1], grains of incense—applying heat to these substances produces not only swaths of smoke but also intense fragrant odors.
These "vibrant matters" have intense impacts on both sight and smell, obscuring vision through billows of smoke and creating, through dominant
odors, an alteration of sensual experience that can shift perception of space,
and even sometimes of time.[1] But these substances, to produce such dazzling
effects, have to be heated by fire. This requires a vessel that can hold the
transformative, but also sinister glow of burning charcoal. Such vessels for
burning resin are called censers, or thuribles, and can come in all kinds of
shapes, sizes, materials, and designs. Some are extremely simple, others
lavishly ornamented. They were made across the globe.

The burning of incense is, in fact, one of the most pervasive religious
practices both today and throughout history. Fragrant incense smoke filling
the air is an aspect found in almost every cultic tradition, whether polytheistic or monotheistic, whether in the ancient Near East, or medieval Europe.[2]
Censers are thus ubiquitous among religious paraphernalia on a truly global scale. They were produced in very simple shapes and materials as well as
elaborate and expensive luxury objects. Surprisingly, however, little scholarly attention has been given to censers and the rituals they facilitate.[3] Censers were involved in rituals of opposed and often very distinct spheres from
the private to the public, from the sacred to the profane. Censers can heal,
cause miracles, cross religious boundaries, or become integrated into new
rituals. Censers and the incense required for their use connect the different
yet intrinsically interlaced spheres of trade, health care, religion, ecology,
philosophy, politics, and art.

Censers therefore invite us to think about the intersection of these
domains. The study of censers is particularly timely in the fields of the history of religion, art history, archeology, material culture, and anthropology.
The combination of the solid censer and the ephemeral smoke produced by
the burning of incense offers a fertile ground for examining questions central to all of these fields of study regarding the relation between the material and the immaterial, and between artifacts, biotic substances, and codified practices. Centering the censer thus not only places the object in a
constellation of other religious artifacts, but also relocates the importance
of rituals that have long been placed at the margins of the study of religion,
art, and cultic practices.

Through these objects we can discern traces of a shifting historical,
artistic, and religious record. This is true in spite of the fact that, where most
pre-modern religious cultures are concerned, we have scant and scattered
written information about their making and use. Yet their forms themselves
reveal the ways in which the contexts and spaces through which the objects
circulated changed over time in response to new patterns of making, consumption, and cultural exchange. These material records of multiple nodes
and modes of contact between people, places, and epistemologies make themselves visible in changes to the censers' morphologies and ornamentation.
Examining this material and visual record can thus suggest not only how
these objects reflect history, but also change how history is perceived and

recounted: an analysis of forms like those of censers demands that we rewrite objects' stories as traces of a lost past, which manifests itself in a variety of structural, ornamental, and material details.

Working in the field of ancient American art, the art historian George Kubler had little recourse to primary sources which described the process of making the objects that he studied. Few textual sources described how these objects were used and received. In the face of these challenges, Kubler introduced a theory of morphology paired with temporality. He suggested that we examine objects as formal chains that stretch over time. Every now and again, he argued, a "prime object" will emerge that seems to have been triggered by a significant change in the trajectory of what he termed "the chain of objects." This object could then trigger a change itself. These prime objects enable us, Kubler suggested, to analytically crack open otherwise "voiceless" objects, since they draw our attention to an event, or a moment of contact/rupture, which demands analysis. He wrote, "The history of art in this sense resembles a broken but much-repaired chain made of string and wire to connect the occasional jeweled links surviving as physical evidence of the invisible original sequence of prime objects."[4]

In a certain way, although Kubler claimed to use morphology as a category, his notion of the prime object nonetheless reintroduced the concept of the creative, individual artistic mind through the back door. In singling out a specific object in a series and attributing uniqueness to that object, as *pars pro toto* of its maker's work, Kubler indirectly claims that change occurs through artistic will and invention, even though the object-makers he studied remained anonymous and forever unknown. Their objects, however, in his analysis, stood in for them. When examining censers, however, we find an abundance of preserved objects that have similar appearances, functions, and modes of production though they also differ in significant ways. Is there a prime object among them, or are subtle changes in the censers *not* attributable to intentional modifications in a morphological chain? Do they demand that the art historian, archeologist, or anthropologist not seek a prime object, or individual artistic will?

Censers are so often objects that come down to us without makers, users, or contexts or documentation. They thereby form an ideal case for inquiry into what is increasingly at the core of important new fields of study in art history, archeology, and anthropology, which seek to address the imbalance of fractured archives as well as disjunctions between cultures of the written word and those that, supposedly, did not have it. We have incredibly large groups of objects. In very few cases, however, do these tell a story of artistic intentionality or of aesthetic choice. In this sense, they ask us to think beyond a Kublerian model, accounting for variability outside of categories that reify the prime object as the only site where meaning is made or where choices matter. It is this volume's contention that censers can tell stories, which the gaps in the written documentation and the lack of historical records and liturgical primary sources have obscured. Censers are a particularly ideal case, because they were so ubiquitous as to not require comment (and this was true across cultures).

Would it not thus be more apt—and more interesting—to try to understand how these objects were not unique, but instead part of an entangled web across space and time? For this, we would have to consider how they were embedded into networks of actions, materials, and knowledge production. We will never fully understand the entire network of objects, or see the full mosaic of moving parts in which entities like the censers examined in the following volume traveled. We will also never fully comprehend the actions or motivations of the human actors involved in their production and distribution. But we can still gather bits and pieces of these stories by reading and inspecting the material objects themselves. By taking the objects themselves seriously as narrators, we can try to clarify parts of their lost histories. While Kubler's focus was on the artist who produced a "prime object," we might gather more analytical results by shifting the focus from a prime object to the dispersed *tesserae* of a mosaic—to be read formally or perhaps with the aid of non-invasive technology—that we can never fully reconstruct. Such was the goal of the conference that generated this volume.

This volume proposes to explore these commonly used yet seldom studied objects from a comparative perspective. This investigation entails consideration of the material fabrication of censers themselves and their subsequent significations, as well as the role of the incense as it vaporizes over the course of religious ceremonies. By comparing censers across cultures, we aim to unveil resemblances and differences in various religions, so that we can better understand the peculiarities and distinct qualities of censers in specific traditions. Through these objects we also hope to interrogate dominant narratives in art history defined by exclusive categories like "the era of art" or by retrospectively delineated periods or artistic developments aligned with specific dynasties, geographic regions, or dates.

Comparing objects with similar functions and comparable uses in different cultures can open up a number of new perspectives: a new usage, or a previously unimagined story or intent, as well as practices that were not recorded in written documentation or specific archives. However, in this volume we have not tried to simply compare censers from different cultures. Rather, we have invited experts to write their histories from specific points of view coined by their particular scholarly subfields. We hope that as a group, the contributions gathered together here will ignite new ideas, point out novel lineages of thought, and develop a power they do not have on their own when relegated to a specific academic niche. We hope to build a basis from which future comparative approaches can depart. Emerging from this volume, we hope, is a better grasp of the role of sensorial elements in the fostering of the devotional practices of world religions. Acknowledging the need for an interdisciplinary approach to the profound questions provoked by the censer as object and as site of action, this book aims to unite scholars from different fields of study in an exploration of the censer and its materiality, ontology, and presence.

My personal interest in this topic was sparked by a group of seemingly inscrutable censers that seemed to be a dead end. A group of early Christian bronze censers with relief scenes depicting the life of Christ on their exteriors plays a unique role in the history of censers, although we cannot say with certainty where, when, or for whom these objects were made. Because of these uncertainties, these censers have often been ignored in spite of their significance as some of the earliest objects to depict key moments of the life of Christ and connect them to liturgical moments in the Christian religious cult. Until now, scholars have assumed that they were produced from the sixth through the twelfth century, probably in the Syro-Palestinian region [Figures 2 and 3].[5] On the basis of their iconography, the dating around 600 for the earliest examples seems plausible. These icono-

Figures 2–3

Figure 2
View of the Crucifixion,
the Women at the Holy
Sepulchre and the
Annunciation from a censer
with New Testament scenes,
6th–9th century,
bronze, 10.9 × 10.8 cm,
Basel, Antikenmuseum,
inv. no. BRE 644.

Figure 3
Baptism of Christ, from censer
with scenes from the life
of Christ, 6th or 7th century,
bronze, 11.43 × 12.1 cm.
Richmond, VA, Virginia
Museum of Fine Arts, inv.
no. 67.27.

graphic details include the long tunic worn by Christ in the scenes of the crucifixion and some potential analogies with the church of the Holy Sepulcher in the scene of the entombment. Certain details, such as the number of angels present in the scene of the baptism and the various positions of Mary in the birth of Christ, could speak of a moment in Christian art when iconographical traditions were not yet precisely fixed. Alternatively, maybe the makers of those censers did not strictly follow their models, or perhaps various workshops and craftsmen modified these models over time. None of the preserved bronze censers are actually very similar to one another. They seem to have *either* been cast with forms that were subsequently lost, *or* their production was so plentiful that a profound loss means many still survive but none of the same model.[6]

These objects thus point to numerous intriguing ambiguities and recent discussions of them situate these objects at the heart of important current discursive debates in art history, including the role of global mercantile exchange, religious intersection (Christian, Islamic, and Jewish), and the junction between the rising Christian cultures of Latin, Greek, and Syrian heirs of the Roman Empire.[7]

These censers inspired me to try to think through these objects by inviting scholars from very different subfields of art history to discuss censers writ large in order to analyze their use and changes in their appearances throughout different time periods and cultural contexts. My hope is that volumes like this initiate, foster, and contribute to a critical dialogue across the subfields of art history—a dialogue that will enable us to develop new narratives and theoretical frameworks based on collaborative empirical analysis in front of the works and within their cultural contexts.

In the following book, Claudia Brittenham's contribution reveals the crucial role that smoke and fire played in the Mesoamerican tradition. She unfolds the multisensory experience of *copal* in rituals that combined the use of censers and braziers with chant, prayers, dance, costumes, offerings, and other potent substances. Her examples, encompassing three millennia, include fixed incense burners, spiked hourglass *incensarios* used in conjunction with ladle censers and portable objects, as well as the reception of the use of incense in the Florentine Codex.

Kiersten Neumann discusses the apparatuses used for burning incense from West Asia, with a focus on censers of the Neo-Assyrian period, but including earlier, contemporary, and later censers from neighboring regions. Written sources show censers were both portable and fixed. Relief sculpture, textual prescriptions, and material culture demonstrate the importance of incense burning in Assyrian rituals.

Karen Stern rethinks the role of censers and ritual acts of burning incense within the devotional practices of Israelites, Judahites, and Jews throughout the ancient, medieval, and modern eras in the Middle East, North Africa, and Europe. Her contribution discusses the design, presentation, and use of censers in writings, as well as floor mosaics, oil lamps, and manuscripts.

Milette Gaifman shows the importance of incense burners in ancient Greek art (fifth century BCE) by analyzing how censers were presented in pictorial imagery. As these depictions reveal, Hellenic censers were variously placed on supports, carried in sacrificial processions, or were freestanding objects that articulated social status and social differences in cultic and profane sites. These *thymiateria* were an essential element of ritual experiences and the incense burner was linked with youthfulness, seduction, and the female sphere.

The chapter by Nathan Dennis discusses the censer's allusion to the womb of the Mother of God in Early Byzantine and Coptic devotion. He emphasizes the strong relationship between sight, sound, and smell for a metaphorical interpretation of censers depicted in wall paintings, as well as censers used in rituals and depicted in written sources such as hymns and songs included in rituals and theological writings.

In her chapter, Margaret Graves uses a close reading of a Middle Eastern censer which surfaced in Sweden in 1943. She suggests that the so-called Gövle censer should be attributed not to Khurasan, but to the metal-casting traditions of the central Islamic lands. She does so by revealing connections between its making and use to practices, formal patterns, and production techniques of the early Islamic era. She supplements the analysis of the censer with thoughts on the role of censers and incense in Islamic magic.

Beate Fricke analyzes depictions of censers in paintings (e.g., by Rogier van der Weyden) as well as written sources describing the use of censers, and a selection of censers to address the shifting roles and forms of censers in late medieval Europe. Between the twelfth and the fifteenth centuries in the Latin West, censers were depicted with increasing frequency, featuring significantly in the ornamentation of liturgical spaces, including glass painting, reliefs on portals and tombs, as well as standing figures that embellished liturgical furniture such as pulpits.

Allison Stielau takes as a starting point Sandro Botticelli's painting depicting *The Punishment of Korah* and continues with an analysis of censers, painted and sculpted altar panels, woodcuts in printed books, and religious tracts. Both Catholic theologians and supporters of the Reformation discussed the role of incense and censers in devotional practice. Embedding censers as "potentially unruly objects" into narratives of rebellion and transgression reveals just how specifically coded messages around censers and their use could be in the early modern period.

Yao Ning focuses on the censer and the visualization of smoke emanating from a censer in a portrait of the Ming emperor Xizong (1605–1627). She connects her observations with the belief that incense smoke has the capacity "to connect the celestial realm with the earthly world." She analyzes the description of incense and its smoke in written treatises and shows that the revival of Daoism and reconsiderations of the renewed interest in Song aesthetics impacted the representation of longevity in the Xizong portrait.

The different types of written sources in Greek and Roman Antiquity as well as in the Middle Ages including the Islamic world are discussed by Beatrice Caseau. She emphasizes the complexity of incense and the important changes regarding the substances used to create fragrant smoke. Her contribution also discusses the recent results from chemical analyses of incense residues from the fourth century BCE to the sixteenth century CE.

Jaś Elsner's afterword points out the synesthesia of religion and the ways "the scent-scape, sound-scape and light-scape in any given site [...] create a powerful sacral atmosphere [...] through collective embodied experience." He considers censers as gadgets "for the instrumental transformation of natural materials into something else," reading censers as devices that link body and embodied subjectivity through material objects to an invisible world and to imaginations of a different kind.

The conference and the book have received substantial support from the European Research Council (ERC) project "Global Horizons in Pre-Modern Art" based at the University of Bern. The initial conference that generated this book was planned and organized by myself together with Ittai Weinryb in Bern, Switzerland, in 2019.[8] Francesco de Angelis, James A. Doyle, Aden Kumler, and Nina Macaraig all participated, but have decided not to publish their conference papers in this volume.

For line- and copyediting I am very grateful to Andrew Sears, Sasha Rossman, and Jonathan Hoare. For their indispensable help with everything from images and assistance with the preparation of the peer review, I am deeply indebted to Alessandra Fedrigo, Elena Filliger, and Joanne Luginbühl. Zumrad Ilyasova oversaw the final stretch of the publication with greatest care and attention. My own contribution to this volume, the discussion of censers in the Latin West, has gained several sparks of inspiration from discussions with my team in Bern—especially valuable were comments and suggestions by Katharina Böhmer, Ivan Foletti, Aaron Hyman, and Carlos Rojas Cocoma. Last, but not least, the entire chapter has particularly benefited from thoughts, ideas, and inspiration from Andrew Sears. Both, Andrew and Zumrad are now moving on to new shores. Andrew Sears to Washington (National Gallery) and Zumrad Ilyasova to London (British Museum)—I will dearly miss them as colleagues in Bern.

Kaj Lehmann has enthusiastically let himself be inspired by ideas from the use of incense for the design of the conference flyer and now the publication of the proceedings. This book, wrapped when sold and shipped, leaves traces of charcoal, as did and do censers. His idea emphasizes the intimate connection of content, containing wrapper, and the bookboards holding the content in place; however, odor and ideas are equally capable of transgressing such thresholds. I am immensely grateful to Elisabeth Rochau-Shalem at Hirmer-Verlag for her support with this project and for guiding me with my team through the production press. There are few presses who are willing to take on an ambitious design for an academic book, and Kaj Lehmann and I are very happy that Rainer Arnold and Hirmer-Verlag supported our ideas and facilitated their realization.

The pandemic not only impacted the writing of several authors gathered in this volume, but also the breadth of the different subfields to be covered in the book. The contributions assembled in this volume are not considered as substitutes for important missing subfields from Asia, Africa, or the Americas. The pandemic and its impact on the ability of scholars to do research on the ground explains some of the gaps in scholarship on the history of censers we could not fill: we had solicited several contributions for which research needed to be done in East and South Asia, as well as in Africa, and the Americas. There is, therefore, a problematic imbalance between the subfields covered in the volume, in which some subfields can draw on long-lasting traditions in scholarship and firmly established archival traditions that are lacking in other fields. We hope, however, that this volume will ignite scholarly interest in these fields so the gaps can be soon be filled.

ENDNOTES

1 Bennet 2010.
2 See the contribution of Beatrice Caseau as well as her important publications on this topic. Furthermore see also Barker 2009; Darvill 2008; Groom 1981; Frère and Hugot 2012; Miller 1969; Montúfar López 2016; Pfeifer 1997. For the history of smell see Robinson 2019.

3 A significant part of the extant scholarship focuses on European and/or Christian censers and the related rituals—for a good overview on the extant scholarship regarding European censers and Christian rituals involving incense see Westermann-Angerhausen 2014, 19–46; for a broader temporal and regional focus see also Caseau and Neri 2021; Le Maguer-Gillon 2022; Sales-Carbonell 2017.
4 Kubler 1962, 40.
5 Richter-Siebels 1990.

6 Ibid., 229–38 and the first chapter in Flood and Fricke 2023, 22–51.
7 Elsner 2022; 2021; Fauvelle 2017; Heng 2014; 2021; Keene 2018; Zimo et al. 2020.
8 The conference was initially organized and held in collaboration with Ittai Weinryb. He was a key part in the conception of the original idea for the conference, and the initial phase of planning the volume. Not editing this volume together was a personal decision by him, and I owe him many important ideas and suggestions.

BIBLIOGRAPHY

Barker, Margaret. 2009. "Fragrance in the Making of Sacred Space: Jewish Temple Paradigms of Christian Worship." *Ierotopija*, 71–83.

Bennet, Jane. 2010. *Vibrant Matter: A Political Ecology of Things*. Durham, NC: Duke University Press.

Caseau, Béatrice, and Elisabetta Neri, eds. 2021. *Rituels religieux et sensorialité (Antiquité et Moyen Age)*. Milan: Silvana.

Darvill, Timothy. 2008. "Copal." In *The Concise Oxford Dictionary of Archaeology*, n.p. Oxford: Oxford University Press.

Elsner, Jas, ed. 2021. *Imagining the Divine: Exploring Art in Religions of Late Antiquity across Eurasia*. London: The British Museum.

Elsner, Jas, ed. 2022. *Landscape and Space: Comparative Perspectives from Chinese, Mesoamerican, Ancient Greek and Roman Art*. Oxford: Oxford University Press.

Fauvelle, François-Xavier. 2017. "Trade and Travel in Africa's Global Age (AD 700–1500)." In *Global Africa: Into the Twenty-First Century*, edited by Dorothy L. Hodgson and Judith A. Byfield, 17–26. Oakland: University of California Press.

Flood, Finbarr Barry, and Beate Fricke. 2023. *Tales Things Tell: Material Histories of Early Globalisms*. Princeton, NJ: Princeton University Press.

Frère, Dominique, and Laurent Hugot. 2012. *Les huiles parfumées en Méditerranée occidentale et en Gaule (VIIIe siècle AV. – VIIIe s. apr. J.-C.)*. Rennes: Presses universitaires de Rennes.

Groom, Nigel. 1981. *Frankincense and Myrrh: A Study of the Arabian Incense Trade*. London: Longman.

Heng, Geraldine. 2014. "Early Globalities, and Its Questions, Objectives, and Methods: An Inquiry into the State of Theory and Critique." *Exemplaria: Medieval, Early Modern, Theory* 26 (2–3): 234–53.

Heng, Geraldine. 2021. *The Global Middle Ages: An Introduction*. Cambridge: Cambridge University Press.

Keene, Bryan C., ed. 2018. *Toward a Global Middle Ages: Encountering the World through Illuminated Manuscripts*. Los Angeles: J. Paul Getty Museum.

Kubler, George. 1962. *The Shape of Time: Remarks on the History of Things*. New Haven, CT: Yale University Press.

Le Maguer-Gillon, Sterenn. 2022. "The Art of Hospitality: Incense Burners and the Welcoming Ceremony in the Medieval Islamic Society (7th–15th Centuries)." In *Mediality of Smells / Médialité des odeurs*, edited by Jean-Alexandre Perras and Erika Wicky, 41–59. Oxford; Bern; Berlin: Peter Lang.

Miller, James Innes. 1969. *The Spice Trade of the Roman Empire, 29 B.C. to 641 A.D.* Oxford: Clarendon Press.

Montúfar López, Aurora. 2016. "Copal de Bursera bipinnata: Una resina mesoamericana de uso ritual." *TRACE* (Mexico City, Mexico) 70: 45–77.

Pfeifer, Michael. 1997. *Der Weihrauch: Geschichte, Bedeutung, Verwendung*. Regensburg: Pustet.

Richter-Siebels, Ilse. 1990. "Die palästinensischen Weihrauchgefäße mit Reliefszenen aus dem Leben Christi." PhD dissertation, Freie Universität Berlin.

Robinson, Kately. 2019. *The Sense of Smell in the Middle Ages*. London: Routledge.

Sales-Carbonell, Jordina. 2017. "'Incensum in monasterium' in Preandalusian Hispania (Centuries 5th–8th)." *Hortus artium medievalium* 23, no. 1: 107–13.

Westermann-Angerhausen, Hiltrud. 2014. *Mittelalterliche Weihrauchfässer von 800 bis 1500*. Petersberg: Imhof Verlag.

Zimo, Ann, Tiffany Vann Sprecher, Kathryn Reyerson, and Debra Blumenthal, eds. 2020. *Rethinking Medieval Margins and Marginality*. London: Routledge.

Incense burner, Northern Italy, ca. 1530–40 CE, bronze, 34.3 × 21.1 × 17.5 cm, The Metropolitan Museum of Art, New York, The Jack and Belle Linsky Collection, 1982.

Circular limestone incense
burner, Cyprus, (year unknown),
limestone, 8.6 × 7.6 cm,
The Metropolitan Museum
of Art, New York, The Cesnola
Collection, Purchased
by subscription, 1874–76.

Censer, Germany, 11th–12th century CE, copper alloy, 23.5 × 11.5 cm, The Metropolitan Museum of Art, New York, Rogers Fund, 1909.

Incense Burner of Amir Saif al-Dunya wa'l-Din ibn Muhammad al-Mawardi, Iran, 1181–82 CE, bronze, 82.6 × 22.9 cm, The Metropolitan Museum of Art, New York, Rogers Fund, 1951.

SMOKE FIRE
BRAZIERS CENSERS

THE ART OF SMOKE AND FIRE: BRAZIERS AND CENSERS IN MESOAMERICAN TRADITION

Claudia Brittenham

Mesoamerican rituals were multisensory experiences: the poetry of chant, prayer, and song accompanied by music, dance, sumptuous costumes, and offerings of food, flowers, blood, and other symbolically potent substances. The sharp and smoky scent of heated copal resin marked a space of ceremony in the ancient Mesoamerican world, as it continues to do today among Indigenous communities in Mexico, Guatemala, Honduras, Belize, and their worldwide diaspora. In this essay, I will describe the uses and properties of burnt aromatics in Mesoamerican societies, trace the development of vessels for these substances over the course of Mesoamerican history, and conclude with some brief reflections about the continuing importance of copal and other kinds of incense in contemporary ritual practice. In this short essay, it is impossible to fully describe the interrelated evolution of censer and brazier forms across numerous cultures and linguistic groups over three millennia, so I will instead focus on some key charismatic moments in the long history of these forms. In the survey of Mesoamerican incense burners, one important continuity that emerges is an inextricable link between copal and people, whether in the form of personified vessels or of vessels intended to be used in concert with the human body.

MESOAMERICAN AROMATICS

In Mesoamerica, the preferred form of aromatic incense was a crystallized tree resin called *copalli* in Nahuatl and *pom* in Mayan languages, commonly referred to as copal. The product of a number of trees in the *Bursera* and *Protium* genera, especially *Bursera bipinnata*, *Bursera copallifera*, and *Protium copal*, copal is produced either by gathering naturally occurring clumps of resin that accumulate where the bark was damaged, or by slashing the tree and collecting the resin that flows from the wounds.[1] Users distinguish among various different kinds and qualities of copal, depending on the color and purity of the resin, which might be presented as small crystals or shaped into pellets, balls, cakes, cones, or other shapes for transport and use. In these forms, copal could be sold in the marketplace, paid as tribute, or deposited as an offering.[2]

Copal was conceptualized as the blood of the tree, just as the bark of the tree, used to make paper, was understood as the tree's skin.[3] The smell of burning copal frequently accompanied or substituted for offerings of blood and human flesh. One story in the seventeenth-century K'iche' Maya sacred text called the *Popol Vuh* makes this kind of substitution explicit (although it features a different tree sap than copal): when the maiden Lady Blood, miraculously impregnated by the skull of One Hunahpu, flees the underworld after the discovery of her pregnancy, the lords of the underworld clamor for her death. The clever maiden suborns the owls sent after her, and they substitute the sap of the croton tree (*Croton sanguifluus*) for her heart and blood. The gods, fooled by this substitution, enjoy the aroma of the heated resin, "Then they dried it over the fire ... [and] savored its fragrance. They all rose up to lean over it, for truly delicious was the smell of the blood to them."[4] Fray Diego de Landa describes a similar substitution of copal for animal hearts in the Maya lowlands, where people "took out a great many of the hearts of the animals and birds and threw them into the fire to burn. And if they were unable to get large animals like tigers (jaguars), lions (pumas) or crocodiles, they made their hearts out of their incense."[5] Copal and other burnt aromatics "pleased the hearts of the gods" not only for their scents but for the logics of substitution that allowed them to stand in for human or animal bodies.

In numerous situations, incense was conceived of as food for the gods.[6] Several of the forms in which copal was prepared—the round balls resembling maize tamales and the flat cakes shaped like maize tortillas—created symbolic equivalences between incense and human food, especially maize, the staple of Mesoamerican diets.[7] As Brian Stross reports, some cones of copal used by the modern Lacandon Maya also have small pellets at the upper end, arranged radially like kernels of maize on a cob, yet another association between copal and maize.[8] In this light, the fact that the small pellets or crystals of naturally occurring copal were often collected, stored, and sold in maize husks or maize leaves created another kind of material equivalence.[9] Copal might also be mixed with maize or other forms of sustenance, such as beans, before burning.[10]

In addition to being burnt as incense, copal had other uses. It could be directly cast into the fire to mark a particularly significant utterance, as described in sixteenth-century Nahuatl sources: "And the casting of incense was thus done when some statement already was to be uttered; perchance a judgement already was to be uttered; first one cast incense into the fire. For whoever already was to speak, just there lay the incense in a gourd vessel. Or else a singer, when already he was to sing, thus would begin: first he cast incense into the brazier."[11] A distinctive bag full of copal was a ubiquitous attribute of priestly attire in many Mesoamerican societies. Offerings of copal or other incense were used to accompany all kinds of events, from daily household rituals to state-level ceremonies.

Copal also had a variety of medicinal uses. It was used to treat diarrhea, fevers, swelling, rashes, insect bites, venereal diseases, and ailments of the eye; the resin might also be applied as a filling for dental cavities or used as an aid in childbirth.[12] At the other end of the life cycle, copal and pine resin were used in preparing bodies for burial, primarily as excipients for cinnabar and hematite pigments that coated Maya corpses. These resins were part of a suite of aromatic substances designed to enrich the sensory experience of the tomb and mitigate the odors of decomposition.[13]

Furthermore, copal had a number of artistic applications. It was a component of varnishes and glues, according to colonial sources, and has been found as a component of the adhesive used to create turquoise mosaics.[14] The resin was mixed with beeswax and used in lost wax gold casting.[15] In the Aztec marketplace, copal was sold alongside pigments by the *tlapalnamacac*, or "vendor of colors," hinting at still other artistic and cosmetic uses.[16] The resin could serve as a medium for sculpture: images of rain, water, and maize deities made from copal were deposited as offerings in caches at the Aztec Templo Mayor.[17] Made in molds, these images were then covered with a thin layer of stucco, painted, and dressed in paper garments.[18] Approximately a century or so earlier, ca. 1225–1475, a number of hand-modeled copal figures of humans and frogs were also deposited in the Sacred

Cenote at Chichen Itza, a site of ritual pilgrimage to request rain even centuries after the great city's abandonment.[19] Copal also coated the wooden cores of sculptures found in the Cenote, serving as the "modeled 'flesh' of wooden idols that were finally covered with a rubber 'skin'," and then frequently painted blue.[20] It additionally served to create other adornments on these figures, such as a line of round balls of copal modeled and painted to look like a necklace of jade beads.[21] Copal balls were also thrown directly into the Cenote, most likely while set alight and emitting fragrant smoke. The copal was often wrapped in rubber or in maize leaves or husks, or provisioned with a wooden wick to produce the necessary heat for the resin to smolder.[22] When placed into simple tripod bowls, sometimes with pieces of precious jade embedded in their surface, these balls of copal might also have provoked a particularly evocative coloristic alchemy: as the copal was heated, causing billowing clouds of resinous smoke, the heat transformed white palygorskite clay and indigo on the outside of the vessels into the brilliant and stable Maya blue pigment.[23]

    Mesoamericans used a wide variety of other aromatics in addition to copal. Slivers of the wood of copal-producing trees could be burnt alongside the resin for a pleasing smell, as could pine needles and a particularly pungent herb called *yauhtli* (*Tagetes lucida*).[24] As mentioned above, agricultural products such as maize and beans could also be mixed with copal resin.[25] Other plant exudates, particularly latex, might also be burnt as aromatics, and, like copal, conceptualized as the blood of the trees from which they were gathered. Particularly common latexes that might be burnt as aromatics included *chicle* (Nahautl *tzictli*, from sapodilla trees, *Manilkara sp.*, also the principal ingredient in chewing gum) and *hule* (Nahuatl *olli*, from rubber trees, *Castilla elastica*).[26] Like copal, these latexes were gathered by cutting into the bark of the tree and collecting the liquids that flowed from them. As Andrea Stone reminds us, the odor of natural burnt rubber "does not smell like burning tires, the bad odor of which comes from the sulfur used in vulcanization."[27] In certain regions of Mesoamerica, tar (Nahuatl *chapohpohtli*) was also burnt for its insistent scent and the clouds of smoke that it generated.[28] Paper, often spattered with rubber or with blood from autosacrificial bloodletting, was also frequently burnt alongside these other substances, and continues to be an important part of Nahua ritual practice.[29]

    The clouds of smoke produced by all burnt aromatics had numerous symbolic properties. The fragrant smells summoned the attention of divine forces; as Alan Sandstrom observes: "According to the Nahua, everything around us is an expression of *totiotzin* [lit. 'our honored divinity or divine forces'], yet it is difficult to perceive this overwhelming presence, much less to summon it to receive a ritual offering. Simply getting the attention of this pervasive spirit presence is a preoccupation of ritual specialists, both ancient and contemporary."[30] As Dominican friar Diego Durán wrote in the sixteenth century, "This ceremony [of burning incense] was in honor of the god and the sun, who were asked to grant that all these prayers and pleas rise to heaven, just as the perfumed smoke rose."[31] In an ethnography of modern Maya community of Zinacantan, Evon Vogt argues that the transformation of incense from solid to gas constitutes "metaphorically crossing the threshold between the material and spiritual worlds."[32] Moreover, the heating of the incense imbues it with a kind of radiant, solar energy which is present everywhere but especially concentrated in sacred things. The swirling clouds of smoke reveal the constantly shifting energies of the universe in motion.[33] Yet another metaphorical association existed between these clouds of smoke and rain clouds, making copal and other kinds of incense particularly powerful elements of rituals seeking to draw the attention of rain deities.[34] The use of aromatics in Mesoamerican ritual was thus ubiquitous and imbued with profound and multifaceted symbolism, tied to the physical, olfactory, and visual qualities of the burnt substances as well as to their origins and methods of processing.

MESOAMERICAN INCENSE BURNERS

No elaborate apparatus was required to burn copal or other aromatic substances. Any clay or wooden cup, plate, or bowl could serve as a support for the smoldering resin, and indeed, some of the earliest examples of incense burners, with extensive traces of burning, closely parallel utilitarian forms.[35] But over time, more elaborate vessels were developed. Clay was the predominant medium—at least among the examples that have survived. The choice of material had pragmatic as well as symbolic aspects; in addition to the ubiquity and durability of clay, Mesoamericans must have appreciated the symmetry between the application of heat to fire clay and to cause copal to produce aromatic smoke. Wood does not preserve well in Mesoamerican climates, but there were likely once wooden vessels for incense as well, perhaps preferentially carved out of hard woods not immediately susceptible to the heat of smoldering coals.[36] There are occasional stone incense burners, or examples made of modeled stucco over a stone core, but they are often closely related to contemporary clay forms, and the logic of accretive decoration seems most natural to the clay medium.[37] One notable exception to this pattern are a series of sculptures made out of volcanic stone at the Central Mexican city of Teotihuacan in the first millennium CE, which depict an aged male deity in a seated position, hunched over and supporting a basin on his head, the interior of which frequently displays signs of burning.[38] Yet even these forms derive from smaller ceramic prototypes.[39] Although metal is a preferred material for censers in many other parts of the world, this is not the case in Mesoamerica, where metallurgy was adopted relatively late, and the use of metal was predominantly confined to small objects of personal adornment. Mesoamerican metalworkers selected for properties of shine, brilliance, and sound rather than durability, hardness, and heat resistance.[40]

A significant distinction can be made between fixed incense burners—perhaps brazier would be the closest word in English, although I will also follow Mesoamericanist usage of the Spanish terms *incensario* or *brasero* to describe such vessels—and portable objects, intended to be in motion during use, for which I will reserve the term censer. Where available, Indigenous terms for these objects will be discussed below. I will begin by considering the less portable *incensarios* and then move on to discuss mobile censers.

INCENSARIOS

The basic forms of Mesoamerican *incensarios* were simple: a cylinder, sometimes with flaring sides, or perhaps an hourglass-like biconical form, sometimes topped with a conical lid. Some *incensarios* could be decorated with openwork sides to allow more smoke to escape, or with protruding spikes

Figure 1

that some have likened to the spines on the ceiba tree, emblematic of the center direction in many spheres of Mesoamerican belief [Figure 1].[41] These unfigured or lightly figured braziers surely characterized much Mesoamerican practice. But more elaborate forms were also possible.

One persistent theme across Mesoamerican history is the association of incense burners with bodies, and especially with human heads. One of the earliest examples of a decorated incense burner is from San José Mogote in the Oaxaca Valley, made ca. 900–600 BCE, where just a few schematic features transform the flaring cylinder into a human head: circular holes for eyes and an elongated rectangle for a mouth, a modeled nose and flanges for

Figure 2

ears [Figure 2].[42] A thin band with knot at the front cinches the flaring cylinder at its narrowest point, serving as a headdress, perhaps a symbol of authority, for the figure beneath. Copal resin is often not burned directly, but instead heated indirectly: the crystals of resin would be placed on the slightly concave upper surface of the flaring cylinder, and the whole hollow configuration would be placed above a small fire or smoldering coals to heat it and release the odor of the resin. In the process, smoke emerging from the eye and mouth holes of the figure would transform it into something otherworldly. As a result, although the whole apparatus is small enough to move from one place to another between uses, it would likely remain fixed in place once the coals were heated. The facial features of this early *incensario* are extremely minimal, but other later braziers from the Valley of Oaxaca feature more elaborately rendered faces, often with supernatural attributes, such as curling upper lips, unusually shaped teeth, or wrinkled cheeks, which suggest that they represent deities or revered ancestors rather than living mortals, since humans rarely show signs of age in Mesoamerican art.

Centuries later, the association of bodies and incense burners also characterized the material culture of the Central Mexican city of Teotihuacan, an urban center of more than 100,000 people that thrived in the first half of the first millennium CE. In a class of objects known as theater-type *incensarios*, an elaborate lid tops a biconical base where the copal resin is heated. The decoration almost entirely conceals the utilitarian conical lid

Figure 3

with a vertical flue conducting the smoke upward [Figure 3]. On the front of the lid an assemblage of clay plaques are arrayed as if a proscenium in front of and around a mask-like human face, which itself often bears ear flares and a nose ornament that conceals the mouth.[43] All of the decorative elements of these objects were made with molds, many of them likely mass-produced in state-sponsored workshops.[44] Although composed of standardized components, no two incensarios were identical; many were found in the residential apartment compounds of the city. It has been proposed that they might commemorate individuals, perhaps warriors, given the prevalence of imagery associated with birds and butterflies, creatures that held martial significance for the Teotihuacanos and their successors.[45] Symbols related to fire also abound, as do clay images of feathered mirror-like disks, often gleaming with mica inlays. Combined with the bright paint of many of the elements, it is easy to imagine how affecting these objects would have been while being used, as fragrant smoke escaping from the juncture of base and lid would have partially obscured the figures, making the mask-like faces and their surrounding symbols appear vibrant and changeable, perhaps even animate. Significantly, Teotihuacan also had a robust tradition of non-figural openwork *incensarios* coexisting with and perhaps even used

Figure 1
Brazier from the La Ventilla apartment compound, Teotihuacan, ca. 170–250 CE, 52 × 28 cm, 4.75 kg, Museo Nacional de Antropología, Mexico City, inv. no. 10-0080675. Archivo Digital de las Colecciones del Museo Nacional de Antropología. INAH-CANON. Reproduction authorized by the Instituto Nacional de Antropología e Historia.

Figure 2
Brazier from Room 1,
Structure 26, San José Mogote,
Oaxaca, Zapotec, ca. 900–
600 BCE. 36.5 × 26.5 cm. Museo
de las Culturas de Oaxaca,
Ex Convento de Santo Domingo
de Guzmán. Photo by Jon G.
Fuller / VWPics / Alamy Stock
Photo. Reproduction authorized
by the Instituto Nacional
de Antropología e Historia.

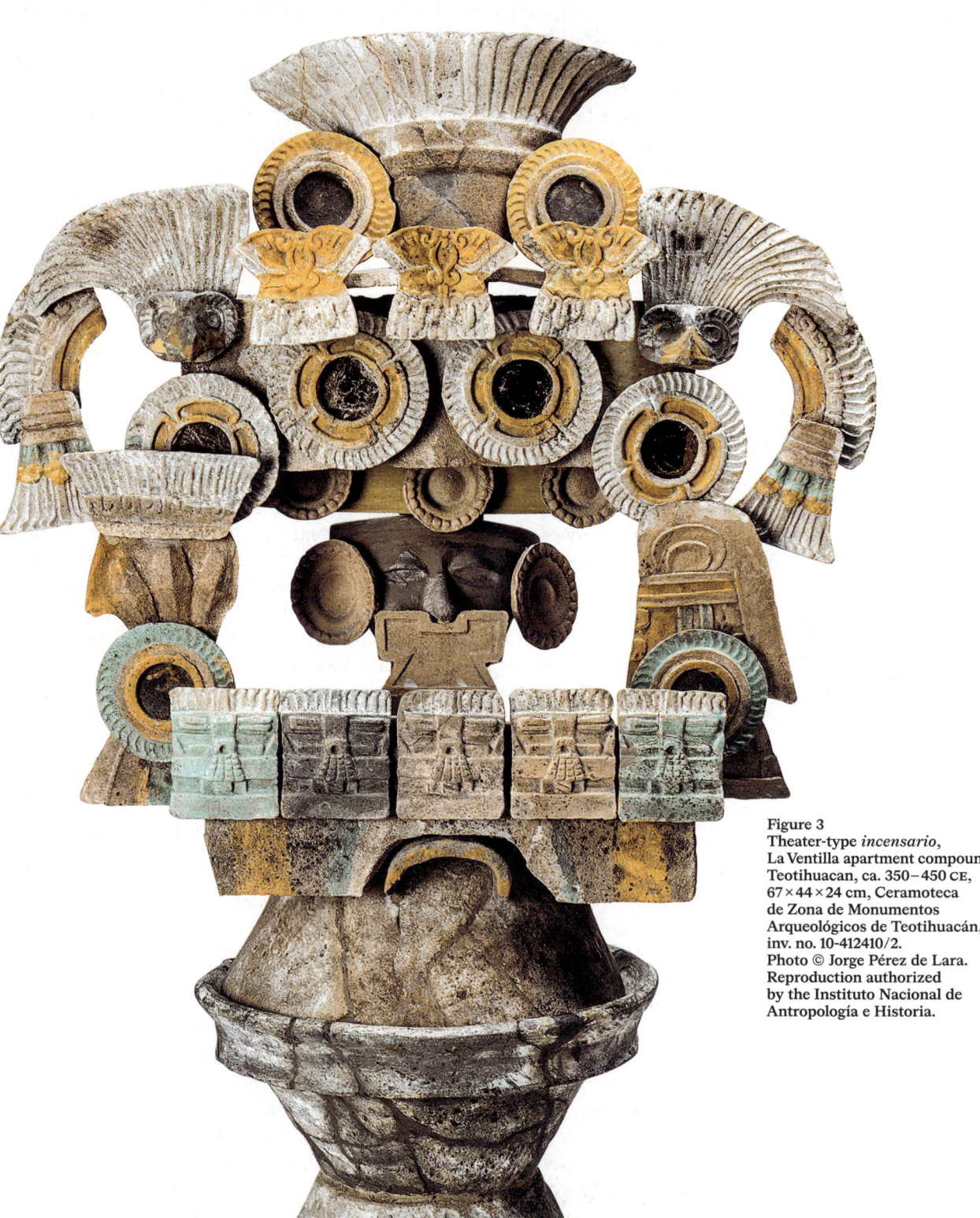

Figure 3
Theater-type *incensario*,
La Ventilla apartment compound,
Teotihuacan, ca. 350–450 CE,
67 × 44 × 24 cm, Ceramoteca
de Zona de Monumentos
Arqueológicos de Teotihuacán,
inv. no. 10-412410/2.
Photo © Jorge Pérez de Lara.
Reproduction authorized
by the Instituto Nacional de
Antropología e Historia.

alongside these more anthropomorphic forms. Indeed, the *incensarios* illustrated in Figures 1 and 3 were excavated from the same apartment compound at Teotihuacan.[46]

Elsewhere in Mesoamerica, artists emulated Teotihuacan theater-type *incensarios* as the city became a major pan-Mesoamerican power, but often with significant changes. One of the most characteristic features of the Teotihuacan *incensarios*, as with so much Teotihuacan material culture, was a persistent emphasis on disembodiment: the masks at the center of the theater *incensarios* were not associated with hands, torsos, or other corporeal elements. Emulations of these objects, however, especially along the Pacific coast of Guatemala in the Escuintla region, often featured more fully embodied busts, marking a fundamental reinterpretation of the format.[47] Other elements of these objects shifted as well, as the bodies represented often were transformed into those of local goddesses.[48] In other instances, the theater-type frame was reinterpreted as an architectural form that could encompass the interactions between multiple figures.[49]

In other parts of the Maya world around this time, the connections between *incensarios* and bodies became even more pronounced. At Tikal in the Central Peten region and Kaminaljuyu in the Guatemalan highlands—both sites with rich histories of Teotihuacan interaction—a supernatural body itself became the container for copal resin. One especially compelling example comes from Tikal Burial 10. It features an old deity, seated on a stool made of crossed bones, holding a severed head in his cupped hands. The head and upper torso can be detached from the rest of the sculpture, allowing copal resin to be placed in the hollow interior, so that billows of smoke might emerge from the figure's gap-toothed mouth.[50] At Kaminaljuyu, figures of aged deities and simian creatures have similar two-part hollow structures; these so-called effigy censers and hourglass-shaped biconical *incensarios* like those from Teotihuacan displaced an earlier tradition of three-pronged censers with minimal figuration.[51]

In other cases, deities and figures of ancestors perched on top of *incensario* lids. At the city of Copan in modern Honduras, for example, a matched set of *incensarios* portraying the twelve kings in the founding lineage was discovered in an elite tomb underneath the Temple of the Hieroglyphic Stairway, where they were deposited, probably ca. 700 CE.[52] Each ruler is rendered as an entire body, seated atop the lid topping a more utilitarian brazier base; the rulers are also rendered with individual details of costume and attributes, permitting identification of the founder and successive rulers. Their bodies are largely the color of the fired clay, with bits of postfire red, blue, and white pigments embellishing key adornments. Similar full-body *incensario* lids have also been found at other Classic-period lowland Maya centers, always rendered in the distinctive local style of the city state.[53]

Figure 4

At the city of Palenque and related sites in the western Maya region, by contrast, tall *incensario* bases grew increasingly ornate between ca. 500 and 800 CE [Figure 4]. From the front, these ceramic bases consist of a human or deity head wearing an elaborate headdress or stack of headdresses; flanges projecting from the sides of the face conceal the utilitarian tube behind.[54] Many depict the patron deities of the city, while others represent deceased rulers of the city, especially King K'inich K'an Bahlam (r. 684–702 CE), whose portraits are immediately recognizable. This entire configuration was not an incense burner itself, but merely a stand into

Figure 4
Incense burner stand with head
of the sun god, Palenque, Maya,
ca. 690–800 CE, 115 × 36 cm,
Museo Nacional de Antropología
e Historia, Mexico City,
inv. no. 10-0009789. Archivo
Digital de las Colecciones
del Museo Nacional de
Antropología. INAH-CANON.
Reproduction authorized
by the Instituto Nacional de
Antropología e Historia.

which a plain conical vessel containing coals and smoking copal would be placed, often with a lid to control or inhibit the flow of smoke. Traces of blood and other plant resins have also been found in the vessels. Over a hundred such *incensarios* were found in the fill of the temples of the Cross Group and associated structures at Palenque; they were especially concentrated on the western sides of each structure. One can imagine a line of smoking braziers on each of the stepped platforms of these tall pyramids, converting the human-made mountains into an elusive vision, wreathed in clouds of fragrant incense. The *incensarios* were likely extinguished and then re-lit at the end of key calendrical periods; they also appear to have been ritually buried each time the pyramid was remade. Simpler versions of the same style of objects, made out of clay or stucco-coated stone, were often found in elite residential compounds, suggesting that the worship of ancestors and lineage patron deities was not a practice restricted to the rulers of the city.[55] Much the same accretive logic and patterns of coloration define a group of incense burner stands from the nearby caves around Tapijulapa and Tacotalpa, Tabasco, although these smaller objects often feature the entire bodies of standing figures, particularly the Jaguar God of the Underworld, the deity of the nocturnal sun.[56] These objects attest both to the power of caves as important sites of pilgrimage and ritual, and also to the regional impact of Palenque's distinctive *incensario* style.

After the fall of the lowland Maya city states in the ninth century CE, figural incense burners became less common for several centuries, replaced by spiked hourglass *incensarios* that were used in conjunction with ladle censers in new ritual choreographies unencumbered by the failed model of divine kingship so intimately associated with previous sculptural forms (see below).[57] Yet the connection between incense burners and bodies was made even more explicit in an extraordinary object found in the Sacred Cenote of Chichen Itza: a human skull that was converted into an incense burner by plugging the eyes with wooden discs, the nasal cavity with resin, and carving a hole in the top of the cranium, which was given a wooden lid.[58] Traces of bright blue and red paint decorated the object when it was dredged from the Cenote but have now faded, while char marks and remains of resin inside the skull make it clear that it had been used to burn incense. Several burnt pearls were also found inside. At this historical remove, it is impossible to tell if the intention was to honor a revered ancestor or revile a defeated enemy; the skull was that of a relatively young individual, perhaps making the latter possibility more likely. In this object, the metaphors of smoke emitting from bodies modeled of clay were literalized in bone.

By the thirteenth century CE, figural censers had returned in force to many areas of Mesoamerica. In the Mixteca-Puebla region (an ethnically and linguistically diverse zone of exchange between Oaxaca, the Gulf Coast, and the Valley of Mexico), a new kind of effigy incense burner, called a *xantil*, became common [Figure 5]. Consisting of a hollow cylindrical body, terminating in a modeled head, with vestigial arms and legs attached to it as if the figure were seated with arms raised and bent, these vessels represented yet another permutation of a familiar Mesoamerican theme. In this case, the entire bell-shaped vessel could be placed over coals and incense, and smoke would be emitted through the open mouth, nose, and other ori-

Figure 5

Figure 5
Incense burner (*xantil*),
Tehuacan Valley, Eastern
Nahua, ca. 1200–1500 CE,
57.5 × 38 × 23 cm,
Metropolitan Museum of Art,
New York, 1978.412.10,
The Michael C. Rockefeller
Memorial Collection, Gift of
Nelson A. Rockefeller, 1969.

fices. Frequently found in caves and on mountain peaks, these *incensarios* embodied deities who became increasingly important during this period, including Xochipilli (lit. "Flower Prince") and the Macuiltonalequeh, patrons of music, feasting, and dance.[59] Finely drawn lines indicate the luxurious ornaments worn by these deities, including gold bells, elaborate textiles and sandals, large earflares, and intricate body paint. Simultaneously an incense burner and a god-image, such vessels focalized new forms of devotion and ritual practice.

At the Maya city of Mayapan on the Yucatan peninsula, a site linked to the Mixteca-Puebla region through ties of trade and diplomacy, another kind of full-body *incensario* became common in roughly the same period,

Figure 6   ca. 1150–1450 CE [Figure 6]. These *incensarios*, often brightly painted with fine details in a range of postfire pigments (including hematite red, Maya blue, yellow, white, orange, and green), frequently depict deities who sometimes hold round balls of copal incense or even spiky *incensarios* in their hands. These bodies are affixed to the front of a brazier in the shape of a footed urn, often with cleverly placed firing holes in eyes, mouth, and elsewhere on the bodies that would allow smoke to be emitted. Products of an interconnected Mesoamerican world, these braziers depict not only deities with long roots in the Maya world, like the maize god, the rain god Chahk, the monkey scribe, and the merchant deity (God M), but also deities more commonly associated with Central Mexico, including Quetzalcoatl, Tlahuizcalpantecuhtli, Xipe Totec, and Tlazoteotl.[60] Likewise, the polychrome decoration, with its finely detailed lines and rapid color changes, as well as the proportions of the bodies, giving unusual emphasis to the head, are typical of the "International Style" of the Late Postclassic period, much like the decoration of Figure 5.[61]

Moreover, the Mayapan *incensarios* are conceptually similar to vessels produced in the Aztec heartland in Central Mexico a century or two later, which also feature deity figures colored with rich polychrome and attached to the front of incense-bearing braziers. The Aztec examples, however, are substantially larger than their Maya counterparts. They are so large that they would require several people to lift and transport them, and the braziers behind them often have a biconical hourglass shape with a long Central Mexican history. Especially notable are a set of braziers from the site of Tláhuac in the Valley of Mexico, each nearly a meter tall and weighing approximately 25 kilograms, that depict a variety of rain and maize deities.[62] Another series of vessels, found during the subway excavations in Mexico City, are ornamented with skeletal and deified warriors in a richly detailed polychrome; this use of color and the position of the arms recall the *xantiles* of Mixteca-Puebla tradition.[63] Behind the figures, the hourglass shape of the brazier recalls other common Aztec brazier forms, while triangular strips of clay surrounding the rims of these braziers may echo a more perishable substance such as leather or paper.[64]

Tenochtitlan, the Aztec capital, was home to a wide variety of *incensario* and brazier forms, used in the continuous succession of ritual observances that defined the solar year. In addition to the full-bodied braziers described in the previous paragraph, other forms also received extensive ritual use. Particularly notable are a series of large braziers, over a meter high and nearly as wide in diameter, painted white, featuring the face of the rain god Tlaloc at large scale, recalling the persistent Mesoamerican associ-

Figure 6
Brazier depicting the deity
Itzamnaj, Mayapan, Maya,
ca. 1200–1450 CE, 23 × 22 × 15 cm,
Museo Nacional de Antropología
e Historia, Mexico City,
inv. no. 10-0001243. Archivo
Digital de las Colecciones
del Museo Nacional de
Antropología. INAH-CANON.
Reproduction authorized
by the Instituto Nacional de
Antropología e Historia.

Figure 7

ation of clouds of incense with rain [Figure 7]. The bodies of these vessels are also decorated all over with spiky protrusions that recall the tradition of spiky hourglass *incensarios* so prevalent during the ninth to eleventh centuries CE throughout Mesoamerica, but with roots that can be traced even further back at Teotihuacan and in the Maya area [see Figure 1]. Other smaller *incensarios* rest on three circular legs that recall the three hearth-stones of creation in Mesoamerican myth.

This survey of Mesoamerican *incensarios* reveals a tremendous diversity of forms, united by deep continuities and shared traditions. We see moments of regional differentiation as well as of pan-Mesoamerican commonality as the inspiration for concepts, vessel shapes, and practices traveled in different directions at different moments in Mesoamerican history, revealing a profoundly interconnected world. In disparate regions across three millennia, artists returned again and again to foundational metaphors: the incense burner as world tree and symbolic center, the incense burner as a human or divine body. Moreover, these fixed forms were often used in conjunction with mobile censers to create powerful multisensory experiences.

CENSERS

Many of the *incensarios* and braziers described in the preceding paragraphs were intermittently mobile. Rarely more than one meter in height and generally weighing less than 10 kilograms, they were easy for a single person to lift and move, even though they would have been dangerously hot to touch while in operation. Even the largest censer bases at Palenque [see Figure 4] or braziers in the Aztec capital of Tenochtitlan [see Figure 7] could be moved by a team of two or three people. Though some buildings featured built-in braziers, fire pits, or other receptacles to receive ceremonial burning, most braziers were designed to be moveable, at least between uses.[65] This may indicate that motion and cyclical renewal were important components of the ritual burning of incense.

Yet these semi-portable objects coexisted with and complemented another even more mobile mode of censing. Smaller vessels, designed to be held with the hand or hands, could be carried while being used to burn copal and other resins. This allowed the user to direct the purifying smoke in multiple directions, cense the boundaries of a territory, or accompany ritual movement. These vessels correspond more closely to what might be properly termed censers and are often known by the Spanish term *sahumador*. Over time, such vessels gradually developed accoutrements dictated by their function, such as handles to insulate the bearer from the heat of the coals burning the resin and perforations to allow the smoke to escape in multiple directions.

Figure 8

A two-handled censer from the region of Cholula, decorated in the cosmopolitan Mixteca-Puebla style, is scaled for human handling [Figure 8]. Twenty-three centimeters wide, twelve centimeters tall, and weighing approximately 735 grams, it has two side flanges that might be held; holes through the flanges might also have allowed the censer to be suspended from two ropes and swung, a practice that might account for some of the wear on the flanges. The vessel is decorated with symbols of fire, including white figures that combine characteristics of butterflies and flames (the forms frequently converge in Postclassic Mesoamerican art), as well as starry eyes that evoke the gleam of the night sky and black spots imitating the pelt of

Figure 7
Brazier with attributes of the
rain deity Tlaloc, found in
the House of the Eagles at
the Templo Mayor, Aztec,
ca. 1400–1521 CE, 72 × 55 cm,
Museo del Sitio del Templo
Mayor, Mexico City.
Photo by Gary Todd from
Xinzheng, China, CC0,
via Wikimedia Commons.
Reproduction authorized
by the Instituto Nacional de
Antropología e Historia.

Figure 8
Censer, Cholula, Nahua,
ca. 1200–1520 CE,
12 × 23.5 × 20 cm, 735 g, Museo
Nacional de Antropología,
Mexico City, inv. no. 10-78081.
Ex-collection of William
Spratling. Archivo Digital de las
Colecciones del Museo Nacional
de Antropología. INAH-CANON.
Reproduction authorized
by the Instituto Nacional de
Antropología e Historia.

jaguars.[66] The head of Xolotl, a canine deity associated with the planet Venus, protrudes from the side of the vessel; similar vessels of this type feature the heads of eagles, jaguars, and other symbolically potent animals.

Still another kind of censer placed the user at an even greater remove from the heated incense. These so-called ladle or frying pan censers, which consist of a bowl for receiving incense and coals attached to a long handle, were also widely used throughout Mesoamerica from at least the first millennium CE onwards.[67] The form became even more common in the upheavals in the ninth and tenth centuries CE, perhaps in conjunction with the spread of what William Ringle, Tomás Gallareta, and George Bey term a new "world religion" tied to the deity Quetzalcoatl.[68] Harbingers of new kinds of devotional practice, these frying pan censers were one element in a suite of ritual implements, which also included openwork censers, a resurgence of spiked hourglass-shaped *incensarios*, and concave-sided braziers decorated with rudimentary features of the rain god Tlaloc. The new ritual practices associated with these objects extended well beyond the borders of Mesoamerica: frying pan censers are found as far south as the Greater Nicoya region of Costa Rica.[69]

By the fifteenth century CE, the form of such ladle censers had become even more attenuated, with an even longer handle and a wide, shallow bowl; this form was ubiquitous from the Mixteca-Puebla region to the Valley of Mexico and beyond. Perforations in the bowl allowed smoke to escape, and often formed significant patterns, such as a configuration of four triangles arranged like a Maltese cross, which Ángel González López and colleagues argue is a symbol associated with fire in the Aztec world.[70] In other cases, perforations constituted ringed eyes and a fang-like mouth for an image of Tlaloc, the rain deity whose fecund clouds are summoned by the clouds of smoke issuing from burning incense [Figure 9]. At the same time, the long handles often ended in clawed feet or in figural heads, shaped like a serpent with open maw and protruding tongue, a wide-eyed eagle or owl, the curled proboscis of a butterfly, or the curl-nosed snout of the Xiuhcoatl, or fire serpent, a deity associated with the Pleiades.[71] These heads are often figured so that they would be inverted while the censer was held during use; between uses, they might have been displayed so that the heads on the handles and bowls were more visible.[72]

Figure 9

These objects had their own faces and embodied identities, yet they also existed as extensions of the person who wielded them, prosthetics that extended the capacities and reach of the human body.[73] The word in Nahuatl (the language spoken by the Aztecs) for such objects is *tlemaitl*, literally "fire-hand."[74] Other terms, such as *tlapopochhuiloni* ("an instrument for causing things to smoke"), alluded to the voluminous quantities of smoke that these vessels would produce.[75] The Florentine Codex, a sixteenth-century cultural encyclopedia compiled by Bernardino de Sahagún and Indigenous Nahua knowledge-holders, describes the practice of burning incense (*tlenamaquiliztli*):

> And thus was the offering of incense performed. It was with an incense ladle made of clay, with [stones/clay pellets in its hollows making] a rattle. There in the ladle they laid live coals. When they had scooped them up, then they filled it with copal incense; with it they came forth before the devil or else

Figure 9
Censer (*tlemaitl*), with Tlaloc
face on the bowl and owl head
handle, excavated by Leopoldo
Batres in the Calle de las
Escallerías, near the Templo
Mayor. Aztec (Mexica), ca.
1400–1521 CE, 9.5 × 62.5 × 25 cm,
1.765 kg, Museo Nacional de
Antropología, Mexico City,
cat. no. 10-0220158. Archivo
Digital de las Colecciones del
Museo Nacional de Antro-
pología. INAH-CANON.
Reproduction authorized
by the Instituto Nacional de
Antropología e Historia.

in the middle of the courtyard where the brazier stood. [This] was made of clay.

And when they came to stand before the devil, then they raised the incense ladle in dedication to the four directions. Thus they offered incense. And when they had raised it in dedication to the four directions, then they threw [the incense and the coals] into the brazier. Then the copal was smoking.

And this was it done: the mothers, the fathers likewise woke the children at dawn, whether men [children] or women [children]; that they might offer incense quickly, they woke them.[76]

As the text describes, the embodied experience of wielding such a prosthetic was a multisensory one. In addition to the smell and texture of the smoke generated by the burning resin, the heat of the coals, as transmitted through the handle, would warm the body, while the clay pellets rattling within the handle added a sonic component. At the main temples, such offerings were made four times each day and five times each night, the ritual rhythms punctuating the day. The practice was also, however, common on a smaller scale in individual households.[77] The embodied and multisensory experience of burning incense united people at all levels of Mesoamerican society.

An image in another section of the Florentine Codex shows the offering of fire and incense to the sun deity, who is rendered in a European-influenced form with little precedent in Mesoamerican tradition [Figure 10]. The offering of incense is conjoined with other forms of ritual observance: the offering of music, in the form of playing conch shell trumpets, and of blood, produced by piercing the ears with sharp thorns.[78] Together, these three offerings constituted different kinds of vital essences: the blood of autosacrifice; the breath necessary to play the conch trumpets; and solar energy or *tonalli* in the flames that produced the pleasing scent of the incense.[79]

Figure 10

Certain pieces of evidence hint at even more complex choreographies. Offering 130, found at the Templo Mayor, the principal temple of Aztec Tenochtitlan, contained thirty-one long-handled censers, laid out in a careful configuration. Placed in a pit right at the foot of the temple along its central axis sometime between 1440 and 1469 CE, the censers showed traces of burning, copal residue, and other signs of use, but very little unburnt copal was found within the pit. It is thus likely that the burning coals and resins had been deposited in a brazier, as described in the Florentine Codex passage cited earlier. The censers, very similar to the object illustrated in Figure 9, were placed in the pit parallel to one another, with the handles facing away from the temple, towards the west. A single censer was oriented in the opposite direction. It is possible to imagine their deposition as part of a coordinated action, where at the conclusion of a ritual, the priests placed their coals in a brazier, then stood facing the stairway of the great temple and the priest before it, before kneeling to put the incense burners in the pit together. This offering suggests how braziers and censers might be used together; it also alerts us to the ways in which incense burning might be a social activity, involving multiple actors, rather than a solitary practice.

Figure 10
Three different kinds of offerings to the sun god: music from conch shell trumpets, incense, and blood, Bernardino de Sahagún and Indigenous collaborators, *Historia general de la nueva España* (Florentine Codex), Book 2, Appendix, fol. 135r, 1575–77 CE. Biblioteca Medicea Laurenziana, Florence, Ms. Med. Palat. 219, fol. 296v. Courtesy of the Ministero della Cultura. Further reproduction by any means is prohibited.

CONTEMPORARY USES

Burning copal remains an essential part of Indigenous ritual practice today. In the rituals of traditional Maya daykeepers, in the churches of Indigenous communities, and in the spaces used by healers to conduct *limpias*, or spiritual cleansings, copal is a ubiquitous presence. Clouds of copal smoke also accompany the rhythm of drums and the flashing costumes of neo-Aztec dance performances. In many cases, the modern vessels for burning incense are far simpler than their premodern counterparts: a hollowed-out wooden cylinder, a clay bowl or saucer, a tin plate. Still, the distinctive scent of heated copal continues to enliven ceremonies and connect people in Mexico, Guatemala, and throughout the world, wherever diasporic communities are found today.

ENDNOTES

I am deeply grateful to Beate Fricke for the invitation to contribute to this volume, and for her patience and generosity during its writing. Thanks also to Ángel González López, Mark Van Stone, Allison Caplan, Felipe Rojas, and Vera Tiesler, whose conversation and vast knowledge enriched this work. All errors that remain are my own.

1 Breedlove and Laughlin 1993, 1:179; Montúfar López 2012, 109–16; Tozzer 1941, 75 n. 338, 197.

2 For tribute, see Codex Mendoza, fols. 35v–37r in Berdan and Anawalt 1997, 4:76–79, see also 2:76, 78, 79, 81, 168 in the same book; for offerings, see Coggins and Ladd 1992a, 345–53; Rice 1999, 27; Victoria Lona 2012.

3 Heyden 1997, 243, 247, 267; Rice 1999, 28. On the metaphorics of paper, see also Mundy 2015.

4 Christenson 2003, 128–34; for commentary, see also García 2022, 32–34. Andrea Stone proposes that the material that is burnt might actually be rubber (Stone 2002, 23).

5 Tozzer 1941, 163, interpolations in Tozzer's translation.

6 Dupey García 2018, 202–3; Graulich and Olivier 2004, 124–25; Olivier 2008, 224–25, 347 n. 103; Rice 1999, 28; Stross 1997.

7 On tamales, see Taube 1989.

8 Stross 1997, fig. 2; see also Thompson 1970, 324.

9 Montúfar López 2012, 115–16.

10 Robb 2017b, 366; Tozzer 1941, 104.

11 Sahagún 1950–82 [1575–77], Book 2, Appendix, 195.

12 Ibid., Book 11, Chapter 7, 187; Ruiz de Alarcón 1987 [1629], 108, 136–38, 171–73, 182–83, 196–97; Breedlove and Laughlin 1993, 1:179; Heyden 1997, 264–65. Modern research has shown that copal smoke has anti-anxiety effects on rats (Merali et al. 2018); for other potential therapeutic properties, see Gigliarelli et al. 2015, 22391–92.

13 Vázquez de Ágredos Pascual et al. 2018, 70–73.

14 Heyden 1997, 244; Stacey, Cartwright, and McEwan 2006.

15 Sahagún 1950–82 [1575–77], Book 9, Chapter 16, 74, 77; for discussion, see Caplan 2019, 177, 197.

16 Sahagún 1950–82 [1575–77], Book 10, Chapter 21, 77.

17 Klein and Victoria Lona 2009, 355–65; Matos Moctezuma and Solís Olguín 2002, 460; Victoria Lona 2012.

18 Victoria Lona 2012, 211–12; see Montúfar López (2012, 117) for an example with well-preserved red and black paint.

19 Coggins and Ladd 1992a, 347–49.

20 Ibid., 351; see also Coggins and Ladd 1992b, 283–97.

21 Coggins and Ladd 1992b, 293–95, fig. 8.67.

22 Coggins and Ladd 1992a, 346, 348, 351, 354; Stone 2002, 23–24.

23 Arnold et al. 2008.

24 Vogt (1976, 49–50) contrasts the wood, "cut directly from the trees, that is, something wild and undomesticated" with the more processed gathered copal resin; see also Breedlove and Laughlin 1993, 1:179.

On *yauhtli*, see Burns 2008; on other plant materials that contributed to the olfactory landscape of Mesoamerican temples and tombs, see Dupey García 2020; McNeil 2021; Vázquez de Ágredos Pascual et al. 2018.

25 Robb 2017b, 366; Tozzer 1941, 104.

26 Carreón Blaine 2006; Stone 2002; Tarkanian and Hosler 2011.

27 Stone 2002, 23.

28 Aguilera 1980; Carreón Blaine 2006, 65–68; Heyden 1997, 247.

29 Sahagún 1950–82 [1575–77], Book 9, Chapter 3, 9–11; 1975 [1575–77], Book 2, Appendix, 166; Arnold 2002; Sandstrom and Sandstrom 2016; Thompson 1970, 156. For modern Nahua ritual uses of paper, which do not include burning the paper, see Sandstrom and Sandstrom 1986.

30 Sandstrom 2021, 42.

31 Durán 1971 [1576–79], 104.

32 Vogt (1976, 207), citing an unpublished BA thesis by Carolyn Pope, who also stresses the properties of heat and light in candles, which the people of Zinacantan call "tortillas for the gods," while incense is their "cigarettes" (ibid., 49).

33 Maffie 2014, 295, 324.

34 Heyden 1997, 247–48; Rice 1999, 28; Stone 2002, 23; Thompson 1970, 166, 264.

35 Rice 1999, 25, 31; see also Rattray 2001, 165, 183, 211, 243, 273, and for an illustrated example, Robb 2017b, 375, although the pattern of burning on the inside of this perforated cup-like vessel suggests that it was placed lip down over a fire or smoking incense, rather than containing the smoldering substance as it was held in the hand.

36 Rice 1999, 25. Wood is a preferred medium for censers among neo-Azteca dance groups today.

37 E.g., Hough 1912, fig. 1; Miller and Martin 2004, 224–25, 230.

38 Robb 2007; 2017a. Examples are illustrated in Berrin and Pasztory 1993, 174–75; Robb 2017b, 232, 284, 385; Solís Olguín 2009, 328–29.

39 Robb 2007, 199–203; 2017a, 143–44.

40 Hosler 1995; 2009; Matos Moctezuma and Solís Olguín 2002, 244–54.

41 On the object illustrated in Figure 1, see Robb 2017b, 387; Solís Olguín 2009, 378–79; for spiky incensarios in the Maya world, see Rice 1999, 30, 32–36, 39.

42 Marcus and Flannery 1996, 131–32.

43 On the object illustrated in Figure 3, see Robb 2017b, 380–81. On the class of objects more generally, see Berrin and Pasztory 1993, 216–21; Pasztory 1997, 167–71; Solís Olguín 2009, 306–11; Robb 2017b, 206, 266–367.

44 Sugiyama 2002.

45 Berlo 1983; Headrick 2007, 124–45.

46 Rattray 2001, 163–65, 359, 363. On the combination of spiky and figural censers in the Maya world, see Rice 1999, 39, 42.

47 Berlo 1980. For a similar process of corporealization in Teotihuacan architectural ornaments at the Central Mexican city of Cacaxtla, see Brittenham and Nagao 2014, 81–84.

48 Chinchilla Mazariegos 2021.

49 Chinchilla Mazariegos 2019.

50 Coe 1990, 2:479–87, fig. 160; Coggins 1975, 150–52; Culbert 1993, fig. 14; Harrison 1999, 86, color plate 2; Martin and Grube 2008, 33.

51 Kidder, Jennings, and Shook 1946, 207–14, figs. 178e–h, 190–91, 201–2, 206c, 207g; Rice 1999, 29–31.

52 Fash et al. 1992, 112–13; Fash 2001, 106–12; Fields and Reents-Budet 2005, 220–21; Martin and Grube 2008, 202. There were also numerous spiked incensarios found at the tomb, see Rice 1999, 34.

53 See Fields and Reents-Budet (2005, 166–67) for one unprovenanced example.

54 Miller and Martin 2004, 226–31; Cuevas García 2004; 2007.

55 López Bravo 2004, 256–58; Miller and Martin 2004, 224–25, 231.

56 Perales Vela, de Paz, and Balán 2010, 129–35; Michelet 2014, 27–28, 296–97; see also Houston 2022, 100, for a similar example from a residential group at Palenque.

57 Ringle, Gallareta Negrón, and Bey 1998, 216–19; Rice 1999, 41.

58 Coggins and Shane 1984, 155; Moholy-Nagy and Ladd 1992, 132–40.

59 Pohl 2007.

60 Milbrath and Peraza Lope 2013, 216–24; Taube 1992, 89–90, 120–29; Thompson 1957.

61 For color, see Houston et al. 2009, 94–97; for the International Style, see Boone and Smith 2003; Robertson 1970; Fields, Pohl, and Lyall 2012.

62 Matos Moctezuma and Solís Olguín 2002, 292–93, 458–59.

63 Ibid., 216–17, 433; for still other genres of Aztec brazier, see also Heyden 1987; Matos Moctezuma and Solís Olguín 2002, 176, 188, 212, 319, 423, 426, 432, 471.

64 Kurella, Berger, and de Castro 2020, 338; Pasztory 1983, 292–93, color plate 25.

65 One example of a fixed stone brazier is illustrated in Heyden 1987, fig. 10; see also the reconstruction of the temple summit at Santa Cecelia Acatitlan in Pasztory 1983, color plate 25.

66 Matos Moctezuma and Solís Olguín 2002, 439; Solís and Velásquez 2006, 118–19. For other examples of the type, see Fields, Pohl, and Lyall 2012, 197; Solís and Velásquez 2006, 91.

67 Rice 1999, 32, 42, 50.

68 Ringle, Gallareta Negrón, and Bey 1998, 216–19; see also Rice 1999, 40–41.

69 E.g., Denver Art Museum 1993.474, https://www.denverartmuseum.org/en/object/1993.474.

70 González López, Turner, and Barrera Rodríguez 2018, 70–75.

71 For Xiuhcoatl, see Taube 2000, 270–89; 2012.

72 I am grateful to Mark Van Stone for this observation (personal communication, 2021).

73 For prosthetics in Mesoamerican context, see Hamann 2004, 81, 94–95.

74 Molina 1970 [1571], *Vocabulario en lengua mexicana y castellana*, fol. 147r.

75 Molina 1970 [1571], *Vocabulario en lengua castellana y mexicana*, fol. 106v.

76   Sahagún 1950–82 [1575–77], Book 2,
Appendix, 194.
77   Durán 1971 [1576–79], 119, 235, 427;
Sahagún 1950–82 [1575–77], Book 2,
Appendix, 216.

78   On Mesoamerican music, see Katz 2018;
on the act of perforating the body, see
Finegold 2021, 89–116.

79   On animic entities, see López Austin 1988;
Furst 1995.

BIBLIOGRAPHY

Aguilera, Carmen. 1980. "Algunos datos sobre el chapopote en las fuentes documentales del siglo XVI." *Estudios de Cultura Náhuatl* 4: 335–43.

Arnold, Dean E., Jason R. Branden, Patrick Ryan Williams, Gary Feinman, and J. P. Brown. 2008. "The First Direct Evidence for the Production of Maya Blue: Rediscovery of a Technology." *Antiquity* 82: 151–64.

Arnold, Philip P. 2002. "Paper Rituals and the Mexican Landscape." In *Representing Aztec Ritual: Performance, Text, and Image in the Work of Sahagún*, edited by Eloise Quiñones Keber, 227–50. Boulder: University of Colorado Press.

Berdan, Frances F., and Patricia Rieff Anawalt. 1997. *The Essential Codex Mendoza*. Berkeley: University of California Press.

Berlo, Janet Catherine. 1980. "Teotihuacan Art Abroad: A Study of Metropolitan Style and Provincial Transformation in Incensario Workshops." PhD thesis, Yale University.

Berlo, Janet Catherine. 1983. "The Warrior and the Butterfly: Central Mexican Ideologies of Sacred Warfare and Teotihuacan Iconography." In *Text and Image in Pre-Columbian Art: Essays on the Interrelationship of the Verbal and Visual Arts. Proceedings of the 44th International Congress of Americanists, Manchester, 1982*, edited by Janet Catherine Berlo, 79–117. Oxford: B.A.R.

Berrin, Kathleen, and Esther Pasztory, eds. 1993. *Teotihuacan: Art from the City of the Gods*. New York; San Francisco: Thames & Hudson; Fine Arts Museums of San Francisco.

Boone, Elizabeth Hill, and Michael E. Smith. 2003. "Postclassic International Styles and Symbol Sets." In *The Postclassic Mesoamerican World*, edited by Michael E. Smith and Frances F. Berdan, 186–93. Salt Lake City: University of Utah Press.

Breedlove, Dennis E., and Robert A Laughlin. 1993. *The Flowering of Man: A Tzotzil Botany of Zinacantán*. 2 vols. Washington, DC: Smithsonian Institution Press.

Brittenham, Claudia, and Debra Nagao. 2014. "Cacaxtla Figural Ceramics." *Anales del Instituto de Investigaciones Estéticas* 36, no. 104: 55–96.

Burns, Corinne. 2008. "Four Hundred Flowers: The Aztec Herbal Pharmacopoeia, Part 1. Yauhtli and Cempoalxochitl." Mexicolore web essay. https://www.mexicolore.co.uk/aztecs/health/aztec-herbal-pharmacopoeia-part-1.

Caplan, Allison. 2019. "Their Flickering Creations: Value, Appearance, Animacy, and Surface in Nahua Precious Art." PhD thesis, Tulane University.

Carreón Blaine, Emilie. 2006. *El olli en la plástica mexica*. Mexico City: Instituto de Investigaciones Estéticas, Universidad Nacional Autónoma de México.

Chinchilla Mazariegos, Oswaldo. 2019. "Temples to the Great Bird: Architecture, Mythology, and Ritual in Teotihuacan-Style Censers from Escuintla, Guatemala." *Res: Anthropology and Aesthetics* 71/72: 78–96.

Chinchilla Mazariegos, Oswaldo. 2021. "The Goddess in the Garden: An Exploration of Gender in the Flower Worlds of the Pacific Coast of Guatemala." In *Flower Worlds: Religion, Aesthetics, and Ideology in Mesoamerica and the American Southwest*, edited by Michael D. Mathiowetz and Andrew D. Turner, 105–28. Tucson: University of Arizona Press.

Christenson, Allen J. 2003. *Popol Vuh: The Sacred Book of the Maya*. Winchester, UK: O Books.

Coe, William R. 1990. *Excavations in the Great Plaza, North Terrace and North Acropolis of Tikal*. 6 vols. Tikal Report 14. Philadelphia: University Museum, University of Pennsylvania.

Coggins, Clemency Chase. 1975. "Painting and Drawing Styles at Tikal: An Historical and Iconographic Reconstruction." PhD thesis, Department of Art, Harvard University.

Coggins, Clemency Chase, and John M. Ladd. 1992a. "Copal and Rubber Offerings." In *Artifacts from the Cenote of Sacrifice, Chichen Itza, Yucatan: Textiles, Basketry, Stone, Bone, Shell, Ceramics, Wood, Copal, Rubber, Other Organic Materials, and Mammalian Remains*, edited by Clemency Chase Coggins, 345–57. Cambridge, MA: Peabody Museum of Archaeology and Ethnology.

Coggins, Clemency Chase, and John M. Ladd. 1992b. "Wooden Artifacts." In *Artifacts from the Cenote of Sacrifice, Chichen Itza, Yucatan: Textiles, Basketry, Stone, Bone, Shell, Ceramics, Wood, Copal, Rubber, Other Organic Materials, and Mammalian Remains*, edited by Clemency Chase Coggins, 235–344. Cambridge, MA: Peabody Museum of Archaeology and Ethnology.

Coggins, Clemency Chase, and Orrin C. Shane. 1984. *Cenote of Sacrifice: Maya Treasures from the Sacred Well at Chichén Itzá*. Austin: University of Texas Press.

Cuevas García, Martha. 2004. "The Cult of Patron and Ancestor Gods in Censers at Palenque." In *Courtly Art of the Ancient Maya*, edited by Mary Ellen Miller and Simon Martin, 253–55. New York; San Francisco: Thames & Hudson; Fine Arts Museums of San Francisco.

Cuevas García, Martha. 2007. *Los incensarios efigie de Palenque: Deidades y rituales mayas*. Mexico City: Universidad Nacional Autónoma de México, Centro de Estudios Mayas and Instituto Nacional de Antropología e Historia.

Culbert, T. Patrick. 1993. *The Ceramics of Tikal: Vessels from Burials, Caches and Problematical Deposits*. Tikal Report 25A. Philadelphia: University Museum, University of Pennsylvania.

Dupey García, Élodie. 2018. "Making and Using Colors in the Manufacture of Nahua Codices: Aesthetic Standards, Symbolic Purposes." In *Painting the Skin: Pigments on Bodies and Codices in Pre-Columbian Mesoamerica*, edited by Élodie Dupey García and María Luisa Vázquez de Ágredos Pascual, 186–205. Tucson: University of Arizona Press.

Dupey García, Élodie. 2020. "Lo que el viento se lleva. Ofrendas odoríferas y sonoras en la ritualidad náhuatl prehispánica." In *De olfato. Aproximaciones a los olores en la historia de México*, edited by Élodie Dupey García and Guadalupe Pinzón Ríos, 83–131. Mexico City: Fondo de Cultura Económica.

Durán, Diego. 1971 [1576–79]. *Book of the Gods and Rites and The Ancient Calendar*. Translated by Fernando Horcasitas and Doris Heyden. Norman: University of Oklahoma Press.

Fash, William. 2001. *Scribes, Warriors and Kings: The City of Copán and the Ancient Maya*. Revised edn. New York; London: Thames & Hudson.

Fash, William L., Richard V. Williamson, Carlos Rudy Larios, and Joel Palka. 1992. "The Hieroglyphic Stairway and Its Ancestors: Investigations of Copan Structure 10L-26." *Ancient Mesoamerica* 3, no. 1: 105–15.

Fields, Virginia M., John M. D. Pohl, and Victoria I. Lyall, eds. 2012. *Children of the Plumed Serpent: The Legacy of Quetzalcoatl in Ancient Mexico*. Los Angeles: Los Angeles County Museum of Art; Scala Publishers.

Fields, Virginia M., and Dorie Reents-Budet, eds. 2005. *Lords of Creation: The Origins of Sacred Maya Kingship*. Los Angeles: Los Angeles County Museum of Art; Scala Publishers.

Finegold, Andrew. 2021. *Vital Voids: Cavities and Holes in Mesoamerican Material Culture*. Austin: University of Texas Press.

Furst, Jill Leslie McKeever. 1995. *The Natural History of the Soul in Ancient Mexico*. New Haven, CT: Yale University Press.

García, Edgar. 2022. *Emergency: Reading the Popol Vuh in a Time of Crisis*. Chicago: University of Chicago Press.

Gigliarelli, Giulia, Judith X. Becerra, Massimo Curini, and Maria Carla Marcotullio. 2015. "Chemical Composition and Biological Activities of Fragrant Mexican Copal (*Bursera* spp.)." *Molecules* 20: 22383–94.

González López, Ángel, Andrew Turner, and Raúl Barrera Rodríguez. 2018. "Un deidad olvidada en el tiempo. Muerte, fuego y transformación en la escultura de Tenochtitlan." *Arqueología Mexicana* 149: 70–75.

Graulich, Michel, and Guilhem Olivier. 2004. "¿Deidades insaciables? La comida de los dioses en el México Antiguo." *Estudios de Cultura Náhuatl* 35: 121–55.

Hamann, Byron Ellsworth. 2004. "'In the Eyes of the Mixtecs/To View Several Pages Simultaneously': Seeing and the Mixtec Screenfolds." *Visible Language* 38, no. 1: 68–123.

Harrison, Peter D. 1999. *The Lords of Tikal: Rulers of an Ancient Maya City*. New York; London: Thames & Hudson.

Headrick, Annabeth. 2007. *The Teotihuacan Trinity: The Sociopolitical Structure of an Ancient Mesoamerican City*. Austin: University of Texas Press.

Heyden, Doris. 1987. "Symbolism of Ceramics from the Templo Mayor." In *The Aztec Templo Mayor*, edited by Elizabeth Hill Boone, 109–30. Washington, DC: Dumbarton Oaks Research Library and Collection.

Heyden, Doris. 1997. "La sangre del árbol: El copal y las resinas en el ritual mexicano." In *Códices y documentos sobre México: Segundo simposio*, edited by Salvador Rueda Smithers, Constantino Vega Sosa, and Rodrigo Martínez Baracs, 243–70. Mexico City: Instituto Nacional de Antropolgía e Historia.

Hosler, Dorothy. 1995. "Sound, Color, and Meaning in the Metallurgy of Ancient West Mexico." *World Archaeology* 27, no. 1: 100–115.

Hosler, Dorothy. 2009. "The Metallurgy of West Mexico: Revisited and Revised." *Journal of World Prehistory* 22: 185–212.

Hough, Walter. *Censers and Incense of Mexico and Central America*. Washington, DC: Government Printing Office, 1912.

Houston, Stephen D. 2022. "Day, Night." In *Lives of the Gods: Divinity in Maya Art*, edited by Oswaldo Chinchilla Mazariegos, James A. Doyle, and Joanne Pillsbury, 85–107. New York; New Haven, CT: The Metropolitan Museum of Art; Yale University Press.

Houston, Stephen D., Claudia Brittenham, Cassandra Mesick, Alexandre Tokovinine, and Christina Warinner. 2009. *Veiled Brightness: A History of Ancient Maya Color*. Austin: University of Texas Press.

Katz, Jared. 2018. "Gentle Flutes and Blaring Horns: An Analysis of Ancient Maya Music and Musical Instruments in Daily and Ceremonial Activities." PhD thesis, University of California, Riverside.

Kidder, Alfred V., Jesse D. Jennings, and Edwin M. Shook. 1946. *Excavations at Kaminaljuyu, Guatemala*. Publication 561. Washington, DC: Carnegie Institution of Washington.

Klein, Cecelia F., and Naoli Victoria Lona. 2009. "Sex in the City: A Comparison of Aztec Ceramic Figurines to Copal Figurines from the Templo Mayor." In *Mesoamerican Figurines: Small-Scale Indices of Large-Scale Phenomena*, edited by Christina T. Halperin, Katherine A. Faust, Rhonda Taube, and Aurore Giguet, 327–77. Gainesville: University Press of Florida.

Kurella, Doris, Martin Berger, and Inés de Castro, eds. 2020. *Aztecs*. Munich: Hirmer.

López Austin, Alfredo. 1988. *The Human Body and Ideology: Concepts of the Ancient Nahuas*. Translated by Thelma Ortiz de Montellano and Bernard Ortiz de Montellano. 2 vols. Salt Lake City: University of Utah Press.

López Bravo, Roberto. 2004. "State and Domestic Cult in Paleque Censer Stands." In *Courtly Art of the Ancient Maya*, edited by Mary Ellen Miller and Simon Martin, 256–58. New York; San Francisco: Thames & Hudson; Fine Arts Museums of San Francisco.

Maffie, James. 2014. *Aztec Philosophy: Understanding a World in Motion*. Boulder: University Press of Colorado.

Marcus, Joyce, and Kent V. Flannery. 1996. *Zapotec Civilization: How Urban Society Evolved in Mexico's Oaxaca Valley*. New York: Thames & Hudson.

Martin, Simon, and Nikolai Grube. 2008. *Chronicle of the Maya Kings and Queens*. 2nd edn. London: Thames & Hudson.

Matos Moctezuma, Eduardo, and Felipe Solís Olguín, eds. 2002. *Aztecs*. London: Royal Academy of Arts.

McNeil, Cameron L. 2021. "The Flowery Mountains of Copan: Pollen Remains from Maya Temples and Tombs." In *Flower Worlds: Religion, Aesthetics, and Ideology in Mesoamerica and the American Southwest*, edited by Michael D. Mathiowetz and Andrew D. Turner, 129–48. Tucson: University of Arizona Press.

Merali, Zul, Christian Cayer, Pamela Kent, Rui Liu, Victor Cal, Cory S. Harris, and John T. Arnason. 2018. "Sacred Maya Incense, Copal (*Protium copal* – Burseraceae), Has Antianxiety Effects in Animal Models." *Journal of Ethnopharmacology* 216: 63–70.

Michelet, Dominique, ed. 2014. *Mayas: Révélation d'un temps sin fin*. Paris: Musée du Quai Branly.

Milbrath, Susan, and Carlos Peraza Lope. 2013. "Mayapán's Chen Mul Modeled Effigy Censers: Iconography and Archaeological Context." In *Ancient Maya Pottery: Classification, Analysis, and Interpretation*, edited by James John Aimers, 203–28. Gainesville: University Press of Florida.

Miller, Mary Ellen, and Simon Martin. 2004. *Courtly Art of the Ancient Maya*. New York; San Francisco: Thames & Hudson; Fine Arts Museums of San Francisco.

Moholy-Nagy, Hattula, and John M. Ladd. 1992. "Objects of Stone, Shell, and Bone." In *Artifacts from the Cenote of Sacrifice, Chichen Itza, Yucatan: Textiles, Basketry, Stone, Bone, Shell, Ceramics, Wood, Copal, Rubber, Other Organic Materials, and Mammalian Remains*, edited by Clemency Chase Coggins, 99–152. Cambridge, MA: Peabody Museum of Archaeology and Ethnology.

Molina, Alonso de. 1970 [1571]. *Vocabulario en lengua castellana y mexicana y mexicana y castellana*. Facsimile of 1571 edn. Mexico City: Editorial Porrúa.

Montúfar López, Aurora. 2012. "El copal: Producción, circulación y usos." In *Humo aromático para los dioses: Una ofrenda de sahumadores al pie del Templo Mayor de*

Tenochtitlan, edited by Leonardo López Luján, 107–20. Mexico City: Instituto Nacional de Antropolgía e Historia.

Mundy, Barbara. 2015. "Representation, Fragments and Nature of the Deity Performer, or Teixiptla, in Sixteenth-Century Mexico." Paper presented at the College Art Association annual conference, New York.

Olivier, Guilhem. 2008. *Mockeries and Metamorphoses of an Aztec God: Tezcatlipoca, the Lord of the Smoking Mirror*. Niwot: University Press of Colorado.

Pasztory, Esther. 1983. *Aztec Art*. New York: Abrams.

Pasztory, Esther. 1997. *Teotihuacan: An Experiment in Living*. Norman: University of Oklahoma Press.

Perales Vela, Rebeca, Héctor de Paz, and Cristina Balán, eds. 2010. *Tiempo soy entre dos eternidades: Piezas selectas del Museo Regional de Antropología Carlos Pellicer Cámara*. Villahermosa: Gobierno del Estado de Tabasco.

Pohl, John M. D. 2007. *Sorcerers of the Fifth Heaven: Nahua Art and Ritual of Ancient Southern Mexico*. Princeton, NJ: Princeton University Program in Latin American Studies.

Rattray, Evelyn. 2001. *Teotihuacan: Ceramics, Chronology and Cultural Trends*. Mexico City; Pittsburgh, PA: Instituto Nacional de Antropología e Historia; University of Pittsburgh.

Rice, Prudence M. 1999. "Rethinking Classic Lowland Maya Pottery Censers." *Ancient Mesoamerica* 10, no. 1: 25–50.

Ringle, William M., Tomás Gallareta Negrón, and George J. Bey. 1998. "Return of Quetzalcoatl: Evidence for the Spread of a World Religion during the Epiclassic Period." *Ancient Mesoamerica* 9, no. 2: 181–232.

Robb, Matthew H. 2007. "The Construction of Civic Identity at Teotihuacan, Mexico." PhD thesis, Yale University.

Robb, Matthew H. 2017a. "The Old Fire God." In *Teotihuacan: City of Water, City of Fire*, edited by Matthew H. Robb, 144–49. Berkeley: University of California Press.

Robb, Matthew H., ed. 2017b. *Teotihuacan: City of Water, City of Fire*. Berkeley: University of California Press.

Robertson, Donald. 1970. "The Tulum Murals: The International Style of the Late Post-Classic." *Proceedings of the International Congress of Americanists (38 Session, Stuttgart and Munich, 1968)* 2: 77–88.

Ruiz de Alarcón, Hernando. 1987 [1629]. *Treatise on the Heathen Superstitions that Today Live among the Indians Native to this New Spain, 1629*. Translated by J. Richard Andrews and Ross Hassig. Norman: University of Oklahoma Press.

Sahagún, Bernardino de. 1950–82 [1575–77]. *Florentine Codex: General History of the Things of New Spain*. Translated by Arthur J. O. Anderson and Charles E. Dibble. 13 vols. Santa Fe, NM: School of American Research.

Sahagún, Bernardino de. 1975 [1575–77]. *Historia general de las cosas de Nueva España*. Mexico City: Editorial Porrúa.

Sandstrom, Alan R. 2021. "Flower World in the Religious Ideology of Contemporary Nahua of the Southern Huasteca, Mexico." In *Flower Worlds: Religion, Aesthetics, and Ideology in Mesoamerica and the American Southwest*, edited by Michael D. Mathiowetz and Andrew D. Turner, 35–52. Tucson: University of Arizona Press.

Sandstrom, Alan R., and Paula Effrein Sandstrom. 1986. *Traditional Papermaking and Paper Cult Figures of Mexico*. Norman: University of Oklahoma Press.

Sandstrom, Alan R., and Paula Effrein Sandstrom. 2016. "Aztec Papermaking."

Mexicolore web essay. https://www.mexicolore.co.uk/aztecs/writing/aztec-papermaking.

Solís, Felipe, and Verónica Velásquez. 2006. "The Polychrome Ceramics from Cholula and Other Sites in the Valleys of Puebla." In *Cholula: The Great Pyramid*, edited by Felipe Solís, Gabriela Uruñuela, Patricia Plunket, Martin Cruz, and Dionisio Rodríguez, 78–129. Mexico City: Grupo Azabache.

Solís Olguín, Felipe, ed. 2009. *Teotihuacan: Cité des Dieux*. Paris: Musée du Quai Branly; Somogy Editions d'Art.

Stacey, Rebecca, Caroline Cartwright, and Colin McEwan. 2006. "Chemical Characterization of Ancient Mesoamerican 'Copal' Resins: Preliminary Results." *Archaeometry* 48, no. 2: 323–40.

Stone, Andrea. 2002. "Spirals, Ropes, and Feathers: The Iconography of Rubber Balls in Mesoamerican Art." *Ancient Mesoamerica* 13: 21–39.

Stross, Brian. 1997. "Mesoamerican Copal Resins." *U Mut Maya* 6: 177–86.

Sugiyama, Saburo. 2002. "Censer Symbolism and the State Polity in Teotihuacán." Report submitted to the Foundation for the Advancement of Mesoamerican Studies. http://www.famsi.org/reports/97050/.

Tarkanian, Michael J., and Dorothy Hosler. 2011. "America's First Polymer Scientists: Rubber Processing, Use and Transport in Mesoamerica." *Latin American Antiquity* 22, no. 4: 469–86.

Taube, Karl A. 1989. "The Maize Tamale in Classic Maya Diet, Epigraphy, and Art." *American Antiquity* 54, no. 1: 31–51.

Taube, Karl A. 1992. *The Major Gods of Ancient Yucatan*. Studies in Pre-Columbian Art and Archaeology 32. Washington, DC: Dumbarton Oaks Research Library and Collection.

Taube, Karl A. 2000. "The Turquoise Hearth: Fire, Self-Sacrifice, and the Central Mexican Cult of War." In *Mesoamerica's Classic Heritage: From Teotihuacan to the Aztecs*, edited by David Carrasco and Lindsay Jones, 269–340. Niwot: University of Colorado Press.

Taube, Karl A. 2012. "The Symbolism of Turquoise in Ancient Mesoamerica." In *Turquoise in Mexico and North America: Science, Conservation, Culture and Collections*, edited by J. C. H. King, Max Carocci, Caroline Cartwright, Colin McEwan, and Rebecca Stacey, 117–34. London: Archetype Publications in association with the British Museum.

Thompson, J. Eric S. 1957. *Deities Portrayed on Censers at Mayapan*. Current Reports 40. Washington, DC: Carnegie Institution of Washington Department of Archaeology.

Thompson, J. Eric S. 1970. *Maya History and Religion*. Norman: University of Oklahoma Press.

Tozzer, Alfred M. 1941. *Landa's Relación de las Cosas de Yucatan: A Translation*. Papers of the Peabody Museum of American Archaeology and Ethnology, Harvard University 18. Cambridge, MA: Peabody Museum.

Vázquez de Ágredos Pascual, María Luisa, Cristina Vidal Lorenzo, Patricia Horcajada Campos, and Vera Tiesler. 2018. "Body Colors and Aromatics in Maya Funerary Rites." In *Painting the Skin: Pigments on Bodies and Codices in Pre-Columbian Mesoamerica*, edited by Élodie Dupey García and María Luisa Vázquez de Ágredos Pascual, 56–74. Tucson: University of Arizona Press.

Victoria Lona, Naoli. 2012. "Objects Made of Copal Resin: A Radiological Analysis." *Boletín de la Sociedad Geológica Mexicana* 64, no. 2: 207–13.

Vogt, Evon. 1976. *Tortillas for the Gods: A Symbolic Analysis of Zinacanteco Rituals*. Cambridge, MA: Harvard University Press.

BURN INCENSE
CENSERS

"I BURN AS INCENSE FOR YOU": CENSERS IN ASSYRIA AND BEYOND

Kiersten Neumann

The cultures of ancient West Asia communicated with divinity in a variety of ways, each determined and supported by an established set of materials, participants, actions, oral recitations, and spatial contexts. The burning of incense was one such avenue of communication. This highly sensorial performance was a fundamental component of ritualized practice, often performed in the vicinity of, if not within, temples—that is to say, the dwelling places of the gods on earth. From the acquisition of the raw materials necessary to create incense to the crafting of the censer upon which the incense was burned, archaeological and textual evidence confirms the widespread importance of this aromatic substance and its experiential phenomena across the temporal and geographical expanse of ancient West Asia. Yet the apparatuses used for burning incense make up a truly heterogenous group—from the small cuboid-shaped burners of the Arabian Peninsula to the sculptured tripod vessels from Guzana (modern Tell Halaf), the censers with stepped covers depicted in early Achaemenid reliefs, and the many instances in between.

Elsewhere I have explored the sensory phenomena of incense and aromatic oils within the context of Assyrian temple practice of the Neo-Assyrian period (934–612 BCE), looking at raw materials and aromatic substances—their origin, manner of acquisition, and production—and their use in practice, considering their affect at an individual, cultural, and social level.[1] Here, I concentrate on evidence from Assyria for the foremost furnishing itself, that is to say, the censer—the intermediary mechanism that facilitated the transformation of incense from tangible material to something aromatic and intangible—and its distinguishing types. While focusing on censers of the Neo-Assyrian period, I also consider earlier, contemporary, and later censers with meaningful similarities from Assyria and neighboring regions, as both consideration of and attestation to the remarkable exchange of materials, technologies, and cultural practices related to this single device across ancient West Asia.[2]

CENSERS IN ASSYRIA

From the tenth through the seventh centuries BCE, the state of Assyria grew into an empire that dominated West Asia and extended into Africa before falling rapidly to the combined forces of the Babylonians and Medes. This was the last stage of a process that can be traced back to the mid-third millennium BCE and the growth of the old trading city and cult center of Aššur on the Tigris River in northern Mesopotamia. By the fourteenth century BCE, a succession of able rulers established a strong Middle Assyrian kingdom, gaining independence from the kingdom of Mitanni. A successful policy of territorial expansion and administration brought stability and wealth to Assyria during the Neo-Assyrian Empire of the first millennium BCE. An abundance of information about this empire has been preserved in the extensive archaeological remains of its capital cities, smaller towns, and provincial centers. In addition to artistic traditions, literary materials in Assyrian—a dialect of Akkadian and official language of the Neo-Assyrian court that was written using cuneiform script and preserved on clay and stone—reflect the centuries of innovations that helped create a distinct Assyrian cultural identity.[3]

Assyria was named after the city Aššur and the god of the same name, who became the supreme deity of the emergent state and subsequent empire. Under the rulers of the Neo-Assyrian Empire, the administrative capital shifted from Aššur (modern Qala'at Sherqat) to Kalḫu (modern Nimrud), then Dur-Šarrukin (modern Khorsabad), and finally Nineveh (modern Mosul including the mounds Kuyunjik and Nebi Yunus), though past capitals remained important for reasons of continuity and their resident divinities. As the high-priest of the god Aššur, responsibility for the construction and maintenance of the land's temples—the dwelling places of the gods on earth, though not places of worship—fell to the king, who similarly played an important role in temple proceedings. Members of the royal court and select temple personnel accompanied the king, filling in for him when necessary.

Aromatic substances and olfaction played a key role in these courtly acts, marking the space and contributing to the overall sensescape of the temple: fumigation offered a way to purify the land prior to laying foundations, while censers emitted potent aromas that both purified and provided nourishment for the gods throughout the life of the temple.[4] An excerpt from the inscriptions of the Assyrian king Esarhaddon (r. 680–669 BCE) on his offering of incense to the gods exemplifies this cultural appreciation and intentionality of burning incense: "the harvest of the sea (and) the abundance of the mountains, I piled up before them. The burning of incense, a fragrance of sweet resin, like heavy fog, covered the wide heavens."[5] Similarly, the scribe Budi-il expresses an appreciation for the sweet smell of burning wood when, in the form of a kind of love poem, he asks the gods Nabu and Tašmetu to let the cult room be filled with the aroma of pure juniper.[6] A line from an explanatory text attributed to Kiṣir-Aššur, a ritual expert (āšipu) of the Aššur temple, communicates the understanding that the aromas had divine associations and purification abilities, here the scent having the ability to drive away the evil gods: "The cedar (resin) which they burn in front of the gods is the loose flesh of the evil gods; they smelled the scent and went into hiding."[7] Several texts also refer specifically to the gods smelling and inhaling incense, the verb eṣēnu, "to smell (an odor)," being combined with qutrinnu, "incense."[8] Comparable practices associated with incense and aromatics, albeit of a smaller scale, were staged by people in domestic spaces throughout Assyrian cities, while others took place in the open air, beyond the urban landscape.

Written sources leave little doubt regarding the essential role played by censers—the specialized apparatuses used for burning incense, which took the form of sweet-smelling resins (the hardened form of liquid gum obtained through an incision made into the bark of a tree) and wood shavings—in fulfilling these cultural expectations for purity, ritualized observance, and caring for the gods in temples and households throughout

Assyria. Akkadian differentiates between different types of censers: *nignak-ku/nidnakku* and *ša tēlilti/tēlissi* refer to smaller, portable censers, the latter used specifically for purification achieved by way of fumigation; *šēḫtu* is used in reference to tall, stationary censers; and *kinūnu/kanūnu* signifies braziers.[9] Texts also reference censers made of stone, clay, and precious and semi-precious metals, including gold (*ḫurāṣu*), silver (*kaspu*), and copper or bronze (*erû*). For example, a votive inscription of king Aššurbanipal (r. 669–631 BCE) tells of a gold censer that he gifted to the god Marduk.[10] Several terms are used for the aromatic substances burnt on censers: *ḫibištu* ("cuttings of resinous and aromatic substances"); *kisittu* ("wood shavings [of aromatic woods]"); *qutāru* ("fumigant"); *qutrīnu/qutrinnu/qutrēnu* ("incense"); *riqqu/rīqu* ("aromatic plant"); *siltu* ("shaving, splinter"); *za'u, ḫīlu,* and *dāmu* ("resin"); and *ziqpu* ("shoot [of a tree or other plant]"). Written sources also employ species-specific terms, that is to say the source of the resins and/or wood shavings. The most commonly cited species are *erēnu* ("cedar"), *šurmēnu* ("cypress"), *burāšu* and *duprānu/daprānu* ("juniper"), *taskarinnu* ("boxwood"), *murru* ("myrrh"), and *labānatu* ("frankincense").[11] Texts also testify to the filling of censers with charcoal (*pēntu/pēmtu*) before the aromatics were added; this would allow for the latter to smolder over a long period of time. Verbs of action employed in the context of burning incense on censers include *sarāqu* ("to strew, scatter, sprinkle") and *qatāru* ("to rise [said of smoke]") in the D-stem, *qutturu* ("to cause something to smoke, to make an incense offering, to cense, to fumigate, to fume incense"), and *ḫâbu* ("to purify by fumigation"). A passage from the ritual instructions of the diviner (*bārû*) makes use of the last verb in the context of burning cedar as incense for the gods: "I burn as incense for you pure cedar, bundles of shavings(?) (with) sweet-smelling resin (and) bundles of pure cedarwood, beloved of the great gods."[12]

Assyrian textual sources also speak to the placement of censers during temple practice: most often they are installed directly in front of the divinity, that is to say, their image, which was located on the dais at one of the narrow ends of the cult room. The following excerpts from a ritual text addressing offerings to the god Nusku from Nineveh stand as example:[13]

> Tukulti-Ninurta (I), king of Assyria, performed and instituted the (following) rites for Nusku:
>
> When you are to perform a sheep offering to Nusku, you go to the house of Sin (and) let sunshine enter it through its doorway.
>
> You set up a chair beside the house under the god, lay clean red wool upon it, and place a bowl of sweet oil, aromatics, juniper, and tufts of red wool upon it.
>
> You set up a table before Šamaš, light a censer (*šēḫtu*), and place it behind the table. You place two libation vessels (and) two libation bowls to the left of the censer (*šēḫtu*), and place a container of brushwood behind the censer (*šēḫtu*).
>
> ...

Ea sets off (in procession). You carry a portable censer (*nig-nakku*) (loaded) with juniper fragrance before him ... (and) sing, "...."

...

You light a censer *(šēhtu)*, pour oil into the container, place ... before the bed (and) before [DN]

...

You offer fatty tissue and roast meat before Šamaš, make a flour/incense-offering, pour oil, honey and beer, and sing, "..., Lord of righteousness, ... god ...."

Included within these prescriptions is the use of both portable (*nignakku*) and stationary (*šēhtu*) censers. Several texts also speak of the bringing in and clearing of censers, offering tables, and altars before and after the presentation of offerings.[14] These textual sources reinforce the importance of understanding censers as being both transient and fixed: some were brought out when needed and stored elsewhere when not in use and others had a more lasting footprint. A royal decree for the Aššur temple refers specifically to an "incense-man" (*ša-emdīšu*) as the one responsible for mixing and placing incense and fumigants on the censers; comparable personnel would have been tasked with moving portable censers in preparation for temple practice.[15] Noteworthy is that the fumigation achieved by way of portable censers was used to cleanse not only spaces but also objects. The following excerpt from a ritual text for the presentation of offerings in the Aššur temple during the Shebat-Adar festival details this use of portable censers by the king:[16]

He swings the censer of purification (*ša-tēlissi*) over the table, saying: "The hand is released."

He swings it in the center of the house, saying "The center of the house is released."

He swings it in the area of the censers (*šēhtu*), saying "The house is seized."

He swings it over the censer (*šēhtu*), saying: "May Fire purify."

He gives incense thrice, saying: "Aššur, accept! Aššur, listen."

Censers also played an important role when laying a temple's foundations, as with those of any house, here incense fulfilling the same dual duty of purifier and offering. As example, ritual instructions for laying the foundations of a temple, *Enūma IM.DÙ.A tappatiqu* ("When you lay the foundations [of the house of a god]"), prescribe censers (*nignakku*) burning juniper resin to be placed on the ground along with food and liquid offerings prior to interring foundation deposits and laying the bricks.[17] Ritual instructions for warding off evil from a house through figurine deposition, *Šēp lemutti ina bīt amēli parārsu* ("to block the entry of the enemy in someone's house"), similarly prescribe the use of censers (*nignakku*) burning various resins in order to purify the raw materials used to manufacture the figurines and again to purify the house during figurine deposition.[18] Textual and archaeological

evidence from Assyrian capital cities confirm that this apotropaic measure
was carried out in private houses, palaces, and temples alike.[19]

The olfactory phenomena produced by burning incense on censers,
as the above asserts, was also employed in practices disconnected from
temples, including (in addition to purifying building foundations and cleansing a house of evil) acts of divination, medicine, and childbirth. Fumigation
and the provision of offerings by way of censers, for example, is ubiquitous
in such ritual texts as *namburbi, maqlû, qutāru,* and *šurpu*.[20] What is more,
there are instances in these texts when a particular type of incense is connected to a specific ailment or desired outcome. Textual sources also speak
to the role of censers at royal audiences and banquets.[21] In these contexts,
the pleasant aroma of the incense likely fulfilled a similar purifying and
votive function—the king understood in the Assyrian world as being an
intermediary between humans and the gods—while simultaneously evincing
his power and strength through the demonstration of his ability to procure
such valued and prestigious resources as the incense itself and the materials
required to craft a fashionable censer.

The textual sources cited above communicate features and functions
of censers in first-millennium BCE Assyria; yet availing oneself of the contemporaneous archaeological evidence and imagery provides an even more
nuanced understanding of this apparatus' place in practice as well as its
forms and styles. Traits of these varying forms and styles, furthermore, support a tripartite classification system: tall circular censers, short circular
censers, and cubic censers. Moreover, certain types are more often attested
for particular spheres of activity than others: tall circular censers are predominantly associated with the presentation of offerings during ritualized
practice; short circular censers are more variable, appearing in both royal
and ritual contexts; and cubic censers are similarly mobile, moving from
temple doorways to gardens and mountain ranges.

TYPES OF CENSERS
Tall Circular Censers

Figures 1A–1G

Imagery from the Neo-Assyrian period identifies a tall, circular, tapered
stand—relatively plain except for the possibility of convex molding—with a
wide top that consisted of either an integral bowl-shaped receptacle or a flat
surface that would have supported objects, likely metal bowls within which
incense was burned.[22] Their represented size—standing around a meter and
a half tall—suggests that this type of censer was largely stationary as opposed
to portable; it is also closely associated with the presentation of offerings,
both within and outside of temple contexts. One of the most well-known
depictions of a tall circular censer is from a series of stone wall panels (or-
thostats) showing a lion-hunt sequence carved in low relief from the North
Palace of Aššurbanipal at Nineveh.[23] The scene shows the king pouring a
libation on the bodies of slain lions; to the left of the lions stand offering
accoutrements, including a table with lion-paw legs that is laden with offerings and a tall censer with conical top [Figure 1A]. Bronze bands that once
adorned a pair of wooden doors in a palace of king Šalmaneser III (r. 858–
824 BCE) at the Assyrian city of Imgur-Enlil (modern Balawat, about 28 kilo-
meters southeast of Nineveh) show in repoussé relief a comparable libation
scene performed by the king and attendants in front of a rock-cut royal stele
at Lake Urmia. Here, the tall censer with conical top is similarly depicted

alongside an offering table, a tall stand with a libation vessel, and a pair of standards [Figure 1B].[24] On a fragmentary piece from this same series of bronze bands is a scene preserving a pair of tall censers—shown with flames in place of the conical top—alongside a pair of standards and a rock-cut royal stele; the scene takes place in the context of a royal campaign in a western mountain range, likely the Amanus [Figure 1C].[25]

Turning back to Assyrian palace relief sculpture, specifically from the reigns of Tiglath-pileser III (r. 744–727 BCE), Sargon II (r. 721–705 BCE), and Sennacherib (r. 704–681 BCE), we see tall censers with covers in offering scenes staged within military camps. These censers are again grouped with laden offering tables and standards and are accompanied by a pair of officiants (some in priestly dress and one of whom raises his hand to the censer).[26] Interestingly, Austen Henry Layard and Paul-Émile Botta with Eugène Flandin all observed in the nineteenth-century red paint on the top of a censer in one such scene in Sargon II's palace at Dur-Šarrukin—an illustration of the heat of the cover caused by the burning of incense within [Figure 1D].[27] Last is a representation of the city of Arbaʻilu (modern Erbil) from the wall reliefs of Aššurbanipal's North Palace: a tall burner and offering table are shown across from the king who pours a libation over the head of a vanquished enemy, the Elamite king Teumman, at the entrance of the Ištar temple.[28]

Similar to the second example from the bronze bands of Imgur-Enlil cited above are scenes from cylinder seals of the Neo-Assyrian period that include censers with flames rising from the stand in place of a conical top.[29] Offering scenes on glazed vessels from Aššur of the same period provide polychromatic representations of tall censers likewise topped by flames [Figure 1E].[30] Such illustrations support the interpretation of the conical top as a cover. When these types of censers were in use, the covers would have helped to control the speed of combustion of the burning aromatic substances.[31] Unfortunately, archaeologists have yet to excavate a cover of this type dating to the Assyrian period (the closest example, albeit from Aššur, dates to the Parthian period[32]); however, examples of the main component of the tall circular censer have been preserved.

In the mid-1950s the Iraq Antiquities Department excavated the temple of the Sibitti, a group of seven deities, at Dur-Šarrukin. In the building's courtyard they uncovered three tall stone stands whose form perfectly matches that of the tall censers represented in the aforementioned scenes: as described by Fuad Safar, "they are in the shape of an elongated chalice with a shallow basin on a column-like base which tapers at the top"[33] [Figure 1F–G]. The one example that was complete when excavated—and was moved to the Mosul Cultural Museum[34]—measured around 1.5 meters tall with a 44-centimeter-deep bowl and slots about 10 centimeters high located at the top of the stand beneath convex molding. In her article on Assyrian temple furniture, Barbara Mallowan suggests that the slots may have been used to move the censer by means of the insertion of sticks.[35] Excavation of the temple also uncovered fourteen large, triangular, solid stone offering tables with three lion-paw legs and circular, flat tops: eleven were found in the cult room and three in the courtyard.[36] The rim of each object was inscribed with a dedicatory text of Sargon II to the Sibitti. These tables are comparable to both those depicted in the offering scenes discussed above and an uninscribed example excavated at Kalḫu, which was repurposed as a censer and is discussed below [Figure 8D].

1A

Figures 1A–1G
Tall circular censers of the
Neo-Assyrian period:

1A
1A Relief panel, North Palace,
Nineveh, British Museum, BM
124887. Photo by author;

1B–1C
Bronze gates, Imgur-Enlil,
British Museum, BM 124662,
after King 1915, pl. I;
Birch and Pinches 1880, pl. N2;

1D
Drawing of a relief panel,
Dur-Šarrukin (after Botta and
Flandin 1849–50, II, pl. 146);

1E
Watercolor of a glazed vessel,
Aššur, Vorderasiatisches
Museum, Berlin, VA 5043,
after Andrae 1925, pls. 29;

1F
Stone censer, Sibitti temple,
Dur-Šarrukin;

1G
Stone censer fragment,
Sibitti temple, Dur-Šarrukin.
Stephen Batiuk, 2022.

1B

1C

1D

1E

1F

1G

Figures 2A–2E

Looking to imagery predating this period, both in Assyria and beyond, reveals that this type of tall circular censer was not unique to the Neo-Assyrian period. Carved in relief on the eleventh-century BCE "White Obelisk," excavated at Nineveh near the Ištar temple, is a scene of the king performing a libation and sacrifice: a censer with flames is among the offering accoutrements, with a temple and divine image shown in the distance [Figure 2A].[37] Earlier Assyrian imagery—specifically glyptic scenes on cylinder seals of the thirteenth to twelfth centuries BCE—also depicts this same style of tall censer, represented both with a cover and with flames [Figure 2B].[38] Comparable hourglass-shaped censers with rising flames, sometimes with an additional shallow bowl and rising smoke, are included on Akkadian and Ur III-period cylinder seals that were in circulation in the Diyala region and southern Mesopotamia—this extends the continuity of practice of tall circular censers back to the third millennium BCE [Figure 2C].[39] The presentation scene carved in low relief on a boundary stone (*kudurru*) of the Kassite king Meli-Šipak (r. 1186–1172 BCE) from southern Mesopotamia includes another notable example. Here, a tall circular censer with cover is situated between the king and goddess Nanaya [Figure 2D].[40] Finally, imagery situates this same style of censer in practices to the west. First are seal impressions from Nuzi clay tablets (texts of the Hurrian kingdom dating from the mid-fifteenth to the mid-fourteenth centuries BCE) that show tall circular censers with flames.[41] Second is a Hittite silver stag vessel of the fourteenth–thirteenth century BCE on which a tall circular censer is shown in front of a seated divinity in a presentation scene [Figure 2E].[42] This last example includes detailed decoration on both the tapered stand, consisting of rows of diagonal hatching and plain bands, and the cover, whose small slits suggest a means by which the scent of the incense burning within was emitted.

Figures 3A–3C

Tall circular censers also continue to appear in visual sources following the Neo-Assyrian period. Of particular interest is a chalcedony cylinder seal whose design combines Assyrian, Babylonian, and Persian motifs. Dominique Collon suggests that the seal was created by a craftsman or workshop at the borders of these three regions in the late ninth–early eighth century BCE.[43] Also striking is the representation of the censer on this seal: positioned between a beardless figure and a kneeling human-headed winged *apkallu* (mythological sage), the censer includes a conical cover with lines rising above—no doubt an illustration of the aroma wafting from the incense smoldering within. Landing at the Late Babylonian-Achaemenid temporal divide (end of sixth–early fifth century BCE) is a stunning, artificially dyed, eyed-sardonyx cylinder seal, excavated at Kalḫu, into which is engraved a double scene of combat and ritualized practice; the latter includes a worshiper standing before a tall circular censer with a somewhat rounded conical cover and a temple-shaped altar with symbols [Figure 3A].[44] Achaemenid glyptic imagery (sixth–fourth century BCE) continues to illustrate censers with tall, circular, tapered stands topped by bowl-shaped receptacles and conical covers, some with articulated stepped covers and fluted rings [Figure 3B].[45] Of particular note is a chalcedony cylinder seal from western Iran whose carving combines Achaemenid and Egyptian motifs: a falcon, a winged ibex, and a tall circular censer with a fitted bowl and two-tiered lid that connects to the stand by way of a chain.[46] Achaemenid seals also prominently feature stepped structures of varying forms with flames rising from the top ("fire

2A

2B

Figures 2A–2E
Tall circular censer from
earlier periods:

2A
Libation scene on the "White
Obelisk", Kalḫu, British Museum,
BM 118807, redrawn after
C. D. Hodder, 1853, published in
Sollberger 1974: pl. XLII.;

2B
Cylinder seal with modern
impression, British Museum BM
85486,A. © The Trustees of the
British Museum;

2C
Cylinder seal impression,
Eshnunna (modern Tell Asmar)
As. 31:275. Courtesy of
the Institute for the Study
of Ancient Cultures;

2D
Boundary stone, Meli-Šipak,
Musée du Louvre, SB 23.
© 2017 Musée du Louvre /
Philippe Fuzeau;

2E
Silver vessel, The Metropolitan
Museum, Met 1989.281.10.
The Metropolitan Museum of
Art, New York.

2C

2E

2D

3A

Figures 3A–3C
Tall circular censer
from later periods:

3A
Cylinder seal, Kalḫu,
British Museum, BM 89324.
© The Trustees of
the British Museum;

3B
Collated line drawing of
PFS 161*s, Persepolis. Courtesy
of the Persepolis Fortification
Archive, Institute for the Study
of Ancient Cultures;

3C
Carved orthostat, Persepolis.
Courtesy of the Institute for the
Study of Ancient Cultures.

3B

3C

altars")—many are comparable to the tall circular censers discussed thus far and therefore may be illustrations of censers specifically.[47]

Representations of tall circular censers are also found in Achaemenid architectural decoration. Exceptionally well preserved on two limestone relief panels from the so-called Treasury at Persepolis in present-day south-western Iran and dating to the reign of Darius I (r. 522–486 BCE) is a royal audience scene with two tall circular censers; albeit shown side-by-side, they represent a pair—likely made of gold or silver—that would have flanked the enthroned king [Figure 3C].[48] The relief sculpture masterfully illustrates, as described by Erich Schmidt—archaeologist and director of the Institute for the Study of Ancient Cultures (formerly the Oriental Institute) excavations at Persepolis[49]—a corrugated base in the shape of a slender truncated cone with flaring bottom, an almost cylindrical upper part, and a ring-shaped rim [carrying] a deeply fluted semiglobe. Above it a short corrugated cylinder—perhaps a continuation of the base—supports a seven-stepped conoid receptacle. Outlets for perfumed smoke, presumably of frankincense, are marked by arrow-shaped slots piercing the five upper steps. The incense burner was fed through its truncated apex, which was closed by an anvil-shaped stopper. The latter was attached by a chain with S-shaped links to a duck's head protruding near the top of the base. Further, Schmidt proposes that the bucket—corrugated in a similar manner and held by the second attendant facing the king—contained the incense used on the censers.[50] A comparable audience scene with a pair of the same albeit slightly shorter censers is preserved on doorjambs of the Hall of 100 Columns at Persepolis, dated to the reigns of Xerxes (r. 486–465 BCE) and Artaxerxes I (r. 465–424 BCE), while doorjambs in the palaces of Darius and Xerxes include beardless attendants carrying in one hand censers, almost identical but much smaller, and incense pails in the other.[51]

Apparent in these later representations is the censers' slender build and reduced height, landing lower on the body of the neighboring figures than most of the Neo-Assyrian examples; these variations suggest a greater ease of portability and likelihood of being crafted of metal. Unfortunately, however, unlike the situation in Assyria, texts that speak to Achaemenid practices involving censers and the burning of incense—and which might offer details regarding these furnishings beyond what can be obtained from imagery—are lacking.[52] The same is true of archaeological evidence, yet material culture from the west offers interesting comparisons. Looted from tumuli at the Lydian site of İkiztepe in western Turkey and dating to about 500 BCE (a time when this region was under Achaemenid rule) are two silver censers of the type depicted in the Treasury reliefs at Persepolis. The more elaborate of the two, which stands 28.8 centimeters tall, has a corrugated tapered stand with an oval lug mid-point, from which hangs a section of chain, and a stepped-cover pierced with arrow-shaped slots that is topped by an open flower and cock—a mix of Achaemenid and Lydian stylistic elements.[53] The collection of preserved visual imagery and archaeological evidence hitherto discussed makes a strong case for the stepped, pierced cover being a unique design introduced during the early Achaemenid period.[54]

Exhibiting some of the same qualities as the tall circular censers of the Neo-Assyrian period and therefore worth including in this section before proceeding to the next type are three cylindrical ceramic stands with flared bases and ornamented exteriors that were uncovered during excavation, Figures 4A–4B

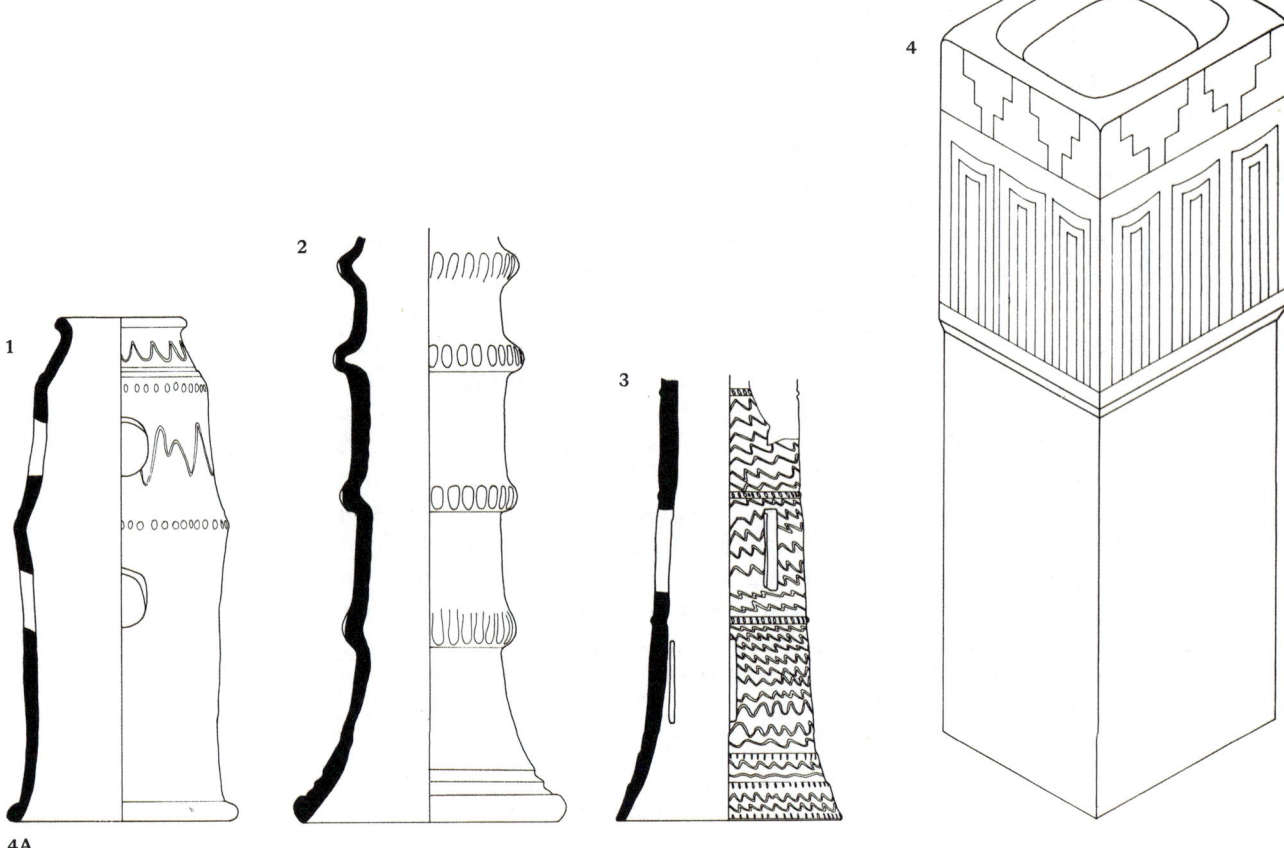

4A

Figures 4A–B
Circular stands:

4A
Isometric drawing of temple
furnishings, Karana, after
Oates 1974, pl. XXVIII;

4B
Two-part ceramic stand,
Megiddo, Institute for
the Study of Ancient Cultures,
A20830A–B. Courtesy of the
Institute for the Study of
Ancient Cultures.

4B

directed by David Oates on behalf of the British School of Archaeology in Iraq, of a Late Assyrian temple at Karana (modern Tell al-Rimah), a provincial town to the west of Nineveh [Figure 4A, nos. 1–2].[55] The stands were among an assortment of temple furnishings, votive offerings, and fixed architectural decorations that included most notably a stele of Adad-nirari III (r. 811–783 BCE); the royal stele was still standing in situ to the side of the raised platform at the end of the cult room, having been erected by the provincial governor of Raṣappa, Nergal-ereš.[56] Unlike the tall stands with integral bowls discussed above, the stands from Karana would have supported bowls into which offerings were placed, possibly incense to be burnt; the two nearly complete examples stood 60.4 and 72 centimeters tall (Figure 4A, nos. 1–2, respectively). As documented by Joan Oates, the closest parallels for this type of ceramic stand are third-to-second-millennium BCE examples from northern and central Mesopotamia and twelfth-to-eleventh-century examples from the Levant. For example, a well-preserved ceramic stand was excavated at Megiddo along with its bowl, which preserved features for fastening it to the stand and discoloration inside from burning [Figure 4B].[57] Second-millennium examples from the Ištar temple at Aššur include a group of what German archaeologist and director of excavations Walter Andrae termed *Räucherstander* that exhibit varying degrees of completeness and ornamentation.[58] The use of this type at Karana in the first millennium BCE may thus reflect a mix of local continuity and western connections.[59]

Short Circular Stands

Figures 5A–5E

Embodying many qualities of the first group and prominent during the Neo-Assyrian period is a shorter type of circular censer with integral bowl, broad case, and modest to more elaborate decoration. These portable censers—measuring at most 25 centimeters though often less—were likely crafted of stone, metal, and clay. The Institute for the Study of Ancient Cultures' excavations of Dur-Šarrukin excavated two short circular censers dating to the seventh century BCE: one stone example—measuring 13.7 centimeters tall and 11.4 wide at the top, with convex molding and a weathered row of drooping petals below the bowl—was excavated in a corridor (29) of Residence Z, an elite building to the east of the citadel [Figure 5A].[60] A second almost complete example was excavated in the forecourt (Court I) of the Nabu temple at the entrance to Room 14, possibly a secondary cult room; excavation documents record that it was made of clay, had decorative molding and a partially preserved inscription on its shaft, and was 25 centimeters tall and 12.5 centimeters wide [Figure 5B].[61] Short circular censers were also excavated at Kalḫu, specifically in the Nabu temple, and at Guzana—an Aramaean state that was incorporated into the Neo-Assyrian Empire by the end of the ninth century BCE—and are now housed in the British Museum. The example from Kalḫu, likely dating to the seventh century BCE, is the more complete of the two: carved from limestone, it measures 21 centimeters tall by 14.5 centimeters wide and has a row of petals and convex molding under the bowl, which is mounted on a fluted circular shaft with broad base; the bowl also preserves traces of burning.[62] The eighth- to seventh-century BCE basalt example from Guzana is fragmentary, consisting solely of a portion of the shaft and a shallow bowl with a row of petals and convex molding below; it measures 16.7 centimeters tall by 13 centimeters wide.[63] Additional basalt censers of this type dating to the Aramaean–Neo-Assyrian

5A

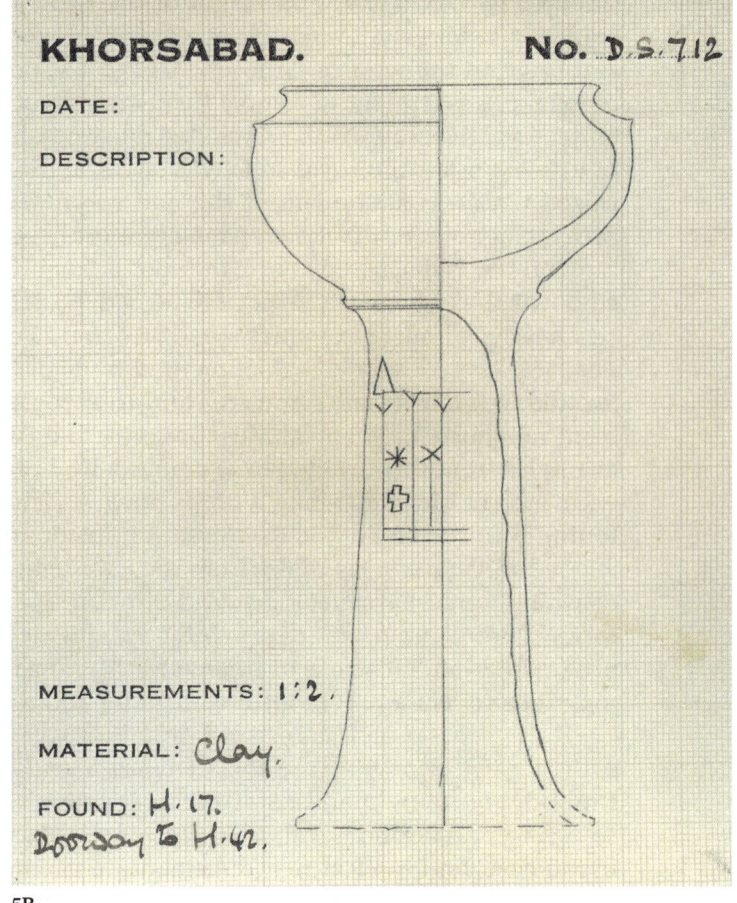

5B

Figures 5A–5E
Short circular censers from
the Neo-Assyrian period:

5A
Stone censer, Dur-Šarrukin,
after Loud and Altman 1938,
pl. 64, no. 263;

5B
Ceramic censer, Dur-Šarrukin,
Khorsabad Expedition Catalog
Card, DS 712, Institute for
the Study of Ancient Cultures
Archives. Courtesy of
the Institute for the Study
of Ancient Cultures;

5C
Stone censer, Guzana,
Vorderasiatisches Museum,
VA 12793. © Staatliche Museen
zu Berlin – Vorderasiatisches
Museum / Olaf M. Teßmer;

5D
Relief panel, North Palace,
Nineveh, British Museum,
BM 124920. Photo by author;

5E
Relief panel, North Palace,
Nineveh, British Museum,
BM 124922. © The Trustees of
the British Museum.

5C

5D

5E

period were excavated at Guzana, including a pair that was found in a ninth- to eighth-century BCE cult room.[64] Some of the examples from this last group had lined decorations on the exterior of the bowls, rows of boss-like projections on the bowl and shaft, and convex molding [Figure 5C].

Representations of short circular censers in Assyrian imagery include examples both without and with a cover over the bowl-shaped receptacle, comparable to the tall censers discussed above; they also appear in contexts outside of offering scenes. For example, short censers are included in the elaborate garden scene from the wall reliefs of the North Palace at Nineveh that shows Aššurbanipal reclining on a couch with bowl in hand, his queen enthroned also with bowl in hand, and between them a laden table (comparable to the offering tables with lion's-paw legs discussed above). In this scene the pair of short censers with covers frames the royal couple.[65] Likely crafted of metal, these examples also appear to have fluted circular shafts with decorative rings and molding [Figure 5D]. A scene to the right in the same relief sequence shows a similarly short circular censer among a group of eunuchs, some of whom play music and others serve as guards for the royal party; the characteristics of this censer, including the fact that it is shown with a bowl above its bowl-shaped top, are similar to the tall circular stands discussed above [Figure 5E].[66] Also worth noting are representations of Assyrian soldiers piling up booty from southern Mesopotamia, including weapons, furniture, vessels, and short circular censers, in the seventh-century BCE reliefs from the Southwest Palace at Nineveh.[67]

Owing to their overall similarities, the *comparanda* discussed above for tall circular censers may also relate to short circular censers. Of note, however, is a group of third–second-millennium BCE objects classified as "pedestal bowls" by Agnieszka Pieńkowska that exhibit parallels to the short circular censers of the Neo-Assyrian period presented here. Fashioned of both clay and stone and excavated at sites throughout Mesopotamia (including Karana, Ur, and Tepe Gawra), these earlier examples consist primarily of simple, tapered stands with integral bowls and at times convex molding— some are also documented as having traces of burning inside.[68]

Cubic Censers

The cubic style of censer of the Neo-Assyrian period consists of a square or rectangular top—whose sides are often decorated with a low-relief, crenellated pattern—with a shallow bowl-like receptacle and a square or rectangular integral shaft. Commonly crafted of stone, this type has a greater range in scale, being both portable and stationary, and was used in both indoor and open-air settings (the latter predominantly at entrances to temples but also contexts entirely divorced from temples).

Figures 6A–6C

A fairly well-preserved seventh-century BCE limestone example of this type was excavated by Reginald Campbell Thompson in the Ištar temple at Nineveh, now in the collection of the British Museum [Figure 6A].[69] The censer stands 41.5 centimeters tall and measures 21 by 22 centimeters across the top. A three-stepped crenellation design decorates one side of the top and carved in low relief on all four vertical faces of the shaft are mythological figures, of the same type that were fashioned by ritual experts in Assyria and interred under the foundations of houses in order to drive away evil.[70] Noteworthy is that a black mark from burning is preserved near the center of the bowl-like top surface and an adjacent area is partly reddened

6B

6A

Figure 6A–6C
Cubic censers of the
Neo-Assyrian period:

6A
Stone censer, Nineveh, British
Museum, BM 1930-5-8, 218.
© The Trustees of
the British Museum;

6B
Drawing by F. Cooper,
Šarrat-niphi temple, Kalhu
after Layard 1853a, 360;

6C
Drawing of a relief panel,
Dur-Šarrukin, after Botta and
Flandin 1849–50, II, pl. 114.

6C

by heat; damage to the surface of one relief figure, including chipping and blistering, was likely also caused by heat.[71] The expedition also found two fragments of seventh-century BCE limestone cubic censers—one clearly exhibiting the crenellation pattern and both a stepped form—when excavating a building northwest of the citadel at Nineveh.[72] In the nearby Nabu temple Thompson excavated another stone censer with a cubic shaft and top with a shallow basin; rather than the crenellated pattern, its cubic top is decorated with upright triangles (likely simplistic acanthus-leaf designs) at the corners, for which reason Anne Searight, Julian Reade, and Irving Finkel date it to the first–second century CE, drawing on comparable censers from Hatra of the Parthian period, also referred to as "incense altars" or "horned altars."[73] For example, Andrae excavated an "incense altar" (*Räucheraltar*) with upright triangles from a Parthian level at Aššur.[74] Notably, the Nabu temple censer measures only half the size of the Ištar temple example, standing 18.9 centimeters tall with a top measuring 7.8 by 7.5 centimeters.

Hormuzd Rassam's excavation documents (including a plan and photograph) and his publications on the Kidmuri temple at Kalḫu record cubic stone censers (which he refers to as square marble pillars) in positions that suggest that they originally flanked the entrance leading from the courtyard into this temple; the photograph indicates a height slightly taller than those from Nineveh above. Finkel reads the fifth and sixth lines, albeit fragmentary, of Rassam's copy of a dedicatory inscription of Aššurnaṣirpal II (r. 883–859 BCE) on one of the censers as follows: "erected that incense-burner in its gates."[75] Additional stone furnishings were recovered in the temple and are visible in the photograph, including a square stone table with lion's feet at the top of the steps that led to the raised platform where the divine statue would have stood, and a "very handsome tripod" made of stone.[76] Reade suggests that the "tripod" may have supported a standard or was an offering table comparable to those represented in libation scenes and found in the Sibitti temple at Dur-Šarrukin, discussed above.[77]

Another pair of tall cubic censers with crenellation designs though uninscribed were excavated at the entrance to the cult room of the Šarrat-nipḫi temple at Kalḫu, here preceding a pair of colossal stone lions that lined the doorway and to the side of glazed-brick panels. Frederick Charles Cooper's drawing, published by Layard, records the crenellated pattern at the top of these censers; it also suggests that their shafts were decorated with vertical lines, comparable to Assyrian temple façades [Figure 6B].[78] Recent excavations of the same temple uncovered an additional pair of the same style of censer in a corner of the temple's courtyard.[79] Worth mentioning—owing to its comparable features and location at a temple doorway (indicating that it probably served as a censer)—is the rectangular stone object published as a "small, much-weathered limestone altar with a circular basin cut into its upper surface"; specifically, it stood at the north entrance to the passage-chamber (NT1) in Ezida (Nabu temple) that gave access from the outer courtyard to the inner courtyard and subsequently the cult rooms of Nabu and Tašmetu (NT2, NT4).[80]

A final example of a cubic censer with crenellation design from Kalḫu was excavated in Room XX of the Northwest Palace; albeit found broken in two, the censer is recorded as being 93 centimeters tall. Room XX was a corridor connecting the Royal Courtyard (AJ) with what was likely a kitchen (Room ZZ) and the rooms beyond—an area that has been interpreted as both women's quarters and storage spaces. Since the censer was the only item connected with ritualized practice in this area, it is likely that it was placed here after the Assyrian royal court's use of the palace.[81]

At Karana excavations uncovered a weathered, limestone cubic censer at the entrance to the Late Assyrian temple [Figure 4A, no. 4]. The censer, which stood 81.3 centimeters tall and whose top measured 23 by 20 centimeters, included a shallow basin in the upper surface and a straight cubic rectangular shaft whose top was decorated on three sides with parallel lines that mimicked columned façades topped by a crenellation pattern.[82]

Depictions of cubic censers with crenellations from Assyrian imagery reflect the variations in size seen in the examples above, supporting the argument that this style was likely used for both portable and stationary censers. The scene of Arba'ilu from the wall reliefs of Aššurbanipal's North Palace, discussed earlier, includes a cubic censer at the front of a small temple situated at the citadel gate, above which (so to be understood as taking place within the citadel wall) is the scene of the king pouring a libation in front of the Ištar temple.[83] Other preserved representations of cubic censers in Assyrian wall reliefs, in contrast, are shown outside of temple contexts: one was featured at the top of a wooded hill amidst a hunting scene in Sargon II's wall reliefs at Dur-Šarrukin [Figure 6C],[84] and another is situated along a path in a park scene that includes trees, canals fed from an aqueduct, and a columned building with a royal stele in the wall reliefs of the North Palace.[85] In these open-air settings, and similarly when stationed outdoors at entrances to temples, the raised sides with crenellation design likely played a functional role in protecting the charcoal and burning aromatics from gusts of wind, as suggested by Julian Reade.[86]

In ancient West Asian studies, small cuboid-shaped censers form a prominent category of portable incense burner, with examples attested from southern Mesopotamia and the Upper and Middle Euphrates, the Levant, and the Arabian Peninsula, dating from the third through the first millennium BCE and continuing through to the present in Arabia.[87] Commonly taking the form of a cube with four stout legs and manufactured of stone or clay, these censers can either be plain or have decorative patterns, including incisions, carvings, and applied elements such as small knobs; some also contain residue of the aromatics burnt within, in particular frankincense (*Boswellia sacra*). The distribution pattern of cuboid censers attests to the widespread trade (both overland and maritime) of Arabian aromatics, which saw a significant increase starting in the Neo-Babylonian period. The censers' excavation contexts also point predominantly to domestic use with some evidence for use in ritualized practices staged within temples and tombs. Remarkably, even though Neo-Assyrian rulers engaged in—and attempted to control sections of—the Arabian aromatics trade,[88] cuboid censers have not been found in Assyria.[89] Notwithstanding, the focus of former excavations of Neo-Assyrian sites on royal built environments may be at play here; as future projects look to non-royal and domestic contexts, attestations of this same type may come to light. For now, as argued by William Zimmerle, the censers here identified as the cubic censer type for the Neo-Assyrian period (what Zimmerle calls "shaft incense altars"), despite similarities between their cubic receptacle and the Arabian style of cuboid censer, "are too generic in shape to suggest that there was cultural interaction between Arabia and Mesopotamia from such evidence."[90]

Hybrids and Analogies

As with any attempt at a system of classification, several censers are known   Figures 7A–7B
from Assyria with features that challenge this tripartite divide. In the Kidmuri temple at Kalḫu, Rassam excavated a cubic top of a censer measuring
8.9 centimeters tall and 9.3 by 8.6 centimeters across, decorated with crenellation pattern, and with traces of burning in the basin cut into the upper
surface; yet rather than a cubic shaft, this fragment preserves part of a circular shaft that forms an eight-pointed star in plan.[91] Like other materials
from this temple, the censer likely dates to the ninth century BCE; it is now
housed at the British Museum. A second comparable hybrid censer, also at
the British Museum, stands 26.5 centimeters tall with a top measuring 11.5
by 13 centimeters; it is carved of limestone and is particularly well preserved:
the crenellation pattern decorates three sides of the top, its vertically fluted
circular shaft has nine faces, and it terminates in a cushion base with square
bottom.[92] Though previously exhibited in the British Museum's Assyrian
Room and published in the 1922 *Guide to the Babylonian Assyrian Antiquities in the British Museum*, the censer's provenience is not stated [Figure
7A]. Another censer with square top and base and a circular shaft decorated
with large drooping petals, altogether measuring 15 centimeters tall, was
excavated in a Late Assyrian level at Khirbet Khatuniyeh in present-day
northern Iraq.[93] A fourth example was excavated at Karana: albeit quite
fragmentary, what remains preserves an incised design on one side of the
top receptacle [Figure 7B].[94] The publication identifies this design as a light-
ning bolt, similar to comparable motifs on other stone objects from the site,
yet one might wonder whether this could be a self-referential illustration
representing smoky emissions, shown as three wavy vertical lines rising
from a censer.

In addition to hybrids, excavations of Assyrian sites have identified
features and objects that probably also relate to the burning of aromatics in
temple contexts but that do not fit into the categories of censers discussed
above. To either side of the principal entranceway to the Ninurta temple at
Kalḫu—preceding the colossal stone human-headed winged lions that lined
the doorway and laying to the side of platforms faced with glazed bricks—
were square stones pierced in the center: these stones likely supported censers, perhaps portable and/or metal versions that were removed when the
temple was sacked during the fall of the empire at the end of the seventh
century BCE, as suggested by Reade.[95] Two additional features likely similarly once supported censers: the first, a square stone base with a circular
groove in its top surface that stood on the main axis of the cult room of
Nabu at Kalḫu, and the second, a broken baked brick with traces of burning
on its surface that was inset in the floor on the main axis preceding the dais
in the Late Assyrian temple at Karana.[96]

The same thinking should be directed toward the stone statues of   Figures 8A–8D
divine attendants recovered from Assyrian temples. The square trays that
topped the heads of the almost life-sized statues from Dur-Šarrukin may
have held burning aromatics themselves or supported bowls within which
incense was burnt; the statues were excavated flanking the doorways of the
temples of Nabu, Sin, and Šamaš [Figures 8A–B].[97] The same can be proposed
for the boxes with open tops held in the raised hands of a pair of statues
from the doorway to the cult room of Nabu at Kalḫu and a pair of basalt
statues that once stood in the Ištar temple at Hadatu (modern Arslan Tash)

Figures 7A–7B
Hybrid censers:

7A
Stone censer, British Museum,
BM 92218. © The Trustees of
the British Museum;

7B
Stone censer fragment, Karana,
Früher Tell-Halaf-Museum,
Berlin, Inv. Nr. 1581, after
Hrouda 1962, pl. 55, no. 211.

7A

7B

8A

Figures 8A–8D
Analogous objects:

8A–8B
Stone statues, Dur-Šarrukin,
Institute for the Study of
Ancient Cultures Museum,
A11808. Courtesy of
the Institute for the Study
of Ancient Cultures.
photo by author;

8C
Stone statue, Hadanu, Musée
du Louvre, AO 7538. © 2005
RMN-Grand Palais (Musée du
Louvre) / Franck Raux;

8D
Stone offering table, Kalḫu,
British Museum, BM 118806.
© The Trustees of
the British Museum.

8C

8B

8D

[Figure 8C].[98] Searight, Reade, and Finkel propose a similar supportive role for the lion-head stands excavated in the cult room of the Late Assyrian temple at Karana where they flanked the entrance to the dais.[99] Also noteworthy is the discovery of a stone offering table—of the same type discussed above from the Sibitti temple at Dur–Šarrukin—flanking the entrance to a secondary cult room (Room c) of the Ninurta temple at Kalḫu [Figure 8D]. The table had been repurposed as a censer, judging by the hole about 20 centimeters deep carved into the top surface: at the bottom of the hole are black stains, which Reade suggests may be traces of the bitumen used to fix a small censer in place.[100]

CONCLUSION

Textual prescriptions and material culture from the Neo-Assyrian period confirm the fundamental contribution and cultural appreciation of the olfactory phenomena produced by the burning of incense to the larger multisensory staging of ritualized practice in Assyria. During these acts, incense fulfilled a truly multifaceted role: fumigation cleansed and purified spaces and objects while the sweet-smelling incense both lured and was consumed by the gods, ensuring their attention and favorable support of the king and state. As the discussion above illustrates, the censers that made this possible were similarly multifaceted, ranging in material composition, size, portability, ornamentation, and cover or no cover, among other attributes. Yet these apparatuses also fit within a broad tripartite classification system that, in addition to responding to contemporary and local needs, suggests continuity of material culture and practice, both temporally and geographically.

In thinking about not only practice but also production, the quality of the censers discussed above attests to their being created at the hands of skilled craftsmen and in workshops with access to the raw materials and necessary tools—and likely with connections to the royal courts, where these furnishings were later used.[101] Alternately, evidence for the manufacture of censers and the burning of incense is not well attested for non-elite levels of society, although these spaces have remained less explored by foregoing excavations. What is more, any type of vessel could have been used for burning incense intended as divine offering and fumigant, or even as air freshener and insect repellent. It is also worth bearing in mind the frequency with which metal objects were melted down and reused in antiquity—and this applies to censers circulating at all levels of society. Last, the corpus of censers discussed above is in no way exhaustive. Notwithstanding, while we may never be able to reconstruct a complete picture of the production and practices associated with censers, there is still room to grow: excavations of non-elite contexts at Assyrian sites and more rigorous scientific investigations, in particular residue analysis and a better understanding of the materials and movements of the Arabian aromatics trade, have the potential to exponentially increase our understanding of censers and the burning of incense across the social and urban landscape of the land of Aššur during the Neo-Assyrian period.

ENDNOTES

1 Neumann 2019a; 2019b; forthcoming a; forthcoming b.

2 On censers of the third and second millennia BCE in Mesopotamia, see Pieńkowska 2018; on cuboid censers (*Räucherkästchen*) from the late third to the late first millennium BCE from southern Mesopotamia, Arabia, and the Levant, see Zimmerle 2014; 2021; on censers of ancient Israel, Nielson 1986; and of the Achaemenid period, Harper 2005. While no prior publication has focused solely on censers in Assyria, I would be remiss to not recognize prior considerations of this topic within studies of a larger scope, most notably Rashid 1981; Mallowan 1993; Reade 2002; 2005; Searight, Reade, and Finkel 2008; Lőrincz 2017.

3 Akkadian is a member of the Semitic language family (Luukko and Van Buylaere 2017). On the history of Assyria, see Postgate 1992b; Radner 2011; Frahm 2017b. On artistic and literary traditions, see Curtis and Reade 1995; Grayson 1991; 1996; and volumes from the Royal Inscriptions of the Neo-Assyrian Period project and the State Archives of Assyria series. Select primary volumes on excavations of Assyrian capital cities are Place 1867–70; Layard 1849; 1853b; Loud 1936; Loud and Altman 1938; Andrae 1938; Mallowan 1966; Oates and Oates 2001.

4 On the connections between the Assyrian court, king, and temple practice, see Neumann 2018; 2019a; 2019b; and on the use of incense in these contexts, Neumann forthcoming b. On religion and ideology in Assyria, see Pongratz-Leisten 2015.

5 Leichty 2011, 127–28 (RINAP 4: Esarhaddon 57, vii 2–8).

6 Livingstone 1989, 35 (SAA 3: no. 14, 8).

7 Ibid., 102 (SAA 3: no. 39, r. 24–25).

8 Oppenheim 1956–2010, E: s.v. *eṣenu* (CAD).

9 For the Akkadian terms listed in this section, see the respective entries in the Chicago Assyrian Dictionary (hereafter CAD) for definitions and references (Oppenheim 1956–2010). On textual references for the use of aromatic substances and fumigation in Assyrian ritualized practice, see further Maul 1994, 52, with references; Finkel 1991; Jursa 2006–2008; Neumann forthcoming b. Many types of texts include references to censers, for example, royal inscriptions, royal correspondence, administrative texts associated with temples and caring for the gods, and ritual, medical, and literary texts. *ša tēlilti/ša tēlissi* is abbreviated from *šēḫtu ša tēlilti*, meaning "censer of purification" (CAD Š: s.v. *šēḫtu* d)). *muqattirtu*, "censer," is attested in one Neo-Assyrian source (Frame 2021, 302 [RINAP 2: Sargon II 65, 361]; see further, CAD M/2: s.v. *muqattirtu*; Unger 1928: § 4–5).

10 Novotny and Jeffers 2018 (Ashurbanipal 225, r. 1′–6′); see also Frame 2021, 302 (RINAP 2: Sargon II 65, 361) (*kaspu*); Fales, Postgate, and Reade 1992, 102 (SAA 7: no. 88, r. 12) (*erû*); Parpola 2017, 142 (SAA 20: no. 50, 10) (*ḫurāṣu*); CAD N/2: s.v. *nignakku* b).

11 On the correlations between the Akkadian terms and known species of trees, which is based on textual descriptions, archaeological evidence, and studies of regional resources, see Postgate 1992a; Zimmerle 2014, 54–71; Neumann forthcoming a.

12 Zimmern 1901, no. 75–78, r. i 57.

13 Parpola 2017, 73–76 (SAA 20: no. 27); see further references to *šēḫtu* and *nignakku* in the volume.

14 van Driel 1969, 128, 200; Parpola 2017, 11 (SAA 20: no. 3).

15 Parpola 2017, 143 (SAA 20: no. 50, ii 5–7). On temple personnel, as well as the restricted access and exclusivity of this space, in Assyria, see Oppenheim 1944, 56; Menzel 1981, 1:4–5; Sallaberger 2011–13, 521; Neumann 2019b, 25–27.

16 Parpola 2017, 4 (SAA 20: no. 1, 14–18).

17 Ambos 2004, 117–25 (II.A.2.1, 20, 23); see also, 155–66 (II.C.2. *Ṭuppi ḫišiḫti uššē bīt ili epēšu enūma uššē bīt ili tanamd*, "Tablet for the materials needed in order to lay the foundations of a house of a god: When you are laying the foundations of a house of a god"); see also, Neumann 2019a.

18 Wiggermann 1992.

19 Ibid.; Schmitt 2004; Nakamura 2005; Neumann 2019a.

20 *namburbi* ("[ritual for] undoing of it") are texts with instructions, including incantations, for averting evil foretold by omens (Maul 1994, and specifically 52); *maqlû* ("burning") is a lengthy anti-witchcraft ritual (Abusch 2015); *šurpu* ("burning") is a series of texts with instructions for absolving patients of a curse resulting from a broken oath (Reiner 1958; Simons 2017); and, *qutāru* ("fumigation") is a medical-fumigation series of texts (Finkel 1991). On incantation series in general, see Mirelman 2018.

21 E.g. Parpola 2017, 91 (SAA 20: no. 33).

22 Reade (2005) suggests that the tall censers from Assyria were used specifically for burning oil while shorter censers, discussed below, were used for burning resins.

23 Aruz, Graff, and Rakic 2014, cat. no. 20 (BM 124886, BM 124887).

24 Schachner 2007, pls. 1, 50b (BM 124662).

25 Ibid., 70, fig. 113, pls. 14, 63a (Band Na) (BM 124662).

26 Reade 2005, figs. 11–15 (including BM 124914, BM 124915).

27 Layard 1849, 2:468; Botta and Flandin 1849–50, II, pl. 146. Despite the minimal traces of color preserved on wall reliefs from Assyrian palaces, temples, and gates, these stone surfaces were once brightly painted in such colors as black, white, red, yellow, and blue (Thavapalan 2019).

28 Place 1867–70, 3: pl. 41; nineteenth-century drawing by William Boutcher (BM 2007-6-24, 450); Barnett 1976, pls. XXV–XXVI.

29 Collon 2001, nos. 130–34, 156 (possibly Neo-Babylonian), 174 (BM 89613, BM 135147, BM 138658, BM 89619, BM 140849, BM 89382, BM 104499).

30 Andrae 1923, pls. 23, 25, 26, 29.

31 Searight, Reade, and Finkel 2008, 87.

32 Andrae 1938, 180, pl. 82a.

33 Safar 1957, 221.

34 This censer was heavily damaged during the destruction and looting of the Mosul Cultural Museum by ISIS in 2015; Brusasco 2016, 235–36, fig. 25; Couturaud et al. 2023.

35 Mallowan 1993, 386.

36 Safar 1957 (what I refer to as the cult room is Safar's antecella); Mallowan 1993, pl. 67, nos. 1–2; Brusasco 2016, 216–17; Frame 2021, 242–44 (RINAP 2: Sargon II 49); Neumann 2023. Nine of the tables from the Sibitti temple went to the Mosul Cultural Museum, of which eight are accounted for following the destruction and looting of the museum by ISIS in 2015 (Couturaud et al. 2023), while others remained on site. Four offering tables of the same type, all likely originating in the Sibitti temple, were found elsewhere at Dur-Šarrukin in the first half of the twentieth century and are now in the Iraq Museum (Loud and Altman 1938, 96, no. 18; 104, no. 3; pl. 48 [DS 1195]), the Istanbul Archaeological Museum (EŞ 4784; Nassouhi 1925), the Musée du Louvre (AO 19900; Pottier 1924, 92–93 n. 58, pl. XXXI), and the Institute for the Study of Ancient Cultures Museum (formerly the Oriental Institute Museum) (A17547; Loud and Altman 1938, 96, no. 19; pl. 48), bringing the total from Dur-Šarrukin to twenty.

37 Watanabe 1992; Pittman 1996 (BM 118807). The caption inscribed above the scene reads, "Bīt-natḫi of the city of Nineveh: I perform the wine libations (and) sacrifices of the temple of the exalted goddess" (Grayson 1991, 254–56 [RIMA 2: A.0.101.18]).

38 Moortgat 1941, figs. 69–72; 1944, figs. 69–70; 1966, nos. 591, 654–55, 748; Collon 1987, no. 285 (BM 89417); Mallowan 1993, figs. 1–5, pl. 68, no. 2.

39 Frankfort 1982, pl. 63, no. 681 (IM 14669 [As. 31:275]); Collon 1982, nos. 186–88 (BM 102511, BM 128597, BM 102521); Pieńkowska 2018, 315–16, fig. 1a–b.

40 Seidl 1989, 23, pl. 11a–b (Louvre SB 23).

41 Mallowan 1993, 386, with reference to Stein 1987, 239, 294–95, no. 68.

42 van den Hout 2018 (Met 1989.281.10).

43 Collon 2001, no. 203 (BM 102495).

44 Ibid., no. 393 (BM 89324).

45 Select examples include Curtis and Tallis 2005, no. 209 (BM 115523); Pedersén 2005, no. 456, fig. 71 (VAT 13190); Garrison 2017, 354, fig. 5.20 (PFS 161*s).

46 Collon 1987, 926 (BM 128865).

47 Garrison 2017, 248–52, figs. 4.1–4.6; 290–95, fig. 4.26. Interestingly, the continuity of this style of tall circular censer from the Assyrian through the Achaemenid period is remarked upon already in the mid-nineteenth century by Layard (1849, 2:467–68) when he writes of "fire-worship" and the "fire-altar" depicted in the palace wall reliefs of Dur-Šarrukin and Nineveh.

48 Schmidt 1953, 162–70, figs., 76F, pls. 119, 121–23.

49 Ibid., 164.

50 Ibid., 167.

51 Ibid., 133, fig. 60C, pls. 91, 96–99 (what is here called the Hall of 100 Columns is referred to in the publication as the "Throne Hall"); 227, pls. 148B, 150; 243, pl. 184.

52 Harper (2005, 53) proposes that the "new stylization of the Achaemenid censer as it appears at Persepolis is an abbreviated but deliberate reference to the cosmos, to heaven and earth, linked by the intermediary of fire."

53 Özgen and Öztürk 1996, 114–17, nos. 71–72 (no. 71: Uşak Archaeological Museum [UAM] 1.55.96); Baughan 2013, 241, fig. 154k; Melekian-Chirvani 1993.

54 Goldman 1991; Harper 2005.

55 Oates 1974 (TR. 4127, TR. 4128, TR. 4129).

56 Oates 1968, 125–32, pls. XXXIIa, XXXVIII; Page 1968 (IM 70543). For a full description of the Late Assyrian temple and its contents, see Oates 1968, 122–33, pls. XXXII–XXXVIII.

57 May 1935, 20, pl. 20 (P6056) (ISAC Museum A20830A–B).

58 Andrae 1922, 19, pls. 18, 20; 1938, fig. 37.

59 Oates 1974, 180–83, with references; and further, Pieńkowska 2018, 318 ("offering stands or potstands"), figs. 2g–h.

60 Loud and Altman 1938, 99, no. 263, pl. 64 (DS 1158).

61 Khorsabad Expedition, Catalog Cards, DS 712, and Object Log, Institute for the Study of Ancient Cultures Museum Archives. Although these excavation documents record DS 712 as being clay, DS 1158 was also recorded in the object log as being of clay and was ultimately published as stone, so DS 712 may also have been of stone. The object log also labels DS 712 as being a "compote," a term for a bowl-shaped desert dish with a stem.

62 Searight, Reade, and Finkel 2008, 88, no. 582, fig. 56 (BM 1994-11-5, 30). Traces of burning in its concave base suggest a later stage of use.

63 Ibid., 88, no. 581, fig. 56 (BM 1920-12-11, 354).

64 Oppenheim 1933, 205, pl. XLIXa, no. 1; Hrouda 1962, 67, 71, nos. 98–113; pl. 52, nos. 98–99, 101 (VA 12793).

65 Barnett 1976, p. 57, pl. LXIV; Reade 1995, 26–27, fig. 29 (BM 124920).

66 Barnett 1976, p. 58, pl. LXIV; Reade 2005, 26, fig. 30 (BM 124922).

67 Reade 1995, fig. 19 (BM 124956, BM 124825).

68 Pieńkowska 2018, 317–18, fig. 2a, c–h, with references.

69 Searight, Reade, and Finkel 2008, 89–90, no. 585, with references, fig. 57 (BM 1930-5-8, 218). The original publication by

Thompson and Hutchinson (1931, 83, pl. XVII) reports that three additional plain examples were excavated, two of which were said to be in Baghdad; their date, however, is unclear.

70 The figures on the incense burner include the *girtablullû* (scorpion-man), *suḫurmāšu* (goat-fish), *kulullû* (merman), and *kusarikku* (bull-man), known from Akkadian texts (Wiggermann 1992; 1993–97; Lőrincz 2017). On the figurines and their deposition, see notes 18–19.

71 Lőrincz 2017, 68–69.

72 Thompson and Mallowan 1933, 78, pl. XXVIII, nos. 29–30.

73 Searight, Reade, and Finkel 2008, 88–89, no. 584, with references (including mention of comparable tenth–seventh-century BCE "incense altars" from the Levant), fig. 56; Safar and Muhammad 1974, 271, figs. 265–66; see further, Foietta 2020.

74 Andrae 1938, 179, pl. 82b.

75 Rassam 1878–79, R 57; Reade 2002, 152, fig. 16; see further the discussion in Zimmerle 2014, 329–30.

76 Rassam 1878–79, 225–26.

77 Reade 2002, 145–54.

78 Layard 1853a, 360; a drawing by Solomon C. Malan, who visited the site in 1850, of the same entrance shows one such censer overturned in front of the colossal lion (Gadd 1938).

79 Hussein, Kertai, and Altaweel 2013, 104, pl. XLIXa.

80 Oates 1957, 27–28; Mallowan 1966, 1:234, figs. 194, 196.

81 Reade 2002, 195–96; Kertai 2015, 42–46, figs. 2.9–2.10.

82 Oates 1968, 123; Oates 1974, 184, pl. XXVIII.5 (TR. 4456).

83 See note 28.

84 Botta and Flandin 1849–50, II, pl. 114; this section is no longer preserved on the relief panel, displayed at the Institute for the Study of Ancient Cultures Museum (A11255).

85 Barnett 1976, 41, pl. XXIII (BM 124939).

86 Reade 2002, 151–52.

87 Zimmerle 2014; 2021 (for distribution, see in particular figs. 1.1, 1.2); and on the Mesopotamian examples, see further Ziegler 1942 (here identified for the first time as *Räucherkästchen*, "fire-boxes" [Sumerian NÍG.NA]); Pieńkowska 2018, 319, fig. 3b.

88 Zimmerle 2014, 128–39, with references; Frahm 2017a; Neumann forthcoming a.

89 In the Mesopotamian assemblage, Ziegler (1942, 233, fig. 52) describes a possible cuboid-censer corner fragment for Aššur (Ass. 16289, now in the Vorderasiatisches Museum, Berlin); this unstratified ceramic fragment is decorated with lines forming an X, a rosette stamp, and small knobs; see further, Zimmerle 2014, 331, table 6.1.2.

90 Zimmerle 2014, 323.

91 Searight, Reade, and Finkel 2008, no. 583, fig. 56 (BM 118372).

92 BM 92218.

93 Hrouda 1962, 72, pl. 55, no. 211; Searight, Reade, and Finkel 2008, 68, pl. 55, no. 211; Curtis and Green 1997, 20–21, fig. 24, no. 84; pl. XIVa–b.

94 Hrouda 1962, 51, nos. 227–28, pls. 37–38.

95 Reade 2002, 168, fig. 31.

96 Oates 1957, 27, n. 2; Mallowan 1966, 1: fig. 194; Oates 1968, 123, pls. XXXIIa, XXXIII.

97 Place 1867–70, 1:122–26; Loud 1936, 98–99, 107, figs. 111, 112, 107, 108; Loud and Altman 1938, 59, pls. 17, 45, 47 (a pair of statues is housed at the Iraq Museum, Baghdad, and another at the Institute for the Study of Ancient Cultures Museum [A11808–11809]).

98 For Kalḫu, see Mallowan 1966, 1:260–63, fig. 243; Brusasco 2016, 242–44, figs. 3–33 (the statues are housed in the Mosul Cultural Museum). For Hadatu, see Thureau-Dangin et al. 1931, 66, pl. 1; Thomas 2016: 159, no. 165 (the statues are housed in the National Museum of Aleppo [no. 51] and the Musée du Louvre [AO 7538]). On Assyrian temple statues overall, see further Reade 2002, 152; Nadali 2013; Neumann 2018.

99 Searight, Reade, and Finkel 2008, 88.

100 Layard 1853b, pl. 4; Reade 2002, 170–71, figs. 6, 32 (BM 118806).

101 On craftmanship and production in the Assyrian court, and specifically with respect to temples, see Neumann 2017; 2018, with references.

BIBLIOGRAPHY

Abusch, Tzvi. 2015. *The Magical Ceremony Maqlû: A Critical Edition.* Leiden; Boston: Brill.

Ambos, Claus. 2004. *Mesopotamische Baurituale aus dem 1. Jahrtausend v. Chr.* Dresden: Islet.

Andrae, Walter. 1922. *Die Archaischen Ischtar-Tempel in Assur.* Ausgrabungen der Deutschen Orient-Gesellschaft in Assur. A: Baudenkmäler aus Assyrischer Zeit IV. Leipzig: J. C. Hinrichs.

Andrae, Walter. 1923. *Farbrige Keramik aus Assur und ihre Vorstufen in altaassyrischen Wandmalereien.* Berlin: Scarabaeus.

Andrae, Walter. 1925. *Coloured Ceramics from Ashur, and Earlier Ancient Assyrian Wall-Paintings, from Photographs and Water-Colours by Members of the Ashur Expedition Organised by the Deutsche Orient-Gesellschaft.* London: K. Paul Trench Trubner & Co.

Andrae, Walter. 1938. *Das wiedererstandene Assur.* Sendschrift der Deutschen Orientgesellschaft 9. Leipzig: J.C. Hinrichs.

Aruz, Joan, Sarah Graff, and Yelena Rakic, eds. 2014. *Assyria to Iberia at the Dawn of the Classical Age.* New Haven, CT; London: Yale University Press.

Barnett, Richard David. 1976. *Sculptures from the North Palace of Ashurbanipal at Nineveh (668–627 B.C.).* London: British Museum Press.

Baughan, Elizabeth P. 2013. *Couched in Death: Klinai and Identity in Anatolia and Beyond.* Madison: University of Wisconsin Press.

Birch, Samuel, and Theophilus G. Pinches. 1880. *The Bronze Ornaments of the Palace Gates of Balawat.* London: Society of Biblical Archaeology.

Botta, Paul-Émile, and Eugène Flandin. 1849–50. *Monuments de Ninève, découvert et décrit par M. P.-É. Botta, mesuré et dessiné par M. E. Flandin.* Paris: Imprimerie nationale.

Brusasco, Paolo. 2016. "The Assyrian Sculptures in the Mosul Cultural Museum: A Preliminary Assessment of What Was on Display before Islamic State's Attack." *Journal of Near Eastern Studies* 75: 205–48.

Collon, Dominique. 1982. *Catalogue of Western Asiatic Seals in the British Museum: Cylinder Seals II: Akkadian, Post-Akkadian and Ur III Periods.* London: British Museum Press.

Collon, Dominique. 1987. *First Impressions: Cylinder Seals in the Ancient Near East.* London: British Museum Publications.

Collon, Dominique. 2001. *Catalogue of the Western Asiatic Seals in the British Museum: Cylinder Seals V: Neo-Assyrian and Neo-Babylonian Periods.* London: British Museum Press.

Couturaud, Barbara, Zaid Ghazi Saadallah al-Obeidi, Ariane Thomas, and Daniel Ibled. 2023. "The Rehabilitation of the Monumental Artworks of the Cultural Museum of Mosul: A Challenge Towards Iraqi Heritage." 13th International Congress for the Archaeology of the Ancient Near East, Copenhagen, May 25.

Curtis, John, and Anthony Green. 1997. *Excavations at Khirbet Khatuniyeh.* Saddam Dam Report 11. London: British Museum Press.

Curtis, John, and Julian Reade. 1995. *Art and Empire: Treasures from Assyria in the British Museum.* London: British Museum Press.

Curtis, John, and Nigel Tallis. 2005. *Forgotten Empire: The World of Ancient Persia.* London: British Museum Press.

Fales, Frederick Mario, John Nicholas Postgate, and Julian E. Reade. 1992. *Imperial Administrative Records, Part I: Palace and Temple Administration.* State Archives of Assyria (SAA) 7. Helsinki: The Neo-Assyrian Text Corpus Project.

Finkel, Irving L. 1991. "*Muššu'u, qutāru* and the Scribe Tanittu-Bēl." In *Velles Paraules: Ancient Near Eastern Studies in Honor of Miguel Civil on the Occasion of His Sixty-Fifth Birthday,* edited by Piotr Michalowski, P. Steinkeller, E. C. Stone, and Richard L. Zettler, Aula Orientalis, 91–104. Barcelona: Editorial AUSA.

Foietta, Enrico. 2020. "Movable Altars and Burners in Stone from Hatra." *Mesopotamia* 54: 197–218.

Frahm, Eckart. 2017a. "Assyria and the Far South: The Arabian Peninsula and the Persian Gulf." In *A Companion to Assyria,* edited by Eckart Frahm, 299–310. Hoboken, NJ: Wiley-Blackwell.

Frahm, Eckart, ed. 2017b. *A Companion to Assyria.* Hoboken, NJ: Wiley-Blackwell.

Frame, Grant. 2021. *The Royal Inscriptions of Sargon II, King of Assyria (721–705 BC).* Royal Inscriptions of the Neo-Assyrian Period (RINAP) 2. University Park, PA: Eisenbrauns.

Frankfort, Henri. 1982. *Stratified Cylinder Seals from the Diyala Region.* Oriental Institute Publications 72. Chicago: University of Chicago Press.

Gadd, Cyril J. 1938. "A Visiting Artist at Nineveh in 1850." *Iraq* 5: 118–23.

Garrison, Mark B. 2017. *The Ritual Landscape at Persepolis: Glyptic Imagery from the Persepolis Fortification and Treasury Archives.* Studies in Ancient Oriental Civilization 72. Chicago: Oriental Institute of the University of Chicago.

Goldman, Bernard. 1991. "Persian Domed Turibula." *Studia Iranica* 20: 179–88.

Grayson, A. Kirk. 1991. *Assyrian Rulers of the Early First Millennium BC Part I (1114–859 BC).* Royal Inscriptions of Mesopotamia Assyrian Periods (RIMA) 2. Toronto; Buffalo, NY: University of Toronto Press.

Grayson, A. Kirk. 1996. *Assyrian Rulers of the Early First Millennium BC Part II (858–745 BC).* Royal Inscriptions of Mesopotamia Assyrian Periods (RIMA) 3. Toronto; Buffalo, NY: Univereisty of Toronto Press.

Harper, Prudence Oliver. 2005. "From Earth to Heaven: Speculations on the Significance of the Form of the Achaemenid Censer." *Bulletin of the Asia Institute* 19, Iranian and Zoroastrian Studies in Honor of Prods Oktor Skærvø: 47–56.

Hrouda, Barthel. 1962. *Tell Halaf IV: Die Kleinfunde aus historischer Zeit.* Berlin: Walter de Gruyter.

Hussein, Muzahim Mahmu, David Kertai, and Mark Altaweel. 2013. "Nimrud and Its Remains in Light of Iraqi Excavations from 1989–2002." In *New Research on Late Assyrian Palaces: Conference at Heidelberg, January 22nd, 2011,* edited by David Kertai and Peter A. Miglus, 91–124. Heidelberg: Heidelberger Orientverlag.

Jursa, Michael. 2006–2008. "Räucherung, Rauchopfer. A. In Mesopotamien." In *Reallexikon der Assyriologie und Vorderasiatischen Archäologie,* edited by Michael P. Streck, 225–29. Berlin: Walter de Gruyter.

Kertai, David. 2015. *The Architecture of Late Assyrian Royal Palaces.* Oxford: Oxford University Press.

King, Leonard W. 1915. *Bronze Reliefs from the Gates of Shalmaneser, King of Assyria, B.C. 860–825.* London: British Museum Press.

Layard, Austen Henry. 1849. *Nineveh and Its Remains*. 2 vols. London: John Murray.

Layard, Austen Henry. 1853a. *Discoveries among the Ruins of Nineveh and Babylon*. New York: Harper & Brothers.

Layard, Austen Henry. 1853b. *A Second Series of the Monuments of Nineveh*. London: J. Murray.

Leichty, Erle. 2011. *The Royal Inscriptions of Esarhaddon, King of Assyria (680–669 BC)*. Royal Inscritions of the Neo-Assyrian Period (RINAP) 4. Winona Lake, IN: Eisenbrauns.

Livingstone, Alasdair. 1989. *Court Poetry and Literary Miscellanea*. State Archives of Assyria (SAA) 3. Helsinki: The Neo-Assyrian Text Corpus Project.

Lőrincz, Huba. 2017. "A BM 1930-5-8, 218-as számú ninivei füstölőállvány funkcionális és ikonográfiai elemzése [The Iconographic and Functional Analysis of the BM 1930-5-8,218 Incense Burner from Nineveh]." In *"Közel, s Távol" VII. Az Eötvös Collegium Orientalisztika Múhely éves konferenciájának elóadásaiból 2016*, edited by Doma Petra and Takó Ferenc, 67–92. Budapest: Eötvös Collegium.

Loud, Gordon. 1936. *Khorsabad I: Excavations in the Palace and at a City Gate*. Oriental Institute Publications 38. Chicago: University of Chicago Press.

Loud, Gordon, and Charles B. Altman. 1938. *Khorsabad II: The Citadel and the Town*. Oriental Institute Publications 40. Chicago: University of Chicago Press.

Luukko, Mikko, and Greta Van Buylaere. 2017. "Languages and Writing Systems in Assyria." In *A Companion to Assyria*, edited by Eckart Frahm, 313–35. Hoboken, NJ: Wiley-Blackwell.

Mallowan, Barbara. 1993. "Assyrian Temple Furniture." In *Aspects of Art and Iconography: Anatolia and Its Neighbors: Studies in Honor of Nimet Özgüç*, edited by Machteld Johanna Mellink and Nimet Oezguec, 383–87. Ankara: Türk Tarih Kurumu Basmevi.

Mallowan, Max E. L. 1966. *Nimrud and Its Remains*. 3 vols. London: British School of Archaeology in Iraq.

Maul, Stefan M. 1994. *Zukunftsbewältigung: Eine Untersuchung Altorientalischen Denkens Anhand der Babylonisch-Assyrischen Löseritual (Namburbi)*. Baghdader Forschungen 18. Mainz: Philipp von Zabern.

May, Herbert G. 1935. *Material Remains of the Megiddo Cult*. Chicago: Oriental Institute of the University of Chicago.

Melekian-Chirvani, A. S. 1993. "The International Achaemenid Style." *Bulletin of the Asia Institute* 7: 111–30.

Menzel, Brigitte. 1981. *Assyrische Tempel*. 2 vols. Studia Pohl, Series Maior 10. Rome: Biblical Institute Press.

Mirelman, Sam. 2018. "Mesopotamian Magic in Text and Performance." In *Mesopotamian Medicine and Magic*, edited by Strahil V. Panayotov and Luděk Vacín, 343–78. Leiden; Boston: Brill.

Moortgat, Anton. 1941. "Assyrische Glyptik des 13. Jarhunderts." *Zeitschrift für Assyriologie und vorderasiatische Archäologie* 47: 49–88.

Moortgat, Anton. 1944. "Assyrische Glyptik des 12. Jarhunderts." *Zeitschrift für Assyriologie und vorderasiatische Archäologie* 48: 23–44.

Moortgat, Anton. 1966. *Vorderasiatische Rollsiegel: Ein beitrag zur Geschichte der Steinschneidekunst*. Berlin: Gebr. Mann.

Nadali, Davide. 2013. "When Ritual Meets Art: Rituals in the Visual Arts *versus* the Visual Arts in Rituals: The Case of Ancient Mesopotamia." *Rivista degli Studi Orientali Supplemento* 2: 209–26.

Nakamura, Carolyn. 2005. "Mastering Matters: Magical Sense and the Figurine Worlds of Neo-Assyria." In *Archaeologies of Materiality*, edited by Lynn Meskell, 18–45. Oxford: Blackwell.

Nassouhi, Essad. 1925. "Les autels trépieds assyriens." *Revue d'Assyriologie et d'Archéologie Orientale* 22: 85–90.

Neumann, Kiersten. 2017. "Gods among Men: Fashioning the Divine Image in Assyria." In *What Shall I Say of Clothes? Theoretical and Methodological Approaches to Dress in Antiquity*, edited by Megan Cifarelli and Laura Gawlinski, Selected Papers in Ancient Art and Architecture 3, 3–23. Boston: Archaeological Institute of America.

Neumann, Kiersten. 2018. "Reading the Temple of Nabu as a Coded Sensory Experience." *Iraq* 80: 181–211.

Neumann, Kiersten. 2019a. "Laying the Foundations for Eternity: Timing Temple Construction in Assyria." In *Sounding Sensory Profiles in the Ancient Near East*, edited by Annette Schellenberg and Thomas Krüger, Ancient Near East Monographs 25, 253–78. Atlanta, GA: SBL Press.

Neumann, Kiersten. 2019b. "Sensing the Sacred in the Neo-Assyrian Temple: The Presentation of Offerings to the Gods." In *Distant Impressions: The Senses in the Ancient Near East*, edited by Ainsley Hawthorn and Anne-Caroline Rendu Loisel, 23–62. Winona Lake, IL: Eisenbrauns.

Neumann, Kiersten. 2023. "Behind-the-Scences: The Assyrian Offering Table at the OI Museum." *The Oriental Institute News & Notes* 253: 14–17.

Neumann, Kiersten. forthcoming a. "'Aššur, accept! Aššur, listen!' Connecting Arabia and Assyria through Aromatics and Olfaction." *Proceedings of the 55th Seminar for Arabian Studies*. Deutsches Archäologisches Institut.

Neumann, Kiersten. forthcoming b. "From Raw to Ritualized: Following the Trail of Incense of the Assyrian Temple." In *Sensing Divinity: Incense, Religion and the Ancient Sensorium*, edited by M. Bradley, A. Grand-Clément, A.-C. Rendu Loisel, and A. Vincent.

Nielson, Kjeld. 1986. *Incense in Ancient Israel*. Leiden: E. J. Brill.

Novotny, Jamie R., and Joshua Jeffers. 2018. *The Royal Inscriptions of Ashurbanipal (668–631 BC), Aššur-etel-ilāni (630–627 BC), and Sîn-šarra-iškun (626–612 BC), Kings of Assyria, Part 1*. The Royal Inscriptions of the Neo-Assyrain Period 5/1. University Park, PA: Eisenbrauns.

Oates, David. 1957. "Ezida: The Temple of Nabu." *Iraq* 19: 26–39.

Oates, David. 1968. "The Excavations at Tell al Rimah, 1967." *Iraq* 30: 115–38.

Oates, Joan. 1974. "Late Assyrian Temple Furniture from Tell al Rimah." *Iraq* 36: 179–84.

Oates, Joan, and David Oates. 2001. *Nimrud: An Assyrian Imperial City Revealed*. London: British School of Archaeology in Iraq.

Oppenheim, A. Leo. 1944. "The Mesopotamian Temple." *The Biblical Archaeologist* 7: 54–63.

Oppenheim, A. Leo. 1956–2010. *The Assyrian Dictionary of the Oriental Institute of the University of Chicago (CAD)*. 26 vols. Chicago: Oriental Institute of the University of Chicago.

Oppenheim, Max von. 1933. *Tell Halaf: A New Culture in Oldest Mesopotamia*. Translated by Gerald Wheeler. London; New York: G. P. Putnam's Sons.

Özgen, Ilknur, and Jean Öztürk. 1996. *The Lydian Treasure: Heritage Recovered*. Ankara: Republic of Turkey, Ministry of Culture, General Directorate of Monuments and Museums.

Page, Stephanie. 1968. "A Stela of Adad-nirari III and Nergal-ereš from Tell al Rimah." *Iraq* 30, no. 2: 139–53.

Parpola, Simo. 2017. *Assyrian Royal Rituals and Cultic Texts*. State Archives of Assyria (SAA) 20. Helsinki: The Neo-Assyrian Text Corpus Project.

Pedersén, Olof. 2005. *Archive und Bibliotheken in Babylon: Die Tontafeln der Grabung Robert Koldeweys 1899–1917*. Abhandlungen der Deutschen Orient-Gesellschaft 25. Saarbrücken: Saarländische Druckerei und Verlag.

Pieńkowska, Agnieszka. 2018. "Mesopotamian Incense Burners from the Third and Second Millennia BC: An Archaeological Approach." In *Proceedings of the 10th International Congress on the Archaeology of the Ancient Near East, 25–29 April 2016, Vienna*, edited by Barbara Horejs and Christoph Schwall, 315–28. Wiesbaden: Harrassowitz Verlag.

Pittman, Holly. 1996. "The White Obelisk and the Problem of Historical Narrative in the Art of Assyria." *Art Bulletin* 78: 334–55.

Place, Victor. 1867–70. *Ninive et l'Assyrie*. 3 vols. Paris: Imprimerie impériale.

Pongratz-Leisten, Beate. 2015. *Religion and Ideology in Assyria*. Studies in Ancient Near Eastern Records 6. Boston; Berlin: De Gruyter.

Postgate, John Nicholas. 1992a. "Trees and Timber in Assyrian Texts." In *Bulletin of Sumerian Agriculture 6*, edited by J. N. Postgate and Marvin Powell, 177–92. Cambridge: Sumerian Agriculture Group.

Postgate, John Nicholas. 1992b. "The Land of Assur and the Yoke of Assur." *World Archaeology* 23: 247–23.

Pottier, Edmond. 1924. *Catalogue des antiquités assyriennes*. Paris: Musées Nationaux.

Radner, Karen. 2011. "The Assur-Nineveh-Arbela Triangle: Central Assyria in the Neo-Assyrian Period." In *Between the Cultures: The Central Tigris Region in Mesopotamia from the 3rd to the 1st Millennium BC*, edited by Peter A. Miglus and Simone Mühl, Heidelberger Studien zum Alten Orient 14, 321–29. Heidelberg: Heidelberger Orient-Verlag.

Rashid, S. A. 1981. "A Study of Some Incense Burners in Ancient Iraq (Arabic)." *Sumer* 41: 162–69.

Rassam, Hormuzd. 1878–79. "Letters and Reports in British Museum Central Archive: *Assyrian Excavations*, Vol. I, and *Original Papers* for 1879."

Reade, Julian Edgeworth. 1995. "The Symposion in Ancient Mesopotamia: Archaeological Evidence." In *In Vino Veritas*, edited by Oswyn Murray and Manuela Tecuşan, 35–56. London: British School at Rome.

Reade, Julian Edgeworth. 2002. "The Ziggurat and Temples of Nimrud." *Iraq* 64: 135–216.

Reade, Julian Edgeworth. 2005. "Religious Ritual in Assyrian Sculpture." In *Ritual and Politics in Ancient Mesopotamia*, edited by Barbara N. Porter, American Oriental Series 88, 7–61. New Haven, CT: American Oriental Society.

Reiner, Erica. 1958. *Šurpu*. Archiv für Orientforschung 11, Beiheft. Paris: Répertoire d'Épigraphie Sémitique.

Safar, Fuad. 1957. "The Temple of Sibitti at Khorsabad." *Sumer* 13: 219–21 [English], 193–96, figs. 1–4 [Arabic].

Safar, Fuad, and Ali Mustafa Muhammad. 1974. *Hatra: The City of the Sun God*. Baghdad: Directorate General of Antiquities.

Sallaberger, Walther. 2011–13. "Tempel. A. I. a. Philologisch. In Mesopotamien. 3. Jt. bis 612 v. Chr." In *Reallexikon der Assyriologie und Vorderasiatischen Archäologie*, edited by M. Streck, vol. 12, 519–24. Berlin: Walter de Gruyter.

Schachner, Andreas. 2007. *Bilder eines Weltreiches. Kunts- und kulturgeschichtliche Untersuchungen zu den Verzierungen eines Tores aus Balawat (Imgur-Enlil) aus der Zeit Shalmaneser III, König von Assyrien*. Turnhout: Brepols.

Schmidt, Erich F. 1953. *Persepolis I: Structures, Reliefs, Inscriptions*. Oriental Institute Publications 68. Chicago: University of Chicago Press.

Schmitt, Aaron W. 2004. “Deponierungen von Figuren bei der Fundamentlegung assyrischer und babylonischer Tempel.” In *Mesopotamische Baurituale aus dem 1. Jahrtausend v. Chr*, edited by Claus Ambos, 229–34. Dresden: Islet.

Searight, Ann, Julian Reade, and Irving L. Finkel. 2008. *Assyrian Stone Vessels and Related Material in the British Museum.* Oxford; Oakville, CT: Oxbow Books; David Brown Book Co.

Seidl, Ursula. 1989. *Die Babylonischen Kudurru-Reliefs: Symbole Mesopotamischer Gottheiten.* Orbis Biblicus et Orientalis 87. Freiburg; Göttingen: Universitätsverlag; Vandenhoeck & Ruprecht.

Simons, Francis James Michael. 2017. “Burn Your Way to Success: Studies in the Mesopotamian Ritual and Incantation Series *Šurpu*.” PhD Dissertation, University of Birmingham.

Sollberger, Edmond. 1974. "The White Obelisk." Iraq 36: 231–238.

Stein, Diana. 1987. “Seal Impressions on Texts from Arrapḫa and Nuzi in the Yale Babylonian Collection.” In *General Studies and Excavations at Nuzi 9/1*, edited by David I. Owen and Martha A. Morrison, Studies on the Civilization and Culture of Nuzi and the Hurrians 2, 225–320. Winona Lake, IN: Eisenbrauns.

Thavapalan, Shiyanthi. 2019. *The Meaning of Color in Ancient Mesopotamia.* Culture and History of the Ancient Near East 104. Leiden; Boston: Brill.

Thomas, Ariane, ed. 2016. *L’histoire commence en Mésopotamie.* Gand: Snoeck Publishers; Musée du Louvre-Lens.

Thompson, Campbell, and M. E. L. Mallowan. 1933. “The British Museum Excavations at Nineveh, 1931–32.” *Annals of Archaeology and Anthropology* 20: 71–186.

Thompson, R. Campbell, and R. W. Hutchinson. 1931. “The Site of the Palace of Ashurnasirpal at Nineveh, Excavated in 1929–30 on behalf of the British Museum.” *Annals of Archaeology and Anthropology* 18: 79–112.

Thureau-Dangin, F., G. A. Barroit, G. Dossin, and M. Dunand, 1931. *Arslan-Tash.* Paris: Librairie orientaliste Paul Geuthner.

Unger, Eckhard. 1928. “Altar.” In *Reallexikon der Assyriologie und Vorderasiatischen Archäologie*, edited by E. Ebeling and Bruno Meissner, 72–74. Berlin: Walter de Gruyter.

van den Hout, Theo. 2018. “The Silver Stag Vessel: A Royal Gift.” *Metropolitan Museum Journal* 53: 115–27.

van Driel, Govert. 1969. *The Cult of Aššur.* Studia Semitica Neerlandica 13. Assen: Van Gorcum.

Watanabe, Chikako E. 1992. “A Problem in the Libation Scene of Ashurbanipal.” In *Cult and Ritual in the Ancient Near East*, edited by H. I. H. Prince Takahito Mikasa, 91–104. Wiesbaden: Harrassowitz.

Wiggermann, Frans A. M. 1992. *Mesopotamian Protective Spirits: The Ritual Texts.* Cuneiform Monographs I. Groningen: STYX & PP Publications.

Wiggermann, Frans A. M. 1993–97. “Mischwesen. A.” In *Reallexikon der Assyriologie und Vorderasiatischen Archäologie*, edited by Dietz Otto Edzard, 222–45. Berlin: Walter de Gruyter.

Ziegler, Liselotte. 1942. “Tonkästchen aus Uruk, Babylon und Assur.” *Zeitschrift für Assyriologie und vorderasiatische Archäologie* 47: 224–40.

Zimmerle, William Gerard. 2014. “Aromatics of All Kinds: Cuboid Incense Burners in the Ancient Near East from the Late Third to the Late First Millennia BC.” PhD Dissertation, University of Pennsylvania.

Zimmerle, William Gerard. 2021. “Frankincense and Its Arabian Burner.” In *All Things Arabia: Arabian Identity and Material Culture*, edited by I. Baird and H. Yağcıoğlu, 23–42. Leiden: Brill.

Zimmern, Heinrich. 1901. *Beiträge zur Kenntnis der babylonischen Religion.* Assyriologische Bibliothek 12. Leipzig: J. C. Hinrichs.

CENSERS

IMAGINED
INCENSE

CENSERS REAL AND IMAGINED: JEWS AND INCENSE FROM ANTIQUITY THROUGH THE PRESENT

Karen B. Stern

Few studies consider censers or practices of thurification among Jews of the premodern world. This neglect reinforces assumptions that Jewish uses of vessels for ritual burning of incense ceased after the Romans destroyed the Jewish Temple in Jerusalem in 70 CE. Yet cursory examination of textual, archaeological, and liturgical data of various sorts complicates the picture: it reveals the persistent resonance of censers and their artistic renderings —in practice and in memory—in Jewish communal and domestic settings through time. This volume thus offers a critical opportunity to rethink roles of censers and ritual acts of thurification (the burning of incense) to contextualize them within the devotional lives and practices of Israelites, Judahites, and Jews throughout the ancient, medieval, and modern Middle East, North Africa, and Europe.

Evidence varies for the design, presentation, and use of censers, as attested in biblical, epigraphic, and rabbinic writings, those found in the Cairo Geniza, and in medieval manuscripts and liturgies. Examples include archaeological vestiges of three-dimensional bronze and ceramic incense shovels and burners and other types of free-standing censers inside devotional, domestic, and mortuary spaces. Others include visual representations of censers and incense shovels, tessellated into mosaic carpets of synagogue floors, embossed onto oil lamps, molded into glass vessels, carved into tombstones or sarcophagi, or painted onto folios of illuminated manuscripts which Jews commissioned. Amulets and shrines offer regional documentation of additional uses of censers; and liturgical references to incense burning proliferated differently in medieval Baghdad and Europe. These diverse data support the argument that, for many Jews, censers and thurification remained varied and potent symbols, if not instruments and activities, well after the destruction of the Jerusalem Temple and the eradication of daily incense sacrifices once conducted within it.

TERMINOLOGY, DEFINITIONS, AND HISTORICAL CONTEXT

Challenges of terminology beset studies of censers and Jews in multiple respects. Foremost, no ancient Hebrew, Aramaic, or Greek terms precisely or consistently correspond with the word censer, let alone when translated into English. Moreover, Israelite, Judahite, and Jewish ritual behaviors and conceptions of thurification, as well as implements associated with incense burning, transformed significantly throughout multiple periods and regions. Even the words used to identify and classify Jews changes diachronically. These factors require preliminary evaluation to frame the discussion that follows.

Censers, commonly defined as three-dimensional objects with multiple components, including a closed metal base and grillwork above, are only attested in a handful of instances in antiquity in places associated with Israelite, Judahite, or Jewish use. The latter populations often preferred to use uncovered and flat metal shovels as censers, which could carry burning coals onto which incense was sometimes placed and ignited for ritual purposes. At other times, metal bowls or ceramic troughs of additional types performed similar functions as thuribles,[1] as did ceramic sets and bronze or iron braziers. This discussion, therefore, deliberately casts a wide net, typologically, geographically, and chronologically, to encompass the breadth of these materials and the activities they facilitated. Functionalities, rather than elusive, emic terminologies, thus predict vessels' considerations below.

The category of censer here incorporates three-dimensional incense burners, composed of ceramic or metal, hanging, free-standing, or propped upright, with or without covers, which were sometimes used for devotional purposes. It also encompasses certain types of uncovered shovels with different handle lengths, often called *maḥtot* in Hebrew (singular: *maḥtah*). Such objects could variously serve as shovels to transport burning or non-burning coals, to carry incense (without coals) or ashes, or to transport incense already burning upon coals. Most related implements of various designations—in Hebrew (*maḥtah, kaf*), Aramaic (*bazih*), and Greek (*thiuskē*)—could be used in corresponding ways.[2] Thus, supplementary information from literary, architectural, and archaeological contexts, as much as construction and design, must qualify an object as a censer in the following discussion.

Yet some of the most powerful representations of censers or incense shovels in Jewish contexts appear in two-dimensions, beside images of other implements historically associated with the Jerusalem Temple, including the *menorah* (seven-branched candelabrum), *shofar* (ram's horn used as a wind instrument), and *ethrog* (citron). These are replicated in multiple media: in stone and glass tesserae of mosaic floors; molded and embossed into ceramic and glass lamps and vessels; impressed into lead sarcophagi; painted onto tombstones; and painted upon illuminated manuscripts rendering the Temple and its environs.[3] Records of incense burning in pilgrimage shrines, as well as descriptions of incense preparation in prayer traditions of Jews of the Middle East and particularly Iraq, also verbally extend the power of censers and thurification through the present day. This breadth of evidence thus demonstrates the durability and resonance of incense and censers, in diverse Jewish contexts, spanning periods of earliest antiquity through modernity.

Terms designating the geographic and political scope of peoples from ancient Israel, Judah, Judaea, Palaestina, and elsewhere, who created and used censers, however, remain commensurately contingent and complex.[4] Indeed, to many non-specialists, corresponding designations of people as Israelites, Judahites, Judeans, or Jews, might seem nearly synonymous and interchangeable. But each term, in turn, refracts distinct chronological, historical, cultural, religious, demographic, and political realities, which require a cursory review to situate the analyses of censers below.

"Israelite," as used here, is a label for Semitic-speaking peoples who inhabited the Iron Age Levant, in regions of ancient Canaan, whose worlds are best (if obliquely) documented in archaeological records of the eleventh through ninth centuries BCE and in biblical texts redacted in later periods. By the ninth century BCE, however, more distinctive administrative entities evolved, with Israel in its northern half (between Mt. Gerizim in the south and Tel Dan in the North) and Judah in its south. "Israelite," after that point, designates inhabitants and objects of the northern kingdom of Israel, while "Judahite," distinguishes those dwelling farther south in Judah, who maintained the central cult center of the Temple in Jerusalem, and whose territories extended southward toward the Negev desert.[5] But regional geopolitics assured rapid demises of both Israel and Judah. The Neo-Assyrian Empire crushed the northern kingdom of Israel in 722 BCE, repopulating the territory with its own constituents, while the Neo-Babylonian Empire overran Judah in the south, destroyed its cult center in Jerusalem, and exiled Judah's elites to Babylon in 587/6 BCE. After this, "Israelite" and "Judahite" become anachronistic labels for corresponding peoples and their material cultures.

In slightly later periods, the modified adjectives "Judean" and "Jewish" replace the former terms, reflecting the changed realities, peoples, languages, and cultures that followed Achaemenid, Hellenistic, and Roman conquests and hegemony in the Levant. Under Achaemenid rulers, including Cyrus the Great and his successors, exiles in Babylon were permitted to return to rebuild their Temple in Jerusalem inside the Persian province of *Yehud*.[6] During this and subsequent periods, when Alexander the Great's political heirs feuded over the same territory throughout the third century BCE, the Greek word "Ioudaios" (frequently translated as "Jew") labeled those who might live in Judea or elsewhere, but worshiped one ancestral Israelite God (YHWH/ YWH), in one Jerusalem Temple, and identified with the same teachings and traditions collected in the Torah.[7] Following the Maccabean revolt and Hasmonean rule (ca. 167–37 BCE), Rome conquered the region (first century BCE and following), and Herod, Rome's client king (r. 37 BCE–4 CE), completed his monumental reconstruction of the Temple that had been rebuilt and modified in Jerusalem throughout the Achaemenid and Hellenistic periods (Josephus *A.J.* 15.396–402).

Sequential Jewish revolts against Rome, however, transformed the lives of Jews in Judea and around the Mediterranean. Rome destroyed Herod's Temple in 70 CE in retribution for the First Jewish Revolt, forcing Jews throughout the empire to develop cultural and religious strategies to accommodate the dramatic loss of their cultic center in Jerusalem and, as some believed, the dwelling of their deity (Josephus *B.J.* 4.388). Punishments for Jewish rebellion multiplied, following the deaths of tens of thousands of Jews (Josephus *B.J.* 6.420). Some Jews were enslaved (Josephus estimates 97,000), while others migrated north or traveled to Africa, Europe, Asia, or Babylonia. Rome redrew regional political boundaries, then, under Hadrian, punitively renamed Judaea "Palaestina," in deference to the Israelites' ancestral enemies, the Philistines.[8] Yet punishments were even more severe following the Second Jewish Revolt (131–38 CE), when Hadrian renamed Jerusalem *Aelia Capitolina* after his own family; he constructed a temple to Jupiter Capitolinus where the Jewish Temple originally stood and expelled Jews from Jerusalem. By the middle of the second century CE, therefore, Jews had lost their eponymous land, their Temple, and their sacred city of Jerusalem. These suddenly became places of collective memory, accessed only through writings, stories, prayers, visual representations, and legends.

In some regions, by later antiquity, synagogues became centers of ritual life and patronage. Elsewhere, the study hall took pride of place, particularly in specific parts of Palestine and Babylonia where rabbinic Jewish cultures flourished (*b. Ber.* 8a; cf. *b. Pesaḥ.* 4:4).[9] And Jewish life in areas that ceded to Arab conquests accommodated different realities than those sustained by Jews who inhabited other regions of Europe, North Africa, or Asia Minor in earlier and subsequent periods of ascendent eastern and western Christianity. These regional histories require notice, because of how profoundly and distinctly they shaped the cultural and religious worlds of Jews throughout premodernity, inclusive of their uses of censers and thurification.

Notably, archaeological documentation for censers in the Jerusalem Temple remains largely absent. This lacuna might seem surprising, given the attention conferred in biblical texts to implements and activities of incense sacrifice in the Jerusalem Temple.[10] Yet multiple historical contingencies account for this lack of archaeological data, which relate to the politics of the modern site where the ancient Temple once stood. Today, the Waqf (endowment to the Muslim religious authority) regulates the area encompassing the Al-Aqsa Mosque and the Dome of the Rock, which Abd al-Malik constructed in the seventh century CE upon the platform that once supported the Herodian Temple. The Waqf's formal prohibitions of excavation in the area dually designated as the Temple Mount/Haram al-Sharif, ensure that any archaeological remains of censers, incense altars, or implements from different iterations of the Jerusalem Temple—let alone any of its architectural features—remain inaccessible for investigation. Biblical texts and subsequent Jewish literatures, as well as archaeological records for censers used and represented in later contexts thus necessarily ground discussions of thurification in ancient Israel, Judah, Judea, and beyond.

CENSERS IN THE BIBLICAL
AND LITERARY IMAGINATION

The nature of biblical sources, including those consulted below, notoriously complicates historians' efforts to reconstruct the Israelite and Judahite past, including the role of censers and incense burning within it.[11] This partly explains why several biblical descriptions of implements and activities of thurification associated with early Israel vary or contradict each other, whether describing practices associated with the portable desert Tabernacle (which predated the construction of the Temple) or the Temple itself. This variability, however, is endemic to studying the Bible for purposes of historiography writ large. Biblical accounts, nonetheless, remain critical for analyzing roles that censers might have played in early Israel and in later Jewish traditions. This is so, not only because they document some historical uses of censers, incense altars, and incense burning, but also because they constitute a core set of texts, which subsequent Jewish populations held dear, studied, and memorized to assist their imaginings of ancient rituals and traditions.

Biblical texts list multiple occasions for thurification in times of ancient Israel and Judah. Twice daily sacrifices of incense in the Jerusalem Temple, in the morning and evening, are described as *ketoret ha-tamid* (Exod 30:7–8). Annual expiatory offerings of incense also took place on the Day of Atonement; unusual events, such as plague, might prompt supplementary sacrifices (Num 10:11–13). Incense offerings, however, are mostly formalized in recipe, procedure, and timing. If dedicants deviated from these procedures, their incense sacrifices could induce divine punishment, rather than favor (Num 16; Lev 26:31).

Discussions of vessels and procedures for incense burning vary.[12] Some texts, for instance, prescribe for pure frankincense (*levonah*) to be burned directly beside bread on the shewbread table (Lev 24:5–9; cf. Josephus *A.J.* 3.10.7).[13] But it is the mixture of pure frankincense with statce, onycha, and galbanum—to be blended in the *ketoret* sacrifice—which distinguished a separate offering on a designated incense altar inside the cultic precinct (Exod 30:34–37). Because biblical descriptions of the latter incense offering are minimal, debates about the weights and proportions of ingredients, as well as augmented lists of aromatics to be blended, abound in subsequent periods. Josephus (*B.J.* 5.5.5), and later the rabbis (*b. Ker.* 6a), enumerated eleven to sixteen distinctive components of incense to be mixed and pulverized, before burning them upon hot coals. These include balsam, onycha, galbanum, frankincense, myrrh, cassia, spikenard, saffron, costus, aromatic bark, cinnamon, lye of Carsina, Cypriot wine, and salt of Sodom (*b. Ker.* 8a).[14] Later rabbinic traditions simultaneously emphasize the significance and esotericism of the Temple incense recipe, whose secrets were allegedly guarded by one family.[15] These elaborations, however, are projected onto past events.

Additional texts primarily link the burning of aromatics and resins to designated altars. When recalling incense sacrifice at the time of the Tabernacle (before the construction of the Temple), for instance, some texts describe burning incense on a portable altar of acacia wood, covered in gold.[16] After the construction of the Temple, other texts prescribe burning incense on a designated limestone altar beside the shewbread table. The architectural position of that altar was debated in texts redacted in later periods, reflecting ongoing rabbinic interests in historical incense sacrifices and their places (both spatially and practically) in Temple cult.[17] Movable implements, such as firepans (*mahtot*), served ancillary roles in these sacrifices. And while the Bible does not describe the manufacture of *mahtot* specifically for the incense altar (e.g., Exod 30:1–10, 37:25–29), rabbinic texts of the *Mishnah* theorized that Temple priests used gold and silver shovels for this purpose (*m. Tamid* 5:5, 6:2).[18] Several other implements, including the ladle (*kaf*), hooks, and bowls are noted, but firepans, or *mahtot*, are most commonly associated with these activities.[19]

So many biblical texts associate the burning of incense with the flat pan of the *mahtah*, however (e.g., Num 16:2, 18; 17:11; cf. Lev 10:1), that it became the Temple implement most visually connected to incense burning in subsequent periods, as discussed below. This connection remained strong, even if certain biblical texts imply that burning incense inside portable vessels, including *mahtot* (as opposed to on the altar itself), was an abhorrent practice, even punishable by death (Lev 10:1–2; Num 16, 17; Ezek 8:11). Some have consequently declared that the *mahtah* never served as a censer in the Temple. Nonetheless, certain biblical texts may implicate an opposite practice, recording that the high priest (Aaron) would bring fistfuls of incense with coals inside *mahtot* on the Day of Atonement, possibly directing its use as a censer (Lev 16:12).

Different biblical passages identify strategic times when censers and acts of thurification served both expiatory and olfactory functions for Israelites and Judahites, whose deity would be "pleased" by their aromas under optimal conditions (Lev 2:2; cf. Lev 26:31). Texts redacted in later periods, which describe the historical activities of the Temple in different ways, however, suggest that not only were the aromas of burning incense instrumental to the efficacy of thurification, but so too was the smoke emitted. For instance, the book of Ezekiel notes that the smoke from the incense sacrifice on the Day of Atonement purposefully veiled the high priest and his actions from public view (Ezek 8:11).[20] Incense burning thus offered multiple benefits, ranging from olfactory emanation to visual obfuscation.

After reconstruction of the Temple began in the Achaemenid period and during periods of Hasmonean and Roman rule, textual evidence for censers and incense practices among Jews appear to broaden and shift somewhat. Texts from the Qumran Library (Dead Sea Scrolls) mostly expound upon biblical discussions of incense altars and services (e.g., 11Q19, III, 9), rather than detail contemporaneous practice. These records thus reflect the distinctive priorities and interests of their sectarian authors.[21]

But Philo and Josephus, Jewish authors of elevated social and economic status, who lived and wrote in first-century Egypt, the Levant, and Rome during periods of Roman hegemony, also consider Temple incense sacrifices, furniture, and implements, if from slightly different vantages. Their writings often aim to favorably translate Jewish practices into the philosophical and cultural idioms of their Roman audiences, who, in turn, would have been otherwise acquainted with practices of incense burning in their own cultic contexts (via firepans, altars, or other types of braziers), in public or domestic spaces.[22] Neither author, however, offers explicit reports about contemporaneous practices of Jewish incense burning. Philo, for instance, prioritizes considerations of philosophical states (*pneuma logikon*) of persons offering incense sacrifices, declaring that these were more important to God than the offerings themselves (*Leg.* 1.273–274). Josephus, by contrast, lists the "censer" as one of the few significant implements contained in the "Holy House" (Temple), alongside the incense altar, the (shewbread) table, and the candlestick (menorah) (Josephus *C. Ap.* 2.8).[23] Josephus, however, fails to describe the physical appearance of this censer. Ensuing literary accounts thus cannot significantly advance historians' understandings of Jewish uses of censers during the Roman period. Even so, they collectively suggest that the presence and use of the censer in Jerusalem—whether imagined as a *maḥtah*, brazier, or something else—remained emblematic of dynamics or features of the Temple cultus, whether to Jews of the Roman period and/or to informed, non-Jewish Roman audiences.[24]

Many have assumed that traditions of using censers to celebrate festivals and sabbaths ceased after the destruction of Herod's Temple.[25] This is partly because of rabbinic proscriptions against conducting certain activities that were once performed inside the Temple, such as animal and incense sacrifices, as well as libations, following the Temple's destruction (*m. Soṭah* 9:12). Nonetheless, rabbinic texts suggest that Jews continued to use makeshift censers of various sorts throughout time, as means to continue to celebrate sabbaths and festivals, even if the occasions, materials, and forms of their censers, in addition to the locations of their use, necessarily diversified after the demise of the Temple.

In rabbinic writings from Palestine and Babylonia from the third through seventh centuries CE, discussions of censers and incense burning are divided into two basic categories: (1) those that consider historical activities associated with incense manipulation in the Temple cult, as seen above and designated as *ketoret* (e.g., *b. Ker.* 6a); and (2) those that reflect, at least obliquely, the historical world that rabbis inhabited, including acts of burning incense in the home and elsewhere, which are differently classified as *mugmar*.[26]

Some rabbinic texts, indeed, describe the continuation of practices of burning incense to celebrate festivals, hundreds of years after the destruction of the Temple, in ways that echo Temple practice. Among these is the following passage from the Babylonian Talmud:[27]

> It is forbidden to lay down incense (*mugmar*) on coals on a festival (*yom tov*), however, the house of Rabban Gamliel they did place it. Thus said Rabbi Eliezer bar Tzadok: Many times, I came in after my father into the house of Rabban Gamliel, and they did not place the *mugmar* [on coal] during a festival, but they would bring perforated iron containers (*'ardaska'ot*), filled them with smoke before sundown on the evening of the festival, and plugged their holes before sundown on the evening of the festival [so that the smoke would not escape]. The following day, when the guests entered, they would unplug them, and the house would be filled with the smell of incense on its own. They [the sages] said to him: if so, also then on the sabbath it is permitted to do this. (*b. Beṣah* 22b)[28]

The story exemplifies a creative response to circumventing biblical prohibitions against igniting coals on a festival or sabbath day (Exod 35:3). The proposed solution—to light coals before the special day begins (the late afternoon/evening before), immediately plug the holes of the surrounding brazier, only to unplug them after the festival or sabbath had begun—thus entailed the release and tacit enjoyment of the aroma in an appropriate way. Burning incense thus is portrayed favorably in this case, as the act of thurification to honor a festival or sabbath moves into domestic settings.[29]

The text quoted above was redacted in Sassanian Babylonia in the fifth through seventh centuries CE. As such, it may reflect imaginings of the Babylonian rabbis concerning how censers might have been used by their predecessors to honor holy days. Alternatively, or in complement, its discussion could reflect their own contemporaneous incense practices. In any case, associated behaviors of incense or spice burning—inside the home or elsewhere—might have transformed or diversified in certain areas of the late ancient Jewish world—in Babylonia or elsewhere—well after the destruction of the Jerusalem Temple.

Final indications, from texts, that some Jews might have continued to use censers and burn incense for ritual purposes as late as the ninth through twelfth centuries CE, include a series of critiques proffered by Karaite polemicists accusing other Jews of burning incense inside their synagogues to celebrate sabbaths and festivals. Karaites celebrated the teachings of the Torah and followed its guidelines, but eschewed the hermeneutical traditions espoused and perpetuated by their "Rabbanite" (rabbinic) Jewish counterparts.[30] Indeed, Karaites frequently critiqued the behaviors of their "Rabbanite" contemporaries, whom they accused of inappropriately performing activities inside their synagogues that resembled too closely those that once took place in the holy Jerusalem Temple.[31] In a textual fragment preserved in the Cairo Geniza, for instance, a ninth-century Karaite writer, Daniel Al-Qumisi, declared: "And it is forbidden in current times to burn incense and to light candles [=*in the synagogue*], [...] as done by the Rabbanites, as it says, 'It is an abomination to me' [Isa 1:13]."[32]

Karaites, such as Al-Qumisi, critiqued the implication that the synagogue was a suitable space to conduct activities that were facsimiles (from both a practical and a sensory standpoint) of those that had once taken place in the Jerusalem Temple, the worldly site of consummate holiness. Al-Qumisi's specific critiques of Rabbanite lamp and incense-lighting on sabbaths, moreover, are echoed by subsequent Karaite writers, including Judah Hadassi in twelfth-century Constantinople.[33] Because of the polemical nature of these criticisms, their contents cannot singlehandedly demonstrate that contemporaneous Jews in Palestine, Egypt, and Constantinople—regardless of whether they participated in rabbinic cultures—burned incense inside synagogues.[34] Only supplementary evidence, including other documents found in Fustat-Cairo and also considered below, can potentially corroborate them. To this point, Karaite writings and accusations against "Rabbanites" demonstrate, at the very least, that uses of censers and thurification were points of contention (in theory, if not in practice) among Egyptian and Levantine Jews in later antiquity.

ARCHAEOLOGICAL EVIDENCE:
CENSERS IN USE

Archaeological data offer critical counterparts to literary information documenting the implements that Israelites, Judahites, and Jews used for thurification through time. As early as the second millennium BCE, for instance, many Levantine peoples, including Israelites, had traded exotic plants and aromatics from Arabia and Africa and cultivated locally produced herbs and resins, to burn in communal cultic and domestic settings upon altars, as well as inside ceramic shovels and braziers.[35] In Philistine and Israelite cult centers in Ekron, Ta'anach, Megiddo, Lachish, and Tel Qedesh, for instance, archaeologists found both unadorned and four-horned limestone incense altars, as well as smaller and portable objects designed and used for the burning of resins and aromatics.[36] At a ninth/eighth century BCE Israelite cultic site in Tel Dan, close to Mt. Hermon, one horn from a four-horned altar was found, directly beside a container and iron shovels used for thurification [Figure 1].[37] Recent botanical analyses, conducted at contemporaneous regional sites, moreover, have revealed that cannabis, as well as various aromatics such as frankincense, were burned inside these types of receptacles, with more definitive tests recently conducted on the remains of a Judahite cult center in Arad from the eighth century BCE.[38] In all cases, in Israelite and Judahite ritual contexts in periods of Iron I and II, both fixed furniture (altars) and movable objects (including censers) are linked to the burning of aromatics (and psychotropics) in regional cult centers.[39]

Figure 1

Discoveries of flattened receptacles, including pans and ladles, also reflect their popularity for cultic use in regions extending from Mesopotamia to the Aegean. Based on the abundance of ceramic or metal versions of these implements discovered in Levantine cultic sites, moreover, Raz Kletter and Irit Ziffer have convincingly argued that flattened fire pans, or fire pans that resembled dippers, were conventionally used for regional thurification.[40] Ambivalence in biblical considerations of altars and implements for incense burning thus likely reflects historical regional variability in associated practices and objects through the first millennium BCE.[41]

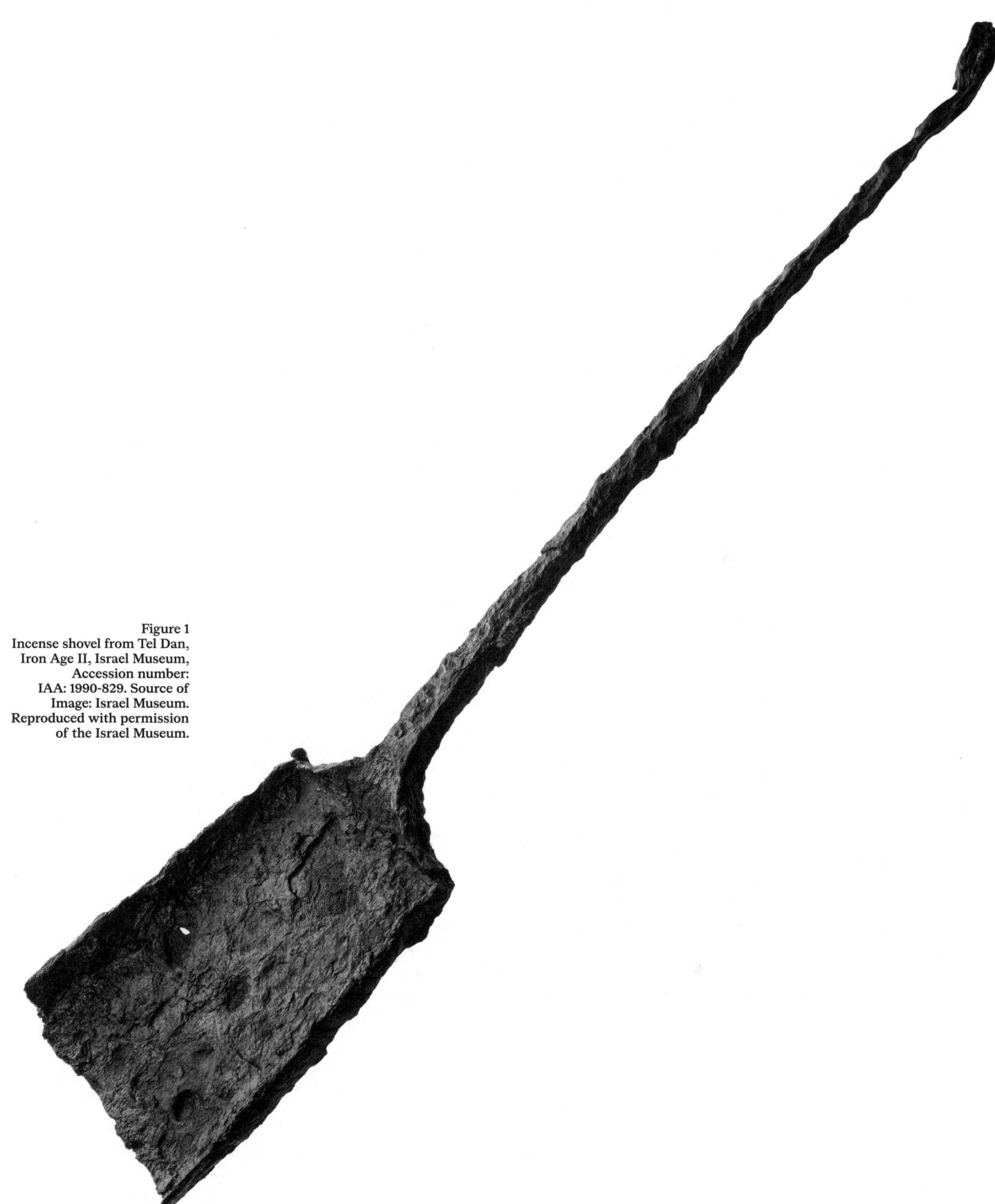

Figure 1
Incense shovel from Tel Dan,
Iron Age II, Israel Museum,
Accession number:
IAA: 1990-829. Source of
Image: Israel Museum.
Reproduced with permission
of the Israel Museum.

Incense sacrifices also occurred outside of communal cultic settings in ancient Israel and Judah.[42] As biblical texts note, the same herbs and resins that could be burned inside the Temple precinct (frankincense, statce, onycha, and galbanum) might be burned in different proportions, by different personnel, for different activities in the home (Exod 30:34; Songs 4:6–15). But humbler materials could also be used. Carol Meyers raises such a possibility in her interpretation of cup-and-bowl ceramics discovered in Israelite domestic contexts in the tenth century BCE. Due to their shapes and signs of burning, she argues that these enigmatic vessels were used for fumigation inside late Bronze and Iron Age homes.[43] The possibility that their uses might have been either practical or devotional, in different contexts, is supported by narratives in later texts, including the Book of Tobit. These describe uses of incense inside homes to cast away demons (Tob 6:1–7) or to perform marriage ceremonies (Tob 11). To ancient populations, such activities simultaneously could commemorate and effect domestic, legal, medical, and religious functions. Women or men could have performed them.[44]

While some evidence exists for uses of incense burners in mortuary contexts and elsewhere, in the sixth through fourth centuries BCE, the archaeological record also attests to diachronic associations between incense shovels and ritual thurification among Jews and their neighbors in the Hellenistic through Roman periods.[45] Recent discoveries of incense shovels in the Galilee document some examples of these. One type was discovered in a fortified city of the Hellenistic period, built upon a hill above the Arbel Valley, called Khirbet el-Eika, approximately 4.3 miles from the Sea of Galilee.[46] Its bronze rectangular pan is textured with slightly rounded edges tapering toward the mouth, with a duck head extending from its handle. Its association with local Jewish populations remains unclear, but the surrounding settlement was destroyed around 140 BCE, possibly by Hasmoneans who were expanding and consolidating their control over the region.[47]

Multiple shovels more closely linked to Jewish populations have been discovered elsewhere in the Galilee. In a storehouse of first-century Migdal (Magdala), close to the ancient shoreline of the sea, excavators recently found a bronze incense shovel and jug. The design of the shovel includes a rectangular pan, which features straighter edges than the example from Khirbet el-Eika and strongly resembles several representations in mosaics from later periods. The proximity of the bronze finds to the local synagogue bolsters their Jewish associations.[48] A set of bronze *mahtot* were also discovered during excavations in Bethsaida, another fishing village beside the Sea of Galilee. Two bronze decorated shovels from that site were found inside the earthen fill of a first-century structure, associated with the Roman Imperial Cult in Bethsaida-Julias.[49] These objects follow regional forms with decorated curving handles and rectangular pans. It remains unclear whether the shovels were of distinctive pagan or non-pagan use, but they were likely associated with the cultic building Herod's son constructed on the site.[50]

It is only after the destruction of the Temple in 70 CE, however, that evidence for the use of portable incense shovels for devotional purposes (rather than, or in complement to, fixed or portable altars) begins to expand. Yigal Yadin discovered the best known and most elaborate examples of bronze incense shovels in his famed excavations of the Cave of Letters in the Judean Desert, which had been a stronghold of Jewish rebels who had perished during the Bar Kohba Revolt in 131–37 CE [Figure 2].[51] Among the dramatic

Figure 2

Figure 2
Batillum (incense shovel)
discovered in Cave of Letters,
bronze, late 1st–early 2nd
century CE, length: 31.8 cm,
Metropolitan Museum of Art,
IAA: 2011-972, Purchase, 1900.

finds in the cave, which included trilingual papyri, were woven baskets that included several implements, including intact glass plates, bronze paterae, and four bronze incense shovels, or *batilla* (singular: *batillum*).[52] The pans of these shovels were rectangular in shape, ranging in length, with "ears" or "cups" extending from the inner corners of the shovel, and whose materials and fine workmanship suggested cultic use.[53] Richard Freund has countered Yadin's earlier claims about these shovels, by arguing that they were of local (rather than foreign) manufacture and exhibited signs of universal wear.[54] This suggested to Freund that families of the Jews who hid themselves in the cave cherished and used them for their own ritual purposes through the late first and early second centuries. The relative abundance of similar fire-pans on the antiquities market, paired with recent discoveries of bronze shovels looted from the Judean desert, suggest that local manufacture and uses of these implements might have been even more widespread than previously assumed among Jews of the first two centuries CE.[55]

The most robust collection of shovels from the region, however, derives from the Roman city of Sepphoris. These vessels have attracted scholarly attention, because they constitute the largest cache of such materials found in controlled scientific excavations of an ancient site populated by Jews in later periods of Roman hegemony. The shovels are composed of ceramic and follow two basic types. One includes a square pan with an open top and another is designed as a rounded pan. Both were originally covered by decorated and perforated lids.[56] Most were discovered around domestic contexts and were used until the middle of the fourth century CE.[57]

Contradictory reports about the condition of these objects upon discovery have yielded disparate interpretations of their original uses. Some initially declared that the vessels were found with traces of burning upon them, while others asserted that they retained no sign of charring.[58] L. V. Rutgers, who has argued for the absence of evidence upon them for burning, drew particular attention to the discovery context of the shovels inside domestic spaces. Rutgers conjectured that families who descended from priests from the Jerusalem Temple once owned these objects, to which they attached great symbolic significance. When these priestly families moved north to the Galilee region after the Temple's destruction, they might have used their possessions (or displays?) of ceramic facsimiles of Temple incense shovels to maintain their historical and familial connection to the (now destroyed) Temple and its cultic activities.[59] Eric Meyers has more recently countered this argument, suggesting that these ceramics were indeed used in elite Jewish homes but possibly for different activities. He theorized that families used them to contain dry fumigants, possibly akin to modern potpourri, as practices are similarly documented in the Iron Age.[60] In any case, the shapes of these shovels were likely significant to their owners. Indeed, and as seen below, their appearances and proportions resemble representations of Temple implements upon decorated floors from contemporaneous synagogues (including that in Sepphoris), and to a striking degree.

Different sorts of coal and incense burners were additionally discovered in cultic, domestic, and mortuary contexts in Roman and Byzantine Palestine and elsewhere.[61] Most are ceramic, rectangular, and stand on four post legs; some are painted, and others are carved with graffiti or superficial decoration. The cultural associations of the owners of these burners remain ambiguous, as some burners may date to the Achaemenid era, while others have been redated to the Byzantine periods (sixth through eighth centuries CE).[62] Certain burners found in mortuary contexts from the late Roman or Byzantine periods, however, may be of clearer Jewish association, including one discovered in the Beth Shearim necropolis.[63] While incense burning, in later antiquity, is deployed in ritual and domestic contexts, discoveries of incense burners in burial caves suggest that related activities (if potentially, for different purposes) occurred in Jewish mortuary contexts as well.[64]

    Continuing practices of thurification, nonetheless, persist in various forms in other contexts, as documented by discoveries of three-dimensional metal censers. One of these is a hanging censer found in the ancient synagogue of Beth Shean A, discovered alongside several other bronze and ceramic objects, including sculpted and molded images of a menorah, hooks, lamps, and jugs. This censer is composed of multiple parts. The square base, which stands on four outturned feet, is punctured by holes. A hook permits the outward hinging of a triangular top, rendered in grillwork, which terminates in a bound point, to which a bronze chain remains affixed.[65] The thurible is associated with sixth- or seventh-century levels of a synagogue, in which images of the Temple *maḥtah*—adorned with particularly colorful renderings of glowing coals or incense—were also found inside floor mosaics. Naveh's identification of a Samaritan inscription in the floor, however, has supported more recent designations of the space as of Samaritan design and use.[66]

Figure 3

    Another example of a free-standing incense burner associated with Jews was purchased in Cairo at the turn of the twentieth century by the Wilbur collection at the Brooklyn Museum [Figure 3]. This fourth–fifth-century bronze vessel is composed in three separate parts, standing on a base with three claw lion feet, topped with a baluster. The upper portion consists of an attached bowl, decorated with sculpted bronze standing birds, which resemble waterfowl. A menorah with seven curved branches, each of which is topped with an incised point that indicates a corresponding light or lamp, precedes a Greek inscription, which encircles the bowl in three registers. K. Herbert has restored and translated it to read: "On behalf of a vow of Auxanon. Blessed, O Lord [thou who is] gracious and ...."[67] The provenance of the censer is unknown, but Coptic analogues for its shape point to an Egyptian origin. The content of the inscription, paired with the menorah, however, suggests it was given to a devotional space—perhaps a synagogue or shrine—following Auxanon's vow.[68] While the classification of the object remains inconclusive, perhaps this censer was the type whose ongoing use Al-Qumisi critiqued in the ninth century—if from his seat in Jerusalem.

    Acts of lighting censers, however, are also connected to Jewish devotional spaces in later periods. On the manuscript of the fourteenth-century List of Yitgaddal, for instance, narrations that accompany illustrated pilgrim's drawings collectively document how inside a synagogue of a shrine dedicated to Moses, Kanīsat Mūsa, in Dummah, Egypt, Jews lit candles and ignited censers. This site constituted a popular place of Jewish pilgrimage through the fifteenth century.[69] The paired image and text thus suggest the historical persistence of practices relating to censers and thurification inside synagogues (and shrines) visited by Levantine and Egyptian Jews through the medieval period. Reported patterns of Jewish pilgrimage and incense burning might contextualize some of the Karaite critiques from similar places,

Figure 3
Standing incense burner
standing on tripod base with
baluster, Egypt, 5th century CE,
Brooklyn Museum, Charles
Edwin Wilbour Fund, no. 41.684.
Photo: Brooklyn Museum.
Reproduced with permission of
the Brooklyn Museum.

if in earlier eras, but more certainly reflect contemporaneous Muslim practices at pilgrimage sites in Egypt and Syria.

ARCHAEOLOGICAL EVIDENCE:
CENSERS IN REPRESENTATION

Preserved examples of censers and incense shovels in the archaeological record, however, wane significantly in periods of later antiquity, just as their two-dimensional representations begin to burgeon. This is particularly so in the context of synagogue decoration. Prayer-houses (*proseuchai*) and synagogues existed long before the destruction of the Temple but grew more ubiquitous, elaborate, and architecturally distinctive in periods of later antiquity, when churches also begin to proliferate.[70] Some features of Levantine synagogue decoration, moreover, grow increasingly stylized throughout these periods, incorporating prominent depictions of implements from the Jerusalem Temple, including menorahs and *mahtot*, upon floor mosaics and wall decoration.[71]

More than twenty-six representations of incense shovels appear inside synagogue mosaics throughout Palestine, particularly beside other symbols associated with the Jerusalem Temple, including the golden menorah, shofar, lulab, and ethrog. Most renderings of these are depicted in mosaic, with sufficient color variation inside their pans to suggest that they sometimes represent burning coals, or incense burning upon them. One example of such a depiction derives from the elaborate polychromatic mosaic floor of the fourth-century synagogue in Hammath Tiberius (stratum IIA), where a symmetrical scene of lulabs, shofars, and *mahtot* each flank large menorahs on opposite sides of a Temple or Torah shrine [Figure 4].[72] Similar but more stylized and abstract representations of incense shovels appear in the upper register of the sixth-century synagogue of Beth Alpha.[73]

Different types of *mahtot* appear in the grand seven-register mosaic carpet from the synagogue in Sepphoris [Figure 5]. In the second band of the mosaic, one flat incense shovel extends beneath a Torah shrine, itself flanked by two menorahs. Its mouth points to the left. Kletter and Ziffer correctly observe that the silver-gray color of the tesserae that form the flat shovel, may mimic one composed of silver or another type of metal, while red colored embers glow inside the pan.[74] Resemblances are apparent between the design of this *mahtah* and the archaeological objects identified above, including the small cup(s), or ears, flanking the base of the pan by the handle. In addition to this representation of a *mahtah*, however, the fourth register of the Sepphoris mosaic also includes two additional ladles flanking the shewbread table, with their heaping contents possibly representing frankincense for that altar (Lev 24:5–9).

Flat and square shovels, however, comprise the most common styles of similar implements depicted in mosaics of synagogues from Roman and Byzantine Palestine, including those in excavated in Beit Shean, Huseifa, Hulda, Gerash, and Beit Shearim.[75] In most instances, pairs of incense shovels form symmetrical scenes flanking images of the Temple or Torah shrine, beside representations of menorah(s), palm fronds, and ethrogs.

Imagery associated with thurification is even more robust in ancient Samaritan contexts, which deploy similar visual idioms in their mosaic floors as do Jews in their synagogues. Indeed, an incense shovel appears in a prominent location between the shewbread table and menorah in the mosaic of

Figure 4
Mosaic from Hammath Tiberias,
upper register of synagogue
floor mosaic. Photo Gilead Peli,
https://synagogues.kinneret.ac.il/
synagogues/hammath-tiberias/

Figure 5
Drawing of mosaic floor of
synagogue in Sepphoris, Israel,
incense shovels indicated in
registers two and four, image
taken from Weiss 2005, 57, fig. 2.
Reproduced with permission
of Ze'ev Weiss.

Figure 7
Repurposed epitaph from the
Gammarth Catacombs in
Gammarth, Tunisia, north of
Carthage, images include
two menorahs, a palm branch,
shofar, and a mahtah on
the left, Carthage Museum.
Photo: Author

Figure 8
Epitaph from Zoara for Sa'dah,
daughter of Pinhas, ochre on
Sandstone, text accompanying
implements from the Jerusalem
Temple, including a menorah,
shofar, and lulab, beside an
incense shovel containing embers
and/or incense, Yeshiva
University Museum, Accession
number 2013.018. Reproduced
with permission of the
Yeshivah University Museum.

the El-Kirbe Samaritan synagogue. Examples from mosaics from the Beit Shean A synagogue similarly emphasize vessels for incense burning.[76] The prominence of images of censers and *maḥtot* inside Samaritan synagogues may reflect the ongoing importance of incense burning in Samaritan traditions; Samaritans burn incense inside their synagogues on holidays and sabbaths through the present day.[77]

Representations of *maḥtot*, moreover, also recur inside architectural decoration and stonework of structures more definitively linked to Jewish (as well as Samaritan) use. In his discussions of the symbolic significance of incense shovels, E. R. Goodenough noted several such representations in synagogues, though additional examples have been found in recent years. One appears on a column capital from the Capernaum synagogue, and another on a stone plaque or screen from Nawa.[78] Still another is carved into a basalt block from Belvoir, found in a secondary context. As in mosaics, these representations all flank larger images of menorahs; some accompany palm fronds or ethrogs.

Still another medium on which images of these shovels appear is embossed onto ceramic oil lamps, and according to Varda Sussman, mostly on Beit Nattif types.[79] Goodenough enumerates six examples of such lamps from Roman Palestine, but others have been discovered more recently. One example appears quite clearly on a lamp with a menorah, round objects, and an image of a shrine. Upon the rectangular pan of the small shovel in relief appear six regularly carved holes, perhaps grillwork placed upon the bottom of the pan.[80] Another four examples of lamps depict *maḥtot* beside elaborate menorahs, which, in turn, face the wick spout of the lamp.[81] Most of these depict the shovels with rectangular pans and shortened handles.[82]

Representations of *maḥtot* additionally appear in mortuary contexts. Some adorn epitaphs, particularly within Levantine cemeteries. Multiple examples are found on epitaphs from Beth Shearim, a sprawling and important necropolis near modern Haifa, which once housed thousands of burials of regional Jewish populations. One lead sarcophagus, found inside Catacomb 20 of that complex, was also embossed with a menorah, shofar, lulab, and *maḥtah* [Figure 6].[83] Similar images appear on painted epitaphs from Zoara, a settlement on the southeastern edge of the Dead Sea, where excavators found hundreds of adjacent Jewish and Christian tombs. Most epitaphs from Zoara are painted with ochre onto sandstone, and several depict images of Temple implements. One tombstone, dedicated to a certain Sa'adah, daughter of Pi[nḥas], dating to 429/430 CE, incorporates a highly detailed presentation of a *maḥtah*, outlining the coals and incense in its pan [Figure 7].[84]

Images of the *maḥtah*, as Hachlili has observed, appear less frequently in devotional or mortuary contexts outside of Palestine.[85] One rare counter example is found on an epitaph from Gammarth in Tunisia, in a necropolis where multiple Jewish graves were discovered. Some have doubted the identification of a figure resembling a shovel on the epitaph. My own direct analysis of the stone, however, reveals that the carving of a *maḥtah* appears clearly and opposite from a shofar, flanking one of two menorahs on the marble. This constitutes an example of a *maḥtah* from a mortuary context that is most distant, geographically, from Levantine examples [Figure 8].[86]

Images of *maḥtot* are combined with those of other Temple vessels on smaller objects used for distinct purposes. These include hexagonal and octagonal molded glass flasks, produced in Palestine during the fifth and

Figure 6

Figure 7

Figure 8

Figure 9

sixth centuries CE [Figure 9]. As depicted in this medium, *maḥtot* often resemble square shovels affixed to extended sticks. Scholars have postulated that these decorated flasks were manufactured by the same workshops as similar vessels bearing Christian symbols, collectively produced for sale to Jewish and Christian pilgrims to the Holy Land. Uses of these flasks largely remain obscure, even if some were ultimately deposited in mortuary contexts.[87]

Certain features of *maḥtah* images in mosaics, on lamps, and upon other vessels thus remain consistent. First, most representations derive from Levantine contexts, but occasionally extend to mortuary contexts from places as far afield as North Africa. Second, images of *maḥtot* are not usually depicted in isolation, but are consistently clustered with other objects associated with the workings of the Jerusalem Temple. Thus, regardless of whether *maḥtot* appear in spaces used for devotional, mortuary, or other purposes, their inclusion in this grouping was deliberate.

Some have theorized, for instance, that ensuing assemblages of images might represent the ritual calendar of the Jerusalem Temple. Indeed, each visual component could emblematize a distinct pilgrimage festival: lulabs and ethrogs might evoke activities associated with the festival of *sukkot* (festival of Tabernacles); the shofar might represent the celebration of the New Year, which entailed the blowing of the ram's horn; and the *maḥtah* could emblematize the Day of Atonement, on which the incense shovel was definitively used also as a censer.[88]

Caution, nonetheless, should be exercised when interpreting these images. Indeed, even if—at times—their representations collectively functioned as a type of visual liturgical calendar, scholars' interpretations of them as an assemblage require attention to the spatial and practical contexts of their appearance. Each figure (whether menorah, ethrog, or *maḥtah*), let alone as part of a collective, might have resonated differently with contemporaneous audiences depending on the period, locality, and region of its appearance, and depending on whether its renderings appeared in devotional or mortuary spaces, or those elsewhere.[89]

In slightly later periods, moreover, this visual assemblage of Temple implements recurs in distinctive media and, presumably, for slightly different purposes. Hebrew Bibles painstakingly copied between the tenth and fourteenth centuries, including those from Fustat-Cairo and Spain, depict the *kaf* or *maḥtah* as censers, situated alongside the menorah, shofar, or other devices, to symbolize the cultic implements and activities once associated with the Temple.[90] Their illustrations are often illuminated and labeled, as exemplified by "frontispieces" of the Parma Bible, Perpignan Bible, and several others [Figure 10].[91] Depictions of these figures in visual inventories and maps of the Jerusalem Temple thus appear to retain a powerful function: they reorient the viewer to a different place and time—to Jerusalem when the Temple still stood—as a locus of worship and ritual memory. Recurring representations of *maḥtot* and ladles inside lavishly illuminated manuscripts, in any case, suggest the ongoing importance of the incense shovel as an element of the Temple assemblage. Its representation simultaneously serves as a visual synecdoche for the Jerusalem Temple and as an aide-memoire for the powerful activities once conducted inside it.

Figure 10

Figure 9
Moulded glass octagonal pilgrim
bottle decorated with Jewish
objects, including menorah and
mahtah, said to be from Kafr
Kama from Byzantine Palestine,
ca. 500–629 CE, Metropolitan
Museum of Art, H. O. Havemeyer Collection, Bequest of
Mrs. H. O. Havemeyer, 1929.

Figure 10
The Duke of Sussex's
Catalan Bible, 1350–1374,
crystalized images of
implements associated with
the Jerusalem Temple,
including mahtot, British
Library, Add MS 15250, f4r.
Public Domain.

CENSERS IN LATER LITURGY, PRAYER, AND PRACTICE

But censers were not only depicted in multiple media from later periods; their descriptions are also absorbed into various Jewish precatory and liturgical practices in late antiquity and beyond. Some Jewish magical invocations and lists designate incense and censers as instruments of attracting both angelic and divine attention, from later antiquity through the medieval and modern periods.[92] References to censers and incense also multiply in other liturgical contexts. As Rachel Elior notes, certain synagogue liturgies integrated a *baraita* about the preparation of incense and its offering in the Temple as early as the ninth century.[93] The repetition of the description of the incense offering is also attested in the ninth-century writings of Rav Amram Gaon, who declared that the timing of the liturgy's recitation corresponds with the timing of the incense sacrifice in the Temple.[94] Comparable traditions persist, even today, in prayers among Iraqi and Mizrahi Jews, recited in the morning and late afternoon as *pittum ha-ketoret*. The prayer pairs the verbal enumeration of eleven components of the ancient *ketoret*, with corresponding bodily movements (pinching fingers in sequence) to manually count its ingredients. Timing of the prayer purposefully aligns the recitation of the incense compounds with the times of the Temple incense sacrifice (morning and late afternoon/twilight; Exod 30:8).

Still others have argued that traditions of incense burning persisted but transformed among Jews of medieval Spain, France, and Ashkenaz. Several scholars suggest, for instance, that practices of using censers to mark the completion of festivals and sabbaths, disaggregated during the medieval period into the Havdalah ceremony—particularly in Ashkenaz—in the form of a ritual which entails lighting a candle beside an elaborate metal spice box, usually crafted in silver.[95] These spice boxes, indeed, often resemble traditional censers with multiple components and decoration, standing on a metal base with covered grillwork. During the Havdalah ceremony, abundant spices fill the designated box. They are not ignited but are often shaken to enhance the release of their scent; moreover, the heat of the flame of the adjacent candle, when held beside the metal container with grillwork, additionally accelerates the emanation of scent from within it.[96]

AFTERLIVES OF CENSERS

Many have neglected the study of censers and incense in Judaism, partly because of the prominence ascribed to such objects and practices in eastern and western Christian traditions. Yet broader considerations of literary and archaeological evidence reveal the enduring significance of censers and thurification in devotional and memorial settings within the Jewish past and imaginary. Closer examinations of biblical texts and later rabbinic commentaries and discussions have demonstrated how central incense sacrifices were in shaping memories of the Jerusalem Temple and notions of Jewish continuity in subsequent periods. After the destruction of the Temple, incense burning might have persisted inside Jewish homes, shrines, or even synagogues to a greater extent than scholars frequently assume.

After the demise of the Temple cult in Jerusalem, moreover, representations of images of censers from it—particularly in the form of *maḥtot*—multiplied among Jews throughout Palestine, Egypt, and Europe, even as some types of thurification ceased. Abundant representations of *maḥtot* and ladles inside synagogue mosaics, on tombstones, lamps, glass vessels, and medieval manuscripts, as well as extended descriptions of thurification in certain forms of medieval and modern Jewish prayer, conjured a common visual and liturgical vocabulary that reinforced the importance of thurification in Jewish ritual life.[97] Serving as both visual and olfactory aides-mémoires, these depictions and descriptions of incense and its burning helped Jews to imagine and commemorate implements, activities, and works of priestly functionaries in the Jerusalem Temple. These efforts, in turn, simultaneously concretized feelings of common ancestry and religious history, while cultivating sensations of connection and continuity between rituals and festivals of later generations of Jews and their Israelite and Judahite predecessors.

What makes the censer—as used, imagined, memorialized, and recalled—so powerful through time, is that its invocations, when paired with that of other Temple implements, conjured for Jews elements of a multisensory past, linked as much to images of historical objects, as to elusive, unrecoverable, but powerful olfactory experiences.[98] While few direct relationships could link Iron Age incense shovels, tessellations of shovels into synagogue floors, visual inventories painted into medieval bibles, synagogue chants, or pinched fingers during daily prayers, each representation or evocation of a censer and its contents reflects a set of shared efforts and mnemonics. Gazing at the form of an incense shovel, or recalling ingredients of incense, as much as using a censer, could invoke, inspire, and remind Jews, from multiple places, cultures, and periods, of the lost and unrecoverable sensorium of the ancient Temple, a space once filled with wafting smoke and tangy and acrid smells and tastes, whose experiences were inextricable from holy encounters with the Divine.

ENDNOTES

1   As listed in Frenkel and Lester 2014, 150–51.

2   Richard A. Freund tabulates terms used for censers and incense shovels in both biblical texts and ancient translations and interpretations (1999, 413–60). The vocabulary for these implements, however, shifts in later Palestinian and Babylonian rabbinic considerations of the *kaf* (spoon or ladle), another the rabbis called a *bazih* (*m. Tamid* 6:3; cf. *t. Sukkah* 4:10), and the *maḥtah* itself. These terms are not necessarily equivalent, but I emphasize the term *maḥtah* here for purposes of general typology, because the linguistic analyses remain inconclusive.

3   Overview of these types and their significance in Hachlili 1988, 234–343.

4   Incisive overviews of these subjects in Baker 2016, 3–16; traditional treatment in Cohen 1998, 276.

5   Miller and Hayes 2006, 221–58. Archaeological overviews of the region and period considered in Finkelstein 2010, 3–28.

6   Miller and Hayes 2006, 497–522.

7   Papyrological evidence in Elephantine in Egypt documents the existence of other temples outside of Jerusalem dedicated to YHWH (Cowley 2005, no. 30). On the complexities and uncertainties in the formation of biblical canon, see Mroczek 2016. Concerning Jews' fealty to one God, one Temple, and one Torah, see the excellent overview in Schwartz 2001. Discussions of who was a Jew in antiquity also remain remarkably vibrant; review of that topic in Schwartz 2001; and Baker 2016.

8   On the making of Palaestina, see discussion in Lapin 2012, 3–20.

9   Syntheses of salient points in Lapin 2012, 16–25; and Schwartz 2001, 162–76.

10   On variability in ancient Israelite cult see Dever 2006.

11   For instance, Numbers 16 critiques the inappropriate burning of incense, but likely reflects concerns about the practice, which date to the Persian period, when the text was redacted. I thank Tracy Lemos for this reminder.

12   Heger 1997.

13   Discussions of the shewbread in Hachlili 1988, 81.

14   Discussions within the Babylonian Talmud illustrate the potency of the incense burned in the Jerusalem Temple, which deprived women in faraway towns of the need to apply their own perfumes (*b. Yoma* 39b). Concerning incense and earlier periods, see Amar 2002; and Nielsen 1992, 404–6.

15   Rabbinic texts ascribe to the House of Avtinas exclusive knowledge and protection of their incense recipe (*b. Yoma* 38a; *b. Šeqal.* 14a).

16   Dimensions and prescriptions for this altar in Exod 30:1–5; and 2 Chron 13:11.

17   Shemesh 2017, 1–3.

18   Shovels of pure gold were prescribed for lamps of the menorah (Exod 25:38) and bronze shovels for holding coals for animal sacrifice (Exod 27:3). Sometimes, in rabbinic texts, the *kaf* (ladle) is described as having both a cover (to prevent the spilling of abundant incense in its bowl) and a cloth upon that (to prevent the smell of incense from escaping at inopportune times (*m. Tamid* 5:4).

19   Kletter and Ziffer 2010, 166; Rutgers 1999, 188.

20   In Ezekiel, the word "*maḥtah*" is not used to describe censers; elders carry the *ketoret* in hand without implements (Ezek 8:11); by contrast, the *maḥtah* is used by the sons of Korah in Num 16:7; cf. Targ. Jonathan on Lev 10:1.

21   See also Elgvin 2002, 20–33. Related discussions in Murphy 2002, 323. Collins (2013) offers an excellent introduction to the library of the Dead Sea Scrolls and the communities that produced them.

22   See discussions of related points in Niehoff 2015; Leonhardt 2001; and Mason 2005, 71–100.

23   This and surrounding sections of *Against Apion* are preserved only in Latin, rather than the typical Greek; the Latin term that designates incense burner or shovel is "*turibulum*" (Josephus *C. Ap.* 2.106).

24   Ibn Ezra was a philologist and grammarian; in his twelfth-century commentary on Leviticus, he equates the word *maḥtah* with "censer"; 16:12.1. Rashi's commentary on II Chronicles (4:22) resembles this reading. Discussion and additional references in Shemesh 2017, 2–6.

25   This differs from the destruction of the First Temple, after which Judahites continued offering incense at its site (Jer 41:5).

26   Practices of burning *mugmar* (incense) after a meal required its own blessing (see *m. Ber.* 6:6; *b. Ber.* 43a–b; *b. Yoma* 38a; *Songs Rab.* 5.1). Additional references in Freund 2000, 660 n. 50.

27   This discussion opens considering which people will be banned from the world to come, including people who misuse Temple incense sacrifices (*b. Ker.* 2a; 6a; cf. Exod 30:23). The Gemara frames such an act as a misuse of smell; see also Freund 2000, 659 n. 47.

28   I thank Ezra Gabbay for his assistance with this translation.

29   Following texts describe acts of placing incense on fragments of hot ceramic, or even directly on bare coals, in domestic contexts to fumigate clothing or surrounding air (*b. Beṣah* 23a).

30   Nemoy 1980.

31   Concerning this point, see Freund 2000, 660; and Zucker 1959, 170–71 n. 666. To the rabbis, the synagogue and the study hall collectively constituted a *miqdash m'at* ("a little sanctuary"); *b. Meg.* 29a; *m. Sotah* 9:12; *b. Ber.* 8a.

32   Texts from Mann 1935, 2:76; Alqumsi 1958, 7; Mann 1922, 277–278; Shemesh 2017, 3–4. For more extensive discussion of this text, see Stern 2023 and concerning Karaite anti-rabbinic polemics, see Rustow 2007, 35–74.

33   Another Karaite scholar and theologian in twelfth-century Constantinople, Judah Hadassi, called "ha-Abel" (the Mourner), similarly proclaims incense burning to be an abomination when conducted inside a synagogue; Shemesh 2017, 4; Ta-Shma 2003, 205.

34   See broader discussion of this topic in Rustow 2007, 35–74. Also worth noting is that censers were commonly also listed as objects from Jewish households in Cairo from contemporaneous periods. See discussion in Frenkel and Lester 2014. Ezekiel 11:16 served as a proof text for rabbinic Jews to suggest that some customs associated with the Temple could be conducted inside the synagogue,

a type of "diminished Temple." Comparison of these methods useful with those of Caseau 2007, 551–79.

35 For regional altars, see Daviau 2007, 125–49; on early uses of shovels and dippers for the purposes of incense burning, see Raz Kletter and Irit Ziffer 2010, 166–87. Concerning the cultivation and trade of aromatics, see. Ben-Yehoshua, Borowitz, and Hanuš 2012, 1–7.

36 See Seymour Gitin 1989; Green 2012, 20.

37 Kletter and Ziffer 2015.

38 Arie, Rosen, and Namdar postulate that the burning of cannabis on the smaller of the two altars was for psychotropic, rather than aromatic purposes, arguing also that different herbs and aromatics required distinct types of fuel (2020, 5–28).

39 Concerning the ancient trade in aromatics and their chemical and psychoactive properties, see Dannaway 2010, 485–97.

40 Kletter and Ziffer 2015, 166.

41 See Ben Yehoshua et al. 2012, 1–12.

42 While biblical texts, including those edited by the Deuteronomistic school, argue that the Jerusalem Temple was the only acceptable location to make sacrifices to YHWH, archaeological evidence attests to historical conduct of similar practices in other cult centers and spaces, as discussed in Herzog 2010, 169–99.

43 Meyers 1998, 30–39; Daviau 2001; and Singer-Avitz 2011, 294.

44 This is so, because from antiquity through the later Middle Ages god(s) were believed to be active in all aspects of day-to-day life. See also Meyers 1998, 30–39 Also worth noting is that, in later periods, the rabbis expressed concern for women burning incense. See discussion in *b. Ber.* 53a in Green 2012, 139; Ahuvia 2021, 76 n. 99.

45 For limestone burners of the Achaemenid period in Sepphoris and elsewhere, as well as other vessels repurposed for thurification, see Dayagi-Mendels 1996; Stern 1982, 182–95. Note the different approach to these in Rahmani 1980, 116–22. Many of these burners resemble Arabian analogues.

46 https://www.biblicalarchaeology.org/daily/ancient-cultures/ancient-israel/duck-shaped-shovel-ancient-galilee/.

47 Some have argued that the presence of this object attests to pagan habitation of the site; several comparable objects have been found in wrecks off the Levantine coast, as in Galili et al. 2010, 125–45.

48 Recent discovery of a second synagogue in Migdal (Magdala), roughly 200 meters from the first known synagogue in the town, reflects the dominance of Jews there and the importance of local places of worship. See broader consideration in Zapata-Meza et al. 2018.

49 The fill of the site was modified in later periods, however, which challenges scholars' abilities to provide dates for its context with greater confidence.

50 Freund 1999; 2000, 644 n. 1.

51 These documents record the legal struggles of a woman named Babatha; Hannah Cotton 1993, 393–420.

52 These shovels resemble what is designated as a *batillum* in Roman contexts, found in the Levant through Syria. See also Freund 2000, 644–60; cf. Yadin 1963, 48–53; nos. 659, 55; Hachlili 1988, 262.

53 Image of Cave of Letters example in Yadin 1963, pl. 16, no. 5.

54 Based on the appearances of these shovels and the elaborate figural decoration of the handle on one example, Yadin asserted that Jewish rebels during the Second Revolt ("Bar Kokhba's troops"), seized them as "from ... Roman Legions or the Auxilia," but speculates that in "the hands of new owners," the "pagan character [of the shovels] was somewhat changed ... having been adapted for Jewish use in keeping with the rulings recorded in the Mishna" (1963, 42, 45). Metallurgical analyses of the shovels, whose poor quality of bronze

included high levels of lead, differently suggested to Freund that these objects were of local, rather than Italian, manufacture; uniform wear across their surfaces suggests serial reuse of a precious object, rather than targeted defacement (2000, 660).

55 Recent confiscations of looted objects from the Judean desert included multiple bronze shovels, resembling those from the Cave of Letters (Gershon 2021). For a similar shovel in a shop in Sardis associated with a certain "Jakob," see Crawford 1990, 15, 61; 71–98.

56 Rutgers 1999, 177–79.

57 Ibid., 192.

58 Ibid., 177.

59 Ibid., 193–96.

60 Meyers 2006, 877; cf. *b. Ber.* 53a.

61 Stern 1982.

62 Stern 1982; cf. Rahmani 1980, 116–22.

63 Avigad 1978, 156; Taxel and Iserlis 2014, 162.

64 For discussions of rabbinic perspectives on incense burning during funerals and in mortuary contexts, see Green 2012, 169–76. The presence of unguentaria in Jewish mortuary contexts, such as Beit Shearim and the Gammarth cemetery near Carthage, demonstrates different ways that scents could be used to honor the dead; Stern 2007.

65 Tzori 1967, pl. 33, 2.

66 Naveh 1981, 220–22.

67 Commentary and bibliography in Fine 1996, 156; and Horbury and Noy 1992, 225–26; Weitzmann 1979, 330, fig. 347; Horbury and Noy 1992, 225–26; Herbert 1972, 61, no. 32.

68 L. V. Rutgers (1999, 186) argued against Roger Bagnall's earlier suggestion of the object's Jewish association, positing that the object was likely associated with Samaritans, because of a lack of precedent for Jewish analogues; Roger Bagnall 1993, 276 n. 105.

69 The five-line text on the lower right on the folio—partly preserved—announces that Jews ignited incense ("*ketoret*") in and around the shrine. The text appears beside a labeled drawing of the synagogue. I thank Ezra Gabbay for his help with reading this manuscript. Egyptian Jews (and Muslims) in the late ancient and medieval periods believed that Moses had traveled through Dummah on the way from Egypt to Canaan. Discussion and analysis of the latter point in Sarfati 2020, 6, fig. 3. Representations of Kanīsat Mūsa in manuscripts include those in British Library Add 27125 fol. 145r (List of Yitgaddal); cf. Florence, BNC, ms. Magl. III, 43 (Florence Scroll), with additional discussion in Reiner 1988, 280–83; and Reiner 2002, 14. Worth noting is that the manuscript collection in which the List appears dates to the sixteenth century.

70 On the latter point, see Schwartz 2001, 179–215; Levine 2012, 225–94. Christians expended efforts to differentiate their own incense traditions from those of Jews; see Tertullian, *Apol.* 2.42.7; Origen, *Contr. Celsus*, XVII.

71 Freund argues that representations in synagogues are better classified by the rabbinic word *bazih*, because he suggests that handles are shorter than they would be for a *maḥtah* (2000, 658–59). The general typology, rather than the precise and elusive vocabulary for these, is a greater priority in this analysis.

72 Discussion in Levine 2012, 245.

73 Image in Levine 2012, 282–83.

74 Kletter and Ziffer 2015; Weiss and Netzer 1998, 18; Weiss 2005.

75 Fine 1996, pl. XXXIX; fig. 66.

76 Tzori 1967, 149–67.

77 Shemesh 2017, 5.

78 See also the example from Pekiin; bereft of a handle that identification is more speculative (Goodenough 1953–68, IV: 193; III: fig. 572; III: 478, fig. 10; III: 618) Updated lists appear in appendices of Rutgers 1999, 187; and Freund 2000.

79 Sussman 2012, 132–33, fig. 100.

80 Goodenough 1953–68, III: fig. 293.

81 Goodenough 1953–68, III: figs. 334–37; according to Goodenough, a bone carving once discovered in Beit Shean, included an image of a menorah with a circular base, a shofar, and other objects, it also bore the image of an incense shovel.

82 The length of these handles need not predict the function of these objects, as in Kletter and Ziffer 2015.

83 Avigad 1978, 269, fig. 130, 4; 178, fig. 89, n. 1; especially pl. 26.2. For a summary of the importance of the necropolis, see also Stern 2018.

84 Misgav 2006, 36.

85 The most explicit depiction of incense and censers in the Dura Europos synagogue appears in the panel depicting the cult of Dagon; Kraeling 1979, 101–2.

86 Rutgers (1999, 180) has dismissed Goodenough's identification of a *maḥtah* here, but I viewed and photographed the Gammarth epitaph in the Carthage Museum in the fall of 2003 and the image is clear. See also Stern 2007, 169.

87 Point discussed in Barag 1970, 35–63; 54, 55, 62; also, Evans and Ratliff 2012, 35, 110, no. 72. Goodenough speculated that these were used for mortuary purposes, but few have been found in situ. An exception includes a fragment from Beth Shearim, Catacomb 20; Avigad 1978, 206, fig. 99a.

88 Rutgers 1999, 181.

89 Concerning context-dependent readings of such representations, see Stern 2019.

90 These include paintings from the opening leaves of Bibles completed between the late 900s and the early 1300s in Fustat-Cairo and Spain, which depicted Temple architecture and implements. These include the Ibn Merwas Bible in 1300 (British Library, MS Or. 2201); and of Joshua Ibn Gaon in Soria, Spain, completed in 1306 (Bodleian Library MS. Kennicott 2, 1v, 2r); discussion in Safarti 2020, 1–23; 14 nn. 58–59; and Kühnel 2007, 177–93, figs. 8.3, 188.

91 Examples abound and include Parma, Bibl. Pal. Ms Parm 2668, fol. 7; Perpignan Bible, Perpignan, 1299. Paris, BNF heb. 7, fol. 12v, fol. 12r; Copenhagen, Roy. Lib. heb. II; see Kogman-Appel 2002, 246–72. See also Rutgers 1999, 181 n. 32.

92 For review see Morgan, transl. *Sepher Ha-Razim*; Kotansky 1994, P. Col XXII/1, 129–31, no. 32, l. 6. Levene and Bhayro (2005/2006, 242–46), argue that an Aramaic incantation bowl, which invokes prayers for good business, concludes by declaring "upon a good smell and upon good fragrances" (l. 11), suggesting that the burning of incense concluded the business deal. Possibly in connection, the modern Israeli Hebrew idiom "to bless over the *mugmar*," is used to describe recognition that a long-sought agreement or achievement has been finalized; the overlap with the Hebrew verbal root "*g-m-r*," which means to finish or conclude, may inform this pattern. I thank Ezra Gabbay for this point.

93 Elior 2002, 117.

94 Gaon 1971, 40.

95 Wieder 1998, 209; Ta-Shma 2001, 59–60.

96 As seen in the Barcelona Haggada, fol. 24v, British Library.

97 Scholars, such as Marianne Hirsch (2012), have long discussed the power of writing and visuality for postmemory—the transfer of memories of events or institutions—to people who had never experienced them directly. Attention to the censer or *maḥtah* benefits from this perspective.

98 Green 2012, 197–201.

BIBLIOGRAPHY

Ahuvia, Mika. 2021. *On My Right Michael, on My Left Gabriel: Angels in Ancient Jewish Culture.* Berkeley: University of California Press.

Alqumsi, D. 1958. *Pitron [=Interpretation] of the Twelfth: Commentary on the Twelfth,* edited by I. D. Merkon. Jerusalem: Mekize Nirdamim.

Amar, Z. 2002. *The Book of Incense.* Tel Aviv: Eretz.

Arie, Eran, Baruch Rosen, and Dvory Namdar. 2020. "Cannabis and Frankincense at the Judahite Shrine of Arad." *Tel Aviv* 47, no. 1: 5–28. doi:10.1080/03344355.2020.1732046.

Avigad, Nahman. 1978. *Beth She'arim: Report on the Excavations during 1953–1958,* vol. 3, *Catacombs 23–23.* New Brunswick, NJ: Rutgers University Press.

Bagnall, Roger. 1993. *Egypt in Late Antiquity.* Princeton, NJ: Princeton University Press.

Baker, Cynthia. 2016. *Jew: Key Words in Jewish Studies.* New Brunswick, NJ: Rutgers University Press.

Barag, Dan. 1970. "Glass Pilgrim Vases from Jerusalem, Part I." *Journal of Glass Studies* 12: 35–63.

Ben-Yehoshua, S., C. Borowitz, and L. O. Hanuš. 2012. "Frankincense, Myrrh, and Balm of Gilead: Ancient Spices of Southern Arabia and Judea." *Horticultural Reviews* 39: 1–7.

Caseau, Béatrice. 2007. "Objects in Churches: The Testimony of Inventories." In *Objects in Context, Objects in Use,* edited by Luke Lavan, E. Swift, and T. Putzeys, 551–79. Leiden: Brill.

Cohen, Shaye. 1998. *The Beginnings of Jewishness: Boundaries, Varieties, Uncertainties.* Berkeley: University of California Press.

Collins, John. 2013. *The Dead Sea Scrolls: A Biography.* Princeton, NJ: Princeton University Press.

Cotton, Hannah. 1993. "The Guardianship of Jesus Son of Babatha: Roman and Local Law in the Province of Arabia." *Journal of Roman Studies* 83: 393–420.

Cowley, A. 2005. *Aramaic Papyri of the Fifth Century B.C.* Oxford: Clarendon; repr., Ancient Texts and Translations, Eugene, OR: Wipf & Stock.

Crawford, J. Stephens. 1990. *The Byzantine Shops at Sardis.* Cambridge, MA: Harvard University Press.

Dannaway, Frederick. 2010. "Strange Fires, Weird Smokes, and Psychoactive Combustibles: Entheogens and Incense in Ancient Traditions." *Journal of Psychoactive Drugs* 42, no. 4: 485–97.

Daviau, M. 2001. "Family Religion: Evidence for the Paraphernalia of Domestic Cult." In *The World of the Arameans II. Studies in History and Archaeology in Honor of Paul Eugène Dion,* edited by P. M. Daviau, J. W. Wevers, and M. Weigl, JSOT Supplement Series 325, 199–229. Sheffield: Sheffield Academic Press.

Daviau, P. M. M. 2007. "Stone Altars Large and Small: The Iron Age Altars from Ḥirbet el-Mudēyine (Jordan)." In *Bilder Als Quellen/ Images as Sources: Studies on Ancient Near Eastern Artefacts and the Bible Inspired by the Work of Othmar Keel* (OBO, Special volume), edited by S. Bickel, S. Schroer, R. Schurte, and C. Uehlinger, 125–49. Göttingen: Vandenhoek & Ruprecht.

Dayagi-Mendels, M. 1996. "Persian-Period Incense Burners." In *Sepphoris in Galilee: Crosscurrents of Culture,* edited by R. M. Nagy, C. L. Meyers, E. M. Meyers, and Z. Weiss, 164–65. Raleigh: North Carolina Museum of Art.

Dever, William. 2006. *Did God Have a Wife? Archaeology and Folk Religion in Ancient Israel.* Grand Rapids, MI: Eerdmans.

Elgvin, Torleif. 2002. "An Incense Altar from Qumran?" *Dead Sea Discoveries* 9, no. 1: 20–33.

Elior, Rachel. 2002. "Hekhalot and Merkavah Literature: Its Relation to the Temple, the Heavenly Temple, and the 'Diminished Temple.'" In *Continuity and Renewal: Jews and Judaism in Byzantine-Christian Palestine,* edited by L. I. Levine, 107–42. Yad Ben Tzvi: Dinur Center for Research in Jewish History; The Jewish Theological Seminary in Jerusalem.

Evans, Helen, and Brandie Ratliff, eds. 2012. *Byzantium and Islam: Age of Transition, 7th–9th Century.* New York: The Metropolitan Museum of Art.

Fine, Steven, ed. 1996. *Sacred Realm: The Emergence of the Synagogue in the Ancient World* New York: Yeshiva University Museum; Oxford University Press.

Finkelstein, Israel. 2010. "A Great United Monarchy? Archaeological and Historical Perspectives." In *One God – One Cult – One Nation: Archaeological and Biblical Perspectives,* edited by Reinhard G. Kratz and Hermann Spieckermann, 3–28. Berlin: De Gruyter.

Frenkel, Miriam, and Ayala Lester. 2014. "Evidence of Material Culture from the Geniza: An Attempt to Correlate Textual and Archaeological Findings." In *Material Evidence and Narrative Sources: Interdisciplinary Studies of the History of the Muslim Middle East,* edited by Daniella J. Talmon-Heller and Katia Cytryn-Silverman, 145–87. Leiden: Brill.

Freund, R. 1999. "The Incense Shovel of Bethsaida and Synagogue Iconography in Late Antiquity." In *Bethsaida: A City by the North Shore of the Sea of Galilee,* edited by Rami Arav and Richard Freund, 413–60. Kirksville, MO: Truman State University Press.

Freund, R. A. 2000. "A New Interpretation of the Incense Shovels in the Cave of the Letters." In *The Dead Sea Scrolls: 50 Years after Their Discovery. Of the Jerusalem Congress, July 20–25,* edited by Lawrence Fishman, 644–60. Jerusalem: Israel Exploration Society, in cooperation with the Shrine of the Book, Israel Museum.

Galili, E., V. Sussman, G. Steibel, and B. Rosen. 2010. "A Hellenistic/Early Roman Shipwreck Assemblage of Ashkelon, Israel." *The International Journal of Nautical Archaeology* 39, no. 1: 125–45.

Gaon, S. Amram. 1971. *Seder Rav Amram Gaon.* Edited by D. S. Goldshmidt. Jerusalem: Massad ha-Rav Kook.

Gershon, Livia. 2021. "Looted Artifacts Recovered from Car Trunk May Be Spoils of War Seized by Jewish Rebels against Rome." *Smithsonian Magazine,* December 17. https:// www.smithsonianmag.com/smart-news/ looted-artifacts-recovered-from-trunk-may-be-roman-spoils-of-war-seized-by-jewish-rebels-180979243/.

Gitin, Seymour. 1989. "Incense Altars from Ekron, Israel, and Judah: Context and Typology." *Eretz-Yisrael: Archaeological, Historical and Geographical Studies* 20: 52–67.

Goodenough, E. R. 1953–68. *Jewish Symbols in the Greco-Roman Period.* 12 vols. New York: Pantheon Books.

Green, Deborah. 2012. *The Aroma of Righteousness: Scent and Seduction in Rabbinic Life and Literature.* University Park: Pennsylvania State University Press.

Hachlili, Rachel. 1988. *Ancient Jewish Art and Archaeology in the Land of Israel.* Leiden: Brill.

Heger, Paul. 1997. *The Development of Incense Cult in Israel.* BZAW 245. Berlin: De Gruyter.

Herbert, K. 1972. *Greek and Latin Inscriptions in the Brooklyn Museum.* New York: Brooklyn Museum.

Herzog, Z. 2010. "Perspectives on Southern Israel's Cult Centralization: Arad and Beer-Sheba." In *One God—One Cult—One Nation: Archaeological and Biblical Perspectives,* edited by R. G. Kratz and H. Spieckermann, Beihefte zur Zeitschrift für die Alttestamentliche Wissenschaft 405, 169–99. Berlin; Boston: DeGruyter.

Hirsch, Marianne. 2012. *Generations of Postmemory: Writing and Visual Culture after the Holocaust.* New York: Columbia University Press.

Horbury, William, and David Noy. 1992. *Jewish Inscriptions of Graeco-Roman Egypt.* Cambridge: Cambridge University Press.

Kletter, Raz, and Irit Ziffer. 2010. "Incense-Burning Rituals: From Philistine Fire Pans at Yavneh to the Improper Fire of Korah." *Israel Exploration Journal* 60: 166–87.

Kletter, Raz, and Irit Ziffer. 2015. "The Yavneh Fire Pans and the Biblical maḥtāh." In *Yavneh II: The Excavation of the "Temple Hill" Repository Pit,* edited by Raz Kletter, Irit Ziffer, and Wolfgang Zwickel, OBO AS 36, 1–2. Fribourg; Göttingen: Academic Press; Vandenhoeck & Ruprecht.

Kogman-Appel, Katrin. 2002. "Hebrew Manuscript Painting in Late Medieval Spain: Signs of a Culture in Transition." *The Art Bulletin* 84, no. 2: 246–72. https://doi. org/10.2307/3177268.

Kotansky, Roy. 1994. *Greek Magical Amulets: The Inscribed Gold, Silver, Coper, and Bronze Lamellae. Part I, Published Texts of Known Provenance.* Wiesbaden: Verlag.

Kraeling, Carl. 1979. *The Synagogue. Excavations at Dura Europos. Final Report VII, Part I.* 2nd edn. New York: Ktav Publishing.

Kühnel, Bianca. 2007. "Memory and Architecture: Visual Construction of the Jewish Holy Land." In *On Memory: An Interdisciplinary Approach,* edited by Doron Mendels, 177–93. Bern: Peter Lang.

Lapin, Hayim. 2012. *Rabbis as Romans: The Rabbinic Movement in Palestine 100–400 C.E.* New York: Oxford University Press.

Leonhardt, J. 2001. *Jewish Worship in Philo of Alexandria.* TSAJ 84. Tübingen: Mohr Seibeck.

Levene, Dan, and Siam Bhayro. 2005/2006. "'Bring to the Gates … upon a Good Smell and upon Good Fragrances': An Aramaic Incantation Bowl for Success in Business." *Archiv für Orientforschung* 51: 242–46.

Levine, Lee I. 2012. *Visual Judaism: Historical Contexts of Jewish Art.* New Haven, CT: Yale University Press.

Mann, J. 1922. "A Tract by an Early Karaite Settler in Jerusalem." *Jewish Quarterly Review* 12, no. 3: 257–78.

Mann, J. 1935. *Text and Studies in Jewish History and Literature,* vol. 2. Philadelphia, PA; Hebrew Press of the Jewish Publication Society of America.

Mason, Steve. 2005. "Of Audience and Meaning: Reading Josephus' *Bellum* in the Context of a Flavian Audience." In *Josephus and Jewish History in Flavian Rome and Beyond,* edited by Joseph Sievers and Gaia Lembo, 71–100. Leiden: Brill.

Meyers, Carol. 1998. "Flumes, Flames, or Fluids? Reframing the Cup-and-Bowl Question." In *Boundaries of the Ancient Near Eastern World: A Tribute to Cyrus A. Gordon,* edited by M. Lubetski, C. Gottlieb, and S. Jeller, *Journal for the Study of the Old Testament Supplement Series* 273, 30–39. Sheffield: Sheffield Academic.

Meyers, E. M. 2006. "The Ceramic Fire Pans from Sepphoris: Another View." In *"I Will Speak the Riddles of Ancient Times": Archaeological and Historical Studies in Honor of Amihai Mazar on the Occasion of His Sixtieth Birthday,* vol. 2, edited by Aren Maier and P. de-Miroschedji, 865–76. Winona Lake, IN: Eisenbrauns.

Miller, J., and John Hayes. 2006. *A History of Ancient Israel and Judah*. 2nd edn. Louisville, KY; London: Westminster John Knox Press.

Misgav, Haggai. 2006. "Two Jewish Tombstones from Zoar." *ISMA* 5: 35–46.

Mroczek, Eva. 2016. *The Literary Imagination in Jewish Antiquity*. Oxford: Oxford University Press.

Murphy, Catherine. 2002. *Wealth in the Dead Sea Scrolls and Qumran Community*. Leiden; Boston: Brill.

Naveh, Naveh. 1981. "A Greek Dedication in Samaritan Letters." *Israel Exploration Journal* 31: 220–22.

Nemoy, Leon. 1980. *Karaites Anthology: Excerpts from Early Literature*. New Haven, CT: Yale University Press.

Niehoff, Maren. 2015. "Josephus and Philo in Rome." In *A Companion to Josephus*, edited by Honora Chapman and Zuleika Rodgers. Wiley Online, 2016. doi:10.1002/9781118325162.

Nielsen, K. 1992. "Incense." In *The Anchor Bible Dictionary*, 6 vols., edited by D. N. Friedman, vol. 2, 404–9. New York: Doubleday.

Rabbi Saadya Gaon's Translation of the Torah, edited by Moses Zucker. 1959. New York: Feldheim.

Rahmani, L. Y. 1980. "Palestinian Incense Burners of the Sixth to Eighth Centuries C.E." *Israel Exploration Journal* 30: 116–22.

Reiner, Elchanan. 1988. "Pilgrims and Pilgrimage to Eretz Yisrael 1099–1517." PhD thesis, The Hebrew University of Jerusalem (Hebrew).

Reiner, Elchanan. 2002. "Traditions of Holy Places in Medieval Palestine—Oral versus Written." In *Offerings from Jerusalem: Portrayals of Holy Places by Jewish Artists*, edited by Rachel Sarfati, 9–19. Jerusalem: The Israel Museum.

Rustow, Marina. 2007. "Karaites Real and Imagined: Three Cases of Jewish Heresy." *Past and Present* 197: 35–74.

Rutgers, L. V. 1999. "Incense Shovels at Sepphoris?" In *Galilee through the Centuries: Confluence of Cultures*, edited by Eric M. Meyers, 177–98. Winona Lake, IN: Eisenbrauns.

Sarfati, Rachel. 2020. "Between Heaven and Earth: Places of Worship in Egypt and Syria through the Mirror of Visual Evidence." *Arts* 9, no. 90: 1–23. doi:10.3390/arts9030090.

Schwartz, Seth. 2001. *Imperialism and Jewish Society 200 B.C.E. to 640 C.E.* Princeton, NJ: Princeton University Press.

Sepher Ha-Razim: The Book of the Mysteries. 1983. Translated by Michael Morgan. Chico, CA: Scholars Press.

Shemesh, Abraham. 2017. "'Those Who Require '[...] the Burning of Incense in Synagogues Are the Rabbinic Jews': Burning Incense in Synagogues in Commemoration of the Temple." *HTS Teologiese Studies/Theological Studies* 73, no. 3: 1–17.

Singer-Avitz, Lily. 2011. "Household Activities in Tel Beersheeba." In *Household Archaeology in Ancient Israel and Beyond*, edited by Assaf Yasur-Landau, Jennie R. Ebeling, and Laura B. Mazow, 275–302. Leiden; Boston: Brill.

Stern, Ephraim. 1982. "Incense Altars." In *The Material Culture of the Land of the Bible in the Persian Period, 538–332 BC*, 182–95. Jerusalem: Israel Exploration Society.

Stern, Karen B. 2007. *Inscribing Devotion and Death: Archaeological Evidence of Jewish Populations of North Africa*. Leiden: Brill.

Stern, Karen B. 2018. *Writing on the Wall: Graffiti and the Forgotten Jews of Antiquity*. Princeton, NJ: Princeton University Press.

Stern, Karen B. 2019. "When Is a Menorah not Just a Menorah? Menorah Graffiti in Jewish Mortuary Contexts." *Near Eastern Archaeology* 82, no. 3: 164–171.

Stern, Karen B. 2023. "Does Smoke Mean Fire? Illumination, Incense and the Senses in Late Antique Synagogues." *Journal of Late Antiquity* 16, no. 1: 189–237.

Sussman, Varda. 2012. *Roman Period Oil Lamps in the Holy Land: Collection of the Israel Antiquities Authority*. Oxford: BAR Archaeopress.

Ta-Shma, I. M. 2003. *The Early Ashkenazic Prayer: Literary and Historical Aspects*. Jerusalem: Magnes Press.

Taxel, Itamar, and Mark Iserlis. 2014. "Two-Part Ceramic Incense Burners in Late Roman and Byzantine Palestine: Technological, Regional, and Ethno-Religious Aspects." In *Roman Pottery in the Near East: Local Production and Regional Trade. Proceedings of the Round Table Held in Berlin, 19–20 February 2010*, edited by Bettina Fischer-Genz, Yvonne Gerber, and Hanna Hamel, 159–169. Oxford: Archaeopress.

Tzori, N. 1967. "The Ancient Synagogue at Beth-Shean." *Israel Exploration Society* 8: 149–67.

Weiss, Ze'ev. 2005. *The Sepphoris Synagogue: Deciphering an Ancient Message through Its Archaeological and Socio-Historical Contexts*. Jerusalem: Israel Exploration Society, Institute of Archaeology, Hebrew University of Jerusalem.

Weiss, Ze'ev, and Ehud Netzer. 1998. *Promise and Redemption: A Synagogue Mosaic from Sepphoris*. Jerusalem: Israel Museum.

Weitzmann, Kurt, ed. 1979. *Age of Spirituality*. New York; Princeton, NJ: Metropolitan Museum of Art; Princeton University Press.

Wieder, N. 1998. *The Formation of Jewish Liturgy in the East and the West: A Collection of Essays*, vol. 2. Jerusalem: Yad Ben Tzvi; Mechon ben Zvi for the Research of Israel Communities; Hebrew University,.

Yadin, Yigal. 1963. *The Finds from the Bar Kochba Period in the Cave of Letters*. Judean Desert Studies 1. Jerusalem: Israel Exploration Society.

Zapata-Meza, M., A. Garza, and A. Sarz-Rincón. 2018. "The Magdala Archaeological Project (2010–2012): A Preliminary Report of the Excavations at Migdal." *'Atiqot* 90: 83–125.

Zucker, M. 1959. *On the Translation of Rabbi Sadiyah Gaon on the Torah*. New York: Feldheim.

THE INCENSE BURNER
IN GREEK ART
OF THE FIFTH CENTURY BCE

Milette Gaifman

What was the place of *thymiaterion*, the Greek incense burner in ritual practice and the visual culture of Greek antiquity? What force did the ancient Greeks ascribe to the smoke it emitted? The significance and impact of incense burners in the ancient Greek world have received relatively little attention in the scholarship of Greek religion and art, particularly when compared to other forms of worship, such as the making of animal sacrifice, the offering of votives, or the pouring of libations.[1] At stake here are not only possible scholarly oversights, but also deeper fundamental questions pertaining to the material and immaterial modes of delineating the sacred and sensorial experiences of Greek antiquity.[2] The subject of incense burners in the ancient Greek world demands further investigation that extends beyond the existing literature and the scope allowed for in a single article.

In this paper, I adopt a visual perspective in response to the fundamental questions raised here above. Focusing on select images from the fifth century BCE, I examine how incense burners were presented in pictorial imagery. I consider here what visual representations may reveal about ancient perceptions of these instruments of cult, and their role in relation to the sacred. I highlight two dominant aspects prominent in this imagery. First, *thymiateria* emerge as integral to ritual experience, particularly to the general framework of animal sacrifice, where they may appear in association with libations. Second, both within and beyond the realm of ritual practice, the incense burner was linked visually with youthfulness, the female sphere, and to seduction. Before turning to look closely at some fifth-century BCE images, it is worthwhile to briefly review some essential evidence on the Greek *thymiaterion* and our broad understanding of this instrument of cult.

THE GREEK THYMIATERION, A GENERAL OVERVIEW

Starting with the material record, we may follow Cristiana Zaccagnino's helpful synthesis of evidence in her study of the *thymiaterion*, in addition to the entries in the *Thesaurus Cultus and Rituum* to note that the earliest documented *thymiateria* in the Hellenic world date to the first half of the seventh century BCE, as seen in the examples uncovered in Athens, in the Kerameikos, northwest of the Athenian Acropolis, which are dated to 680–670 BCE.[3] Visual representations of the instrument first appear in the second half of the sixth century BCE, and become more frequent in the fifth century BCE.[4] The assessment of texts—and whether they specifically reference the burning of incense or usage of censers—is somewhat more complex. It has also generated some debate, as some have hypothesized that the adoption of the practice of burning incense is documented in the Aegean on inscribed tablets already in the second millennium BCE, although this position may be questioned.[5] The explicit mention of frankincense in Greek is first witnessed in the sixth century BCE in Sappho's evocative description of the wedding celebrations of the Trojan prince Hektor to Andromache. Fragment 44 tells how upon Andromache's arrival to Troy the entire city was overjoyed in song and "myrrh, cassia and frankincense (*libanos*) mingled" (line 30).[6] The Greek term, which specifically references the incense burner, *thymiaterion*, is first attested in the fifth century BCE, in the writings of the Greek historian Herodotos, who mentions the marvelous *thymiaterion* dedicated in Delphi by a Cypriot ruler.[7] Notably, from the fifth century BCE onward, the term appears in inscribed texts, and is documented among dedications and cult instruments listed in the inventories of temples, as seen, for instance, in the lists from the fifth and fourth centuries BCE, where *thymiateria* of gilded wood, bronze, and stone are recorded among the items kept on the Athenian Acropolis by the Treasurers of Athena.[8] Other Greek words were also used to a censer or brazier. For instance, *escharis* or *bomiskos* may reference either a type of an altar or an incense burner, depending on the context.[9]

Zaccagnino also provides a helpful overview of the range of forms and types of incense burners used in Greek antiquity. These vary in height and shape. Some are relatively small and others may reach human height. The vast majority consists of a type of a leg or a stand topped by a bowl or conical chamber for the placement of biotic material. Zaccagnino's helpful study is notable for the context of the present volume as it suggests that Greek censers were designed so that they could stand firmly on a surface without additional support, as, for example, the clay *thymiaterion* from Corinth [Figure 1]. Unlike in other traditions, Hellenic censers were not conceived to be hung or swung from a chain, but either to be placed on the ground or on some platform, or to be carried by their support.

Figure 1

The variety of Greek censers correlates with the variety of contexts in which one could have encountered them, ranging from domestic spaces, where they could emit sweet smoke in the *symposium*, to public sanctuaries where they were both instruments of cult and gifts to the gods.[10] Zaccagnino's work also provides an overview of the deities with whom incense is associated, showing that incense burners and the practice of burning incense are attested to in relation to a broad range of divinities including Zeus, Hera, Apollo, Artemis, Dionysos, and others.[11] Among these, Aphrodite appears to have held a particularly strong affinity with the burning of incense, as seen for instance in the so-called Ludovisi Throne, which features the iconic image of the goddess at her birth on its central panel while on an adjacent side it depicts a fully draped female figure adding some material to the burner [Figure 2].[12]

Figure 2

Overall, the evidence indicates that *thymiateria* were used in the Hellenic world at least from the seventh century BCE onward, and sources attest that they continued to be used for centuries well into the Roman era. Still, there is more to explore about these cult instruments. For instance, we could further our understanding of their role and significance within specific contexts and explore possible changes in their function over time. There are various potential reasons why *thymiateria* have not attracted much scholarly attention. One that comes to mind has to do with our general conception of Greek religion, according to which sacrificial practice is understood to have been the central ritualistic focus of Greek religion *par excellence* and the sacrificial altar the quintessential locus of worship.[13] This

Figure 1
A clay incense burner from
Corinth, mid-5th century BCE,
height: 9.6 cm, Excavations
of the American School
Classical Athens, Inventory
no KP1045. Image source:
American School of
Classical Studies Athens.

Figure 2
Aphrodite emerging
from the sea (main panel)
and a figure adding incense
to an incense burner
(side panel), the so-called
Ludovisi Throne, Marble,
ca. 460 BCE, height: 104 cm.
Rome, Palazzo Altemps.
Wikipedia Commons

idea is captured in the Homeric image of the fragrant altar emitting smoke that brings joy to the gods.[14] In fact, the primary meaning of the verb, θύω (*thuō*), to make a sacrifice, is to produce smoke.[15] Typically, one thinks of animal sacrifice; however, vegetal offerings and plants were also placed upon the burning altar.[16] The key role of smoke and scent in Greek religious experience thus invites—if not demands—further exploration of the role of the instruments especially designed to produce fragrant fumes, namely incense burners.[17]

There is another possible reason why *thymiateria* have received relatively little attention within the broader study of Greek art and religion. Of all ritual practices, the burning of biotic material is perhaps the one most often associated with non-Greek regions, specifically with the Near East.[18] This notion is not without warrant, as some of the most renowned plants used in censers are native to the Near East. The Greek word for frankincense, λίβανος (*libanos*), stems from the Semitic root *lbn* (lebona), an etymology which correlates with the origins of the frankincense bush in the Arabian Peninsula. Herodotos reveals his knowledge of frankincense as a plant native to Arabia:

> Again, Arabia is the most distant to the south of all inhabited countries: and this is the only country which produces frankincense (*libanotos*) and myrrh and casia and cinnamon and gum-mastich. All these except myrrh are difficult for the Arabians to get. They gather frankincense by burning that storax which Phoenicians carry to Hellas; they burn this and so get the frankincense; for the spice-bearing trees are guarded by small winged snakes of varied color, many around each tree; these are the snakes that attack Egypt. Nothing except the smoke of storax will drive them away from the trees.[19]

In another passage the Greek historian further describes the use of frankincense as integral to non-Greek customs. Writing of the Scythians he comments:

> The Scythians howl in their joy at the vapor-bath. This serves them instead of bathing, for they never wash their bodies with water. But their women pound cypress and cedar and frankincense wood on a rough stone, adding water also, and with the thick stuff thus pounded they anoint their bodies and faces, as a result of which not only does a fragrant scent come from them, but when on the second day they take off the ointment, their skin becomes clear and shining.[20]

This passage is more than a record of the habits and behaviors of those whose language is not Greek. Mist, perfume, and oiled skin speak to the allure of the foreign.[21] The scent of frankincense is deeply intertwined with lands east of the Aegean, contributing to a view of incense burners as essentially foreign within an ancient Greek context.

Some (or all) Greek customs of burning plants for the sake of generating special smoke and odors may have been adopted through interaction with non-Greek cultures. Yet, as noted above, incense burners are attested to in Athens already in the early seventh century BCE, and by the fifth century BCE they emerge as part and parcel of Greek ritual practice and visual culture. A prime example is the depiction of the incense burner at the very heart of one of the most celebrated monuments of Greek religious art, the Parthenon frieze [Figure 3].

Figure 3

In what follows I turn to depictions of *thymiateria* in different contexts. First, I will examine them as implements carried in sacrificial processions. I then turn to their portrayal as freestanding objects in spaces of ritual. While both of these contexts foreground the censer as an object, in the final section I turn to the force of scent and consider the power that was ascribed to the smoke emitted from these instruments. The cases presented here hardly cover the wide range of contexts in which we find Greek *thymiateria*. At the same time, these examples speak to the incense burner's role as a significant instrument in its own right, particularly in ritual practice. The *thymiaterion* emerges as an object whose olfactory impact could be transformative; it may enhance the allure of the sacred.

AT THE PROCESSION

Figure 4

An oil flask, or *lekythos*, from the turn of the fifth century BCE features one of the earlier Attic depictions of the *thymiaterion*, seen here in the context of a sacrificial procession [Figure 4].[22] The fragrance-producing instrument is carried by a worshiper who holds branches in her right hand. She is followed by a bull, the sacrificial offering, which is accompanied by a fellow worshiper who also holds branches. The bearer of the *thymiaterion* follows the bearer of the *kanoun*, or the ritual basket. In Greek antiquity, the basket bearer, also known as the *kanephoros*, was a key participant in ritual processions.[23] On the vase, a fellow male marcher blows into a wind instrument as he leads the group, heralding the sacrifice to come. We cannot tell whether, in addition to the sound of music, we ought to imagine fragrant smoke in the air. We can, however, note that in the context of the depicted event, the *thymiaterion* appears as a visual marker which distinguishes between different roles within the procession. The elongated object separates the bearer carrying offerings in her basket from the sacrificial victim and its attendant. While all of the participants are presumably moving towards the altar, which is not shown here, the nature of their activities at the upcoming sacrifice is fundamentally different. Unlike those behind her, the *kanephoros* was not involved in the handling of the animal. She was charged with bringing necessary items including, garlands, grains, first fruits, and the sacrificial knife. The *thymiaterion* thus articulates distinctions among those at the sacrificial procession, between the one charged with the victim and the one carrying utensils and gifts for the ritual.

Looking more closely, we may note that the elongated censer frames the *kanephoros*, nearly touching her basket. This visual proximity suggests a link between the instrument and the central figure who is shown here in a role that in the Athenian context of the turn of the fifth century BCE was of prime significance for girls and women as they came of age. Serving as a basket bearer was an honor bestowed upon maidens who then took center-stage in a public religious ritual. On this occasion, these unmarried young women served their community and simultaneously were put on display.[24] On the oil flask in question, the maiden at the heart of the depicted procession stands out thanks both to the basket that she carries and the *thymia-*

Figure 3
A female figure carrying an
incense burner ahead of
maidens with jugs and libation
bowls. Parthenon Frieze,
East Block VIII, Marble,
ca. 447–438 BCE, height: 106 cm,
London, British Museum.
© Trustees of the British Museum

Figure 4
A figure carrying an incense
burner in a procession, Attic,
white ground oil flask (lekythos),
ca. 500 BCE, London, British
Museum, B648. © Trustees of
the British Museum

terion behind her. The image links the young woman at a moment in which she may be admired by society for her youthful attractiveness, with the instrument designed to produce enchanting odors.

The foregrounding of young women in the sort of religious practice depicted here is also relevant to the type of vessel upon which the image of the *thymiaterion* is found, namely the *lekythos*. This type of vessel is most frequently found in and associated with funerary contexts,[25] and women are typically the ones shown in Athenian imagery as the primary performers of funerary rites.[26] The procession depicted here does not necessarily portray an event in honor of a deceased. However, women took on the religious roles of carrying ritual gifts to the central locus of ritual both in sacrificial processions, as seen in our example, and in funerary rituals, which were also deeply associated with the kind of object (*lekythos*) upon which this image appears.

One of the most notable representations of a *thymiaterion* in Greek art of the fifth century BCE lies at the heart of the Parthenon frieze. In this representation, on the frieze's east-facing side a female worshiper standing at the head of a group of maidens holding libation vessels carries the object [Figure 2]. Compared to other aspects of the famed frieze, this portrayal of a *thymiaterion* has not received much attention,[27] presumably because it appears to be just one among many similar depictions of similar items that appear in the frieze as a whole. Much like the bowls and jugs for libations depicted on its east side, or the musical instruments and vessels shown on the north and south sides, the incense burner is one among numerous accoutrements used for the occasion featured on the frieze, which most scholars presume is a procession in honor of Athena.[28]

Like the *thymiaterion* that appears on the oil flask discussed above, the one depicted on the Parthenon's east frieze is shown being carried in the context of a procession. Here too, the instrument is associated with maidens in a ritual context. The *thymiaterion* is carried by the female figure (seen in block E VI, conventionally numbered 57) who is the first in a group of four libation bearers carrying jugs and libation bowls (these figures appear on the same block). She is facing another female participant, who stands directly in front her (seen on block E VII numbered 56) who follows another group of maidens, one of them carrying a libation bowl. While not exclusively limited to women, the offering of libations was often portrayed as being performed by maidens.[29] The *thymiaterion* punctuates this part of the procession: the tall instrument marks a separation between one group of libation bearers and another set of female participants ahead of them, and thereby visually articulates the groupings of female participants within the grand event.

However, the Parthenon's image of the *thymiaterion* also differs dramatically from the small oil flask. In the frieze the incense burner appears at the heart of the grandest architectural structure of fifth-century BCE Athens. Notably, among its various meanings and functions, the Parthenon served for safekeeping treasured objects dedicated to Athena and her worship. The inscribed inventory lists of the Athenian treasurers that record objects offered as gifts and kept inside the Parthenon and the Erechtheion include *thymiateria*.[30] In fact, incense burners made of precious metals emerge as one of the largest groups of inventoried items inside the Parthenon.[31] The epigraphic record thus emphasizes an additional dimension of the *thymia-*

terion depicted on the frieze; the elaborate relief on the building's exterior echoes some of the items that were kept inside.[32] The Parthenon's depiction of the incense burner presents it as having two roles, simultaneously: an implement of ritual and a treasured gift to the divinity.

IN RITUAL SPACE

The image depicted on a grand mixing bowl attributed to the Kleophon Painter features a sacrificial procession to Apollo at Delphi [Figure 5]. Here, within a ritual setting, the *thymiaterion* takes center stage.[33] On the far right, a youthful male figure is seated on a decorated throne within an architectural structure supported by Doric columns. He holds a laurel branch in his hand and wears a laurel wreath on his head; a quiver hangs above him. We may, thus, recognize him as none other than Apollo in his abode. Two tripods stand on either side of the temple with the *omphalos*, the Delphic navel of the world, in front. This is the Pythian Apollo, the deity of the oracle at Delphi. A bearded man stands in front of the god, looking left towards a richly dressed young woman with a ritual basket on her head. We may recognize her as the *kanephoros* who faces the temple. Behind her stands a laurel-wreathed man who turns towards the *thymiaterion*. The youthful, beardless worshiper looks towards fellow laureled participants who stand beyond the incense burner. This group includes youths of various heights, one of whom carries a libation bowl, while others lead cattle, the sacrificial victims that are to be offered to the seated deity within his sacred domain.

Figure 5

In light of the vase's clear visual references to Delphi, particularly the tripods and the *omphalos*, one may be tempted to relate the scene to the cultic actualities of fifth-century BCE Delphi.[34] More specifically, the vase may bring to mind the Herodotean account noted above regarding the "marvelous incense burner" that was dedicated at Delphi in the second half of the sixth century BCE by King Evelthon from Salamis in Cyprus, which the historian notes was stored in the treasury of the Corinthians.[35] One may also be reminded of a bronze incense burner in the shape of a female figure holding up a bowl that was unearthed in Delphi [Figure 6].[36] Additionally, one may link the depiction of the instrument to the possible use of certain fragrances during practices of divination.[37] Yet rather than trying to connect the image to the realities and practices at fifth-century BCE Delphi, it might be more fruitful to examine how it presents the incense burner visually within the representation of the sacred space of Pythian Apollo.

Figure 6

Recalling the depictions of the processions discussed above, the *thymiaterion* shown on the vase attributed to the Kleophon Painter articulates distinctions among participants in a sacred ceremony. On its right, we find a youth, the basket bearer, and a bearded man. This group is closer to the god in the temple and the *omphalos* as well as the tripods. On its left, we find a group of youths: a young man carrying a libation bowl in the lead, followed by those attending to the cattle. Although the entire occasion is dedicated to the god, there is no interaction between the devotees and Apollo inside his temple. Rather, the participants look at each other and the tall incense burner stands at the center of the scene, at the heart of a meeting between two young men.

While marking social distinctions, the *thymiaterion* therefore also demarcates the depicted sacred landscape. Unlike in our previous examples, the burner is placed on the ground. Its positioning on the vase's curved

Figure 5
Sacrificial processional in the sanctuary of Apollo, mixing bowl (volute krater), attributed to the Kleophon Painter, ca. 440–430 BCE, Ferrara, Museo Archeologico Nazionale di Spina T57CVP. Wikipedia Commons.

Figure 6
Bronze incense Burner from Delphi, ca. 450 BCE, height: 16 cm, Delphi Archaeological Museum. © National Archives of Monuments – the Hellenic Ministry of Culture and Sports

surface roughly in the middle of the register presents it as the central axis of the entire composition. In this set-up, the *thymiaterion* thus serves as a landmark that articulates a divide between the area closest to the god, one occupied by few figures, and the rest of the scene where most of the participants gather. It appears as the major milestone that punctuates the way to the holiest part of the sanctuary, the seat of the god. We cannot tell whether any odors are emitted from the burner as there is no indication of smoke. In fact, no libations, sacrifice, or any other ritual take place. Rather, the impending ritual is implied, as the cattle are brought forth. Within this context, the *thymiaterion* appears as a central feature of the sanctuary in its own right, even if it does not produce any scents. It marks spatial distinctions while serving as a meeting point on one's way to a possible encounter with the god.

By contrast, the inside of a cup attributed to Makron Painter features a ritual unfolding in front of our eyes [Figure 7].[38] A woman pours liquid onto a flaming blood-stained altar. Her hair is bound, her body covered by the rich drapery of her tunic and mantle, and a fillet is tied around her head. In her left hand she carries a large ritual basket, the *kanoun*, while performing a holy rite. The red line emerging from the mouth of her jug delineates the flow of liquid from the vessel onto the flaming surface. She adds fuel to the fire, making a wine libation at the sacrificial platform. The simple red lines on the face of the altar denote blood, presumably of victims who were brought forth.[39] These marks also allude to past and future offerings to a deity whose identity remains unknown. The bloodstains, libation, and flame, along with the ritual basket are all part of the sacrificial setting.

A *thymiaterion* stands on a pedestal behind her. The vertical object on the right is juxtaposed with the voluted altar set on a two-stepped platform on the left. Recalling our last example, the incense burner appears as a signpost that frames the primary area of ritual, the space occupied by the libation bearer who also carries the ritual basket. In contrast to our previous examples, however, it appears as if it is physically embedded in its pedestal, a stationary signpost which demarcates the primary area of ritual.[40] This rendition recalls listings from the Athenian Acropolis noted above. Specifically, records from the fourth century BCE list a gold incense burner that was set into the floor of the Erechtheion. Unfortunately, no traces of this instrument have been detected.[41] The cup highlights the role that certain incense burners could assume in Greek religious contexts, independently of other functions they may have. Thanks to their form and placement, *thymiateria* appear to have demarcated certain spaces of worship.

Upon further examination, one may note another significant feature of the cup's *thymiaterion*. Gentle and barely visible lines emerge from its conical chamber. The incense burner is active. While we can only imagine the scent it produces, the depiction of its fumes asserts its olfactory function. The vase presents two types of smoke and scent within the single setting: that of the blazing altar on the left and the nearly invisible one to the right. The two complement each other. The primary locus of devotion is on the left; it is the one whose fire is visible, demanding the addition of wine. This is the focus of the pious worshiper's attention. The other locus of attention is on the right—and it is far subtler: hardly visible but already in action, the *thymiaterion* emits its gentle fumes without any additional action or attention. As the incense burner signals the sanctity of the depicted space, its

Figure 7

Figure 7
A woman pouring libation
at an altar, inside of a red-figure
cup (kylix) attributed to
Makron Painter, ca. 490–480 BCE.
Toledo Ohio, Toledo
Museum of Art 1972.55.
© Toledo Museum of Art.

fragrant smoke may have a further effect; it could invite us to imagine the possibility of a fragrant yet invisible divine presence in this space.[42]

THE SCENT OF DESIRE

The cup attributed to Makron Painter also highlights the power of scent. As we turn to its exterior, we encounter dramatically different scenes [Figure 8]. Here, in contrast to the solitary figure pouring liquid at the altar, women are approached by men, some of whom extend satchels that may contain some goods, while others gesture in a way that implies some form of exchange. The women's femininity is underscored in their attire, as their bodies may be detected beneath their garments, which in some instances appear intentionally diaphanous. It is no surprise that some scholars have interpreted the cup's exterior as depicting scenes of courtship or even prostitution.[43] Among the women, the one holding the double-flute may be taken to be a musician, potentially a performer in the Greek banquet, or female entertainer, known as a *hetaira*. The cup's exterior, however, presents more than a simple scene of courtship or prostitution. Rather, it integrates various areas of intersection between male and female realms. The allusion to male spaces, specifically the *symposium*, is indicated by the objects filling the setting such as the bench with the striped pillow, the double-flute, or the men's walking sticks. The reference to the female sphere is made through the depiction of objects typically shown in fifth-century BCE depictions of women, namely the mirror and the chairs. The male world of the *symposium* intersects with women's everyday experiences.

At first glance, the cup's two sides may appear widely divergent. There is, however, a common thread. In its entirety, the vessel brings together male perspectives onto female experience. The exterior presents encounters in daily life, as men may view women being preoccupied with their appearance, they may court them, and may enjoy their presence as entertainers. The interior features an encounter in the religious sphere, as men may see women in the public taking on primary religious roles serving as libation bearers and carriers of the ritual basket, such as the figures seen in the earlier examples discussed above. The cup's surfaces also share the allusion to scent. The interior's incense burner emits smoke, whereas many of the exterior's figures handle flowers. We may note the standing youth with a flower in his right hand who approaches a seated woman who also carries a flower in each hand, or the bearded man who turns to the seated woman while holding out a plant with his fingertips. The association of delicate blooms with desirability and sweet scents is a commonplace in Greek culture.[44] Here, on the vase's exterior, the protagonists' gentle handling of flowers suggests delicacy and preciousness. Even if we cannot discern their odors, in the context of male-female interactions, the flowers connote sweetness, desirability, and a fragrant smell.

The cup—an object whose form suggests the potential consumption of wine—alludes to the context of the Greek *symposium*, whose primary participants were men. As such it offers its potential male handler a vantage point onto the female realm, particularly onto those spaces in which men may view women. The cup's exterior, which could be seen by more than one banqueter at once, features direct male-female interactions in a group setting. The interior, on the other hand, would be available to a single viewer and offer a privileged vantage point through the cup's circular frame onto the

Figure 8

Figure 8
Exchanges between men and
women, exterior of a red-figure
cup (kylix) attributed to the
Makron Painter, ca. 490–480 BCE,
Toledo Ohio, Toledo
Museum of Art 1972.55.
© Toledo Museum of Art.

solitary libation bearer. Women's spaces are infused with pleasant scents, those of flowers and those of the *thymiaterion*'s smoke.[45]

Figure 9

The final example considered here articulates the power ascribed to the *thymiaterion*'s smoke. It is found on a water vessel, today in the British Museum [Figure 9].[46] Although parts of the vase are now lost, we may note an incense burner on the vase's upper register. This censer is smaller than the ones we have seen so far. It consists of a broad open bowl supported by a stand. Unfortunately, its lower part has not survived. Careful examination reveals that the incense is being burned, as faint lines indicating smoke emerge from the burner, which is placed at the heart of the scene. Directly above the fumes, crouching in mid-air, is a nude, winged male figure. He ties a fillet around the head of the seated female figure on the left. The primary focus of attention, she stands out among all other figures. Her light skin, which has been rendered in added white, distinguishes her from the rest. She wears a radiating crown around her gathered curls, and is dressed in layers of rich garments, whose edge she holds in her left hand. In the vase's current condition, it is difficult to detect her tunic, which is rendered in light brown. The mantle that covers her lower body, in contrast, is notable for the rich patterns enveloping her legs. The central figure's radiating crown and elaborate dress recall depictions of brides.[47] Based on the iconography alone, we may see her as a young woman about to enter a new stage in life; surrounded by a crowd of female attendants she sits in her bridal chamber. The realm of youthful female appeal is filled with fragrant smoke.

The inscriptions accompanying some of the figures layer the image with additional meanings. Two of the female attendants looking upon the central young woman are named ΚΑΛΗ, καλή (*kale*), or beautiful, while another is named ΚΛΕΩ, Κλε(ι)ώ *(Kleiō)*, fame or glory. The central figure is also labeled. The name ΕΛΕΝΗ, Ελένη written above the figure's head, identifies her as Helen. The inscription ΠΟΘΟΣ, Πόθος (*Pothos*), identifies the winged male as the personification of yearning, longing, or desire.[48] The vase presents us with the figure of myth, who in her very essence embodies irresistible erotic allure; at the moment in which wafts of sweet scent fill the air, Pothos himself crowns the Queen of Troy in her nuptial chamber.[49] The positioning of the censer on the vase's shoulder and the placement of Pothos directly above, closer to the vessel's neck, emphasize the link between the smoke and the strong emotions personified by the crouching diminutive figure. We are invited to imagine the scents moving upward along the surface of the vase as if they uphold the winged figure in the air. The *thymiaterion* emits Desire.

This final example situates the censer in the realm of nuptials, and renders the power of its fumes as explicitly erotic. Such rendition fits a larger pattern of associations between the *thymiaterion* and attraction. Along these lines, it is no wonder that of all divinities, Aphrodite, the goddess of love, had a particularly strong affinity with the instrument.[50] The *thymiaterion*, however, is not necessarily connected to desires of the body specifically. The earlier examples discussed here present it in religious contexts, as seen on the oil flask or the grand mixing bowl attributed to the Kleophon Painter. In these instances there is no reference to physical allure, specifically. Rather, the *thymiaterion* is shown here, as it may be found elsewhere, in connection with the realms of maidens, women, and young men, who are endowed with charm and attractiveness.

Figure 9
Helen with attendants,
Attic red-figure water vessel
(hydria), attrbitued to the
Painter of the Athens Wedding,
ca. 450–400 BCE. London,
British Museum, E226.
© Trustees of the British Museum

* *
*

The images discussed here can hardly offer complete answers to the range of questions raised by our evidence for the use and meaning of *thymiateria* in the ancient Greek world. Still, they provide some initial responses to the queries posed here at the outset. The *thymiaterion* was conceived as an instrument that could structure social groupings within a ritual procession. It could serve to demarcate spaces and point to the primary locus of a ritual within a sanctuary. Additionally, its smoke could be conceived as having the power to provoke longing and desire. The *thymiaterion* thus contained the force to mark holy spaces and potentially make these sites of worship desirable to mortals and to the immortal gods themselves.

ENDNOTES

I am grateful for the comments and discussions from the participants at the conference where this paper was originally presented in Bern 2019: Beatrice Caseau, Franceso De Angelis, Nathan S. Dennis, James Doyle, Margaret Graves, Stephen Houston, Aden Kumler, Nina Macaraig, Yao Ning, Allison Stielau, and the co-organizer of that event Ittai Weinryb. Above all, my deep gratitude to Beate Fricke, for co-organizing the conference, hosting us in Bern, and for her careful editing of an earlier draft.

1 For incense and incense burners, see Fritze 1894; Burkert 1985, 62, 73; Detienne 1977; Zaccagnino 1998; Simon 2005; Krauskopf 2005; Mehl 2008; Prost 2008. Note also the emphasis on incense in Naiden 2013. Publications of *thymiateria* are often found in catalogue entries, e.g., Testa 1989; or in publications related to specific contexts, see for instance, Shevchenko 2020.

2 For sacred spaces, see e.g., Alcock and Osborne 1994; Burkert 1996; Rask 2016; Petrovic and Petrovic 2016. Sensorial experiences in antiquity have received more scholarly attention in recent decades. See e.g., Hamilakis 2013; Bradley 2015; Squire 2016; Bellia and Angliker 2021.

3 See incense burners uncovered in the Athenian cemetery the Kerameikos. The Kerameikos Archaeological Museum, nos. 144 and 145. See further, Zaccagnino 1998, 192–93, catalogue numbers CT159–161; Krauskopf 2005; Simon 2005.

4 For an overview, see Zaccagnino 1998. Also, note that as of the writing of this article, the Beazley Archive, the online database of Greek vases, does not list any depictions of incense burners earlier than ca. 550 BCE.

5 See discussion with further references in Zaccagnino 1998, 36.

6 Sappho, Fragment 40, line 30: μύρρα καὶ κασία λίβανός τ' ὀνεμείχνυτο. For further discussion of the poem and the myth, see Spelman 2017.

7 See Herodotos, Histories 4.162, with discussion in Zaccagnino 1998, 42, 105.

8 Zaccagnino 1998, 11–114; Harris 1995.

9 Zaccagnino 1998, 46–48.

10 See discussion in Simon 2005, 257–61; Naiden 2013, 72–76. The sixth-century BCE description of the symposium by the philosopher and poet Xenophanes (Fragment 1, cited in Athenaeus Deipnosophistae, 11.462.c) mentions frankincense among other elements. See discussion of the poem and the role of perfumes in sympotic contexts in Briand 2008.

11 Zaccagnino 1998, 52–62.

12 Rome, Museo Nazionale Romano, 8670, 475–450 BCE; Delivorrias 1984, 114, no. 1170; Guarducci 1985.

13 See e.g., Burkert 1985, 55–59; Parker 2011. For discussions of this perception, see Faraone and Naiden 2012; Lincoln 2012.

14 See e.g., Iliad 8.43; Odyssey 8.363; with discussion in Naiden 2013, 111–13.

15 Chantraine 1968, 360, θύω.

16 See for example the burning of barley by the priests in the Homeric Hymn to Apollo, 491, 509; see also numerous references in Naiden 2013.

17 On scents in Greek religious experience, see Burkert 1985, 62; Prost 2008; Mehl 2008; Bodiou and Mehl 2008.

18 Simon 2005, 263; Zaccagnino 1998.

19 Herodotos, Histories 3.107. All Herodotos translations adopted from A. D. Godley. (Cambridge, MA: Harvard University Press, 1920).

20 Herodotos, Histories 4.75.

21 On the association between Arabia and fragrant smells and plants, see Detienne 1977, especially 3–36. On Herodotean approaches of the non-Greek, see Hartog 1988.

22 London, British Museum B 648, ca. 500 BCE, attributed to the Beldam Painter; Haspels 1936, 267, no. 14; Van Straten 1995, 199, no. V30; Gebauer 2002, 96–97, no. P46; Bundrick 2014, 689, no. 40.

23 See in general Roccos 1995, with reference to this vase at 654–55.

24 See e.g., Dillon 2002, 37–39; Gebauer 2002, 169–71; Connelly 2007, 33–39.

25 See e.g., Oakley 2004; Kurtz and Boardman 1971.

26 See e.g., Lefkowitz 1996; Dillon 2002, 268–92. Note, however, that the depiction of female involvement in funerary rites does not necessarily reflect ancient realities; on this issue see in particular, Sourvinou-Inwood 2004.

27 See discussion of this feature in the frieze in Neils 2005, 208; Mehl 2008, 173.

28 The subject of the Parthenon frieze has been a source of scholarly contention, and while there are notable variations in interpretation, most scholars see it as a rendition of a ritual procession in honor of Athena and connected to her festival in Athens. See e.g., Boardman 1984; Harrison 1996; Jenkins 2005; Neils 2001; Palagia 2008; Neils 2005. For a different interpretation, which takes it as a representation of a myth, see Connelly 1996; 2014. For further discussion, bibliography, and assessment of the arguments, see Shear 2016.

29 Gaifman 2018a.

30 See in general, Harris 1995; Linders 1975. See discussion of thymiateria as gifts to the gods in Prost 2008.

31 Harris 1995, 114.

32 Similarly, libation bowls were also dedicated as gifts to the gods. See, for example, on the Athenian Acropolis, Harris 1995, with further discussion in Gaifman 2018b.

33 Ferrara, Museo Nazionale di Spina: T 57 C VP; red-figure volute krater attributed to the Kleophon Painter, ca. 440–420 BCE; Beazley 1963, 1114, no. 1; Matheson 1995, 139–40, 406, no. KL 1. This vase is often cited in discussions of sacrificial rituals; see Van Straten 1995, 20–21, 207, no. V78; Parker 2005, 225; Gebauer 2002, 701–2. For discussion of its depiction of the thymiaterion, see Mehl 2008, 177–78.

34 See in general, Scott 2014.

35 Herodotos, Histories 4.162.

36 Bronze thymiaterion in the form of a female figure holding up a bowl. Delphi, Archaeological Museum, 7723. ca. 450 BCE, H: 26 cm. Amandry 1939, 112–13; Zaccagnino 1998, 193, no. CT 164; Naiden 2013, 73–74.

37 Krauskopf 2005.

38 Toledo Museum of Art (Ohio), no. 1972.55; Attic red-figure kylix, attributed to Makron Painter, 490–480 BCE. Boulter and Luckner 1976, 34, pls. 53–54; Kunisch 1997, 179, no. 179.

39 For detailed discussion of staining altars with blood, see Ekroth 2005.

40 I thank Savannah Marquardt for this observation, and the students in my seminar on art and ritual for their helpful remarks on this issue.

41 Linders 1975, 215, 218.

42 See similarly, Mehl 2008, 184–85.

43 See e.g., Keuls 1985, 167–68.

44 Bodiou and Mehl 2008, especially 150–54; Kéi 2021.

45 Further on the association between thymiateria and flowers, see Kéi 2021, particularly 176, 182–86.

46 London, British Museum E226; red-figure hydria; attributed to the Painter of the Athens Wedding, ca. 450–400 BCE. Beazley 1963, 1318, no. 3; Williams et al. 1925, vol. 6, III.I. C.8.

47 See e.g., Oakley and Sinos 1993.

48 On Pothos in Greek art, see Shapiro 1993; Smith 2011.

49 On Pothos and Helen particularly in nuptial contexts, see e.g., Stanford 1983; Sutton 1997.

50 Zaccagnino 1998, 53–54; Bodiou and Mehl 2008, 141–148.

BIBLIOGRAPHY

Alcock, Susan E., and Robin Osborne. 1994. *Placing the Gods: Sanctuaries and Sacred Space in Ancient Greece.* Oxford: Clarendon Press.

Amandry, Pierre. 1939. "Rapport préliminaire sur les statues chryséléphantines de Delphes." *Bulletin de Correspondance Hellénique* 63: 86–119. https://www.persee.fr/doc/bch_0007-4217_1939_num_63_1_2676.

Beazley, John D. 1963. *Attic Red-Figure Vase-Painters.* 2nd edn. Oxford: Clarendon Press.

Bellia, Angela, and Erica Angliker, eds. 2021. *Soundscape and Landscape at Panhellenic Greek Sanctuaries, Telestes.* Pisa: Istituti editoriali e poligrafici internazionali.

Boardman, John. 1984. "The Parthenon Frieze." In *Parthenon-Kongress Basel: Referate und Berichte, 4. bis 8. April 1982,* edited by Ernst Berger, 210–15. Mainz: von Zabern.

Bodiou, Lydie, and Véronique Mehl. 2008. "Sociologie des odeurs en pays grecs." In *Parfums et odeurs dans l'antiquité,* edited by Lydie Bodiou, Dominique Frère, and Véronique Mehl, 141–63. Rennes: Presses universitaires de Rennes.

Boulter, C. G., and Kurt T. Luckner. 1976. *Corpus vasorum antiquorum. The Toledo Museum of Art,* fasc. 1 [*United States of America,* fasc. 17]. Toledo, OH: Toledo Museum of Art.

Bradley, Mark, ed. 2015. *Smell and the Ancient Senses.* Abingdon; New York: Routledge.

Briand, Michel. 2008. "Du banquet d'éros au printemps des immortels: Parfums et senteurs dans la poésie mélique archaïque grecque." In *Parfums et odeurs dans l'antiquité,* edited by Lydie Bodiou, Dominique Frère, and Véronique Mehl, 129–39. Rennes: Presses universitaires de Rennes.

Bundrick, Sheramy, D. 2014. "Selling Sacrifice on Classical Athenian Vases." *Hesperia* 83, no. 4: 653–708.

Burkert, Walter. 1985. *Greek Religion: Archaic and Classical.* Oxford: Basil Blackwell.

Burkert, Walter. 1996. *Creation of the Sacred: Tracks of Biology in Early Religions.* Cambridge, MA: Harvard University Press.

Chantraine, Pierre. 1968. *Dictionnaire étymologique de la langue grecque, histoire des mots.* Paris: Klincksieck.

Connelly, Joan B. 1996. "Parthenon and Parthenoi: A Mythological Interpretation of the Parthenon Frieze." *American Journal of Archaeology* 100, no. 1: 53–80.

Connelly, Joan Breton. 2007. *Portrait of a Priestess: Women and Ritual in Ancient Greece.* Princeton, NJ: Princeton University Press.

Connelly, Joan Breton. 2014. *The Parthenon Enigma: A Journey into Legend.* London: Head of Zeus.

Delivorrias, Angelos. 1984. "Aphrodite." In *Lexicon Iconographicum Mythologiae Classicae* vol. II.1, 2–150. Zurich; Munich: Artemis Verlag.

Detienne, Marcel. 1977. *The Gardens of Adonis: Spices in Greek Mythology.* European Philosophy and the Human Sciences. Hassocks, Sussex: Harvester Press.

Dillon, Matthew. 2002. *Girls and Women in Classical Greek Religion.* London; New York: Routledge.

Ekroth, Gunnel. 2005. "Blood on the Altars?" *Antike Kunst* 48: 9–29.

Faraone, Christopher A., and Fred. S. Naiden. 2012. *Greek and Roman Animal Sacrifice: Ancient Victims, Modern Observers.* Cambridge: Cambridge University Press.

Fritze, Hans von. 1894. *Die Rauchopfer bei den Griechen.* Berlin: Mayer and Müller.

Gaifman, Milette. 2018a. *The Art of Libation in Classical Athens.* New Haven, CT: Yale University Press.

Gaifman, Milette. 2018b. "The Greek Libation Bowl as Embodied Object." In *Art History* 41, no. 3, special issue *The Embodied Object in Classical Antiquity,* edited by Milette Gaifman, Verity Platt, and Michael Squire: 444–65.

Gebauer, Jörg. 2002. *Pompe und Thysia: Attische Tieropferdarstellungen auf schwarz- und rotfigurigen Vasen.* Eikon 7. Münster: Ugarit-Verlag.

Guarducci, Margherita. 1985. "Il 'Trono Ludovisi' e l'Acrolito Ludovisi': Due pezzi insigni del Museo Nazionale Romano." *Bollettino d'Arte* 70: 1–20.

Hamilakis, Yannis. 2013. *Archaeology and the Senses: Human Experience, Memory, and Affect.* New York: Cambridge University Press.

Harris, Diane. 1995. *The Treasures of the Parthenon and Erechtheion.* Oxford Monographs on Classical Archaeology. Oxford: Clarendon Press.

Harrison, Evelyn B. 1996. "The Web of History: A Conservative Reading of the Parthenon Frieze." In *Worshipping Athena: Panathenaia and Parthenon,* edited by Jenifer Neils, 198–214. Madison: University of Wisconsin Press.

Hartog, François. 1988. *The Mirror of Herodotus: The Representation of the Other in the Writing of History.* The New Historicism. Berkeley: University of California Press.

Haspels, C. H. Emilie. 1936. *Attic Black-Figured Lekythoi.* Paris: E. de Boccard.

Jenkins, Ian. 2005. "The Parthenon Frieze and Perikles' Cavalry of a Thousand." In *Periklean Athens and Its Legacy: Problems and Perspectives,* edited by Judith M. Barringer and Jeffrey M. Hurwit, 147–62. Austin: University of Texas Press.

Kéi, Nikolina. 2021. *L'esthétique des fleurs: Kosmos, poikilia et kharis dans la céramique attique du VIe et du Ve siècle av. n. ère.* Berlin: De Gruyter.

Keuls, Eva C. 1985. *The Reign of the Phallus: Sexual Politics in Ancient Athens.* New York: Harper & Row.

Krauskopf, Ingrid. 2005. "Rauchopfer; Griechisch und etruskisch." In *Thesaurus Cultus et Rituum Antiquorum (ThesCRA),* vol. 5, 212–23. Basel; Los Angeles: Getty Publications.

Kunisch, Norbert. 1997. *Makron.* 2 vols. Mainz: P. von Zabern.

Kurtz, Donna C., and John Boardman. 1971. *Greek Burial Customs.* London: Thames and Hudson.

Lefkowitz, Mary. 1996. "Women in the Panathenaic and Other Festivals." In *Worshipping Athena: Panathenaia and Parthenon,* edited by Jenifer Neils, 78–91. Madison: University of Wisconsin Press.

Lincoln, Bruce. 2012. "From Bergaigne to Meuli: How Animal Sacrifice Became a Hot Topic." In *Greek and Roman Animal Sacrifice: Ancient Victims, Modern Observers,* edited by A. Christopher Faraone and Fred. S. Naiden, 13–32. Cambridge: Cambridge University Press.

Linders, Tullia. 1975. *The Treasurers of the Other Gods in Athens and Their Functions.* Beiträge zur klassischen Philologie 62. Meisenheim am Glan: Hain.

Matheson, Susan B. 1995. *Polygnotos and Vase Painting in Classical Athens.* Wisconsin Studies in Classics. Madison: University of Wisconsin Press.

Mehl, Véronique. 2008. "Parfums de fêtes: Usage de parfums et sacrifices sanglants." In *Le sacrifice antique: Vestiges, procédures et stratégies,* edited by Véronique Mehl and Pierre Brulé, 167–86. Rennes: Presses universitaires de Rennes.

Naiden, Fred S. 2013. *Smoke Signals for the Gods: Ancient Greek Sacrifice from the Archaic through Roman Periods.* New York: Oxford University Press.

Neils, Jenifer. 2001. *The Parthenon Frieze.* Cambridge; New York: Cambridge University Press.

Neils, Jenifer. 2005. "'With Noblest Images on All Sides': The Ionic Frieze of the Parthenon." In *The Parthenon: From Antiquity to the Present,* edited by Jenifer Neils, 199–223. New York: Cambridge University Press.

Oakley, John Howard. 2004. *Picturing Death in Classical Athens: The Evidence of the White Lekythoi.* Cambridge: Cambridge University Press.

Oakley, John Howard, and Rebecca H. Sinos. 1993. *The Wedding in Ancient Athens.* Wisconsin Studies in Classics. Madison: University of Wisconsin Press.

Palagia, Olga. 2008. "The Parthenon Frieze: Boy or Girl?" *Antike Kunst* 51: 3–7.

Parker, Robert. 2005. *Polytheism and Society at Athens.* Oxford; New York: Oxford University Press.

Parker, Robert. 2011. *On Greek Religion.* Townsend Lectures/Cornell Studies in Classical Philology 60. Ithaca, NY: Cornell University Press.

Petrovic, Andrej, and Ivana Petrovic. 2016. *Inner Purity and Pollution in Greek Religion.* New York: Oxford University Press.

Prost, Francis. 2008. "Encens, parfums et statues de culte." In *Parfums et odeurs dans l'antiquité,* edited by Lydie Bodiou, Dominique Frère, and Véronique Mehl, 97–103. Rennes: Presses universitaires de Rennes.

Rask, Katherine. 2016. "Devotionalism, Material Culture, and the Personal in Greek Religion." *Kernos* 29: 9–20.

Roccos, Linda Jones. 1995. "The Kanephoros and Her Festival Mantle in Greek Art." *American Journal of Archaeology* 99, no. 4: 641–66.

Scott, Michael. 2014. *Delphi: A History of the Center of the Ancient World.* Princeton, NJ: Princeton University Press.

Shapiro, Harvey Allan. 1993. *Personifications in Greek Art: The Representation of Abstract Concepts, 600–400 B.C.* Zurich: Akanthus.

Shear, Theodore Leslie. 2016. *Trophies of Victory: Public Building in Periklean Athens.* Princeton, NJ: Department of Art and Archaeology, Princeton University in association with Princeton University Press.

Shevchenko, Tetiana. 2020. "Thymiateria and the Cult of Aphrodite in Olbia Pontica." *Annual of the British School at Athens* 115: 379–99.

Simon, Erika. 2005. "Rauchopfer." In *Thesaurus Cultus et Rituum Antiquorum (ThesCRA),* vol. 1, 255–68. Basel; Los Angeles: Fondation pour le lexicon iconographicum mythologiae classicae; Getty Publications.

Smith, Amy C. 2011. *Polis and Personification in Classical Athenian Art.* Leiden; Boston: Brill.

Sourvinou-Inwood, Christiane. 2004. "Gendering the Athenian Funeral: Ritual Reality and Tragic Manipulations." In *Greek Ritual Poetics,* edited by Dimitrios Yatromanolakis and Panagiotis Roilos, 161–88. Washington, DC: Center for Hellenic Studies.

Spelman, Henry. 2017. "Sappho 44: Trojan Myth and Literary History." *Mnemosyne* 70, no. 5: 740–57.

Squire, Michael, ed. 2016. *Sight and the Ancient Senses.* Abingdon; New York: Routledge.

Stanford, William Bodell. 1983. *Greek Tragedy and the Emotions: An Introductory Study*. London: Routledge & Kegan Paul.

Sutton, Robert F. 1997. "Nuptial Eros: The Visual Discourse of Marriage in Classical Athens." *The Journal of the Walters Art Gallery* 55/56: 27–48.

Testa, Antonella. 1989. *Candelabri e thymiateria*, vol. 2, *Cataloghi / Monumenti, musei e gallerie pontificie, Museo gregoriano etrusco*. Rome: "Erma" di Bretschneider.

Van Straten, F. T. 1995. *Hiera Kala: Images of Animal Sacrifice in Archaic and Classical Greece*. Leiden: Brill.

Williams, Dyfri, A. H. Smith, Frederick Norman Pryce, H. B. Walters, Edgar John Forsdyke, and Robert Manuel Cook. 1925. *Corpus vasorum antiquorum. Great Britain. British Museum (Department of Greek and Roman Antiquities)*. Corpus vasorum antiquorum. Great Britain, fasc. 1–2, 4–5, 7–8, 10, 13, 17, 20, 25 London: Printed by order of the Trustees of the British Museum.

Zaccagnino, Cristiana. 1998. *Il thymiaterion nel mondo greco: Analisi delle fonti, tipologia, impieghi*. Studia archaeologica. Rome: "L'Erma" die Bretschneider.

FIRE

VESSELS
CENSER

FIRE

VESSELS
CENSER

VESSELS OF HOLY FIRE:
THE CENSER AND THE WOMB
OF THE MOTHER OF GOD
IN EARLY BYZANTINE AND
COPTIC DEVOTION

Nathan S. Dennis

The censer held a privileged position within early Christian and Byzantine liturgy from at least the late fourth or early fifth century, and references to incense-burning in Christian ritual appear as early as the second century,[1] even though it was regarded as a controversial practice by some of the earliest Christian theologians.[2] Incense-burners were far more than objects that stimulated only the olfactory imagination of both clergy and laity alike. Their ability to contain the burning embers of incense, distribute aromas, and present a dramatic visual display of smoke-trails throughout a sacred space facilitated a multisensory experience that encouraged theological interpretations of censers as objects of divine engagement.

Figure 1

The senses of sight and smell were the most obvious conduits for this level of engagement, but hearing was equally a catalyst for promoting metaphorical interpretations of censers. Bishops, priests, and deacons would swing or shake censers to create the staccato sound of a censer's body clanging against the chains that were often attached to it. When paired with liturgical chant, these sounds were amplified, transforming the censer into a makeshift musical instrument for the performance of psalms, hymns, odes, and prayers. An undated papyrus fragment in the Papyrus Carlsberg Collection at the University of Copenhagen seems to show this type of performative movement [Figure 1].[3] A Byzantine or Coptic monk—rendered nearly as a stick-figure— wields a processional cross in his left hand and swings an incense-burner erratically in his right while two indeterminate animals with crosses mounted on their heads stand at his side, possibly as apotropaic symbols. His wide-eyed, piercing gaze almost suggests a moment of religious epiphany amid a cloud of smoke and the rhythmic, perhaps clanking, sound of the censer being shaken. Of course, not all censers were handheld, and some would have hung from canopies or wall mounts in late antiquity and the Middle Ages, but for those employed in more performative ritual movements, the sound would have reverberated throughout the space, accentuating the hypnotic, animated smoke unfurling and rising toward the sky.

The sense of taste was also affected. Clouds of incense smoke, especially in large concentrations, emitted the aroma of the substance burning within the censer, but the airborne molecules also stimulated the sense of taste, thanks to the proximity of the olfactory nerve and the taste buds of the mouth.[4] And finally, the sense of touch, whether real or imagined, was central to the censing performance. To touch or to be enveloped by the smoke of burning incense was to engage with the very materiality of an otherwise ephemeral substance. In medieval Orthodox liturgies, the smoke was often interpreted metaphorically as the visible, divine presence of God or the Holy Spirit,[5] or as the visual manifestation of the prayers of the faithful ascending into heaven.[6] Yet the prospect of "touching" the smoke or being the recipient of its spiritually rejuvenating properties can only be described as a form of haptic desire. How do you touch something that cannot be felt through the tactility of flesh, although you can see its material form with your own eyes? Censers and incense, therefore, were ripe for metaphorical interpretation in the medieval world, where the spiritual was made manifest through sensory engagement.

Figure 1
Undated papyrus fragment
showing a monk with censer
and processional cross,
P. Carlsberg 443, Papyrus
Carlsberg Collection,
University of Copenhagen.
Courtesy of the Papyrus
Carlsberg Collection.

This chapter is focused on just one of those metaphors: the Virgin Mary, or Theotokos (God-Bearer or Mother of God) in the Orthodox tradition, as the so-called "golden censer" in both art and literature, particularly within early Byzantine and Coptic traditions. The trope emerged in the aftermath of the Council of Ephesus in 431, which is when the Virgin Mary was officially given the title of Theotokos. The symbolism, however, was also deeply rooted in late antique phenomenology, whereby sensory engagement with liturgical objects redefined their meaning for the Christian communities that used them. The materiality of the bronze censer, quite often gilded, was conflated with the imagined physicality—even anatomy—of the Virgin herself. The censer assumed the generative agency of the Virgin's womb, which held the fiery divinity of Christ *in utero*, yet was neither consumed by that holy fire, nor was its virginity compromised.[7] The censer distributed a sweet fragrance that Orthodox worshipers frequently interpreted as a foretaste or pleasing aroma of paradise, and medieval theologians interpreted the burning embers of Christ within the Virgin's womb as the odor of salvation.

The emergence of the golden censer motif in Byzantine theology highlighted the importance of feminine agency in Christian salvation history. Mary's pivotal role in many of Christ's most significant life events (Annunciation, Visitation, Nativity, Presentation, Crucifixion, Deposition and Entombment, Ascension) meant that iconography traditionally interpreted as scenes from the life of Christ was equally illustrative of the life of the Theotokos. And these scenes were often depicted on actual censers used in service of the Byzantine liturgy. Christ's narrative is also Mary's narrative. The salvific body of Christ is therefore intimately and inextricably connected to Mary's salvific womb. The censer as emblem of Mary's virginity and the Incarnation of Christ would become particularly important in late antique and early Byzantine Egypt and the Levant, where we find the earliest and most diverse expressions of the incarnational censer motif.

THE GOLDEN CENSER AS SALVIFIC WOMB IN EARLY CHRISTIAN AND BYZANTINE THEOLOGY

The origins of Mary's womb as incarnational censer developed in the fourth century as Christian theologians began associating the Virgin with the golden incense-altar in the Holy of Holies in the Jewish Tabernacle (Exod 30:1): the sacrificial incense, which facilitated communion with the divine, was contained within a holy and inviolable sanctum.[8] Christ became the incense of sacrifice that created a path to salvation for humanity, and through the Incarnation he was contained within the virginal womb of the Theotokos. A golden incense-altar, however, is obviously not a golden censer, but the New Testament had already paved the way for such an interpretation. The original Hebrew phrase used to describe the furnishings of the Tabernacle in Exod 30:1, "מִזְבֵּחַ מִקְטַר קְטֹרֶת" ("*mizbeach miqtar qetoret*," "altar for making smoke from incense") that was covered in gold ("זָהָב," "*zahab*"), was translated into Greek as "χρυσοῦν … θυμιατήριον" ("*chrusoun … thumiaterion*," "golden censer") in Heb 9:4, whereas the earlier Septuagint translation of the Hebrew Bible kept the more literal "θυσιαστήριον θυμιάματος" ("*thusiasterion thumiamatos*," "altar of incense") for Exod 30:1. This interpretive decision in the New Testament is significant since θυμιατήριον was more commonly associated with a portable censer than a large altar in a fixed position.[9] This inevitably gave license to early Christian theologians to reformulate the concept of the Tabernacle altar into that of a more contemporary censer, which was already being used in church services in the fourth century.

Ephrem the Syrian, who was active in the fourth century, is generally credited as the first Christian theologian to apply the metaphor of the golden censer to the generative womb of the Virgin, referring to it as the "golden censer exhaling the sweetest perfumes."[10] In his hymns on the Nativity and faith, Ephrem would further his application of the coal or fire imagery, at times in pseudo-sexual language, such as his description of Ruth in the Hebrew Bible: "The fiery coal that crept into the bed of Boaz / ... She saw the Chief Priest / hidden in his loins, the fire for his censer."[11] The Chief Priest in this context is Christ, whose lineage is traced through Ruth and Boaz in Matt 1:5 and Luke 3:32. When referring to the Theotokos, however, Ephrem writes, "The firstborn entered the womb / And the pure [woman] did not suffer ... / For he is God in his entrance, / And human in his exit. / It is a wonder and a bewildering thing to hear: / Fire entered the womb, / Put on a body and went forth."[12] Ephrem repeats the trope of Christ as the burning fire within the Virgin's womb in his *Homily on the Nativity*, where he writes:

> It is a source of great amazement, my beloved,
> that someone should enquire into the wonder
> of how God came down
> and made His dwelling in a womb,
> and how that Being
> put on the body of a man,
> spending nine months in a womb,
> not shrinking from such a home;
> and how a womb of flesh was able
> to carry flaming fire,
> and how a flame dwelt
> in a moist womb which did not get burnt up.
> Just as the bush on Horeb bore
> God in the flame, so did Mary bear
> Christ in her virginity.[13]

Just a few decades later in the fifth century, Ephrem's fellow Syrian, Rabbula of Edessa, in his fourth *Supplication*, writes "Who is able to extol your Edenic qualities, pure and holy Virgin? Who can speak of your conception and of your wondrous birthgiving, pure and holy Virgin, you who received the living fire in your womb of flesh but were not consumed by it?"[14] Ephrem and Rabbula, in particular, were part of a much larger theological phenomenon in late antique Syria and southern Anatolia, whereby metaphors for either the Virgin Mary or *Mater Ecclesia* (Mother Church) became increasingly bodily, sometimes even sexual.[15]

As Maria Evangelatou has documented, the censer-based imagery for the Virgin Mary and her womb was bolstered by the Council of Ephesus and a widespread proliferation of the cult of the Virgin across the Mediterranean and Middle East in the fifth and sixth centuries. By the seventh century, Andrew of Crete, in his fourth homily on the birth of the Virgin, writes "Hail, golden censer of truly spiritual fragrances in which Christ, the rational incense, formed from divinity and humanity, displayed the fragrance of his living and rational flesh, without confusion and without separation, on fire by his divinity!"[16] By the eighth century, the motif was firmly embedded in Byzantine Mariology. Patriarch Germanos I of Constantinople, who wrote an ecclesiastical history in the seventh or early eighth century, noted this of the symbolism of the liturgical thurible:

> The censer demonstrates the humanity of Christ, and the fire his divinity. The sweet-smelling smoke reveals the fragrance of the Holy Spirit which precedes ... Again, the interior of the censer ... is understood as the (sanctified) womb of the (holy) virgin (and Theotokos), who bore the divine coal, Christ, in whom "the whole fullness of deity dwells bodily" (Colossians 2:9). All together, therefore, give forth the sweet-smelling fragrance. Or again, the interior of the censer points to the font of holy baptism, taking into itself the coal of divine fire, the sweetness of the operation of the Holy Spirit, which is the adoption of divine grace through faith, and exuding a good odor.[17]

Germanos would use the same trope in his *Oration on the Annunciation of the Supremely Holy Theotokos*, writing "Hail, favored one, the spice-bearing earth and life-bearing container and new vase of unguent for the Spirit, that filled the whole universe with a perfumed scent! Hail, favored one, truly the golden censer and the pure and all-holy and spotless treasury of purity!"[18] At the end of the eighth century, Patriarch Tarasios of Constantinople described the womb of the Theotokos as a censer of radiant light, as opposed to the more standardized rhetoric of heat.[19] In the eighth and ninth centuries, both John of Damascus and Joseph the Hymnographer would refer to the Theotokos as either the golden censer[20] or a censer bearing a luminous ember.[21] And among two of the great twelfth- and thirteenth-century Byzantine theologians, Neophytos of Paphos and Iakobos of Kokkinobaphos, Neophytos labels the Theotokos as the golden censer three times in his homilies,[22] and Iakobos comes full circle to the early Christian Marian metaphor, writing "Today there is received into the Holy of Holies the golden censer, in which the *Logos* setting light to the flesh filled the world with its fragrance."[23]

To this day, the Coptic Church in Egypt still sings a hymn at the ninth hour of Good Friday during Passion Week, which states that, "The golden censer is the Virgin; her aroma is our Savior. She gave birth to Him. He saved us and forgave us our sins."[24] Another traditional Coptic hymn begins with, "The fine incense of your virginity, Virgin Mary, rose more still than that of the Cherubim and Seraphim up to the throne of the Father."[25] The Ethiopian Church also incorporates Mary's womb as incarnational censer in its liturgical "Prayer of the Incense."[26] Although it is notoriously difficult to date the origins of specific Coptic and Ethiopic hymns since they were originally passed down orally in medieval monasteries, the origins have long been traced to a common Byzantine orbit.

THE CENSER AND MARIAN ICONOGRAPHY
IN NORTH AFRICAN CHURCHES

One of the earliest pictorial associations of the Theotokos and the censer can be found in a sixth-century frescoed semidome apse within the Red Monastery at Sohag in Upper Egypt, painted, in all likelihood, within a century of the Council of Ephesus [Figure 2]. This northern Marian apse is one of three painted apses in a triconch formation within the monastery's church, which is dedicated to the late fourth- to early fifth-century Egyptian cenobitic monk, St. Pshoi (or Bishay; Coptic Ⲡⲓϣⲱⲟⲓ), who founded the monastery. The other two adjacent semidome apses depict Christ Enthroned on the southern side and, on the eastern side, a palimpsest of a late fifth-century painting of the Ascension and three sixth-century versions of Christ in Majesty.[27] In the northern semidome, which is the only one to feature the Theotokos, Mary nurses the infant Christ seated in her lap, appearing as the *Galaktotrophousa* (Παναγία Γαλακτοτροφούσα), "She Who Nourishes with Milk" or "Milk-Giver." She is surrounded by Archangels Gabriel and Michael above her jeweled throne, along with smaller figures of Joseph and Salome in the upper corners. Biblical prophets and apostles flanking her throne on the ground level are grouped in thematic and/or theological pairs, including Elijah on the far left and Moses on the far right, who act as compositional bookends that, when viewed together, allude to the Transfiguration of Christ. Old Testament prophets Ezekiel and Jeremiah appear on the left and Isaiah and Daniel on the right as larger figures, whose open scrolls present to the viewer prophetic announcements of the Incarnation of Christ or the virginity of the Theotokos. And finally, Peter and Paul, the chief apostles of Christ, are rendered on the columns immediately flanking Mary's throne.

The composition is exceptionally rich in late antique Mariology and Christology,[28] but for our purposes, the twenty-eight censers and lamps depicted in the scene are a key element in this early presentation of Marian devotion. The semidome contains six opposed-beak bronze lamps on the ground level, three on each side of the Virgin's throne. The golden pigment suggests that the lamps are either gilded or at least burnished. A combination of lamps and censers hang from the jeweled arcades in the background. There are seven white bulbous-bodied lamps that appear to be made of either ceramic or alabaster.[29] Flanking these lamps are ten gilt-bronze open-bowl and funnel-shaped censers, two of which are held by the archangels. And then four translucent funnel-shaped censers (possibly intended to represent glass or crystal) are positioned around the heads of the archangels. All six opposed-beak bronze lamps on the level of the Virgin's throne emit white flames, whereas the white bulbous-bodied lamps hanging overhead emit red-orange fire. Only the two white lamps positioned immediately to the sides of the Virgin's head (the one on the left is partially obscured by the Virgin's nimbus) deviate from this pattern by emitting white, rather than red, flames.

From as early as the late fourth and early fifth centuries, the Virgin Mary was compared metaphorically to a lamp that illuminated the path to salvation. Cyril of Alexandria calls her the "inextinguishable lamp" (λαμπὰς ἄσβεστος, *lampas asbestos*), and she is described as the "golden lamp ... who carries every righteous lamp" in the Ethiopic *Liber requiei Mariae*, which was likely based on a late fourth- or fifth-century tradition, possibly from Greek and Syriac sources.[30] And certainly after the Council of Ephesus proclaimed Mary the Theotokos, whose virginal womb contained the full divinity of Christ, her association with censers, and especially golden ones, reinforced her position in Christian salvation history. She is both luminous lamp and fiery container of the divine Godhead. The designer of the Red Monastery apse emphasizes this dual nature of the Theotokos, much like the dual nature of Christ himself, with his full divinity and full humanity remaining

Figure 2

Figure 2
Virgin as *Galaktotrophousa*
in the northern semidome of
the eastern triconch apse
at the Church of St. Pshoi,
Red Monastery, Sohag, Egypt,
6th century. Courtesy
of James VanRensselaer.

intact within the blessed womb of the Virgin. This creates a mirror image of sorts, whereby the salvific identity of Christ is mapped onto the body of the Virgin. This pairing is made even more manifest by the fact that the Theotokos in the northern semidome looks immediately across to Christ her son in the southern semidome, where the same opposed-beak lamps (though only four) flank the enthroned Savior, and the same bronze censers and white lamps hang from the background arcades, although there are only about half as many represented in the Christological scene compared with the Marian one [Figure 3]. Mary's white flames, likely alluding to her purity and the preservation of her virginity through the Incarnation, are contrasted with the deep-red flames of Christ's censers, which may allude both to the fire of his divinity—a common conceit in early Christian and Byzantine theology—and his blood sacrifice on the cross. But only when combined across the space of the triconch apse do the white and red flames of mother and son become entwined in a shared trajectory of salvation through sacrifice, to which the Old Testament prophets and New Testament apostles positioned around them bear witness through prophecy and revelation. Moreover, only the lamps closest to Mary in the composition emit white flames; the rest emit reddish-orange flames, perhaps suggesting that the Incarnation has inextricably fused their destinies as bearers of divine light.

Figure 3

The Red Monastery is unique in the sheer number of censers and lamps represented alongside the Theotokos, as well as the symbolic pairing of the two liturgical vessels. Many Byzantine, Coptic, and Nubian monasteries and churches would eventually *only* show golden or bronze censers in Marian iconography, particularly of the Annunciation and Nativity, where the emphasis on the Virgin's womb as incarnational vessel better exemplified Mary's role in the life of Christ and the salvation he promised. But the motif of the censer as Marian womb would largely be confined to Orthodox traditions in North Africa and the Eastern Mediterranean over the next 700 years. The explicit pairing of censer and Theotokos is conspicuously missing from monumental representations of the Virgin in the Latin West in late antiquity and the early Middle Ages, such as the apse mosaics at Santa Maria Maggiore or Santa Maria in Trastevere in Rome or the Basilica Eufrasiana in Poreč. It is even missing from the prominent sixth-century apse at Angeloktisti in Kiti on Cyprus, which is not far removed from the North African Byzantine orbit where the pictorial motif seems to have emerged. The incarnational censer motif appears nowhere in the earliest portable icons of the Virgin or the wall mosaic or fresco icons of Sant'Apollinare Nuovo in Ravenna or Santa Maria Antiqua, the Catacomb of Commodilla, or the lower church of San Clemente in Rome. In the Nilotic lands of northeastern Africa, however, the motif seems to have thrived.

At the Egyptian monastery of Deir al-Surian at Scetis in the Wadi al-Natrun, the western apse inside the church dedicated to the Theotokos features a large encaustic painting of the Annunciation with the Virgin enthroned, flanked by Moses, Isaiah, Ezekiel, and Daniel, all of whom were thought to have prophesied the Virgin's agency in facilitating Christ's Incarnation [Figure 4].[31] Mary is seated precariously on the edge of her throne, presumably shocked by the news that the Archangel Gabriel just revealed to her. At the same time, she also appears to lean forward to inhale the fragrant incense wafting up from the bronze censer placed somewhat suggestively between her open legs, just below her knees. The gleaming censer,

Figure 4

Figure 3
Christ in Majesty in the
southern semidome of the
eastern triconch apse at
the Red Monastery, Sohag,
Egypt, 6th century.
Courtesy of
James Van Rensselaer.

Figure 4
Annunciation in the
western semidome of
the Church of the
Holy Virgin at Deir
al-Surian, Scetis, Egypt,
8th (or 10th?) century.
Courtesy of the
Deir al-Surian
Conservation Project.

painted a deep reddish-orange, likely to accentuate the fiery embers it contained, is positioned on top of an elaborately carved white marble column,
with ghostly white smoke trailing upward between the Theotokos and Gabriel. Both Paul van Moorsel and Lucy-Anne Hunt have examined the iconography of the apse in context of both Coptic and Jacobite Syrian liturgies
that would have been performed below the apse (including actual censing),
noting that metaphors of the Theotokos as aromatic incense of the Incarnation, the golden censer, and the fragrance of salvation appear frequently
in both liturgical traditions for communal prayers.[32]

The burning censer, however, is not the only container metaphor in
the composition. The background cityscape of Nazareth, Mary's hometown,
is an enclosed city filled with equally enclosed gardens, out of which a lush,
almost paradisiacal, landscape emerges.[33] The trees that sprout from the
gardens have been intentionally highlighted with red pigment, suggesting
the iconography of the burning bush in Exod 3:2, the very passage in Coptic
that appears on Moses's unfurled scroll below: "I saw the bush burnt with
fire, and it was not consumed."[34] The burning bush, like the golden censer,
was a common metaphor for the Theotokos and her virginal womb, which
contained the power of the Godhead yet was not destroyed by its consuming
fire.[35] The metaphor had become codified in Byzantine liturgy by at least
the tenth century—the date of the earliest surviving copies of the *Typikon
of the Great Church*—but the trope itself can be traced back to the fourth
century.[36] Although the earliest pictorial representations of the burning bush
omit any overt references to the Theotokos, later icon traditions such as
those at St. Catherine's Monastery at Mt. Sinai would largely supplant the
presence of God in the burning bush with an image of the Virgin [Figure 5].

Figure 5

The burning bush motif clearly is not a golden censer, but it shows
that Orthodox communities were increasingly eager to identify new ways of
characterizing the holy fire that grew within the Theotokos's womb and
apply them not only to biblical narratives but also to objects and iconographies appropriate to the liturgical offices. Therefore, the layers of metaphor
in the Annunciation apse at Deir al-Surian—the censer that contains the fiery
embers of devotion, the city that contains the life of the people, the gardens
that contain the fertility of the land, the burning bush that is not consumed—
make the scene one of the most complex medieval programs on the salvific
agency of Mary's womb, especially when combined with the representation
of the exact moment when Gabriel announces Mary's pregnancy.

Although the precise chronology is unclear, not long after the installation of the Annunciation, the monks of Deir al-Surian added to the nave a
fresco of the Dormition in a different style [Figure 6]. Here, Mary reclines on
her deathbed as six women holding censers shake them vigorously over the
Virgin's body.[37] The presence of censers in Dormition scenes would seem a
natural complement to the funeral liturgy, where incense is burned, candles
are lit, and smoke rising upward has long been a Christian metaphor for the
soul's ascent into heaven. By the end of the twelfth and beginning of the
thirteenth centuries, Byzantine Dormition scenes regularly represented hier-
archs wielding censers that functioned both as emblems of the liturgy and
as metaphors of the salvific agency of the Theotokos.[38] However, at Deir al-
Surian, there are six figures wielding censers, and they are all women, with a
partial inscription labeling them as virgins ("ΝΙ ΠΑΡΘΕΝ [...]," *Ni Parthen [...]*).
Karel Innemée and Youhanna Nessim Youssef have argued that this unprec-

Figure 6

Figure 5
Icon of St. Catherine with
the Virgin of the Burning Bush,
thirteenth century.
Mt. Sinai, St. Catherine's
Monastery. Courtesy of the
Michigan-Princeton-Alexandria
Expeditions to Mount Sinai.

Figure 6
Dormition on the eastern nave
wall of the Church of the
Holy Virgin at Deir al-Surian,
Scetis, Egypt, 8th (or 10th?)
century. Courtesy of the Deir
al-Surian Conservation Project.

edented detail is most likely a reference to Theodosius of Alexandria's sixth-century homily on the Dormition, where he describes "many virgins from the Mount of Olives having choice censers and lamps in hand," who were dedicated to the Theotokos.[39] Nevertheless, in Orthodox traditions, liturgical censing is almost always assigned to men. This would suggest in the painting a much more intimate connection to female agency, the power and fertility of Mary's womb through which Christ entered the world, and the centrality of the incarnational censer in Byzantine Egyptian theology.

Although censers in Dormition scenes would become much more popular outside of North Africa from the eleventh century onward, their presence in Annunciation and Nativity scenes would remain a more regional concern, largely because Mary's fertility and maternal role were of central importance, which made the censer-as-womb motif easily recognizable in those narrative depictions. At the Cathedral of Faras (ancient Pachoras), now at the bottom of Lake Nasser on the border of Sudan and Egypt, one of the largest collections of Nubian Christian frescoes was discovered, excavated, and removed to the National Museum in Warsaw and the Sudan National Museum in Khartoum in the 1960s, just prior to the construction of the Aswan Dam.[40] Although the church was replete with Marian iconography, the

Figure 7

large fresco depicting the Theotokos in the Nativity [Figure 7] on the eastern wall of the northern aisle is one of the most iconographically and stylistically unique among medieval examples.[41] The cathedral is a palimpsest of frescoes ranging from the eighth to the fourteenth century, but the Nativity is from Layer III and dates to approximately 1000.[42] There are obvious Byzantine and Coptic influences in the composition of the scene, with the hierarchically oversized Theotokos reclining on her birthing bed while a cow and donkey watch over the Christ child in the manger and a diminutive Joseph holding a cross-staff gazes upward to the Virgin's smiling face. However, other iconographical decisions seem to be more localized, such as the inclusion of the Archangel Raphael alongside both Gabriel and Michael; the three Magi, labeled Batousora, Melcheon, and Thaddasia, galloping across the landscape on horseback; the named shepherds, Lekotes and Arnias, dressed as indigenous Nubian herders, seemingly running and gesturing excitedly toward the Virgin; a host of angels soaring across the heavens to pay tribute to Mary; and a prostrate Salome below the bed of the Theotokos. The Magi, angels, and Salome all carry olive branches laden with fruit.

Such an extraordinary display of veneration for the Theotokos is complemented by the Archangels Michael and Raphael on the right side of the Virgin. Each archangel holds a golden censer—the pigment used for the censers is the same used for the wings of the angels, Mary's jeweled crown, and the golden threads of the cushioned bed. And each archangel points with an index finger toward the Virgin herself, using the same hand that wields the censer.[43] If the golden censer motif for the incarnational womb of the Virgin were not immediately recognizable on its own, then the hand gestures of Michael and Raphael make the meaning more explicit. The radiant bodies of the two golden censers are equated with the radiant body of the Theotokos on her birthing bed. This is similar in composition to the Marian semidome at the Red Monastery, where both Gabriel and Michael held censers close to the Virgin's body while she held her infant son, emphasizing the metaphor of the fiery womb that offered salvation to the world. The sixth- or seventh-century prayer niche in Chapel XXVIII at Apa Apollo

Figure 7
Nativity on the eastern wall of
the northern aisle of the
Cathedral of Faras, Sudan,
ca. 1000, Khartoum, Sudan
National Museum. Courtesy of
the Polish Centre of Mediterra-
nean Archaeology of the
University of Warsaw, Tomasz
Jakobielski, and the Sudan
National Museum, Khartoum.

Figure 8

at Bawit contains a similar arrangement, with two winged figures labeled "Angel of God" ("ΑΓΓΕΛΟC ΘΕΟΥ," "*Angelos Theou*") and "Angel of the Lord" ("ΑΓΓΕΛΟC ΚΥΡΙΟΥ," "*Angelos Kyriou*") flanking the Theotokos with censers as she sits on a throne, holding the Christ child in a mandorla [Figure 8].[44]

Representing the censer alongside the Theotokos was not the only strategy for emphasizing the power of her incarnational womb. Actual censers played a significant role, too, of course, especially those adorned with scenes from the life of Christ such as the Annunciation and Nativity, which presented a more obvious iconographical connection to the generative womb of the Virgin. As Béatrice Caseau and Susan Ashbrook Harvey have noted of the extant literature—and the archaeological and art historical evidence attests to this as well—prior to the Theodosian Dynasty at the end of the fourth century, there is limited evidence that the Christian liturgy incorporated the use of incense and censers on a large scale. This is partly because of a lingering Neoplatonic distrust of sensory perception as something carnal and counterproductive to communing with the divine, and partly as a way to distinguish the burgeoning Christian community from both Jewish and ancient polytheistic worship practices.[45] Censing was inherently a multisensory and at times hypnotic experience for both the clergy, who interacted bodily with the censer, and the laity, whose senses of smell, sight, and hearing were the primary conduits for reimagining the presence of God in sacred space. By the end of the fourth century, however, attitudes moved toward a cultural and theological embrace of the physical senses as catalysts for the attainment of spiritual perception.

REFRAMING CHRISTOLOGY ON BYZANTINE CENSERS

The Theotokos as golden censer was a near-perfect articulation of this process of transitioning from carnal to spiritual perception, whereby the rigid materiality of bronze (gilded or burnished) could be reimagined as the metaphysical flesh of the holy Virgin. This form of object alchemy effectively bridged past, present, and future into an atemporal, eschatological moment. The virgin birth of Christ was understood as a historical event in the past, the burning of incense in the liturgy occurred in the present, and the salvific womb of the Theotokos promised redemption through the sacrifice of Christ for the future, but all three moments were expressed simultaneously. The salvific agency of the Theotokos, therefore, was inextricably connected to the agency of Christ himself. In approximately the seventh or eighth century, an archetype for a bronze censer emerged that included scenes from the life

Figure 9

of Christ around the exterior of the censer's body [Figure 9].[46] Dozens of these censers have survived, and the selection of narrative scenes from the life of Christ overlap remarkably well with the life of the Theotokos. The fact that so many of the censers have survived and/or have been discovered *in situ* in the Eastern Mediterranean, Levant, and Caucasus regions would suggest a broad appeal and successful distribution network over several centuries.

Syria-Palestine is almost universally accepted as the origin-point for these censers, which were probably mass-produced for pilgrims or exported to areas such as Egypt, where there was a ready market within monasteries that practiced the liturgical offices daily. And Christians were likely not the only patrons of these vessels. The tenth-century geographer Ibn Rustah, writing on the seventh-century Rashidun caliph ʿUmar ibn al-Khattab, notes that ʿUmar gave to the Mosque of Medina a censer made of silver and covered

Figure 8
Watercolor reproduction of
the Virgin and Child
fresco in Chapel XXVIII at
Apa Apollo, Bawit, Egypt,
6th or 7th century.
Courtesy of Clédat 1904,
pl. XCVIb.

5 cm

Figure 9
Drawing of scenes from the
Life of Christ (above) and
detail of the Nativity (below)
on a bronze censer, 7th to
9th century, Cambridge,
Arthur M. Sackler Museum.
Courtesy of the Harvard
Art Museums/
Arthur M. Sackler Museum.

in human figures, which he had procured in Syria.[47] Assuming there is some truth to the account, Islamic metal workshops in the seventh century were limited, and they were not generally known for depicting the human form at this early date. Therefore, it seems very likely that the censer was produced by a Christian workshop in Syria.

Although occasionally there are substitutions for some of the scenes, including the Visitation or Three Magi, most of the censers from this corpus include five distinct scenes: Annunciation, Nativity, Baptism of Christ, Crucifixion, and Entombment with two or three Marys visiting the sepulcher of Christ. Of those five scenes, Mary appears in four of them—the only scene in which she does not appear is the Baptism of Christ. For the Annunciation scene, the Archangel Gabriel rushes toward Mary (usually from the left), who subtly turns away from God's messenger, indicating a sense of discomfort. Christ is completely missing from that scene, although it sets the stage for the drama of the Incarnation and the subsequent narratives that follow, one after another, around the body of the censer. Christ in the manger, with a donkey and ox presiding over him, is the central motif in the Nativity scene. However, Mary on her birthing bed, located on the right of the composition, occupies an almost equally prominent space and forms a visual transition that leads the viewer into the Baptism of Christ scene. For the Crucifixion, Mary stands resolutely with John the Evangelist by Christ's side as a prominent figure in a triangular formation. And at the sepulcher of Christ, which suggests his body without representing it explicitly, Mary is almost as tall as the tomb itself, making her impossible to overlook.

Many of the censers also include the Virgin and Child Enthroned on the underside of the central roundel [Figure 10]. The presence of the Theotokos here validates her association with the burnished censer itself, with the coals inside the censer literally pressing against the bottom seal that bears her image. Censers featuring the life of Christ were not all produced in the same workshop. Style and quality vary considerably across the corpus, suggesting that local workshops could copy the formulaic archetype and use the basic shape, low-relief style, and Christological emphasis to manufacture their own distinct versions of the bronze censer.[48]

Figure 10

The widespread distribution and imitation of these censers point to a robust market for the objects. Probably more frequently than not, they were intended or acquired for liturgical use as handheld instruments. The cult of the Theotokos from the fifth century onward, which paralleled the development of a certain fetishization of her womb as generative agent of salvation, would suggest that the emergence of these gilded- or burnished-bronze censers mirrored the theological development of the Theotokos as golden censer in the Orthodox liturgy. Moreover, they coincide with the beginning of the golden censer motif in monumental painting cycles inside Byzantine churches, most notably along the Nile in Egypt and Nubia. The relatively contemporaneous appearance of censers showing the life of Christ and monumental paintings of the Theotokos as the golden censer was likely a response to changes occurring in the Byzantine liturgy in late antiquity and the early Middle Ages. If so, then the divinely sanctioned power of the Theotokos's womb was implicit to the salvation history on display through the life of Christ.

Figure 10
Detail of the Virgin and Child
Enthroned on a bronze censer,
7th to 8th century, Baltimore,
Walters Art Museum. Courtesy
of the Walters Art Museum.

ENDNOTES

1 On the use of incense in the early Christian church, see Caseau 2007, 75–91; and 2012, 535–48. For more general discussions of the role of scent and/or incense in medieval theology and liturgy, see especially Walter 1982, 137–63; Albert 1990; Caseau 1994; Pfeifer 1997; Ashbrook Harvey 2006; Pentcheva 2010, 17–44; and Caseau Chevallier 2021, 431–46.

2 Some of the earliest Christian references to incense in ritual contexts are pejorative, largely due to the association of incense with non-Christian religious sacrifice and prayer in Greco-Roman temples, as well as worship of the *Lares* and *Penates* in domestic shrines. See, for instance, the *Letter of Barnabas* 2.5; Justin Martyr, *Apologia prima* 13, 37; Athenagoras, *Legatio pro Christianis* 13; Tertullian, *De idololatria* 2; idem, *Apologeticum* 30; Jerome, *Epistula* 14; Augustine, *Epistula* 87; idem, *Epistula* 102.

3 P. Carlsberg 443, Papyrus Carlsberg Collection, University of Copenhagen. The Egyptian fragment, which is unpublished and has yet to be translated, is presently undated.

4 On the eucharistic implications of smell and taste as *synaesthesis* in the liturgical use of incense, see Pentcheva 2010, 39–40.

5 Pentcheva 2010, 36–44, 54–55.

6 As Maria Evangelatou notes, this symbolism seems to have been well developed in Byzantine theology by at least the sixth century, based on its appearance in Pseudo-John the Evangelist, *Liber de dormitione Mariae* 1, 4, 8–10, 26, and 38. Cf. Evangelatou 2005, 119. The trope itself, however, can be found as early as Ambrose of Milan's letter to Felix, bishop of Como, in ca. 380 CE (*Epistula* 4).

7 Evangelatou 2005, 117–31.

8 Evangelatou 2005, 121; and 2019, 84–85.

9 Biblical translators and exegetes have debated the meaning of θυμιατήριον in Heb 9:4 since at least late antiquity, with the Latin Vulgate version of Heb 9:4 using *turibulum* ("censer") over other words that could have made an "altar" interpretation more explicit. Even if the word does suggest an altar in the Hebrews passage, θυμιατήριον was generally used to indicate a handheld censer, not only in extra-biblical Greek literature (including pseudepigraphal texts such as 4 Macc 7:11), but also in the Greek text of the Septuagint itself. In 2 Chr 26:19 of the Septuagint, the word is used to describe King Uzziah's handheld censer. θυμιατήριον is also used in Ezek 8:11 to describe the handheld censers of the seventy elders in Ezekiel's heavenly vision.

10 Ashbrook Harvey 1998, 109–28.

11 Ephrem the Syrian, *Hymn* 9; English translation in McVey 1989, 127.

12 Ephrem the Syrian, *Hymn* 4; English translation in Wickes 2015, 71–72.

13 Ephrem the Syrian, *Homily on the Nativity*; English translation in Brock 2013, 62. On the broader context of Ephrem's fertility imagery and the motif of the Virgin's womb, see especially Weedman 2014.

14 Rabbula of Edessa, *Supplication* 4.9; English translation in Phenix Jr. and Horn 2017, 299.

15 See, for instance, Theodore of Mopsuestia's fifth-century catechetical homily on baptism, where he describes the baptismal font as Mother Church's salvific womb and baptismal initiates as the impregnating semen that result in the birth of a new creation—*Homiliae de baptismo* 4.9.

16 Andrew of Crete, *On the Nativity* 4.5. English translation in Cunningham 2008, 136. For similar references to the Theotokos as the golden censer, see Andrew of Crete, *On the Nativity* 4.2 and idem, *Canon in beatae Mariae nativitatem, PG* 97, 1324C.

17 Germanos, *On the Divine Liturgy* 30; English translation in Meyendorff 1984, 81. See also Ashbrook Harvey 2006, 142–43.

18 Germanos, *Oration on the Annunciation of the Supremely Holy Theotokos* 3; English translation in Cunningham 2008, 224–25.

19 Tarasios of Constantinople, *In SS. Deiparae Praesentationem, PG* 98, 1489A–C.

20 John of Damascus, *In dormitionem B. Mariae* III, *PG* 96, 756D–757A; idem, *In nativitatem B. Mariae* II, *PG* 96, 689C.

21 Joseph the Hymnographer, *Mariale, PG* 105, 1160B and 1397A.

22 Neophytos of Paphos, *Homily on the Presentation of the Virgin* 1; *Homily on the Annunciation* 5; *Catechesis on the Presentation of the Virgin* 1. In Toniolo 1974, 210, 244, and 300.

23 Iakobos of Kakkinobaphos, *In praesentationem SS. Deiparae, PG* 127, 609B; English translation in Evangelatou 2005, 124.

24 Holy Pascha 2008, 550. See also Kyrillos 1963, 67.

25 van Moorsel 1992a, 9 n. 17; see also Muyser 1935, 237.

26 Ethiopian Liturgy 2010, 63. See also Mercer 1915, 323–24; Sumner 1958, 21; 1963, 40–46, especially 42; and Daoud 2005, 33–34.

27 For a more general discussion of the interior frescoes, see Bolman 2009, 9–13; 2010, 119–40, 563–74; and 2012, 75–81. For a more specific discussion of the triconch semidome frescoes, see Laferrière 2008, 22–32, pls. III–IV; and Bolman 2016, especially 129–49.

28 For a fuller exposition of the theology of the apse, see Bolman 2016, 141–46.

29 The eighth bulbous-bodied censer is missing from the upper-right corner of the semidome, where the painting is damaged.

30 Cyril of Alexandria, *Homilia XI: Encomium in sanctam Mariam Deiparam, PG* 77, 1031D; *Liber requiei Mariae* 99; English translation in Shoemaker 2002, 345, which also contains the most extensive discussion to date of the development of the Ethiopic *Liber requiei Mariae*, but additional commentary can be found in Shoemaker 2009, 1–30.

31 Paul van Moorsel and Athanassios Semoglou have dated the encaustic painting to the tenth century, attributing it to the renovations conducted under Abbot Moses of Nisibis—cf. van Moorsel 1992a, 1–16; and Semoglou 2000, 35–41. Karel Innemée, however, pushed the date back to the early eighth century—cf. Innemée 2003, 1–24; 2016. And Lucy-Anne Hunt dated the painting to the 1170s or 1180s—cf. Hunt 1995, 182–232. For broader discussions of the semidome painting, see also van Moorsel 1992b, 5–23; Innemée 1995, 129–32; 2006, 133–41; Kessler 2007, 57–72; and Innemée 2016.

32 van Moorsel 1992a; Hunt 1995.

33 Hunt 1995, 202–10.

34 Hunt 1995, 198.

35 On the Theotokos as the burning bush, see Ledit 1976, 68–70. See also Brubaker and Cunningham (2016) for several chapters addressing the burning bush metaphor in Byzantine art and literature, particularly those by Barker (2016, 91–108), Linardou (2016, 133–49), and Louth (2016, 153–61).

36 Mateos 1962, 254. For early literary examples, see, for instance, Gregory of Nyssa's development of the trope in *Oratio in diem natalem Christi, PG* 46, 1136B and *De vita Moysis* 2.21; and commentary in Gordillo 1960, 117–55. Ephrem the Syrian also uses the metaphor in his fourth-century homily *De nativitate* (not to be confused with his hymn of the same name), as do fifth-century theologians Proclus of Constantinople, *Oratio* 1, and Theodoret of Cyrrhus, *Quaestiones in Octateuchum* 2.6 (*Quaestiones in Exodum*), and sixth-century theologian Severus of Antioch, *Homilia* 67.

37 Cf. Innemée and van Rompay 2002; and Innemée and Nessim Youssef 2007, 69–85.

38 Cf. Evangelatou's analysis of the Dormition scene at Panagia Arakiotissa at Lagoudera, Cyprus, in Evangelatou 2005.

39 Innemée and Nessim Youssef 2007, 72–73. See also Chaîne 1933–34, 272–314.

40 For a catalogue of the frescoes, see especially Michałowski 1966; 1967; 1974; and Jakobielski et al. 2017. For a discussion of the corpus of commemorative wall paintings, see Ochała 2022.

41 Cf. Bentmann 1965, 24–26, 55–56; Michałowski 1966, 18–19, pl. XII; 1967, 63–69, 143–47; 1970, 11–28; 1974, 29, 32, 39, 48, 53, 56–63, 69, 166–68 (earlier tenth-century Nativity as predecessor to the eleventh-century version), 281–83, and 289; Innemée 2013, 187–99; and Jakobielski et al. 2017, 240–47.

42 Although fragments of an eighth-century Nativity on the eastern wall of the northern vestibule of the cathedral show some compositional similarity to the late tenth- or early eleventh-century version, there appears to be less innovation in the earlier design—cf. Jakobielski et al. 2017, 128–31. Only the Nativity scene at the Central Church of Abdallah Nirqi, just north of Faras and which also dates to the late tenth or early eleventh century, is close in composition and, to a lesser degree, style to the Nativity at Faras—cf. van Moorsel, Jacquet, and Schneider 1975, 89–92, pl. 77.

43 For a broader discussion of the Coptic influences at Faras, see Michałowski 1966; 1967; Weitzmann 1970, 325–46; Michałowski 1974; Łaptaś 2003, 137–43; and 2008, 75–85.

44 Cf. Clédat 1904, 153–64, pl. XCVIb.

45 Caseau 1994, 282–92; Ashbrook Harvey 2006, 75–82; and Caseau 2007.

46 For broader studies on the typology of this corpus of bronze censers, see especially Wellen 1960, particularly Appendix Table II (Der christologische Zyklus) and its catalogue of censers; Elbern 1972–74, 447–62; Hamilton 1974, 53–65; Billod 1987, 39–56; and Richter-Siebels 1990.

47 de Goeje 1892, 66. See also Aga-Oglu 1945, 28.

48 Or merely the shape could be appropriated while introducing more indigenous Christian preferences for the iconography. See, for instance, a Nubian censer discovered in a salvage excavation at Old Dongola in 1968—Wyżgoł 2018.

BIBLIOGRAPHY

Aga-Oglu, Mehmet. 1945. "About a Type of Islamic Incense Burner." *Art Bulletin* 27, no. 1: 28–45.

Albert, Jean-Pierre. 1990. *Odeurs de sainteté: La mythologie chrétienne des aromates.* Paris: Éditions de l'École des hautes études en sciences sociales.

Ashbrook Harvey, Susan. 1998. "St Ephrem on the Scent of Salvation." *Journal of Theological Studies* 49: 109–28.

Ashbrook Harvey, Susan. 2006. *Scenting Salvation: Ancient Christianity and the Olfactory Imagination.* Berkeley: University of California Press.

Barker, Margaret. 2016. "Wisdom Imagery and the Mother of God." In *The Cult of the Mother of God in Byzantium: Texts and Images*, edited by Leslie Brubaker and Mary B. Cunningham, 91–108. London: Routledge.

Bentmann, Reinhard. 1965. *Nubien und Byzanz.* Ludwigsburg: Die Karawane.

Billod, Carole. 1987. "Les encensoirs syro-palestiniens de Bâle." *Antike Kunst* 30: 39–56.

Bolman, Elizabeth S. 2009. "Reflections on the Red Monastery Project: 2000–2008." *Bulletin of the American Research Center in Egypt* 194: 9–13.

Bolman, Elizabeth S. 2010. "Painted Skins: The Illusions and Realities of Architectural Polychromy, Sinai and Egypt." In *Approaching the Holy Mountain: Art and Liturgy at St Catherine's Monastery in the Sinai*, edited by Sharon E. J. Gerstel and Robert S. Nelson, 119–40, 563–74. Turnhout: Brepols.

Bolman, Elizabeth S. 2012. "The White Monastery Federation and the Angelic Life." In *Byzantium and Islam: Age of Transition, 7th–9th Century*, edited by Helen C. Evans and Brandie Ratliff, 75–81. New York; New Haven, CT: Metropolitan Museum of Art; Yale University Press.

Bolman, Elizabeth S., ed. 2016. *The Red Monastery Church: Beauty and Asceticism in Upper Egypt.* New Haven, CT: American Research Center in Egypt; Yale University Press.

Brock, Sebastian, ed. and trans. 2013. *The Harp of the Spirit: Poems of Saint Ephrem the Syrian.* 3rd edn. Cambridge: Aquila Books for the Institute for Orthodox Christian Studies.

Brubaker, Leslie, and Mary B. Cunningham, eds. 2016. *The Cult of the Mother of God in Byzantium: Texts and Images.* London: Routledge.

Caseau, Béatrice. 1994. "Εὐωδία: The Use and Meaning of Fragrances in the Ancient World and Their Christianization (100–900 AD)." PhD diss, Princeton University.

Caseau, Béatrice. 2007. "Incense and Fragrances: From House to Church. A Study of the Introduction of Incense in the Early Byzantine Christian Churches." In *Material Culture and Well-Being in Byzantium, 400–1453: Proceedings of the International Conference, Cambridge, 8–10 September 2001*, edited by Michael Grünbart et al., 75–91. Vienna: Österreichischen Akademie der Wissenschaften.

Caseau, Béatrice. 2012. "Constantin et l'encens. Constantin a-t-il procede à une revolution liturgique?" In *Costantino prima e dopo Costantino / Constantine Before and After Constantine*, edited by Giorgio Bonamente, Noël Lenski, and Rita Lizzi Testa, 535–48. Bari: Edipuglia.

Caseau Chevallier, Béatrice. 2021. "Odorat, encensement et encensoirs. Le paysage olfactif des espaces sacrés dans les églises tardo-antiques et byzantines." In *Rituels religieux et sensorialité (Antiquité et Moyen Âge). Parcours de recherche*, edited by Béatrice Caseau Chevallier and Elisabetta Neri, 431–46. Milan: Cinisello Balsamo.

Chaîne, Marius. 1933–34. "Sermon de Théodose, Patriarche d'Alexandrie, sur la dormition et l'assomption de la Vierge." *Revue de l'Orient chrétien* 29: 272–314.

Clédat, Jean. 1904. *Le monastère et la nécropole de Baouît.* Mémoires publiés par les membres de l'Institut Français d'Archéologie Orientale du Caire 12. Cairo: L'Institut Français d'Archéologie Orientale.

Cunningham, Mary B., ed. and trans. 2008. *Wider than Heaven: Eighth-Century Homilies on the Mother of God.* Crestwood, NY: St. Vladimir's Seminary Press.

Daoud, Marcos, trans. 2005. *The Liturgy of the Ethiopian Church.* London: Kegan Paul; reprinted from the original 1954 version, Addis Ababa: Berhane Selam Printing Press.

de Goeje, M. J., ed. 1892. *Kitâb al-A'lâk an-Nafîsa VII, auctore Abû Alî Ahmed ibn Omar ibn Rosteh, et Kitâb al-Boldân, auctore Ahmed ibn abî Jakûb ibn Wâdhih al-Kâtib al-Jakûbî.* Leiden: E. J. Brill, 1892.

Elbern, Victor H. 1972–74. "Zur Morphologie der bronzenen Weihrauchgefässe aus Palästina." *Archivo español de arqueología* 45–47: 447–62.

Ethiopian Liturgy. 2010. መጽሐፈ ቅዳሴ በግእዝ፣ በአማርኛና በእንግሊዝኛ [The Liturgy of the Ethiopian Orthodox Church]. Addis Ababa: ትንሣኤ ማሳተሚያ ድርጅት [Tensae Publishing House].

Evangelatou, Maria. 2005. "The Symbolism of the Censer in Byzantine Representations of the Dormition of the Virgin." In *Images of the Mother of God: Perceptions of the Theotokos in Byzantium*, edited by Maria Vassilaki, 117–31. London; New York: Routledge.

Evangelatou, Maria. 2019. "Krater of Nectar and Altar of the Bread of Life: The Theotokos as Provider of the Eucharist in Byzantine Culture." In *The Reception of the Virgin in Byzantium: Marian Narratives in Texts and Images*, edited by Thomas Arentzen and Mary B. Cunningham, 84–85. Cambridge: Cambridge University Press.

Gordillo, Mauricio. 1960. "La virginidad transcendente de María Madre de Dios en San Gregorio de Nisa y en la Antigua tradición de la Iglesia." *Estudios Marianos* 21: 117–55.

Hamilton, R. W. 1974. "Thuribles: Ancient or Modern?" *Iraq* 36, no. 1–2: 53–65.

Holy Pascha. 2008. *Holy Pascha: Order of Holy Week Services in the Coptic Orthodox Church: Coptic – English – Arabic.* 2nd edn. Jersey City, NJ: Coptic Orthodox Church of Saint Mark.

Hunt, Lucy-Anne. 1995. "The Fine Incense of Virginity: A Late Twelfth Century Wallpainting of the Annunciation at the Monastery of the Syrians, Egypt." *Byzantine and Modern Greek Studies* 15: 182–232.

Innemée, Karel C. 1995. "Deir al-Sourian: The Annunciation as Part of a Cycle?" *Cahiers archéologiques* 43: 129–32.

Innemée, Karel C. 2003. "Keynote Address: Mural Painting in Egypt, Problems of Dating and Conservation." In *Living for Eternity: The White Monastery and Its Neighborhood. Proceedings of a Symposium at the University of Minnesota, Minneapolis, March 6–9, 2003*, edited by Philip Sellew, 1–24. Minneapolis: University of Minnesota.

Innemée, Karel C. 2006. "Encaustic Painting in Egypt." In *L'apport de l'Égypte à l'histoire des techniques: Méthodes, chronologie et comparaisons*, edited by Bernard Mathieu, Dimitri Meeks, and Myriam Wissa, 133–41. Cairo: Institut français d'archéologie orientale.

Innemée, Karel C. 2013. "The Word and the Flesh." In *Christianity and Monasticism in Aswan and Nubia*, edited by Gawdat Gabra and Hany N. Takla, 187–99. New York: American University in Cairo Press.

Innemée, Karel C. 2016. "Dayr al-Suryan: New Discoveries." *Claremont Coptic Encyclopedia*, January 29. https://ccdl.claremont.edu/digital/collection/cce/id/2137/rec/1.

Innemée, Karel C., and Youhanna Nessim Youssef. 2007. "Virgins with Censers: A 10th Century Painting of the Dormition in Deir al-Surian." *Bulletin de la Société d'Archéologie Copte* 46: 69–85.

Innemée, Karel C., and Lucas van Rompay. 2002. "Deir al-Surian (Egypt): New Discoveries of 2001–2002." *Hugoye: Journal of Syriac Studies* 5, no. 2. https://hugoye.bethmardutho.org/article/hv5n2innemeevanrompay.

Jakobielski, Stefan, et al. 2017. *Pachoras Faras: The Wall Paintings from the Cathedrals of Aetios, Paulos and Petros.* Warsaw: Polish Centre of Mediterranean Archaeology, University of Warsaw.

Kessler, Herbert L. 2007. "'Byzantine Art and the West': Forty Years after the Athens Exhibition and Dumbarton Oaks Symposium." In *Medioevo mediterraneo. L'Occidente, Bisanzio e l'Islam. Atti del Convegno internazionale di studi, Parma, 21–25 settembre 2004*, edited by Arturo Carlo Quintavalle, 57–72. Milan: Electa.

Kyrillos, Abba VI. 1963. *The Coptic Liturgy.* Cairo: Coptic Orthodox Patriarchate.

Laferrière, Pierre. 2008. *La bible murale dans les sanctuaires coptes.* Cairo: Institut français d'archéologie orientale.

Łaptaś, Magdalena. 2003. "Representation of the Angelic Hierarchy in a Nativity Scene from Faras Cathedral." *Gdańsk Archaeological Museum African Reports* 2: 137–43.

Łaptaś, Magdalena. 2008. "A Feast of the Archangel Michael? A New Interpretation of a Mural Painting from Old Dongola." *Eastern Christian Art* 5: 75–85.

Ledit, Joseph. 1976. *Marie dans la liturgie de Byzance.* Paris: Beauchesne.

Linardou, Kallirroe. 2016. "Depicting the Salvation: Typological Images of Mary in the Kokkinobaphos Manuscripts." In *The Cult of the Mother of God in Byzantium: Texts and Images*, edited by Leslie Brubaker and Mary B. Cunningham, 133–49. London: Routledge.

Louth, Andrew. 2016. "John of Damascus on the Mother of God as a Link between Humanity and God." In *The Cult of the Mother of God in Byzantium: Texts and Images*, edited by Leslie Brubaker and Mary B. Cunningham, 153–61. London: Routledge.

Mateos, Juan, ed. and trans. 1962. *Le typicon de la Grande Église: Ms. Sainte-Croix nº 40, Xᵉ siècle*, vol. 1. Rome: Pont. Institutum Orientalium Studiorum.

McVey, Kathleen E., ed. and trans. 1989. *Ephrem the Syrian: Hymns.* New York: Paulist Press.

Mercer, Samuel A. B. 1915. *The Ethiopic Liturgy: Its Sources, Development, and Present Form.* Milwaukee, WI; London: The Young Churchman Company; A. R. Mowbray & Company.

Meyendorff, Paul, ed. and trans. 1984. *Germanus of Constantinople: On the Divine Liturgy.* Crestwood, NY: St. Vladimir's Seminary Press.

Michałowski, Kazimierz. 1966. *Faras, centre artistique de la Nubie chrétienne.* Leiden: Nederlands Instituut voor het Nabije Oosten.

Michałowski, Kazimierz. 1967. *Faras: Die Kathedrale aus dem Wüstensand.* Zurich: Benziger Verlag.

Michałowski, Kazimierz. 1970. "Open Problems of Nubian Art and Culture in the Light of the Discoveries at Faras." In *Kunst und Geschichte Nubiens in christlicher Zeit: Ergebnisse und Probleme auf Grund der jüngsten Ausgrabungen*, edited by Erich Dinkler, 11–28. Recklinghausen: Verlag Aurel Bongers.

Michałowski, Kazimierz. 1974. *Faras: Wall Paintings in the Collection of the National Museum in Warsaw*. Warsaw: Wydawnictwo Artystyczno-Graficzne.

Muyser, Jacob. 1935. *Maria's heerlijkheid in Egypte: Een studie der koptische Maria-literatuur*. Leuven: Sint-Alfonsusdr.

Ochała, Grzegorz. 2022. "The Cathedral of Faras as a Monument of Medieval Nubian Memory." *Dumbarton Oaks Papers* 76: 31–68.

Pentcheva, Bissera V. 2010. *The Sensual Icon: Space, Ritual, and the Senses in Byzantium*. University Park: Pennsylvania State University Press.

Pfeifer, Michael. 1997. *Der Weihrauch: Geschichte, Bedeutung, Verwendung*. Regensburg: Verlag Friedrich Pustet.

Phenix, Robert R. Jr., and Cornelia B. Horn, eds. and trans. 2017. *The Rabbula Corpus: Comprising the* Life of Rabbula, *His Correspondence, a Homily Delivered in Constantinople, Canons, and Hymns*. Atlanta, GA: SBL Press.

Richter-Siebels, Ilse. 1990. "Die palästinensischen Weihrauchgefässe mit Reliefszenen aus dem Leben Christi." PhD diss., Freie Universität Berlin.

Semoglou, Athanassios. 2000. "L'Annonciation de Deir es-Souriani en Égypte." *Cahiers archéologiques* 48: 35–41.

Shoemaker, Stephen J. 2002. *Ancient Traditions of the Virgin Mary's Dormition and Assumption*. Oxford: Oxford University Press.

Shoemaker, Stephen J. 2009. "The Virgin Mary's Hidden Past: From Ancient Marian Apocrypha to the Medieval *Vitae Virginis*." *Marian Studies* 60: 1–30.

Sumner, Claude. 1958. *The Ethiopic Liturgy*. Addis Ababa: Artistic Printing Press.

Sumner, Claude. 1963. "The Ethiopic Liturgy: An Analysis." *Journal of Ethiopian Studies* 1, no. 1: 40–46.

Toniolo, Ermanno M. 1974. "Omelie e Catechesi mariane inedite di Neofito il Recluso (1134–1220 c.)." *Marianum* 36: 184–315.

van Moorsel, Paul. 1992a. "Deir es Souriani Revisited." *Nubian Letters* 17: 1–16.

van Moorsel, Paul. 1992b. "Une Annonciation faite à Marie au Monastère des Syriens. (une découverte de l'IFAO en mai 1991)." *Bulletin de la Société Française d'Égyptologie* 124: 5–23.

van Moorsel, Paul, Jean Jacquet, and Hans Schneider. 1975. *The Central Church of Abdallah Nirqi*. Leiden: E. J. Brill, 1975.

Walter, Christopher. 1982. *Art and Ritual of the Byzantine Church*. London: Variorum Publications.

Weedman, E. Michelle C. 2014. "Mary's Fertility as the Model of the Ascetical Life in Ephrem the Syrian's *Hymns of the Nativity*." PhD diss., Marquette University.

Weitzmann, Kurt. 1970. "Some Remarks on the Sources of the Fresco Paintings of the Cathedral of Faras." In *Kunst und Geschichte Nubiens in christlicher Zeit: Ergebnisse und Probleme auf Grund der jüngsten Ausgrabungen*, edited by Erich Dinkler, 325–46. Recklinghausen: Verlag Aurel Bongers.

Wellen, G. A. 1960. *Theotokos. Eine ikonographische Abhandlung über das Gottesmutterbild in frühchristlicher Zeit*. Utrecht; Antwerp: Uitgeverij het Spectrum.

Wickes, Jeffrey T., ed. and trans. 2015. *St. Ephrem the Syrian: The Hymns on Faith*. Washington, DC: Catholic University of America Press.

Wyżgoł, Maciej. 2018. "A Decorated Bronze Censer from the Cathedral in Old Dongola." *Polish Archaeology in the Mediterranean* 26, no. 1: 773–86.

MATTER MAGIC

CENSER

MATTER MAGIC

CENSER

BETWEEN MATTER AND MAGIC, OVER LAND AND SEA: A MIDDLE EASTERN CENSER IN SWEDEN

Margaret S. Graves

In 1943, so the story goes, two boys playing in a forest in eastern Sweden uncovered a remarkable cache of metalwork. Hidden in a crevice between two boulders [Figure 1], partially buried under a layer of earth and stones, were an extraordinary censer, three pairs of tongs, and a lidded spout apparently detached from a larger object [Figure 2].

The trope of the small boy who unearths a fantastic treasure by accident is a popular one with dealers seeking to explain the mysterious appearance of previously undocumented objects. In this case, however, the whole find seems to have gone straight into the hands of the local authorities. They placed it in the Gävleborg County Museum, where it remains to this day. No interview with the boys is recorded in the museum's archives and recent efforts to contact them revealed that both are now dead, but there seems no reason to doubt the story.[1] The findspot, then, can be fixed securely enough to the woods near the parish church at Hamrånge, north of the port town of Gävle on Sweden's Baltic coast. The cache itself, though, has remained something of a puzzle since its first publication by the Swedish archaeologist of Iran and Central Asia, Ture J. Arne, in the year of its discovery.[2]

The most impressive object in the group is the spectacular cast copper-alloy censer.[3] Taking the form of a domed cuboidal building mounted on four hooved feet, with a long projecting handle, it stands an imposing 34.5 cm high. The three pairs of simple beaten copper-alloy tongs found with it proved, when squeezed in 2018, to have maintained their springiness up to the present; presumably they were once used to manipulate burning charcoal and aromatics inside the censer. Those few scholars who have written about the Gävle censer agree it is from the Middle East and probably eighth or ninth century in date, but geographic attributions have ranged from the eastern Mediterranean to Afghanistan.[4]

The singularity of the Gävle censer and the debates about its site of manufacture reveal how fragile the taxonomies of medieval Middle Eastern metalwork really are. Statements of origin that appear on museum labels, their beguiling confidence only occasionally hampered by a question mark, mask countless hours of scholarly labor and are fraught with contingencies. The Gävle censer has a documented findspot—a rare and precious thing in a corpus stuffed with objects that surfaced through the art market—but it does not tell us where it was made. It has cognates of a sort, but there is nothing else that looks exactly like it. It merges elements that appear elsewhere, but to what end? Above all, what was it for? What did it do before it came to rest between two rocks in Sweden? And what can be told from an architectonic form for emitting smoke that lurches up on four hooved feet, with walls and dome animated by a vibrant flow of palmette openwork?

This essay will take the Gävle censer as its primary focus in an exploration of incense burners in the Middle East during the early and medieval Islamic eras, scrutinizing the material body of the censer itself for traces of its production and first stages of existence. In the course of this exploration, the chapter will look across sacred and quotidian censing, the Viking contacts with the Islamic world that must have brought the censer to Sweden, and medieval Middle Eastern metalworking traditions. Finally, it will turn to the rather overlooked roles of both incense and metalcasting

Figure 1
Findspot of the Gävle censer:
woods near Hamrånge
parish church, Sweden.
Photo taken ca. 1943.
Image: Länsmuseet Gävleborg.

Figure 2
Cast copper alloy censer and
beaten copper alloy tongs,
found together (lidded spout
from same cache not pictured),
8th or early 9th century,
height of censer 34.5 cm.
Image: Länsmuseet Gävleborg.

in Islamicate occult practices as possible factors in the formation of this enigmatic object. The Gävle censer is at once a "type"—one of the many domed censers made in metalwork across the early Islamic world—and a unicum; a primer and a puzzle.

CENSING THE EARLY ISLAMIC WORLD

The dense materiality and idiosyncratic form of the Gävle censer open several questions about the use of incense burners (Arabic: *majmar* or *mijmara*, *mabkhara* or *mibkhara*; Persian: *'ūd-sūz*; Turkish: *buhurdan*) in the early Islamic era. Used across almost all social and sectarian groups in Western Asia to demarcate special occasions and states of being through scented smoke, censers were employed to burn a variety of woods and resins. Aloeswood was one of the more common substances for censing (hence its place in the Persian word for censer, *'ūd-sūz*, literally "aloes burner"), but many others were also burned for their scent, singly or in combination.[5] Scholarly discussion has long focused on the pious and social uses of incense in Islam—liturgical, funerary, domestic—and has often tended to treat censers themselves as largely fungible when it comes to categories of use.[6] This is perhaps understandable when one looks at the scant textual evidence, which very rarely gives any description of what an incense burner was like when mentioning that one was used. Censers are normally known in the textual sources by what they *do*, in the most general sense, not by how they *are*.

For example, the extensive use of censers in scenting the sacred spaces of early Islam—including the Ka'ba itself—is implicit in reports of the use of incense as part of the perfuming of those sites, a form of pious patronage. Rarely, however, are the censers themselves mentioned.[7] In this aspect the historical texts are similar to those that describe the scentworld of Paradise, which such perfumed earthly spaces intentionally evoke. The Hadith tell us that the people of Paradise will burn aloeswood (*'ūd*) in their censers, but not what those censers look like, nor what they are made from.[8] Only for very exceptional objects do the historical texts provide any significant record of the instruments of censing, like the silver censer (*mijmara*, lit. "place of burning") with modeled forms (*tamāthīl*) that was donated to the mosque at Medina by the caliph 'Umar (r. 634–44).[9]

Similarly, textual sources attest to the widespread funerary, hygienic, and domestic uses of incense in the pre-modern Middle East, from the Prophetic tradition advising Muslims to perfume the shrouds of the deceased with *bakhūr* (or *bukhūr*: incense, sometimes specifically frankincense) to the sweet scents of incense and other perfumes used at social gatherings. Those sources rarely describe the censers used for these practices in even the most perfunctory terms.[10] There are some exceptions where materials are mentioned and incense burners are noted as being made of gold, silver, or clay, and there is even a late eleventh-century Arabic mandate on image production that mentions the tops of censers made in the form of birds (a widespread phenomenon in the medieval material record, from Central Asia to Coptic Egypt and beyond).[11] For the most part, however, the authors of the medieval textual records were apparently unconcerned with recording things like form, decoration, or how censers were held or manipulated.

The material evidence is quite different. The clattering masses of surviving censers from the early and medieval Middle East and North Africa range from simple fired earthenware dishes to carved stone to masterpieces of metalcasting, revealing the richly variegated material dimensions of censing within pre-modern Islam.[12] Any attempt to parse through the great variety of manufactured forms used for burning incense usually ends in the creation of typologies that, while useful for understanding regional trends in portable objects, do not necessarily do much to illuminate individual censers or their immediate contexts of use. To take only metalwork, the most plentiful surviving medium in which incense burners were made, we find a profusion of extant formal types from the medieval Middle East: standing; handled; mounted on three feet or four; suspended from chains; bowl-shaped; lidded; domed; spherical; zoomorphic; arcaded; with drawers for incense and without, etc. Each of these types becomes its own taxonomic endpoint in catalogues and inventories, strengthening the tendency to understand individual censers as exemplars of morphological categories rather than autonomous objects with individuated relationships to human life and ritual.

One way to overcome the reductive regime of the inventory is to consider other means by which censers connect with human life and ritual, beyond the well-canvassed realms of sensate piety and social hygiene. A further important role for censing in the pre-modern regions dominated by Islam is the connection between suffumigation and the occult sciences (ʿulūm al-ghayb). The occult applications of incense in pre-modern Islam have received very scant attention until quite recently and are yet to appear in art historical scholarship on the large, heterogenous corpus of Islamic-era censers.[13] There are several reasons for the longstanding exclusion of the occult in Islamic studies at large. Early Orientalist scholars often sidelined anti-rationalist practices, regarding them as a sort of folkish static to be cleared off more important things, like court histories and "proper" science, while modern orthodox Islamic movements have frequently sought to de-legitimize magic practices within the faith. Moreover, some of the surviving written sources from the medieval era emphasize orthopraxy and seek to discredit the occult practices of their own and earlier times, further obscuring the historical integration of such things into Islamic practice. However, a major upsurge in scholarship on the Islamic occult sciences in recent years has started to bring magic practices back into the purview of historians, and the time is ripe for integrating these new investigations into the art historical study of objects of use.[14]

While this essay does not seek to make a definitive statement on the Gävle censer as an instrument of magic, the censer's early date, striking morphology, and enigmatic itinerary, along with its inscription and material, all encourage a line of questioning that probes more deeply into the occult dimensions of censing in Islam. This makes it possible to set the material remains of medieval censing—the incense burners themselves—back into a discourse around substance, smoke, and efficacy that includes magical practices. Before turning to the occult, however, this essay will first consider the censer's possible route to Sweden, as well as its manufacture and material qualities, and the ongoing question of its geographical area of origin.

THE NAME OF GOD AND THE MOBILITY OF METAL

The identification of the Gävle censer as something that belongs to the Islamic world rests on stylistic analysis and an inscription in Arabic incised into the only blank surface of the object visible during use, the space underneath the joint between the handle and the main body [Figure 3]. The words

Figure 3

"*bi-ism/illāh al-raḥmān*"—with the "*al-raḥmān*" inverted and sandwiched between the two parts of *bi-ism/illāh*—inscribe the object with the first part of the formula that opens every sura of the Qur'an but one: *bi-ismillāh al-raḥmān al-raḥīm*, "In the name of God, the compassionate, the merciful."[15] The bismillah is one of the most extensively used pious phrases in Muslim life, traditionally invoked before any significant act. Epitaphs and graffiti from the first century of Islam include the bismillah as an opening formula, although Leor Halevi has argued that the earliest uses of the bismillah in epitaphs are not absolute indicators of Muslim identity and should instead be viewed as markers of the gradual process of Islamization.[16] In spite of its cultural centrality the bismillah is not very often found inscribed alone on objects of use, with the exception of some engraved gemstones and seals.

The epigraphy on the censer is scratched in a rather awkward rectilinear script, the letter shapes and baselines rendered slightly uneven and rigid. The result is a script that follows some archaic Kufic conventions but confounds any precise dating through calligraphic style. In this respect it is similar to inscriptions seen on some hardstone seals and amulets.[17] In fact the script is close to Linear Kufic, where all letters are shown on one leveled line without following the conventions of ligature and letter separation that normally govern Arabic script. Linear Kufic was often used for magical inscriptions from the early Islamic period up to the thirteenth century (by which latter point it was quite archaic, and presumably used for that reason); the script of the *bi-ism/illāh* on the Gävle censer is formally similar to that used for magical letter sequences on some medieval Arabic amulets and sealstones.[18] Differences in the letter forms (especially evident in the letter *mīm*) suggest that the inverted *al-raḥmān* was possibly added post-production, by a different hand.

By contrast with the inscription, the fine lines feathering the cast openwork palmettes on the censer—which were probably present on the original model but enhanced with a sharp instrument after casting was complete—are so fluid and accomplished from top to bottom that it is hard to believe the inscription could have been made by the same hand, even allowing for a craftsman who was not fully literate. Accumulated corrosion and dirt make it hard to distinguish fine work on the mold from cold-worked incising on early bronzes, and it is difficult to tell if the *bi-ism/illāh* was incised into the casting model or if it was driven into the bronze surface after the projecting handle was attached.[19] It is possible that the whole inscription is a post-production addition to the object, date uncertain but made prior to the object's departure from the Islamic world. On the other hand, it is also quite possible that the *bi-ism/illāh*, at least, was incised on the model, but was just not very neatly executed.

As Arne and others have already noted, the censer's discovery near the Swedish coast surely indicates that it is one of a sizable corpus of objects, including vessels, items of adornment, and huge numbers of coins, brought to Scandinavia during the Viking Age through trade connections with the Middle East and Central Asia.[20] These transregional routes were chronicled most famously by Ibn Fadlān (d. ca. 960) in his vivid account of a mission from Baghdad to the Volga region in 921–22.[21] Ibn Fadlān's encounters with the tattooed and unwashed people he called the *Rūs*, believed to be Norsemen, made an indelible impression on the caliphal envoy, while contemporary Persian authors also report *Rūs* traders selling slaves along the Volga.[22]

Prior to the tenth-century reports of the Volga trade routes, however, the earliest appearance of the *Rūs* in Arabic literature is found in the mid-ninth-century geography of Ibn Khurradadbih (d. ca. 912). This text describes *Rūs* traders traveling the Black Sea as well as the Caspian and sometimes transporting their merchandise—furs and swords—by camel all the way from Gurgan, on the southern edge of the Caspian, to Baghdad.[23] The numismatic evidence from Sweden also suggests Viking connections with the ʿAbbasid center into the ninth century: coins minted in Iraq and (to a lesser extent) the western provinces of the Islamic world have been found in significant numbers in Swedish coin hoards. By the time of Ibn Fadlān's mission in the tenth century, however, central ʿAbbasid coinage had been overtaken by a flood of silver dirhams from Central Asian mints, seemingly reflecting shifting trade routes and a reorientation toward the Samanid territories of eastern Iran and Central Asia in the later part of the Viking Age.[24]

Identifying the Gävle censer with the Islamic world in the age of Viking contact is logical and undoubtedly correct. However, the intercontinental community of faith referred to as "the Islamic world" is a very big field. Arne, in the first published study of the censer, compared it with objects from Egypt, Iraq, and Iran and suggested a manufacture date no later than 800 CE.[25] In the last thirty-five years attributions for the Gävle censer have swung around rather wildly. Karin Ådahl initially followed Arne in suggesting that it could be from either Iran or the eastern Mediterranean; however, in a later publication (with input from the specialist in Persian metalwork Assadullah Souren Melikian-Chirvani) she fixed on Khurasan, a historic region encompassing northeastern Iran and much of Afghanistan.[26] Ådahl also expanded the possible date range slightly, but believed the piece to date from no later than the end of the ninth century—a *terminus ante quem* with which I would concur on stylistic grounds. Vladislav Darkevic attributed it to Iraq.[27] James Allan and Almut von Gladiss both placed it in Iran: "the old Sasanian heartlands," in Allan's words.[28]

The arguments for Iran/Khurasan rest primarily on the numismatic evidence of significant Viking trading contact with the eastern Islamic world—which is indisputable but does not negate the possibility of objects from the central Islamic lands making their way to Sweden in the eighth or ninth century—and on stylistic assertions. I believe the latter to be mistaken. The palmette designs of the openwork and the stepped merlons have been linked by Ådahl and others with late Sasanian architectural decoration in Iran, but the exchange of ideas between late Sasanian Iran and the lands to the west meant that similar forms are present in architectural decoration in Greater Syria and Mesopotamia by the seventh century.[29] Similarly, the lobed finial of the censer, linked by Ådahl with Central Asian lotus designs, is in fact closely comparable with forms found on censers from Egypt or Greater Syria.[30] Moreover, there is little complex relief decoration on the cast copper-alloy objects that survive from early Islamic Iran, apart from the almond-shaped bosses appearing on some vessels.[31] The modeled openwork of the Gävle censer does not, to my knowledge, resemble anything else that can be attributed to the metalworking traditions of early Islamic Iran. I first suggested in 2018 that the censer should probably be attributed to the eastern Mediterranean region or Mesopotamia.[32] While I will not repeat my earlier arguments in detail here, I will lay out some additional material for the case for an origin in Greater Syria or Mesopotamia, using this as an opportunity to probe deeper into the material and religio-occult histories of metalcasting in the region. This question of geographic origin is not just a fussy scholar's sticking point. The mobility of handled censers certainly means that such objects are often hard to pin down to precise sites of origin, but there are questions about use, valency, and cultural resonance that can only be furthered by some sense of locale, with more specificity than just the pan-Islamic context. To steal a line from Borges, "To investigate its precursors is not to subject oneself to a miserable drudgery of legal or detective work; it is to examine the movements, probings, adventures, glimmers, and premonitions of the human spirit."[33]

OPENWORK AND METALCASTING IN
THE MEDIEVAL MIDDLE EAST

The attribution of orphaned artifacts like the Gävle censer is a funny business. The process relies heavily on matching formal and material elements with those of other objects that can (hopefully) be tied more securely to a place and date of origin. However, because most medieval censers from the Middle East first appeared not via scientific excavation but on the art market without any reliable information about findspots, this kind of connoisseurship can easily create echo chambers when speculative attributions start to amplify each other. Caution is always necessary.

A major part of the problem in determining the origins of medieval Middle Eastern metalwork is the limited number of documentary sources available versus the mass of undocumented objects. As a result of this, a somewhat lopsided picture has emerged in scholarship, with the metalworking industry of medieval Khurasan (northeastern Iran and northern Afghanistan) receiving more attention than that of almost any other area of the Middle East or Central Asia. The material and the textual sources do seem to be plentiful for this region, but the situation is complicated by longstanding scholarly and commercial tendencies to attribute everything that is remarkable in Islamic-era metalwork to Khurasan—including many objects of uncertain provenance. James Allan noted long ago that some scholars "have been at pains to emphasise the role of Khurasan as the metalworking center *par excellence* of Islamic Iran, if not of the whole of eastern Islam," but, he continues, this should not be allowed to overshadow the fact that in the first centuries of Islam extremely fine cast copper-alloy wares were produced in Mesopotamia, Greater Syria, and elsewhere.[34] This is unsurprising when one considers that metalworkers in the region were using the lost-wax casting technique to create complex three-dimensional objects before the end of the fourth millennium BCE, as seen from artifacts excavated in modern-day Israel and Iraq.[35] The spectacular brazier excavated at Mafraq, Jordan in 1986 shows that the ancient Near Eastern tradition of lost-wax casting survived in the region into the Islamic period.[36] Moreover, a famous early Islamic cast copper-alloy ewer, now in the Georgian National Museum in Tbilisi, names its own place of manufacture as Basra (in modern Iraq) and showcases the virtuosity and versatility of metalcasters working in the central Islamic lands of the eighth and ninth centuries.[37]

In terms of manufacture, the Gävle censer has been cast, using the lost-wax technique, in three main openwork parts: the upper section (including the domed top and finial), the body, and the handle. The quantities of highly skilled labor and copper alloy expended in the successful casting

3

4

5

6

7

Details of the Gävle censer:

Figure 3
Inscription under handle,
reading *bi-ism/illāh al-raḥmān.*

Figure 4
Domed lid with a corner hole
revealed where part of the
"parapet" section has broken off.

Figures 5 and 6
Base viewed from inside
and outside.

Figure 7
Detail of cast openwork.

Images: Margaret S. Graves.

of these three sizable, complex, and richly decorated forms are noteworthy. Next, the handle was soldered onto the body, as were the separately cast feet, while the top and bottom parts of the body were once jointed by a simple hinge now missing its upper section and pin. The parapet of stepped merlons around the outer edge of the lid is a separate stage of production. It has been cut from beaten sheet metal and bent to wrap around the object, fixed to the flat top surface of the cast lid's square section with four pins running through soldered corner braces [Figure 4]. Four cast "pomegranate" finials, a form found quite frequently on Middle Eastern metalwork of the early Islamic era, were once soldered onto the corner merlons of the parapet, amplifying the sculptural extravagance of the object's upper section.[38] However, there are four small holes cast in the flat surface of the lid section, one of which is visible in Figure 4. These suggest the piece might once have had, or been intended to have, some other kind of projecting component set into each corner. The parapet section might therefore be a later addition to the object, making up for the loss (or non-realization) of whatever was originally supposed to occupy the four corners. Finally, opening the Gävle censer reveals the contradiction of the cast openwork, between the delicacy of the external designs and the roughness of the back surface. A kind of figure/ground effect unfolds when viewing the openwork design on the base from inside and outside [Figures 5 and 6]. Openwork in the base of an incense burner as an aid to air circulation during use is perhaps unusual but certainly not unheard of—as shown by the celebrated thirteenth-century cast and inlaid handled censer made at Damascus and signed by Muḥammad ibn Khutlakh al-Mawṣilī, which also has an openwork base.[39]

Having briefly considered what it took to make the Gävle censer, how should we approach the *unheimlich* semiotic register of its form, an architectonic domed cube mounted on feet that look like they are ready to walk across the room? We can begin—quite traditionally—by generating a material context—i.e., looking for other censers like it.[40] The Gävle censer has a small number of close comparators: a very famous incense burner in the Freer Gallery [Figure 8], and two in the Coptic Museum in Cairo, one of which is in exceptional condition [Figure 9] while the other is more degraded, with only the lid surviving.[41] The Freer censer has been subject to varying attributions but the consensus is largely settled on Egypt,[42] while the more complete of the two examples in the Coptic Museum was reportedly found at Ahnas in Middle Egypt.[43] The four corner domes on these two examples suggest that something similar might originally have been planned for the Gävle censer. The overall architectonic form of the piece, then, can be fairly confidently connected with Egyptian/eastern Mediterranean metal-casting, in spite of attempts to link it to later Central Asian architecture.[44] The very striking architectonic form of a domed cube has, as I have discussed elsewhere, immediate parallels in ciboria, baldachins, and other honorific structures of the late antique Mediterranean world; these preceded the domed cube's later ascent in the funerary architecture of the eastern Islamic world from the tenth century onwards.[45] The imposing form of the Gävle censer thus taps into the gravity of the domed cube as an honorific architectonic unit, at a moment when experiments with this form in metalcasting ran alongside experiments with it in masonry architecture, across a range of scales.

Figure 4

Figures 5 and 6

Figure 8
Figure 9

Figure 8
Cast copper alloy censer,
8th or 9th century,
height 31.5 cm,
National Museum of
Asian Art, Washington D.C.,
F1952.1. Image: National
Museum of Asian Art.

Figure 9
Cast copper alloy censer,
reportedly found at Ahnas,
Egypt, 8th or 9th century,
height: 27 cm,
Coptic Museum, Cairo, 5205.
Image: Eternal Egypt.

Looking toward the eastern Mediterranean context, recent excavations indicate that metalcasting practices were more deeply entangled around the region in the late antique and early Islamic periods than was once believed. Early cast censers excavated in Jordan and Israel suggest that the conventional attribution of some celebrated domed openwork censers to Egypt should be revisited, and contexts in Greater Syria considered.[46] Excavations in Israel have also revealed major finds of medieval cast copper-alloy materials: the metalwork hoards uncovered at Tiberias and Caesarea between 1989 and 1998 include large numbers of copper-alloy objects made with lost-wax casting.[47] These are mostly from the tenth and eleventh centuries but suggestive of older prototypes that can be traced to Roman and Coptic traditions.[48]

In the Gävle censer lost-wax casting is the technique, and openwork is the product of that technique. There is more than one way, though, to produce openwork in cast metal. The thick cast and detailed surface patterning of the openwork on the Gävle censer, with its rip and roughness around the voids on the reverse, is different from that seen on the cast copper-alloy vessels of medieval Khurasan, where there is a greater propensity for closely knotted designs and much simpler surface decoration within the openwork.[49] To coin a textile analogy, where the cast openwork on the Gävle censer hangs with a bulky flatness, like a thickly embroidered textile, Khurasanian cast openwork tends to operate more like a three-dimensional net. Yet another mode of openwork characterizes many of the cast censers from the eastern Mediterranean/Egyptian littoral. These are typified by more open scrolling vegetal forms based on late antique vinescroll designs, like those that delicately web the domes of the Freer censer and the sides of the example in the Coptic Museum, and are quite distinct from the dense winged palmettes of the Gävle censer. There do, however, seem to be parallels in manufacturing between the Gävle and Freer censers, where the fine recessed lines that enhance so much of the design were cast in place but possibly also further defined with a sharp instrument after casting.[50]

While it is dense, the openwork of the Gävle censer is certainly not clumsy. Over much of the surface of the object the scrolling openwork design of the repeating winged palmette pattern is executed with a captivating skill. Its power lies not in perfect symmetry but in its modeling of surface, the plastic capture of a delicate organicist growth that is at once vegetal and completely removed from the natural world. In some passages of the openwork the surface seems almost mobile, oscillating through sharply defined

Figure 7

s-curves with indented lobes and fine, feathery incisions [Figure 7]. At points it almost seems to capture the flow of molten material and the changing states of bronze, recalling some of the alchemical dimensions of metalcasting and metal alloys in early and medieval Arabic literature—a point that will be discussed further below.[51] In other places the design is less fluid, and the eye is drawn to the spaces between the palmettes.[52]

The Gävle censer is unique, then, and it draws the eye and the fingers towards itself, but where was it made? On the basis of technique, morphology, and design I think this object should be attributed not to Khurasan but to the metalcasting traditions of the "central Islamic lands," Greater Syria or Mesopotamia, in the early Islamic era. It is instructive to look to the so-called "Marwan ewer" found south of Cairo, and its cognates. The cast copper-alloy ewers in this group, with their elaborate piece-cast bird-shaped spouts and openwork neck sections, have been attributed at various points to both Syrian and Mesopotamian workmanship of the eighth or early ninth century.[53] It is here that we find the closest parallel in metalcasting for the oscillating palmette designs of the Gävle censer. These are found in the winged palmettes, cast in relief and crowned with pomegranates, that adorn the Metropolitan Museum's cockerel-spouted copper-alloy ewer, below its handle [Figure 10]. The palmettes on the Metropolitan Museum's ewer are larger than those on the Gävle censer and have been executed with greater freedom—afforded by their liberation from any structural role—but the close formal and technical similarities between the two sets of palmette designs solidify the link between the Gävle censer and the Mesopotamian or Syrian traditions of metalcasting that produced complex, piece-cast copper-alloy vessels in the early Islamic period.

Figure 10

This parsing of comparanda, of formal elements and production techniques, allows us to set a profoundly mysterious censer in Sweden back into the production context of eighth- or early ninth-century Mesopotamia or Syria. It's not a very precise attribution, but it's an acceptable one for an orphaned piece of early metalwork, and more tenable than Khurasan. This matters not so much as a taxonomic pursuit in its own right, but as a means of orientation towards the cultural environment and intellectual currents that could have given rise to such a remarkable object. And so, with the Gävle censer now linked to a milieu where early Islamic practices comingled with deeply embedded traditions of astrological and occult science, we turn finally to the last part of this analysis.

SMOKE AND METAL, MATTER AND MAGIC

In use, the extraordinary form of the Gävle censer would have been partially dematerialized and destabilized through the emission of smoke, a seemingly substanceless yet visually perceptible phenomenon. Attempting to imagine the appearance of the object in use, with smoke curling upwards from the openwork of the dome, leads to my last consideration in this study: the roles of incense and censers in Islamicate magic. There are two important aspects of the Gävle censer that should be considered in relation to occult science. One is the centrality of thurification to early Islamicate occult practices. The other is the very strong connection between the art of skilled metalcasting and the occult science of talismans.

First, smoke. That inherently mysterious and liminal entity assumes forms, seems to touch, obscures matter, and affects vision—all instantaneously, perpetually changing and then dispersing entirely, leaving only an olfactory trace of itself behind. Long associations between the unfurling of incense smoke and the occult take many forms. For example, libanomancy, or divination from incense smoke, was evidently a significant practice in ancient Babylonia and the Greco-Roman world.[54] There is far less textual documentation of it in the Islamic era, although Ibn Khaldūn, writing in the fourteenth century and from a largely anti-occultist position, describes something that might be libanomancy or might equally refer to a form of narco-hypnosis, whereby censing and music are deployed to induce a trance-like state and see visions.[55] It is also true that incense smoke seems to have associations in some quarters with chicanery, specifically as a substance that could be used to befuddle the senses and create an otherworldly atmosphere. This much can be seen from the thirteenth-century *Kitāb al-mukhtār fī kashf al-asrār* of al-Jawbarī, a remarkable work that details all kinds of fraudulent practices from a perspective claiming insider knowledge. Strikingly, the appearance of incense in this text is largely limited to the section on "spirit conjurers" (*al-muʿazzimīn*), where it is repeatedly cited as a routine element in the bogus conjuration of jinns.[56] At one point al-Jawbarī describes a hypothetical charlatan "taking only his incense burner [*majmara al-bakhūr*] with him" to fake the slaughter of a jinn inside a locked house.[57]

These somewhat peripheral concerns should not overshadow the very significant role played by censing in seemingly all aspects of life in the early Islamic period, including efficacious practices. As mentioned above, the pious use of perfumed smoke to scent the spaces of early Islamic pilgrimage is represented in some early and medieval texts as an act that connotes the scents of paradise, creating proximity to the spaces of the blessed.[58] This is, in its way, an efficacious practice. Disagreement in the early sources about whether the smoke perfuming the Kaʿba was ritually contaminating or purifying demonstrates how far those sources lie from any consensus around categories of permissible and impermissible practice that would come to calcify later on.[59] Rather than treating the occult uses of incense as entirely distinct from the pious, we should instead consider both as part of a spectrum or continuum of efficacious censing, the whole of which is subject to debates about orthopraxy. This reframing exposes smoke as a pervasive entity across a range of early Islamicate encounters with the world, giving it substance.

The Islamicate occult sciences may have a vexed historiography, but the textual record is rich and generates a distinct picture of an evolving discourse, with regional trajectories as well as some commonalities.[60] Magic (*siḥr*) in the early Arabic tradition is variously defined in the textual sources but repeatedly brings together three core practices: alchemy (*kīmiyāʾ*), talismans (*ṭilasm*), and ritual and incantations (*nīranjāt*).[61] Each of these is a process that mediates between matter and spirit. Liana Saif persuasively argues that magic practices in the first centuries of Islam were strongly connected with natural philosophy, stressing causation and knowledge of natural and astral signs.[62] The early Islamic period that produced the Gävle censer was witness to occult practices built on principles of magical efficacy through correspondences that "pivoted on the intermediary function of the celestial world between God and the terrestrial world."[63] For the purposes of sympathetic magic, this meant that the astral forces corresponding to the Divine also corresponded to things on earth—stones, metals, plants, animals, human actions—and these could be harnessed through the alignment of materials and ritual acts with the correct astrological power for the intended outcome. Suffumigation was an integral stage of many of these processes and appears over and over again throughout the Arabic literature of instruction in occult practices. It can be understood as a vital component of *nīranjāt*, a critical conduit for invoking celestial forces and a means of suffusing spirit into matter (especially in the creation of talismans). At their simplest these practices of suffumigation generate lists of planetary incense, like that given in the shorter epistle on magic in the *Rasāʾil* of the Ikhwān al-Ṣafāʾ (probably written in early tenth-century Basra), that tabulate the heavenly bodies with the aromatics used to attract their power: the Sun with aloeswood, the Moon with frankincense, Saturn with storax, Jupiter with ambergris, and so forth.[64]

Far more complex are the fumigation recipes in the tenth-century *Ghāyat al-ḥakīm* of Maslama al-Qurṭubī (d. 964), the Arabic original for the

Figure 10
Detail of cast copper alloy
ewer with a cockerel-shaped
spout, 8th or early 9th century,
height of ewer: 39.4 cm,
Metropolitan Museum of Art,
New York, 41.65,
Samuel D. Lee Fund, 1941.

Latin *Picatrix*.[65] This compilation of magic, which incorporates several earlier Arabic writings in the occult tradition, gives instructions for producing benefic or malefic outcomes through sequences of actions that almost invariably include suffumigation. The recipes for these fumigations in the *Ghāyat* often require rather exotic materials. Many call for the blood and brains of various animals (one wonders if some of these could be *Decknamen*, code names for plants recognizable to the initiated) as well as toxic or psychoactive plants such as mandrake, henbane, wormwood, and datura, along with more standard scented aromatics—especially aloeswood, the most frequently cited fumigation material in the text.[66] These combinatory recipes usually result in the creation of little pellets that the practitioner is instructed to burn on the charcoal of the censer as required (hence the usefulness of the tongs found with the Gävle censer).

It would be easy to suggest that these processes represent the far fringes of heterodoxy. Perhaps they were not necessarily followed to the letter. But the historical presence of such occult practices is beyond doubt. The processes described in the *Ghāyat al-ḥakīm* are attested not only in many other textual sources, but also in the preserved material outcomes of occult practices, a large and diverse surviving corpus of talismans, amulets, geomantic devices, and magic bowls.[67] There is even the documented case of the aforementioned thirteenth-century metalworker, Muḥammad ibn Khutlukh al-Mawṣilī, who made and signed both a geomantic divination device and a handled incense burner, including on the latter the location of production as Damascus.[68] These surviving objects in their turn must represent only a small fraction of a total body that would once have included countless perishable or ephemeral artifacts: scraps of paper or parchment, pieces of wax or wood, or marks simply traced upon the ground. To ignore the pre-modern occult practices that took place in the lands under Islamic rule is to ignore a whole swathe of human activity—activity that is of direct relevance both to metalcasting traditions in the Middle East and to the cultural context that gave rise to the Gävle censer.

But to locate occult practices is not simple; even the textual record is full of ambivalences. When it comes to material culture, the questions of not just *when* and *where*, but also *who*, are even more opaque. There are exceptional cases like Muḥammad ibn Khutlukh al-Mawṣilī, whose self-inscribed name opens some windows onto his identity. His *nisba, al-mawṣilī,* connects his origins to the city of Mosul in northern Iraq, even as he worked in Damascus, while the unusual appellative *khutlukh* likely indicates Turkic descent—which would fit with the cosmopolitan and multiethnic environment of thirteenth-century Mosul.[69] More generally, the question of who was responsible for making the artifacts of occult science has received important attention in Kristina Richardson's recent work. She proposes that early blockprinting practices were created, propagated, and transmitted from the Islamic world to Europe through amulet-making, and that this was propelled by the multiethnic, multiconfessional tribal entity known in classical Arabic as the *ghurabā*, or "strangers"—that is, so-called "gypsies."[70] Richardson's research on the *ghurabā* identifies them with the production of amulets for urban client groups and shows how they pioneered block printing techniques to produce printed amulets at scale, bringing into view one of the various minority labor groups delineated along linguistic, ethnic, and/ or confessional lines in the medieval Middle East. These groups are often missing from the canonical histories of the region. In Richardson's account we see how such minority labor groups could be imbricated with both craft and occult practices, and also how they could propel important technological advances seemingly from the social margins. Like Thābit ibn Qurra (d. 901), who will be discussed below, the "otherness" of the *ghurabā'* was probably understood to be part of their efficacy in occult production.

As for *where*, occult practices in the Islamic world were undoubtedly regionally inflected. One of the most direct lines of regional descent can be traced in northern Syria and Mesopotamia, where astral magic practices inherited from pagan Babylonia continued well into the Islamic period. A local blend of pagan practices and Hellenistic philosophy, centered on a syncretistic astral cult and regarded by medieval Arab authors as somewhat exotic and curious, flourished at Harran (now in northern Syria) into at least the tenth century.[71] Another group, in the countryside of Mesopotamia, seems to have blended biblical tradition with Assyro-Babylonian religion.[72] Arab authors of the time often applied the label "Sabians" to these groups, although as Michael Noble and others have observed, "the Sabians came to represent any form of learned pagan culture—be it Greek, Indian, or Mesopotamian—that was versed in natural philosophy and steeped in the worship of heavenly bodies."[73] Importantly, adherents of so-called Sabian religion did not exist only on the very margins of Islamic society. The young Thābit ibn Qurra, author of treatises on astronomy and talismans and translator of Euclid and Ptolemy from Greek to Arabic, was brought from Harran to Baghdad in the ninth century for his skills as a translator, astrologer, and physician. He ended up as court physician to the 'Abbasid caliph. Thābit ibn Qurra did not convert to Islam and retained a Sabian identity to the end of his life—in fact, it has recently been argued that his Sabian identity and first-hand knowledge of pagan magic practices probably helped rather than hindered his success at court. Various of his descendants maintained their Sabian identities through six generations even as they held positions of note within the 'Abbasid elite of Baghdad.[74]

The astrological cult practices associated with the so-called Sabians made great use of suffumigation in ritual, along with incantation, invocation, diet, sacrifices, and so forth.[75] Among the scattered sources on the Sabians, the Ikhwān al-Ṣafā' describe the cult practices at the temple of Jurjis, probably at Harran, in the tenth century: particular kinds of incense (*bakhūrāt*) were burned in front of each of seven images of the seven planets, in "a new censer made from red clay (*mijmaratun jadīdatun ma'mūlat min ṭīnin aḥmara*), each one of these being made in the name of one of the seven planets."[76] The virgin earthenware censers in the text probably represent simple fired clay dishes, quite different from the magisterial form and high material value of the Gävle censer. However, their presence in the Ikhwān's compendium gives us a rare glimpse of the instruments of censing within a literature that is liberally wreathed in references to thurification.

Unsurprisingly, these practices were not limited to Harran. Vestiges of pagan occult practices can be traced across Syria and Mesopotamia, later giving rise, predictably, to the wrath of orthodox jurists. As is so often the case, the writings of those who sought to forbid transgressions of orthodoxy give helpful insight into popular practices. For example, the thunderous denunciations of heterodoxy from the Syrian Hanbalite theologian Ibn Taymiyya (d. 1328), who moved as a child from Harran to Damascus, are illuminating in their portrayal of popular censing rituals. In addition to condemning the Christian use of incense—"they consider incense burning as sacrifice, as animal offering"—Ibn Taymiyya also points an angry finger at the popular occult uses of incense among the Syrian Muslim population, linking these with Sabian magic as well as Christian saint-worship:

> [A]ll or most of the common people [...] are given the explanation that incanted incense-burning, by virtue of its blessing, neutralizes the effects of the "evil eye," sorcery, ailments, and pests. They draw pictures of scorpions and snakes and paste them into their houses, believing that these pictures—cursed be he who draws them, and angels do not enter the house where they are found—prevent pests from coming inside. This is a kind of Sabian sorcery.[77]

> The various acts connected with [the week leading up to Easter Sunday] are disreputable, for example: women strolling outdoors; burning incense on graves; spreading clothes on rooftops; attaching inscribed sheets of paper to the doors; turning this period into a season for the buying and selling of incense; [...] the magic use of incense in general, at this time or another, or the intention to buy incense for magical purposes, for it is the cult of the Christians and Sabians to use incense and incantations as a sacrifice.[78]

His condemnation of those who claim to be Muslim and yet "prostrate before the sun and other planets, turn to them with various invocation formulas and chanting, wear in honour of them clothes and rings which are considered suitable, and seek times, place, and incense proper to them" clearly implicates an ongoing legacy of pagan astral cults and sympathetic magic within popular religious practice in Syria into at least the fourteenth century.[79]

Ibn Taymiyya repeatedly connects the apotropaic and magic uses of incense with talismanic images and inscriptions. This is not happenstance. It reflects the longstanding integration of fumigations and talismanic arts not merely as adjacent subjects in the written sources, but as practices. This brings us to the second important point of potential connection between the Gävle censer and occult sciences: the demanding art of skilled metalcasting.[80] The craft of talismans denotes an art of process, of which suffumigation is an essential component. What is usually left at the end is the physical embodiment of the process, the talisman. This is an object that could be made from various materials but in the ninth- and tenth-century texts is most often cast in metal.[81] Described by the scholar Fakhr al-Dīn al-Rāzī (d. 1210) as the peak of Sabian science and the pinnacle of human achievement, the talismanic art involves metalcasting within a regimen of ritual preparation and astrological observation, to blend "heavenly active forces with elemental passive forces" in the creation of efficacious artifacts.[82]

It is hardly surprising that the craft of metalcasting should lie near the heart of popular magic. The conjoined trajectories of alchemy, talismans, and *nīranjāt* in the Arabic tradition are further entwined with the history of the practical arts, especially the arts of fire: metalworking, ceramics, glass, and pigments. As Paola Carusi poetically observes, "This link to the practical arts is the origin and also the history of alchemy: a discipline which even when it takes on more spiritual dimensions can never be divorced from matter."[83] The same can be said of the other branches of Islamicate occult science, and indeed magic practices in general. Carved stone or engraved or cast metal, materials of the earth, are substrates of choice for talisman production in the *Ghāyat al-ḥakīm*. The instructions for making them typically begin with the instruction to "craft" (*ṣana'a*), to "make" (*'amal*), or to "engrave" (*naqasha*) an image. (The idea of image, "*ṣūra*," in tenth-century Arabic discourse could refer to both two- and three-dimensional forms of representation.)[84] Hence two different recipes for talismans to ward off scorpions, one of which begins "craft an image of a scorpion in gold," while the other instructs the reader to "engrave an image of a scorpion into a bezoar stone."[85] Other talismans in the *Ghāyat al-ḥakīm* require small human figures made from various substances, usually wax or metal, such as that which begins with the instruction to craft the figures of a man and a woman from copper (*aṣna' tamathālīn min nuḥās 'alā ṣūrat rajul wa āmrāa*).[86] The use of *ṣana'a* ("to craft," "to fabricate") for objects in metal like the gold scorpion or the copper man and woman—in contrast to *naqasha* ("to engrave," "to draw") for images applied to metal or stone, and *'amal* ("to make," "to work") for figures in wax—indicates that in the *Ghāyat*, *ṣana'a* is understood to mean making three-dimensional forms in metal, through casting.[87]

This type of production is also described in quite specific terms in a Judaeo-Arabic fragment of Thābit ibn Qurra's ninth-century treatise on talismans, which gives instructions for a talisman to create friendship between a ruler and one of his officers. After delineating the correct astrological circumstances for successful production, it continues:

> And when you have finished the engraving [*naqsh*] of the mould [*al-qālib*], according to the aforementioned conditions, complete the form of the man from lead, tin, or copper, whichever agrees for you with the ascendant of the nativity [horoscope] of the man, if you know it, or the ascendant of his question.[88]

The description of casting metal in molds that have been made by engraving or incising, cited by an author with direct experience of the so-called Sabian magical tradition, confirms the centrality of the metalcaster's art to occult practices. Furthermore, it shows some understanding of what is actually involved in metalcasting—i.e., the absolute importance of the successfully crafted mold—adding further weight to the argument that the occult sources describe real, not merely theoretical, practices.

The last example I will cite from the occult sources comes from the *Ghāyat al-ḥakīm*. Within this text there are instructions for making a complex device that unites talismanic imagery with metalcasting practice and suffumigation, creating it from the desired mix of metals for your chosen planet of influence. The device consists of a cast metal cross onto which talismanic images are mounted, the cross to be set above a censer made from the same alloy, with a hole in the domed top of the censer (*yakūn fī ā'lā qubba al-mijmara thuqb*) that will release upward the smoke from the incense (*bukhur*) burned in it, so it curls around the images on the cross.[89] This complex three-dimensional form provides a concrete reference to the domed tops of cast metal censers—a feature of multiple surviving censers from the medieval Middle East that is splendidly represented on the example now in Gävle. *Qubba,* the word used in the *Ghāyat* to denote the dome on the censer, is the word for an architectural dome and is sometimes used metonymically in the medieval sources to denote a domed building.

The intriguing artifact described in the *Ghāyat*'s instructions is emblematic of early Islamicate occult practices *in toto.* It mediates matter through the central processes of magic—metalcasting, astrological observation, image production, *nīranjāt,* suffumigation—to create a putative "influencing machine" that harnesses the forces of the universe.[90] In the light of such an object, then, we can understand the Gävle censer as perhaps something more than just a fungible object of use. Its large, heavy, deep brazier section and attendant copper tongs would work well for censing with unusual materials as well as the more standard aloeswood or frankincense; its portable but monumental form is designed to create a powerful and somewhat forbidding impression in use, with smoke rising through the openwork of the dome and threading from the mobile surface of winged palmettes; its facture advertises it as a virtuosic example of the metalcaster's art, a marvel of the mold. Any censer can theoretically be used for any act of censing, and it would be impossible to say definitively that the Gävle censer was created as an instrument of magic. And yet, after examining the texts of occult instruction, it is hard to imagine a censer that would suit the part better than this one. Perhaps a different deduction is more important: any pre-modern censer could have been used for occult suffumigation, and doubtless some of them were. This aspect of censing in the early Islamic world is ubiquitous in the medieval occult sources, yet almost nowhere in the existing art historical literature on censers. In the end there is more to be gained not by attempting to reclassify the Gävle censer as a definitively magical artifact, but by exposing the powerful potential resonances of occult practices in all such objects.

To that end, I wish to close this exploration of the occult by returning to the inscribed text of the bismillah on the body of the Gävle censer. If it is a post-production addition, it is possible that on the Gävle censer this represents what we might call an act of consecration, with a later user taking an object that they view as ambiguous and reorienting it towards the faith. But it is equally possible to understand the bismillah within an Islamicate occult framework. Two identical early so-called "magic bowls," now in the Khalili Collection and the Bumiller Collection, where seemingly struck from lead like coins from a die. Each bears on its base the bismillah and the Qur'anic phrase *ḥasbiya llāhu* (God is sufficient for me) in an early rectilinear script [Figures 11 and 12].[91] The juxtaposition of the pious phrase on the bowl with astrological and magical imagery indicates an attitude to occult practices that was by no means rigidly exclusionary; it harnesses "the mystery of the One God who is Lord of the Mercies" which gives the bismillah its power of benediction.[92] Emilie Savage-Smith, discussing the lead bowl in the Khalili Collection, proposes that it may have been intended for magical-medicinal purposes—although, as she notes, it is curious that on this piece the pious words are on the outside rather than the inside. The configuration suggests a variation on the practice of drinking water in which the inked words of the Qur'an had been dissolved, or from bowls inscribed inside with Qur'anic verses, which is debated in various medieval juridical texts relying on the authority of earlier jurists such as Ibn Ḥanbal (d. 855).[93] Some

Figures 11 and 12

early Islamic magical-medical bowls even include instructions for use within their inscriptions, instructing the patient to drink water from the bowl in order to gain relief from fever, repel scorpions, or ease childbirth.[94] Like the pious words on the magic bowl, the inscription of the bismillah on the Gävle censer was intended to produce a beneficent effect, in an environment where the efficacious practices of religion and occult science were thoroughly intertwined.

EPILOGUE:
A MIDDLE EASTERN CENSER WALKS TO SWEDEN

Cast, incised, heavy, and treasured, the Gävle censer is a monumental material presence. But its openwork is permeable, while its hooved feet intimate animation and ambulation—appropriately enough for an object that traveled so far in its lifetime. The censer's dense layering of seemingly contradictory material expressions is perhaps the most compelling aspect of this puzzling object. Combining the vocabulary of monumental architecture with the paratactical elements of hoofed feet and handle, its dense materiality showcases the seeming contradictions of bronze, delicacy of design co-existing with the pierced rip of thick cast openwork. In this essay I have used diverse forms of evidence to place the censer into Syro-Mesopotamian metalcasting traditions and expose its resonances with early Islamicate occult practice, but an obvious question remains: what happened next? How did it come to rest between two boulders in a remote parish in Sweden?

Beyond the likelihood that it was brought to Sweden during the Viking Age, there is precious little of the censer's long journey that can be reconstructed. The fact that it was secreted together with those three pairs of tongs strongly suggests that it continued to be used for censing during and after its migration. If those who transported it had valued it solely for its material, its workmanship, or its exoticism, and not as a masterfully produced object of use, the tongs would be superfluous. The other part of the cache, the lidded spout, is harder to interpret, but it is possible that it once figured in some arrangement of use with the censer and the tongs. Once again, we should consider the possibility of censing within pagan ritual. The region in which the cache was found has its own intriguing history of occult practices. Hamrånge parish, an area rich in iron ore deposits and traces of iron production, has also furnished an enigmatic toothed iron ring, found in 1887 and speculated to be a pre-Christian cult object or amulet.[95] Traces of a nearby stone circle suggest cult activity in the local area, which was not Christianized until the twelfth century or later and likely retained pagan practices alongside the new religion for much longer than that. The censer, then, seems to have arrived into another landscape of efficacious pagan practices, one with its own influencing machines at work.

Ultimately, it will never be possible to answer every question raised by the Gävle censer. But this does not mean we should not continue to try to better understand both the material artifact and the cultural currents that gave rise to it and carried it from one place to another. This essay will close with a note of caution about fetishizing the transregional movement of the Gävle censer and objects like it, at a time when there is much appeal in constructing a pre-modern globalism that satisfies postmodern sensibilities. In our desire to access pre-modern mobility—and so demonstrate the long histories of interconnectedness that have shaped all human societies—we

Figure 11
Die-struck lead vessel,
8th or 9th century, 6.8 × 6.8 cm,
Bumiller Collection, Bamberg
University Museum of Islamic
Art, 2.389. Image courtesy of
the Bumiller Collection.

Figure 12
Underside of vessel.
Image courtesy of
the Bumiller Collection.

sometimes risk losing sight of the artifacts themselves. This can lead to two separate problems that run counter to the work of art historical scholarship: first, misinterpreting and mischaracterizing artifacts (which is often followed by instrumentalizing them within narratives informed by contemporary politics), and second, reducing them to fungible markers in a giant game of transregional checkers.

In an example of the first problem, Stephennie Mulder recently showed how a quest for headlines about medieval multiculturalism resulted in the sensationalized misinterpretation of a tenth-century Scandinavian textile band.[96] In reality the textile fragment was a wonderful product of medieval tablet-weaving all by itself; press-release fantasies about Muslim Vikings were quite superfluous. The whole episode was a timely reminder that if one is going to try to incorporate historical artifacts into contemporary narratives about identity, one must first make a sincere and informed effort to understand the artifact on its own terms—and to accept that what emerges from that effort might not accord with what twenty-first-century audiences most desire to see.

In reference to the second problem: objects move, but they are not just nodal points on a web of connections. It is exciting and illuminating that the Gävle censer (and its attendant objects) traveled from the Middle East to Sweden, but the object itself should not be allowed to disappear behind its remarkable—if still obscure—itinerary. Person or persons as yet unknown, somewhere in the Middle Eastern heartlands of the early Islamic empire, labored over the production of a complex and unique piece of lost-wax casting, modeling its dense palmette openwork down to the gently indented lobes and incised linear web of leaf veins. Those unknown craftsmen pursued a remarkable vision of a domed, footed building, materialized in bronze yet penetrable and porous, woven from fantastic foliage and wreathed in smoke and inscribed ultimately to the name of Allah. Their creation was valued and protected enough at every stage of its existence to make the long journey to Sweden intact, eventually to be concealed in a crevice by someone who perhaps intended a recovery that never happened. Finally, it was uncovered by children who must have enjoyed their moment of celebrity in the bleak year of 1943. In the moments of its casting, an object was created that has outlasted many generations of men and women. Today it stands patiently and silently in a vitrine in Gävle, meters away from the river that flows out endlessly into the Bothnian sea. The censer endures.

ENDNOTES

1 I am deeply grateful to Anna Larsdottor, Richard Schill, and Anki Börjeson for hosting my visit to the Länsmuseet Gävleborg in 2018. I also thank the participants in the 2019 workshop at Bern for their comments on my paper there, and the two anonymous peer reviewers for their perceptive and extremely helpful comments on an earlier draft of this chapter. Ittai Weinryb, Meekyung MacMurdie, Yael Rice, and Matt Melvin-Koushki all provided suggestions and/or answered queries along the way, for which I thank them. Information about the find supplied by Anna Larsdottor and Richard Schill.

2 Arne 1943, 7–24. Arne is probably best remembered for his excavations at Shah Tepe in northeastern Iran and his work on the so-called Luristan bronzes: see Nylander 2009.

3 In the pre-modern era the distinction between copper alloys, especially those now classified as "bronze" (i.e., copper-tin alloy) and "brass" (copper-zinc alloy), was more elastic than it is now: see Aga-Oglu 1944, 218–23; Allan 1976, 1:146–65; Weinryb 2016, 4–5. See also the appearance of a term that seems to designate high-tin bronze in Davis 2020, 3.

4 Arne 1943; Arbman 1955, 142; Ådahl 1985, 34; Darkevic 1985, 390; Allan 1986, 25–26; Jansson 1988, 623–24; von Gladiss 1989, 523–24; Ådahl 1990, 333–45; Graves 2018, 159–63.

5 Allan 1976, 1:83.

6 Although not always: see Nina Ergin's discussion of Ottoman censer typologies and their specific uses in Ergin 2014.

7 Bursi 2020, 200–234; George 2009, 106.

8 *Ṣaḥīḥ al-Bukhārī*, vol. 4, book 55, hadith 544 [https://sunnah.com/bukhari:3327].

9 Ibn Rustah 1891, 66. See also Flood 2002, 644.

10 Thurlkill 2016, 111–58; Aga-Oglu 1945, 28–29.

11 Graves 2018, 151–52; 2020, 199–214.

12 See the overviews of use presented in Kühnel 1920, 4–8; Aga-Oglu 1945, 28–29; Allan 1986, 22–34; Ward 1991, 67–69; Canby 2012, 119–27.

13 The major study on incense in occult practices in Islam is Coulon 2016, 179–248. See also Ducène 2016, 159–78.

14 The bibliography on Islamicate occult sciences that has emerged over the last ten years alone is remarkable: some representative recent titles are Coulon 2017; Saif et al. 2020; and two special issues of *Arabica*: see Gardiner and Melvin-Koushki 2017; de Callataÿ 2021.

15 Ådahl and her colleagues read it as *bi-ismillāh al-raḥīm* (Ådahl 1990, 336). However, a terminal *nūn* (here looking rather like a *rāʾ*) is visible and I have read this word as *raḥmān*—which is usually written, as it is on the censer, without its superscript alif—rather than *raḥ[ī]m* followed by an isolated letter. Compare the inscription on the censer with that

seen in an onyx seal inscribed *bi-ismillāh al-raḥmān al-raḥīm* (Content 1987, 268), and with the shape of the terminal *nūn* in the word *ibn* on several early stone seals (Porter 2011, nos. 41, 43, 46, 48).

16 Lindstedt 2019, 147–246; Halevi 2004, 120–22; see also Ory 1990, 31–32. In other contexts, the bismillah would also be used to begin medieval letters written in Arabic by, and to, non-Muslims. Almbladh 2010, 45–60.

17 I would concur with the suggestion by Michael Rogers (cited in Ådahl 1990, 336) that the script looks "relatively late [for so-called archaic Kufic] but not later than around 1000 A.D. and probably earlier." For seals, see some examples in Content 1987, 268–69, 278.

18 Porter 2010, 131–40; Heidemann et al. 2018, 225–39.

19 Collinet 2021, 79–80.

20 Arne 1943; Jansson 1988. Only Arbman (1955, 142) suggests that it was brought to Sweden in the modern era as an antique: as Jansson observes, this is hard to refute, but hardly seems likely given the circumstances of its discovery.

21 Ibn Fadlān 2012.

22 See Jonsson Hraundel 2013, 71.

23 Ibn Khurradadhbih 1865, 116 and 514.

24 Metcalf 1997, 296; see also Raby 1986, 179–203; Michailidis 2012, 315–38.

25 Since the amplification of Persian products within the canon of Islamic art is a part of this story, it is worth mentioning that of the six plates of comparable censers Arne included in his publication, five are identical with—and were presumably copied from—plates in the multi-volume *Survey of Persian Art*, first published in 1938–39 (Pope and Ackermann 1938–39). Arne's figs. 13, 14, 15, 16a, and 16b are, respectively, Pope and Ackermann 1938–39, vol. 13, plates 1278 C, 1278 B, 1299 A–D, 1352 C, and 1352 D. Two of these also appeared earlier in Kühnel's short foundational essay on the morphology of Islamic incense burners, "Islamische Räuchergerät" (Kühnel 1920), indicating that they were probably the standard object "portrait shots" taken by the museum. Some of the same images appear yet again in Aga-Oglu's seminal essay, "About a Type of Islamic Incense Burner" (Aga-Oglu 1945). Even a cursory survey of the illustrations used in publications on Islamic art from 1939 onwards reveals the impact of Pope and Ackermann's compendium on the scholarly canon.

26 Ådahl 1985, 34; 1990.

27 Darkevic 1985, 390.

28 Allan 1986, 25–26; von Gladiss 1989.

29 Canepa 2009, 188–223; Graves 2018, 159–63.

30 Ådahl 1990, 342; see an example in the L. A. Mayer Museum attributed to eighth-century Egypt, illustrated in Hasson 2000, 16.

31 Allan 1976, 1:382; see also Ward 1993, 31–33.

32 Graves 2018, 159–63.

33 He was talking about Dante's *Divine Comedy*. Borges 2000, 291.

34 Allan 1976, 1:390.

35 Bagley 1987, 16–17; de Laperouse 2008.

36 Humbert n.d., 18–19; 1989, 125–31; 1986a, 267–69. A humbler spouted cast copper-alloy pouring vessel of the Umayyad era, excavated at al-Fudayn, Jordan, has a grooved, lipped domed lid with knob finial reminiscent of that on the mysterious spouted fragment accompanying the Gävle censer, and could strengthen a possible Syrian connection for the Gävle hoard. Humbert n.d., 20; 1986b, 269.

37 Evans 2012, 219–20; Flood 2016, 88–93.

38 Evans 2012, 180–81. See for example the abundant use of the form on the brazier excavated at Mafraq: Humbert 1989, 125–31.

39 Allan 1986, 66–69. This piece is now in the Museum of Islamic Art, Doha, no. MW.584.2009.

40 There are of course latter-day forms that could also be brought in for comparison: see for example the architectonic Arabian frankincense burners in clay: Zimmerle 2021, 23–42.

41 Bénazeth 2001, nos. 299 and 300.

42 Atıl, Chase, and Jett 1985. Eva Baer and Géza Fehérvári both suggested the Freer censer might be from Khurasan. Baer's suggestion was rather speculative. Fehérvári was trying to reattribute the Freer censer to Khurasan as part of his case for the medieval Afghan origins of a puzzling object in the Tareq Rajab Museum. See Baer 1983, 45–50; Fehérvári 2005, 138–40; 2007, 46–50.

43 Bénazeth 2001, 358–59.

44 See the summary of previous scholarship and the arguments against this interpretation in Graves 2018, 157–68.

45 Ibid.

46 Humbert 1989, 130; Harding 1951; Khamis 2013, 49 and 289; Evans 2012, 180–81, 215–16. See also an example from a scientific excavation in Fustat: Scanlon 1984, 16–18; Evans 2012, 216.

47 Lester 2004, 59–68; Lester, Arnon, and Polak 1999, 233–48; Ziffer 1996, 51–57, 111; Khamis 2013. A lampstand of the same type was found at 'Ayn Dara in northwestern Syria in 1956: al-Sirafi 1960, 93 and fig. 16.

48 For example, Ayala Lester has related a square brazier from Caesarea, mounted on four hooved feet, with one uncovered at Pompeii that boasts four lion feet and a design of stepped merlons around the sides. Lester 2017. See also Lester 2014, 441 and fig. 8b, on an Arabic inscription that she reads as *'amal 'Abbās bi-dimashq* ("the work of 'Abbās in Damascus").

49 See examples in Rashidi 2020; Melikian-Chirvani 1982, 23–54; Collinet 2021. The only object I have found attributed to medieval Khurasan bearing openwork even partly comparable to that on the Gävle censer is an unusual oil lamp and stand in the Louvre, OA 7890, attributed on the museum's website to twelfth- or thirteenth-century Iran. See Fontana 2019, 5–26; Collinet 2021, 224–25. Bought by the Louvre from the Indjoujian brothers in Paris in 1927, it seems to have been first attributed to Khurasan, eleventh or twelfth century, in the Burlington House Exhibition of Persian Art in 1931 (*Catalogue of the International Exhibition of Persian Art* 1931, p. 48, no. 74 B).

50 Atıl, Chase, and Jett 1985, 60.

51 Graves 2018, 45–46; Elias 2012, 175–88.

52 The closest parallel for the palmette forms of the Gävle piece that I have found in cast openwork is a censer in the Khalili Collection, attributed to Syria, eighth or ninth century, which combines symmetrical winged palmette openwork with a frieze of stepped merlons and a further frieze of openwork arcade: Rogers 2010, 40–41. A similar arcade design can be seen on a handled cast censer attributed to Islamic Spain, Metropolitan Museum of Art 67.178.3a,b: Canby 2012, 122–23.

53 Rubensohn and Sarre 1929, 85–95; Sarre 1934, 10–16; Dimand 1941, 203; David-Weill 1948, 79–85; Fehérvári 1976, 27–28; Piotrovsky and Rogers 2004, 29; Allan 2004, 355; O'Kane 2006, 21.

54 Cryer 1994, 148; Lawson Younger Jr. 2012, 212; Finkel 1983/1984, 50–55; Pettinato 1966, 308; Luck 2006, 484.

55 Ibn Khaldun 1958, 1:217. On Ibn Khaldūn and the occult, see Melvin-Koushki 2017, 346–403. A widely circulated study published in 2008 has suggested that frankincense, or at least some varieties of it, are indeed mildly psychoactive: Moussaeiff et al. 2008, 3024–34.

56 Al-Jawbarī 2020, 229–50.

57 Ibid., 236.

58 Bursi 2020.

59 Ibid., 216–17.

60 For the early medieval Islamic period, some of the key texts are the Arabic Pseudo-Aristotelian hermetic corpus (probably ninth century); Pseudo-Plato's *Liber Vaccae (Kitāb al-Nawāmīs)* (Arabic

original probably late ninth century); the epistle on magic in the *Rasā'il* of the Ikhwān al-Ṣafā' (tenth century); the *Ghāyat al-ḥakīm* of Maslama al-Qurṭubī (d. 964); the *Kitāb sharāsīm al-hindiyya* (late tenth century or later).

61 Burnett 2020, 43–56; Zadeh 2020, 614–22.

62 Saif 2017, 297.

63 Ibid., 305.

64 al-Safa 2011, 135–36; Coulon 2016, 191–92, 195–98, 207–21. On the longer epistle, see Saif 2020, 162–206.

65 On the authorship of the *Ghāyat al-ḥakīm*, see Fierro 1996, 87–112; Coulon 2014, 99–106.

66 Ritter 1933; Prado 2020, 98–111. On *Decknamen* in Babylonian and Greek magic practices, see Reiner 1995, 32–33.

67 See Maddison and Savage-Smith 1997; Flood 2019, 123–32.

68 Smith and Savage-Smith 1980; 2004, 211–76; Allan 1986, 25–34 and 66–69.

69 "Kutluğ," in Clauson 1972, 601; Kana'an 2012, 67–78.

70 Richardson 2022.

71 Hameen-Anttila 2002, 89–108; Treiger 2021, 239 n. 24.

72 Hameen-Anttila 2002, 96. See also Green 2002, 215–17.

73 Noble 2020, 207–8; Saif 2021, 50–52.

74 Roberts 2017, 253–77.

75 Noble 2020, 212–13.

76 al-Safa 2011, 135.

77 Ibn Taymiyya 1976, 210.

78 Ibid., 221; Troupeau 1979, 800–801.

79 Ibn Taymiyya 1976, 306.

80 For example, the original Arabic of the *Kitāb al-Nawāmīs* attributed to Plato is largely lost, but translations and later compilations suggest that the section on talismans was followed by a section on "wicks and fumigations" (*fatīla* and *dukhna*): Coulon 2020, 352–53. See also Saif 2016, 1–47; 2021, 52.

81 On related questions of talismanic iconography in the medieval Islamic world see Berlekamp 2016, 59–109.

82 Noble 2021, 1.

83 Carusi 2016, 318.

84 See Graves 2020.

85 Ritter 1933, 33 and 34.

86 Ibid., 246.

87 However, a skim through L. A. Meyer's *Islamic Metalworkers and Their Works* (1959) suggests that in signatory formulae on metalwork *'amal* is the more common verb of making, though *ṣana'a* is sometimes used.

88 Following Burnett and Bohak 2012, 191, and Bohak and Burnett 2021, 160–61. An additional section of the text, found in the Latin translations but not in the Judeo-Arabic version of the text studied by Burnett and Bohak, goes into more detail about the manufacture of the mold (Bohak and Burnett 2021, 179–81).

89 Ritter 1933, 185.

90 I have borrowed the "influencing machine" from early twentieth-century studies of schizophrenia: see some of the creations in Busine 1996.

91 Maddison and Savage-Smith 1997, 74–75.

92 Carra de Vaux and Gardet n.d., "Basmala."

93 Maddison and Savage-Smith 1997, 72–75; Zadeh 2009, 464–66; Flood 2019, 123–32.

94 Savage-Smith 2003, 1–6; Maddison and Savage-Smith 1997, 72–75.

95 Sundström 2006.

96 Mulder 2017; Samuel 2017.

BIBLIOGRAPHY

Ådahl, Karin. 1985. "Islamisk konst i Svenska samlingar / Islamic Art in Swedish Collections." In *Islam: Konst och Kultur / Islam: Art and Culture*, 31–47. Stockholm: Statens Historiska Museum.

Ådahl, Karin. 1990. "An Early Islamic Bronze Incense Burner in a Swedish Collection." *Proceedings of the First European Conference of Iranian Studies* 2: 333–45.

Aga-Oglu, Mehmet. 1944. "A Brief Note on Islamic Terminology for Bronze and Brass." *Journal of the American Oriental Society* 64, no. 4: 218–23.

Aga-Oglu, Mehmet. 1945. "About a Type of Islamic Incense Burner." *The Art Bulletin* 27, no. 1: 28–45.

Allan, James. 1976. "The Metalworking Industry in Iran in the Early Islamic Period." PhD thesis, University of Oxford.

Allan, James. 1986. *Metalwork of the Early Islamic World: The Aron Collection*. London: Sotheby's.

Allan, James W. 2004. "Metal Vessels." In *Serçe Limani: An Eleventh-Century Shipwreck*, vol. 1, *The Ship and Its Anchorage, Crew, and Passengers*, edited by George F. Bass et al., 345–60. College Station: Texas A&M University Press.

Almbladh, Karin. 2010. "The 'Basmala' in Medieval Letters in Arabic Written by Jews and Christians." *Orientalia Suecana* 59: 45–60.

Arbman, Holger. 1955. *Svear i österviking.* Stockholm: Natur och kultur.

Arne, Ture J. 1943. "Ett gästrikefynd från Kalifen Harun ar-Raschids välde." *Från Gästrikland:* 7–24.

Atıl, Esin, W. Thomas Chase, and Paul Jett. 1985. *Islamic Metalwork in the Freer Gallery of Art.* Washington DC: Smithsonian.

Baer, Eva. 1983. *Metalwork in Medieval Islamic Art.* Albany, NY: SUNY Press, 1983.

Bagley, Robert W. 1987. *Shang Ritual Bronzes in the Arthur M. Sackler Collections.* Washington, DC; Cambridge, MA: Sackler Foundation; Sackler Museum.

Bénazeth, Dominique. 2001. *Catalogue général du Musée copte du Caire: 1. Objets en metal.* Cairo: Institut français d'archéologie orientale.

Berlekamp, Persis. 2016. "Symmetry, Sympathy, and Sensation: Talismanic Efficacy and Slippery Iconographies in Early Thirteenth-Century Iraq, Syria, and Anatolia." *Representations* 133: 59–109.

Bohak, Gideon, and Charles Burnett. 2021. *Thābit ibn Qurra On Talismans and Ps.-Ptolemy On Images 1–9 Together with the Liber prestigiorum Thebedis of Adelard of Bath.* Florence: Galluzzo.

Borges, Jorge Luis. 2000. "Dante and the Anglo-Saxon Visionaries." In *Selected Non-Fictions,* edited by Eliot Weinberger, 287–91. London: Penguin, 2000.

Burnett, Charles. 2020. "The Three Divisions of Arabic Magic." In *Islamicate Occult Sciences in Theory and Practice,* edited by Liana Saif, Francesca Leoni, Matthew Melvin-Koushki, and Farouk Yahya, 43–56. Leiden: Brill.

Burnett, Charles, and Gideon Bohak. 2012. "A Judaeo-Arabic Version of Ṯābit Ibn Qurra's *De Imaginibus* and Pseudo-Ptolemy's *Opus Imaginum.*" In *Islamic Philosophy, Science, Culture, and Religion: Studies in Honor of Dimitri Gutas,* edited by Felicitas Opwis and David Reisman, 179–200. Leiden: Brill.

Bursi, Adam. 2020. "Scents of Space: Early Islamic Pilgrimage, Perfume, and Paradise." *Arabica* 67: 200–234.

Busine, Laurent. 1996. *Beyond Reason: Art and Psychosis, Works from the Prinzhorn Collection.* Berkeley: University of California Press.

Canby, Sheila. 2012. "The Scented World: Incense Burners and Perfume Containers from Spain to Central Asia." *Arts of Asia* 42, no. 5: 119–27.

Canepa, Matthew. 2009. *The Two Eyes of the Earth: Art and Ritual of Kingship between Rome and Sasanian Iran.* Berkeley: University of California Press.

Carra de Vaux, B., and L. Gardet. n.d., "Basmala." *Encyclopaedia of Islam,* 2nd edn. online.

Carusi, Paola. 2016. "Iznīqī and Jābir, *Sirr* and *Miftāḥ:* Two Authors, Four Titles, One Alchemical Treatise." *Al-Qanṭara* 37, no. 2: 299–327.

Catalogue of the International Exhibition of Persian Art. Revised 3rd edn. 1931. London: Office of the Exhibition.

Clauson, Gerard. 1972. *An Etymological Dictionary of Pre-Thirteenth-Century Turkish.* Oxford: Clarendon.^

Collinet, Annabelle. 2021. *Précieuses matières: Les arts du métal dans le monde Iranian médiéval.* Paris: Louvre; Faton.

Content, Derek J., ed. 1987. *Islamic Rings and Gems in the Benjamin Zucker Collection.* London: Philip Wilson.

Coulon, Jean-Charles. 2014. "Autour de Ġayat al-ḥakīm (Le but de sage) (Compte rendu critique des actes du colloque Images et magie)." *Arabica* 61: 89–115.

Coulon, Jean-Charles. 2016. "Fumigations et rituels magiques: La rôle des encens et fumigations dans le magie arabe médiévale." *Bulletin d'études orientales* 64: 179–248.

Coulon, Jean-Charles. 2017. *La magie en terre d'Islam: 8–13ème siècle.* Paris: CTHS.

Coulon, Jean-Charles. 2020. "The *Kitāb Sharāsīm al-Hindiyya* and Medieval Islamic Occult Sciences." In *Islamicate Occult Sciences in Theory and Practice,* edited by Liana Saif, Francesca Leoni, Matthew Melvin-Koushki, and Farouk Yahya, 317–79. Leiden: Brill.

Cryer, Frederick H. 1994. *Divination in Ancient Israel and Its Near Eastern Environment.* Sheffield: Sheffield Academic Press.

Darkevic, V. P. 1985. "Mezdunarodnye svjazi." In *Drevnjaja Rus': Gorod, zamok, selo,* edited by B. A. Kolchin, 387–411. Moscow: Izd-vo "Nauka."

David-Weill, J. 1948. "Cinq aiguières de bronze archaïques: Unité de l'art musulman." *Semitica* 1: 79–85.

Davis, Humphrey. 2020. "Appendix 1: Vocabulary of Rare Words and Phrases Occurring in *The Book of Charlatans.*" New York: Library of Arabic Literature. Online book supplements, https://www.libraryofarabicliterature.org/extra-2/.

De Callataÿ, Godefroid, ed. 2021. *Arabica* 68, no. 5–6, *Occult Sciences and the Transmission of Knowledge in al-Andalus.*

De Laperouse, Jean-Francois. 2008. "Metallurgy: Early Metallurgy in Mesopotamia." In *Encyclopaedia of the History of Science, Technology, and Medicine in Non-Western Cultures,* edited by Helain Selin, 1624–34. Dordrecht: Springer. https://doi.org/10.1007/978-1-4020-4425-0_8548.

Dimand, Maurice. 1941. "A Review of Sasanian and Islamic Metalwork in 'A Survey of Persian Art'." *Ars Islamica* 8: 192–214.

Ducène, Jean-Charles. 2016. "Des parfums et des fumées: Les parfums à brûler en Islam médiéval." *Bulletin d'études orientales* 64: 159–78.

Elias, Jamal J. 2012. *Aisha's Cushion: Religious Art, Perception, and Practice in Islam.* Cambridge, MA: Harvard University Press.

Ergin, Nina. 2014. "The Fragrance of the Divine: Ottoman Incense Burners and Their Context." *The Art Bulletin* 96, no. 1: 70–97.

Evans, Helen, ed. 2012. *Byzantium and Islam: Age of Transition, 7th–9th Century.* New York: Metropolitan Museum of Art.

Fehérvári, Géza. 1976. *Islamic Metalwork of the 8th to the 15th Century in the Keir Collection.* London: Faber & Faber.

Fehérvári, Géza. 2005. "Islamic Incense Burners and the Influence of Buddhist Art." In *The Iconography of Islamic Art: Studies in Honor of Robert Hillenbrand,* edited by Bernard O'Kane, 127–42. Edinburgh: Edinburgh University Press.

Fehérvári, Géza. 2007. "Samanid or Ghaznavid? An Early Islamic Incense-Burner from the Iranian World." *Hadeeth ad-Dar* 23: 46–50.

Fierro, Maribel. 1996. "Bāṭinism in al-Andalus. Maslama b. Qāsim al-Qurṭubī (d. 353/964), Author of the 'Rutbat al-Ḥakīm' and the 'Ghāyat al-Ḥakīm (Picatrix)'." *Studia Islamica* 84: 87–112.

Finkel, Irving L. 1983/84. "A New Piece of Libanomancy." *Archiv fur Orientforschung* 29/30: 50–55.

Flood, Finbarr Barry. 2002. "Between Cult and Culture: Bamiyan, Islamic Iconoclasm, and the Museum." *The Art Bulletin* 84, no. 4: 641–59.

Flood, Finbarr Barry. 2016. "The Flaw in the Carpet: Disjunctive Continuities and Riegl's Arabesque." In *Histories of Ornament: From Global to Local,* edited by Gülru Necipoğlu and Alina Payne, 82–93. Princeton, NJ: Princeton University Press.

Flood, Finbarr Barry. 2019. *Technologies de dévotion dans les arts de l'Islam. Pèlerins, reliques et copies.* Paris: Hazan; Musée du louvre.

Fontana, Maria Vittoria. 2019. "La rara iconografia di un auriga su une lampada ad olio in lega di rame dal Khurasan (Iran), XII secolo." *Mantua Humanistic Studies* 6: 5–26.

Gardiner, Noah, and Matthew Melvin-Koushki, eds. 2017. *Arabica* 64, no. 3–4, *Islamicate Occultism: New Perspectives.*

George, Alain. 2009. "Calligraphy, Colour and Light in the Blue Qur'an." *Journal of Qur'anic Studies* 11, no. 1: 75–125.

Graves, Margaret S. 2018. *Arts of Allusion: Object, Ornament, and Architecture in Medieval Islam.* New York: Oxford University Press.

Graves, Margaret S. 2020. "Casting Shadows." In *The Seljuqs and Their Successors: Art, Culture and History,* edited by Sheila Canby, Deniz Beyazit, and Martina Rugiadi, 199–214. Edinburgh: Edinburgh University Press.

Green, Tamara. 2002. *The City of the Moon God: Religious Traditions of Harran.* Leiden: Brill.

Halevi, Leor. 2004. "The Paradox of Islamization: Tombstone Inscriptions, Qur'anic Recitations, and the Problem of Religious Change." *History of Religions* 44, no. 2: 120–52.

Hameen-Anttila, Jaakko. 2002. "Continuity of Pagan Religious Traditions in Tenth-Century Iraq." *Melammu Symposia III (Milano 2002):* 89–108.

Harding, Lankester. 1951. "Excavations on the Citadel, Amman." *Annual of the Department of Antiquities of Jordan* 1: 7–16.

Hasson, Rachel. 2000. *Masterworks of the L.A. Mayer Museum of Islamic Art.* Jerusalem.

Heidemann, Stefan, et al. 2018. "A Magical Rock Crystal Gem from Apollonia-Arsūf, Israel." *Journal of Islamic Archaeology* 5, no. 2: 225–39.

Humbert, Jean-Baptiste. n.d. *el-Fedein, Mafraq, Jordanie: Rapport preliminaire de la campagne de fouilles 1986.* Jerusalem: École Biblique et Archéologique Française de Jérusalem.

Humbert, Jean-Baptiste. 1986a. "Brasero." In *La Voie royale: 9000 ans d'art au royaume de Jordanie,* exhibition catalogue, Musée national du Luxembourg, 267–269. Paris: Association française d'action artistique.

Humbert, Jean-Baptiste. 1986b. "Cassolette et pot a verser." In *La Voie royale: 9000 ans d'art au royaume de Jordanie,* exhibition catalogue, Musée national du Luxembourg, 269. Paris: Association française d'action artistique.

Humbert, Jean-Baptiste. 1989. "El-Fedein-Mafraq." In *Contribution française a l'archéologie jordanienne,* edited by François Villeneuve, 125–31. Amman: IFAPO.

Ibn Fadlān. 2013. *Ibn Fadlān and the Land of Darkness: Arab Travellers in the Far North.* Translated by Paul Lunde. London: Penguin.

Ibn Khaldun. 1958. *The Muqaddimah: An Introduction to History.* Translated by Franz Rosenthal. New York: Pantheon.

Ibn Khurradadhbih. 1865. *Kitāb al-masālik wa'l-mamālik* (Book of Itineraries and Kingdoms). Edited and translated by C. Barbier de Meynard. *Journal Asiatique* 5.

Ibn Rustah. 1891. *Kitāb al-'alāq al-nafīsa.* Edited by M. J. de Goeje. Leiden: Brill.

Ibn Taymiyya. 1976. *Ibn Taimīya's Struggle against Popular Religion: With an Annotated Translation of his Kitāb iqtiḍā' aṣ-ṣirāṭ al-mustaqīm mukhālafat aṣḥāb al-jaḥīm.* Edited and translated by Muhammad Umar Memon. The Hague; Paris: Mouton.

Ikhwan al-Safa, 2011. *Epistles of the Brethren of Purity: On Magic I, An Arabic Critical Edition and English Translation of Epistle 52a.* Edited and translated by Godefroid de Callatay and Bruno Halflants. Oxford: IIS.

Jansson, Ingmar. 1988. "Wikingerzeitlicher orientalischer Import in Skandinavien." *Bericht der Römisch-Germanischen Kommission* 69: 564–647.

Al-Jawbarī, Jamāl al-Dīn ʿAbd al-Raḥim. 2020. *The Book of Charlatans*. Edited by Manuela Dangler, translated by Humphrey Davies. New York: NYU Press.

Jonsson Hraundel, Thorir. 2013. "The Rus in Arabic Sources: Cultural Contacts and Identity." PhD dissertation, University of Bergen.

Kanaʿan, Ruba. 2012. "Patron and Craftsman of the Freer Mosul Ewer of 1232: A Historical and Legal Interpretation of the Roles of *Tilmīdh* and *Ghulām* in Islamic Metalwork." *Ars Orientalis* 42: 67–78.

Khamis, Elias. 2013. *The Fatimid Metalwork Hoard from Tiberias: Tiberias, Excavations in the House of the Bronzes, Final Report*, vol. 2. Jerusalem: Hebrew University of Jerusalem.

Kühnel, Ernst. 1920. "Islamische Kunstabteilung: Islamisches Räuchergerät." *Berliner Museen* 41, no. 6: 4–8.

Lawson Younger, K. Jr., 2012. "Another Look at an Aramaic Astral Bowl." *Journal of Near Eastern Studies* 71, no. 2: 209–30.

Lester, Ayala. 2004. "Glass and Metal Objects." In *Excavations at Tiberius, 1989–1994*, edited by Yizhar Hirschfeld, 59–68. Jerusalem: Israel Antiquities Authority.

Lester, Ayala. 2014. "Reconsidering Fatimid Metalware." In *Proceedings of the 8th International Congress on the Archaeology of the Ancient Near East*, vol. 3, edited by Piotr Bieliński et al., 437–54. Wiesbaden: Harrassowitz.

Lester, Ayala. 2017. "Hellenistic, Roman, and Byzantine Influence in the Consolidation of Fatimid Metalware." In *Artistry in Bronze: The Greeks and Their Legacy, XIXth International Conference on Ancient Bronzes*, edited by Jens M. Daehner, Kenneth Lapatin, and Ambra Spinelli, online publication. J. Paul Getty Trust.

Lester, Ayala, Yael D. Arnon, and Rachel Polak. 1999. "The Fatimid Hoard from Caesarea: A Preliminary Report." In *L'Égypte Fatimide: Son art et son histoire*, edited by Marianne Barrucand, 233–48. Paris: Paris-Sorbonne.

Lindstedt, Ilkka. 2019. 'Who Is In, Who Is Out? Early Muslim Identity through Epigraphy and Theory." *Jerusalem Studies in Arabic and Islam* 46: 147–246.

Luck, Georg. 2006. *Arcana Mundi: Magic and the Occult in the Greek and Roman Worlds*. Baltimore, MD: Johns Hopkins University Press.

Maddison, Francis, and Emily Savage-Smith. 1997. *Science, Tools and Magic: The Nasser D. Khalili Collection of Islamic Art*, vol. 12. London: Nour Foundation.

Melikian-Chirvani, A. S. 1982. *Islamic Metalwork from the Iranian World, 8–18th Centuries*. London: Her Majesty's Stationary Office.

Melvin-Koushki, Matthew. 2017. "In Defense of Geomancy: Šaraf al-Dīn Yazdī Rebuts Ibn Ḥaldūn's Critique of the Occult Sciences." *Arabica* 64: 346–403.

Metcalf, D. M. 1997. "Viking Age Numismatics 3: What Happened to the Islamic Dirhams after Their Arrival in the Northern Lands?" *The Numismatic Chronicle* 157: 295–335.

Meyer, L. A. 1959. *Islamic Metalworkers and Their Works*. Geneva: Albert Kundig.

Michailidis, Melanie. 2012. "Samanid Silver and Trade along the Fur Route." *Medieval Encounters* 18: 315–38.

Moussaeiff, Arieh, et al. 2008. "Incensole Acetate, an Incense Component, Elicits Psychoactivity by Activating TRPV3 Channels in the Brain." *FASEB Journal* 22, no. 8: 3024–34.

Mulder, Stephennie. 2017. "The Rise and Fall of the Viking 'Allah' Textile." *Hyperallergic*, October 27. https://hyperallergic.com/407746/refuting-viking-allah-textiles-meaning/.

Noble, Michael. 2020. "Sabian Astral Magic as Soteriology in Fakhr al-Dīn al-Rāzī's *al-Sirr al-maktūm*." In *Islamicate Occult Sciences in Theory and Practice*, edited by Liana Saif, Francesca Leoni, Matthew Melvin-Koushki, and Farouk Yahya, 207–29. Leiden: Brill.

Noble, Michael-Sebastian. 2021. *Philosophising the Occult: Avicennan Psychology and the "Hidden Secret" of Fakhr al-Dīn al-Rāzī*. Berlin: de Gruyter, 2021.

Nylander, Carl. 2009. "Sweden iii. Swedish Archaeological Missions to Iran." *Encyclopedia Iranica* [online]. Accessed December 1, 2020. http://www.iranicaonline.org/articles/sweden-iii-swedish-archeological-missions-to-iran.

O'Kane, Bernard, ed. 2006. *The Treasures of Islamic Art in the Museums of Cairo*. Cairo: American University in Cairo Press.

Ory, Solange. 1990. "Aspects religieux des textes épigraphiques du début de l'Islam." *Revue du monde musulman et de la Méditerranée* 58: 30–39.

Pettinato, Giovanni. 1966. "Libanomanzia presso i Babilonesi." *Rivista degli studi orientali* 41, no. 4: 303–27.

Piotrovsky, M. B., and J. M. Rogers, eds. 2004. *Heaven on Earth: Art from Islamic Lands*. Munich; Berlin; London; New York: Prestel.

Pope, Arthur Upham, and Phyllis Ackermann, eds. 1938–39. *A Survey of Persian Art from Prehistoric Times to the Present*. London; New York: Oxford University Press.

Porter, Venetia. 2010. "The Use of Arabic Script in Magic." *Proceedings of the Seminar for Arabian Studies* 40, supplement *The Development of Arabic Script as a Written Language*: 131–40.

Porter, Venetia. 2011. *Arabic and Persian Seals and Amulets in the British Museum*. London: British Museum.

Prado, Shalen. 2020. "Esoteric Botanical Knowledge-scapes of Medieval Iberia." *Archaeological Review from Cambridge* 35, no. 2: 98–111.

Raby, Julian. 1986. "Looking for Silver in Clay: A New Perspective on Samanid Ceramics." In *Pots and Pans: A Colloquium on Precious Metals and Ceramics in the Muslim, Chinese and Graeco-Roman Worlds, Oxford 1985*, edited by Michael Vickers, 179–203. Oxford: Oxford University Press.

Rashidi, Koroush. 2020. "Openwork in Early Islamic Metalwork from Khorasan and Transoxiana." PhD dissertation, University of Bamberg.

Reiner, Erica. "Astral Magic in Babylonia." *Transactions of the American Philosophical Society* 85, no. 4: 1–150.

Richardson, Kristina. 2022. *Roma in the Medieval Islamic World: Literacy, Culture, and Migration*. London: I. B. Tauris.

Ritter, Helmutt, ed. 1933. *Pseudo-Magrīṭī: Das Ziel des Weisen*. Leipzig; Berlin: Teubner.

Roberts, Alexandre M. 2017. "Being a Sabian at Court in Tenth-Century Baghdad." *Journal of the American Oriental Society* 137, no. 2: 253–77.

Rogers, J. M. 2010. *The Arts of Islam: Masterpieces from the Khalili Family Collection*. London: Nour Foundation.

Rubensohn, Otto, and Friedrich Sarre. 1929. "Ein Fund frühislamischer Bronzegefäsze in Ägypten, vermutlich aus dem Besitz des letzten Omajjaden Marvan II." *Jahrbuch des Preuszischen Kunstsammlungen* 50: 85–95.

Saif, Liana. 2016. "The Cow and the Bees: Arabic Sources and Parallels for Pseudo-Plato's *Liber Vaccae (Kitāb al-Nawāmīs)*." *Journal of the Warburg and Courtauld Institutes* 79, no. 1: 1–47.

Saif, Liana. 2017. "From *Ġāyat al-ḥakīm* to *Šams al-maʿārif*: Ways of Knowing and Paths of Power in Medieval Islam." *Arabica* 64, 297–345.

Saif, Liana. 2020. "A Study of the Ikhwān al-Ṣafāʾ's Epistle on Magic, the Longer Version (52b)." In *Islamicate Occult Sciences in Theory and Practice*, edited by Liana Saif, Francesca Leoni, Matthew Melvin-Koushki, and Farouk Yahya, 162–206. Leiden: Brill.

Saif, Liana. 2021. "A Preliminary Study of the Pseudo-Aristotelian Hermetica: Texts, Contexts, and Doctrines." *Al-ʿUṣūr al-Wusṭā* 29: 20–80.

Saif, Liana, Francesca Leoni, Matthew Melvin-Koushki, and Farouk Yahya, eds. 2020. *Islamicate Occult Sciences in Theory and Practice*. Leiden: Brill.

Samuel, Sigal. 2017. "The Strangely Revealing Debate Over Viking Couture." *The Atlantic*, October 17. https://www.theatlantic.com/international/archive/2017/10/viking-couture-allah/543045/.

Sarre, Friedrich. 1934. "Die Bronzenkanne des Kalifen Marwān II im arabischen Museum in Kairo." *Ars Islamica* 1: 10–16.

Savage-Smith, Emily. 2003. "Islamic Magical Texts vs. Magical Artefacts." *Societas Magica Newsletter* 11 (Fall): 1–6.

Scanlon, George T. 1984. "Fusṭāṭ Expedition: Preliminary Report 1978." *Journal of the American Research Center in Egypt* 21: 1–38.

Al-Sirafi, Faisal. 1960. "Hafriyat ʿayn dāra." *Les Annales Archéologiques de Syrie* 10: 87–102.

Smith, Marion B., and Emily Savage-Smith. 1980. *Islamic Geomancy and a Thirteenth-Century Divinatory Device*. Malibu, CA: Undena Publications.

Smith, Marion B., and Emily Savage-Smith. 2004. "Islamic Geomancy and a Thirteenth-Century Divinatory Device: Another Look." In *Magic and Divination in Early Islam*, edited by Emily Savage-Smith, 211–76. London: Routledge.

Sundström, Ulla. 2006. "En järnrings förbannelse en studie i religionshistoria om en ring från Gästriklands Vikingatid." Master's thesis, University of Gävle.

Thurlkill, Mary. 2016. *Sacred Scents in Early Christianity and Islam*. London: Lexington Books.

Treiger, Alexander. 2021. "Plato and Aristotle Holding Scrolls: An Arabic Ekphrasis of a Christian Painting?" *Studia graeco-arabica* 11, no. 1: 229–40.

Troupeau, Gérard. 1979. "Les fêtes des Chrétiens vues par un juriste musulman." In *Mélanges offert à Jean Dauvillier*, edited by Germain Sicard et al., 795–802. Toulouse: Toulouse Centre d'Histoire Juridique Méridionale.

Von Gladiss, Almut. 1989. "Räuchergefäß mit Zange." In *Europa und der Orient, 800–1900*, edited by Gereon Sievernich und Hendrik Budde, 523–24. Berlin: Bertelsmann Lexicon Verlag.

Ward, Rachel. 1991. "Incense and Incense Burners in Mamluk Egypt and Syria." *Transactions of the Oriental Ceramics Society* 55: 67–82.

Ward, Rachel. 1993. *Islamic Metalwork*. London: British Museum.

Weinryb, Ittai. 2016. *The Bronze Object in the Middle Ages*. Cambridge: Cambridge University Press.

Zadeh, Travis. 2009. "Touching and Ingesting: Early Debates over the Material Quran." *Journal of the American Oriental Society* 129, no. 3: 443–66.

Zadeh, Travis. 2020. "Postscript: Cutting Ariadne's Thread, or How to Think Otherwise in the Maze." In *Islamicate Occult Sciences in Theory and Practice*, edited by Liana Saif, Francesca Leoni, Matthew Melvin-Koushki, and Farouk Yahya, 607–50. Leiden: Brill.

Ziffer, Irit. 1996. *Islamic Metalwork*. Tel Aviv: Eretz Israel Museum.

Zimmerle, William Gerard. 2021. "Frankincense and Its Arabian Burner." In *All Things Arabia: Arabian Identity and Material Culture*, edited by Ileana Baird and Hülya Yağcıoğlu, 23–42. Leiden: Brill.

TIME

CENSERS

SWINGING THROUGH TIME: CENSERS IN THE LATIN WEST

Beate Fricke

In the left panel of Rogier van der Weyden's *Bladelin Altarpiece* (ca. 1460), the Roman emperor Augustus holds a censer and swings it with his right hand, while the fingers of his left touch the fur around the brim of his hat [Figure 1]. His fixed right elbow appears to be stopping the movement of the vessel, which continues to sway from the four metal chains held together at the top. The gray hairs of his beard and the foliated decoration of the censers' handle intersect, as if the shock of the vision appearing in front of the kneeling emperor has caused a sudden movement or, rather, an abrupt standstill; he has sunk to his knees in adoration of what he sees in front of his inner eye.

What he sees is the Madonna seated on a stone bench surrounded by a golden mandorla. Rays of light emanate from the Virgin's apparition, pouring through the window frame into the domestic interior in which Augustus kneels. Mary appears to the emperor in the right part of the window, which comprises a series of frames: the opened wooden shutters, the vertical axis of the central mullion, and the glass tracery at the top embellished with an eagle on each side. Below Mary's stone throne, these frames guide the viewer's eyes from the interior into the exterior, encouraging the eye to wander through the fertile fields of a cultivated landscape with soft hills and a few bushes and trees.

This painted scene is a fiction inspired by the widely circulated *Legenda Aurea* (*Golden Legend*), a collection of Christian legends of saints with a detailed account of Christ's life compiled by Jacobus de Voragine in the second half of the thirteenth century. According to Stephan Kemperdick, van der Weyden relied heavily on Voragine's text, which states that the emperor had been urged by the senators to ask the Tiburtine Sibyl whether a more powerful ruler than himself would ever be born. Then at noon on the day of Christ's birth, the Madonna and Child appeared on an altar in the sky. The Sibyl revealed the power of the child to Augustus, and as a reaction to this divine revelation he made a sacrifice of incense, a Roman practice for worshiping the gods, thus implying that he no longer wished to be worshiped as a god himself. In van der Weyden's painting we see the emperor kneeling before this vision, framed and offset by the window, while making his offering and holding his crown in reverence. The Sibyl stands to the side, interpreting the heavenly sign while three men from the emperor's entourage act as witnesses.[1]

Voragine's legend is just one source of inspiration among many; as Hiltrud Westermann-Angerhausen has emphasized, the altarpiece's overall composition combines events from different times and regions in a kind of atemporal "super-vision" framed by the fifteenth-century Flemish cityscape in the background [Figure 2].[2] In the central panel, the commissioner—the wealthy Pieter Bladelin (ca. 1410–72), who climbed Bruges' social ladder from a city tax collector to the treasury secretary of Burgundy and the

Figure 2

Figure 1
Rogier van der Weyden,
Bladelin Altarpiece, left wing
panel: Vision of Augustus,
ca. 1460, oil on oak panel,
93.5 × 41.7 cm, Berlin,
Gemäldegalerie, in
Dirk de Vos, *Rogier van der
Weyden. Das Gesamtwerk*
(Hirmer 1999), 242.

Figure 2
Rogier van der Weyden,
Bladelin Altarpiece, ca. 1460,
oil on oak panel, 107.7 × 218.8 cm,
Berlin, Gemäldegalerie, in
Dirk de Vos, *Rogier van
der Weyden. Das Gesamtwerk*
(Hirmer 1999), 242–43.

treasurer of the Order of the Golden Fleece—is shown in a scene that exists beyond time and space, as he kneels and venerates the birth of Christ and wears a dark robe that suggests his humility. On the right wing is yet another vision: the celestial apparition of the Christ Child as the star guiding the three kings of Bileam from the east towards Bethlehem. Each of these depictions revolves around various valences of visual revelation. At the same time, the altarpiece reveals the Flemish painter's knowledge regarding how to use a censer. Some painters might even have been involved in designing these liturgical tools, as possibly suggested by the print by Martin Schongauer [Figure 3], while others demonstrate in their painting evident ignorance of the role of the middle chain to lift the lid, the metal cover would be too hot to touch in this case. [Figure 4].

Yet if we return to the left panel featuring Augustus, we can see how this artwork's metanarrative depends on more than things seen or witnessed. Shifting our attention from the window frame and lighting effects—painterly strategies that privilege the visual—and instead pursue the traces of painted smoke and their imagined scent, we encounter another layer of sensory meaning. A fine line of smoke billows out of the top of the censer's flamboyant metal tracery and wafts in the air towards the open windows, although it does not overlap with the rays of light emanating from Mary. Rather, smoke and light encounter each other at the window frame, which reveals itself as a threshold between the visible world and the imaginary realm of the emperor's vision, between the carefully depicted reality of a private sleeping chamber in the house of a very wealthy tradesman and the divine sphere of Mary and Christ's apparition. At the same time, these categories of visible and invisible are at odds with each other, since according to the painting's system of artifice it is the vision that is most "real" and illuminating compared to the earthly space that is shown to be as ephemeral as the disappearing smoke. Light and smoke's intersection thus highlights both a connection as well as a disjunction between spheres of reality and its perception. It is the censer and its smoke that links and calls into question notions of order: between the real and imaginary, past and present, spaces of the profane and sacred.

This chapter will explore how censers came to take on this type of mediating function and how their transcendental liturgical function came to elide with their role as "art" objects that, whether real or depicted, innately challenged spheres of perception and depiction. By tracing the *longue durée* history of censers' uses in Latin liturgies from Late Antiquity to the time around 1500, this contribution seeks to probe how the functional and ritual came to inflect late medieval notions of the artistic.

The extant corpus of censers is quite heterogeneous because of differing materials, locations, and original contexts; numerous objects can hardly be contextualized at all since they have lost any record of their provenance. Yet as we shall see, a close reading of the use, shape, and materiality of specific examples of censers are allowing us to better understand the original functions they might have had.

The initial close reading of the fifteenth-century painting showing a Roman emperor leads us to brief remarks on the use of censers and incense in the first centuries of Christianity in the Latin West in both public and private realms. After looking into the written sources describing the use of the censers, this chapter turns to the analysis of selected censers. Particularly lavishly ornamented censers with complex iconographical programs

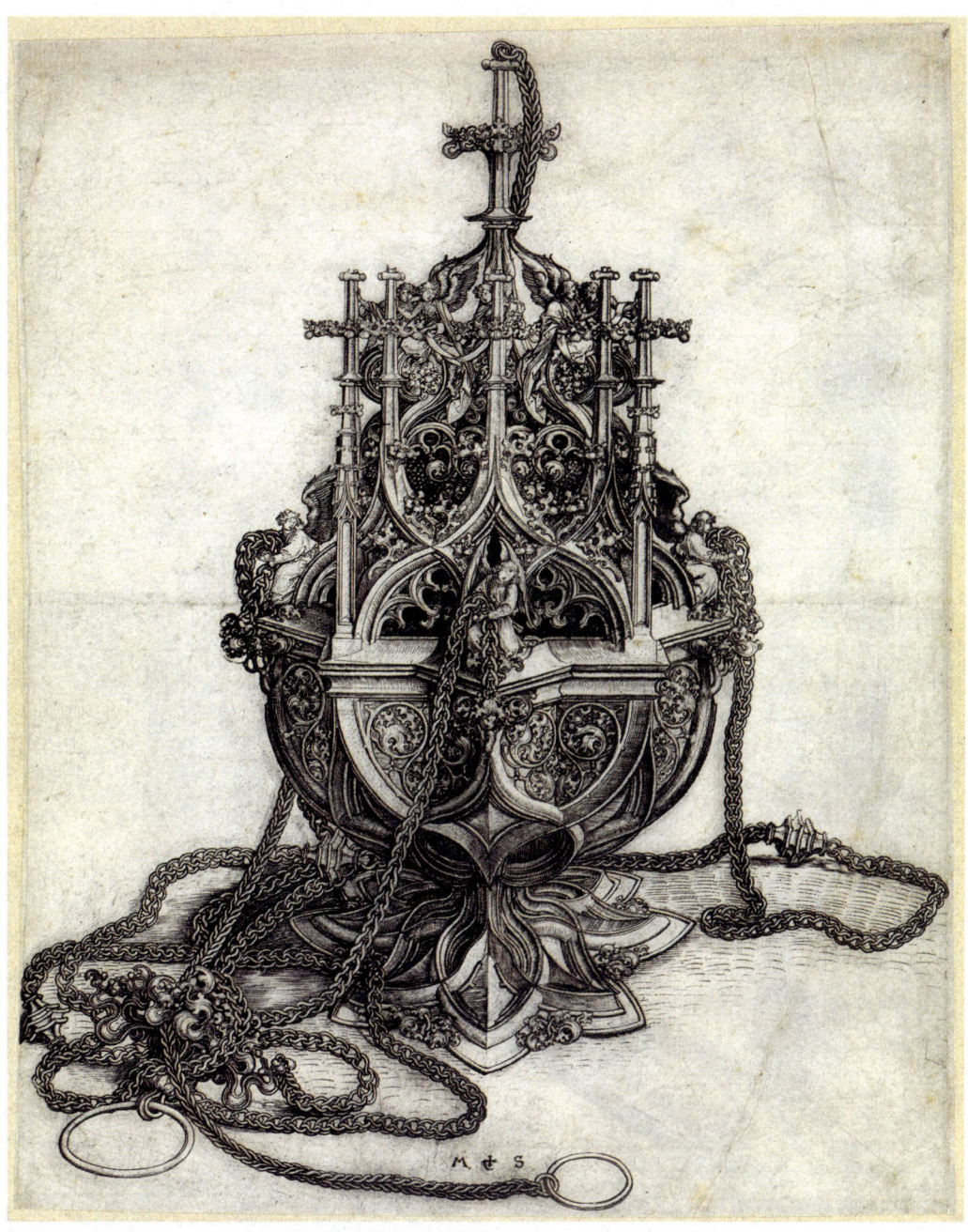

Figure 3
Martin Schongauer, censer,
second half of the 15th
century, copper engraving,
26 × 20.7 cm, Kunsthalle
Karlsruhe, inv. no.1953-37.

Figure 4
After Hugo van der Goes,
Death of the Virgin, last quarter
of the 15th century, panel,
25 × 36 cm, Prague,
Prague Castle Picture Gallery.

have survived from two periods in the Latin West: the twelfth and the fifteenth centuries. Therefore, especially during the twelfth century, and again in the fifteenth, such use came to be understood on a metalevel, i.e., the censers refer in their decoration to mankind's relationship between micro-macrocosmos, as well to the actual practices in which they were involved, and this was especially the case for liturgical censers in sacred contexts, whose makers seem to have understood the ways in which their creations navigated and connected object, ritual, space, art, and ideas about creation. Emphasizing the symbolic function of the liturgically used object, these craftspeople invited the user/beholder of their vessels to transgress thresholds, like the smoke emanating from their artful creations.

Between the twelfth and fifteenth centuries, in the thirteenth and fourteenth centuries, the censers experience a significant rise in being depicted in the ornamentation of liturgical spaces, they feature prominently in glass painting, are depicted in reliefs on portals, and on tombs, and decorate standing figures embellishing liturgical furniture such as pulpits. This overview about censers in Latin liturgies shows that the relationship between the Roman and the Christian use, and the profane and sacred realms much like in the painted altar wing by Rogier van der Weyden (Figure 1), hinges upon the relationship between vision, smoke, and smell. Connecting these different periods in one painting created a unique kind of visual timewarp. This timewarp enables the beholder of the Flemish altar to travel into the past, not only pre-Christianity but also to switch mentally between Roman/pagan and Christian/sacred religious practices, as well as between religious and profane customs in which the use of incense, and therefore objects like the censer, played an important role.

PRIVATE AND PUBLIC USES OF INCENSE
ACCORDING TO WRITTEN SOURCES

Van der Weyden's altarpiece, rather than showing an incense offering in its usual medieval pictorial form, a gift from the Magi, presents us with a quite unique scenario that blends time and space. On the one hand, we see incense used by Augustus in the private, domestic, and pagan space of a bed chamber. On the other, this vignette appears on an artwork made for a public Christian altar; it asks us to consider the typological relationship between the pagan past and the liturgy taking place before the painting. While this entanglement of pagan and Christian, private and public, might seem to be at odds with each other, censers have a long history of use between these contexts, as evidenced by extant written sources from Roman and Christian contexts alike.

Censers were made for daily use in private and public rituals such as caring for the ill or tending to the soul of the deceased; they were also deployed in profane and sacred spaces, from churches, chapels, or tombs to households, public monuments, and baths. This multifunctional context contradicts much early scholarship by both historians and art historians, both of whom dealt little with interrogating the origins of censers' uses and often assumed that sacrificing incense was generally condemned by Christians and not practiced in early liturgical performances.[3] In Pliny's letter to Trajan that was written during prosecutions of Early Christians in the Roman Empire, for instance, Pliny suggested that people suspected of being Christians were encouraged to venerate images and offer incense and wine:

Those who denied being or having been Christians I thought
I should release, since they called upon the gods with a formula recited by me and offered incense and wine before your
image, which I had brought for this purpose together with
the images of the gods, and also reviled Christ—things which
real Christians, it is said, cannot be forced to do.[4]

The extraordinary variety of extant incense burners in various forms (some
open, some closed) and made from an array of materials including precious
metal suggest that they were, in fact, widely used in both Christian empires
succeeding the Roman Empire—the Latin West and in the Greek East—since
antiquity.[5] Many of the early censers, whether in box form with animals on
top of them, or those shaped like fruits, heads, or busts, were probably intended for private environments as quality functional objects, rather than

Figure 5

for religious services [Figure 5]. This is likely also the case with so-called
"smoking pans" with handles or stems.[6] Especially towards the fifth and
sixth centuries we can observe an increase in ornaments on censers that
can clearly be identified as Christian, such as the Chi-Rho sign, heads of
saints, or inscriptions. However, neither their decoration nor their form tell
us how and where they were used.

Egon Wamers has shown in his survey of pre-Carolingian censers
that open bowls as well as rarer examples with a hinged top were often

Figure 6

outfitted with three chains conjoined in a stable hook [Figure 6].[7] Regardless
of iconography, the types of contexts and performances within which such
early examples were used cannot be determined.[8] What is certain, however,
is that many were discovered in subsequent centuries as burial accessories;
while this does not necessarily aid in deciphering their initial uses and contexts, it does help to situate their ritual potential.[9] Less often, one finds
vessels in the form of heads. Either faces or masks, usually four on one object,
can sometimes be found as adornments of censer basins with and without
chains. The preserved Early Christian censers could have been used in both
sacred and profane contexts; together with the depictions of their usage,
most of them relate to burial practices and ideas of cleansing.

Some censers can indeed be attributed to Early Christian contexts.
While the earlier Christian examples often feature hexagonal forms, with

Figure 7

saints depicted in medallions on their lateral sides [Figure 7], later examples
from the sixth through the twelfth century favored depictions of Christ's
life unfolding as a story around their bodies [Figure 6]. Considering the
implications of this shift in form and decoration might also help us to better
understand their intended function. Hexagonal forms with figural decoration,
common among censers produced up to the sixth century, suggest a strong
connection to the architectural spaces in which they were likely used, such
as baptisteries, mausolea, martyria, or church buildings with a hexagonal
footprint or a rotunda at their core. Such a shape eventually disappeared
around the turn of the seventh century and gave way to rounded forms
bearing figurative ornamentation, yet another indication that censers engendered reflection upon not only the spaces and ways that they were deployed, but also their status as artwork able to transcend the geographical
and temporal.[10]

Figure 5
Censer, Italy (?), 11th to
14th century (?), copper alloy,
10 × 11.9 cm, New York,
Metropolitan Museum of Art,
Rogers Fund, 1967.

Figure 6
Censer, Byzantium, Syrian (?),
Palestinian (?), 7th century,
cast bronze, engraved,
9.2 × 10.3 cm, Geneva, Musées
d'art et d'histoire. © MAH
Genève. Photo: Bettina Jacot
Descombes.

Figure 7
Hexagonal censer, 582–602,
sheet silver and copper,
13.9 × 9.5 cm, Munich,
Bayerisches Nationalmuseum,
inv. no. 65/46. Photo
no. D96442, Bastian Krack.

Figures 8–9

Figures 10–11

In particular in the twelfth century [Figures 8 and 9], and especially since then (Figures 10 and 11), censers became nodal points in the liturgy with the potential to build bridges between the beholder and the event. Such a role is echoed in their decoration, with certain examples bearing references to the Heavenly Jerusalem and scenes embellishing the lunettes circling the base that show the Old Testament events thought to foretell Christ's sacrifice. Such typologies might be understood to bridge not only time but also the object with the spectators and building surrounding it.

Because of the transgressive properties of the censers themselves, the sparse medieval textual sources like inventories can limit interpretation, but the availability of written records around the use and meaning of incense itself can help us to better understand how the vessels might have been understood. Towards the late eighth century, the Carolingian liturgical use seems to have evolved from the stationary installation of vessels for burning incense towards a more active mobilization of the "moving parts" of Christian liturgy; liturgical spaces, in other words, came to be filled with movement and sound (sung and spoken words) as well as odor and smoke. The fire-safe use of liturgical handheld censers stands in a direct relationship to the "dramatization of the liturgy" in ninth-century France, to use Jungmann's words.[11] One decisive moment in this shift was the instruction given in the primary source describing the liturgy to wave censers in a motion drawing a cross and crown in the air.[12] Unlike previously, when they were either placed or hung at prominent places in the church and carried only during celebratory processions, around the turn of the millennium they were more often dramatically swung during mass and had to be frequently opened up to be refilled with fresh incense. An *ordo* from the end of the ninth century describes that two *thuriferari* ("incense-bearers") with a censer should stand next to the lector while he reads the text of the gospel.[13]

Aligning with this handheld use came, too, innovations in censers' designs. Earlier examples from the fourth through the eighth century had chains fixed to the edge of the bowl, thus precluding the placement of a lid (Figure 6). This particular example must have been stationary because it offered its user no protection against heat and fire and, moreover, such an open composition would have made it impossible to move the censer around or swing it while in use. According to surviving censers and depictions showing their use during the period, the chains on most surviving vessels rarely exceeded double the height of the bowls. These kinds of short chains would have sufficed to carry the burner, but they would not have been ideal for swinging the bowl; they would quickly have become dangerous and caused a fire. Other censers from this earlier period that did have lids connected the upper and lower portions with a hinge (Figure 8).[14] In order to refill these and place new incense on the hot coals, one would have had to open the censer from a particular position, a difficult task to accomplish without burning oneself and certainly clumsy if it were incorporated into the liturgical performance. Finally, the fixed placement of these pre-1100 examples was also a priority when the objects were not in use. While the bases are generally quite heterogeneous, from socle-like rings to sets of feet, almost all censers from this period feature some kind of integrated component at the bottom that allows them to stand in one place.

Figure 8
Gozbert-Censer, Cologne,
end of the 12th century,
bronze, 21.6 × 14.2 cm,
Trier, Domschatz, in
Hiltrud Westermann-
Angerhausen, 2014, S. 14.

Figure 9
Reiner of Huy, censer, second
quarter of the 12th century,
bronze, 16 × 10 cm, Lille, Musée
des Beaux-Arts, in *Ornamenta
ecclesiae. Kunst und Künstler
der Romanik* (exh. cat. Cologne,
Schnütgen Museum), ed.
Anton Legner, vol. 1 (Cologne,
1985), 477.

Figure 10
Arnolfo di Cambio, Tomb of
Riccardo Annibaldi, frieze
fragments, marble, Basilica
di San Giovani in Laterano,
Rome. © Katharina Böhmer.

Figure 11
Arnolfo di Cambio, column,
1265–67, marble, 105 cm,
Florence, Palazzo del
Bargello o del Podesta
gia del Capitano del Popolo.
Creative Commons 4.0.

MATERIALITY AND MORPHOLOGY

The use, function, and performative capacity of medieval censers was also intimately intertwined with the materials out of which they were made. While most of those that survive are bronze or ceramic, as Westermann-Angerhausen has demonstrated, according to medieval textual sources like inventories, it seems as though precious metals were used most often. Censers made of precious metal were, however, a short-lived phenomenon, their material composition making their status all the more fleeting; they were an easily financially convertible resource, resulting in them being subject to theft and looting; they were also lost to accidents such as a fire. Of the approximately 110 incense burners that appear in treasury inventories of churches between 800 and 1300, Bernhard Bischoff has counted nine golden ones, forty-four silver, and some others that were gilded with an unknown substrate.[15] Only thirteen incense burners of non-precious metal are listed in the inventory, though five of those are specifically mentioned as gilded. Around fifty censers are listed with no material assigned. Several of these, however, correspond in terms of content or context with other silver objects listed in the inventory, so it can be deduced that the majority of these were also made of silver. Since some church inventories were used or made in overlapping contexts, it could well be that some objects are named multiple times; the mention of censors in these sources thus has little statistical value and only helps us to gain a general impression about the types of materials used. It seems as though bronze was the most common material of choice for censers not made of precious metals, as evidenced by their use in rural and urban parish churches across Scandinavia, the Lower Rhine region, Westphalia, and south into Switzerland.[16] There are strikingly few preserved medieval bronze censers, especially in the Catholic regions of Western Europe, since in the early modern period they were often replaced with more expensive works made from the new reserves of precious metal coming from the Americas. Despite this historical and historiographical bias against purportedly lesser materials, there is evidence from early in the Middle Ages that censers' perceived value did not necessarily come from the raw material. In an 811 inventory of Staffelsee, a partially gilt silver censer is described as presented on the altar together with another made of non-precious metal.[17] The latter had an antique pedigree and was probably perceived to have had the same value or status.

The written source that speaks most elaborately and knowledgably about the materiality, shape, and by extension performativity of medieval censers comes from Theophilus Presbyter.[18] The pseudonym veils a craftsperson and monk who compiled detailed descriptions of medieval arts and the techniques of their making, from painting, to glass painting, to metalwork. Composed of three volumes with elaborate accompanying prologues, his tract is commonly known under the title the *Schedula diversarum artium* ("List of Various Arts") or *De diversis artibus* ("On Various Arts") and was probably written down between 1100 and 1120. The prologue for the third book shifts the attention of the reader from the ceiling, walls, and windows of the liturgical built environment towards the "vessels of the House of God without which the divine mysteries and services of the offices cannot continue." He continues by listing them: "These are they: Chalices, candlesticks, censers, cruets, shrines, reliquaries for holy relics, crosses, covers for gospel books and the rest of the things which custom necessarily demands for the ecclesiastical rites."[19]

After a long description of a goldsmith's workshop, he turns to a description of technologies with so much detail that the author clearly speaks from the perspective of significant experience in executing these techniques and observing their making. The same attention is given to the description of making two censers in chapters 60 and 61, one repoussé and the other cast. Both censers consist of a central core and hang from four chains, with a fifth chain included to lift the lid. The forms, Theophilus notes, take the shape of complex "architecture" and are inhabited by two different types of figurines. In the case of the repoussé censer, adornments come in sets of fours; the four rivers of paradise pour water from their vessels, and below are the four symbols of the evangelists.[20] The two stories of a cruciform architectural structure form the upper part of the censer's body and are crowned with a central octagonal tower, whose openings are animated by winged angels. Theophilus concludes this passage with a fictive dialogue with himself as a student, wherein it is discussed that a censer could take a form that would represent Heavenly Jerusalem: "but if anyone wants to put more work into it so as to make the censer of more precious craftsmanship, he can represent the city which the prophet saw on the mountain in the following way."[21]

The architectural form in Theophilus's description of the repoussé censer in chapter 60 also shows strong analogies, as Westermann-Angerhausen has pointed out, to what is probably the most sophistically elaborated cast censer still extant from the Latin West: that crafted by a certain Gozbertus [Figure 8]. The censer surfaced in a parish church in a village in the Ardennes in 1845 and was brought to the cathedral of Trier, where it has been kept since. Although the architectural structure resembles Theophilus's description, the iconography of the Gozbertus censer reveals striking differences. At the core of the Gozbertus censer are scenes related to the Eucharist: Melchizedeck with bread and wine; Solomon's throne on the top. The round bottom half, surmounted by a three-leveled structure with a cruciform ground plan, houses thirty-seven figures: twelve prophets on the bottom half, twelve apostles, and eight angels in half figures on the crenellated upper part surround Solomon on his throne at the top. The last five of the thirty-seven figures are represented in scenes of offering: Abraham's sacrifice of Isaac, Abel with the lamb, and Jacob receiving Isaac's blessing. Prophets and apostles adorn the lower and upper parts, but now with a typological structure, linking figures from the Old and New Testaments. The cast censer emphasizes a strong connection between the cast, connections between liturgy, and the connection of different layers of time (Old and New Testaments).

In juxtaposing Theophilus's passage with the Gozbertus censer in Trier, we begin to see how even detailed written sources describing objects differ to the still extant objects. Yet there is also evidence to suggest that the censer not only linked temporal and liturgical spheres, but rather embodied the combining of the spheres through its own materiality and form. In another contemporary text also written in the twelfth century, Honorius of Autun draws a parallel between the body of Christ and a censer, since both were material entities in their own right as well as vessels. According to Honorius, if the fire inside the censer represented the Holy Spirit within Christ, the incense was his divinity:

And indeed, the thurible [censer] signifies the body of the Lord; the incense, his divinity; the fire, the Holy Ghost. If the thurible is golden, it points to his divinity, which surpasses all things. If it is silver, it shows his humanity, shining with the holiness of all. If it is of copper, it declares his flesh, frail for our sake. If it is of iron, it represents his dead flesh which overcame death in resurrection.

If the thurible has four chains, it signifies that four elements composed the body of the Lord, which was full of the four virtues: prudence, fortitude, justice, and temperance. A fifth chain, which separates the thurible into two parts, designates the soul of Christ, which was separated from his body by death. If, however, the thurible has three chains, it signifies that human flesh, a rational soul, and the divinity of the Word become the one person of Christ, and the fourth chain which separates the parts is the power which in death laid down the soul for the sheep. But if the thurible is held by only one chain, it designates that he himself was born of a virgin without stain, and alone is said to be free among the dead.

The ring, which ties all these together, is the divinity by which all these things are contained, and whose majesty is in no sense confined.[22]

Honorius interprets the different materials from which a censer could be made and the number of chains as different potential representations of Christ's appearance. The twelfth century is the period in which the materials used for the creation of liturgical objects were often chosen according to an allegorical meaning and interpreted accordingly. Several texts such as the short tracts on "The twelve stones" describing the qualities of twelve different kinds of stone or school texts produced for Latin students, such as Alain de Lille's *Complaint of Nature* or his *Anticlaudian*, employ such iconographic readings of the qualities of materials for understanding the creation of liturgical objects.[23]

Particularly emphasized in the written primary sources, and equally striking and characteristic for the use of censers in Latin liturgies, is that ornamentation of the censers themselves evoke the actions in which they were involved and the experiences that they allowed: the sensorial perception of smoke, its smell, and the invisibility caused by the smoke juxtaposed with the material sheen of the metal. For example, the connection of the prayer with the liturgical sacrifice of the Eucharist aligns with the depicted moments of sacrifice on the censers. According to Honorius of Autun "the smoke of the spices represent[s] the prayers of the saints."[24] In a long line of clerical writers, Durandus, bishop of Mende, follows in his symbolic interpretation of incense his predecessors such as Gregory the Great and Bede the Venerable; according to his description, the censer was the heart of man that should be "open above to look upward and closed below to retain."[25]

MERGING MOMENTS OF TIME—CONNECTING SPHERES
THROUGH CENSERS AND SENSES

During the twelfth century, the censer made by Reiner of Huy placed not a king from the Old Testament, but an angel on the tip of the bronze censer with the Hebrews, who refused to worship the statue of the Babylonian king Nebuchadnezzar [Figure 9]. He threw them into a burning furnace, where flames instead spared their flesh:

> The angel of the Lord went down with Azarias and his companions into the furnace: and he drove the flame of the fire out of the furnace and made the midst of the furnace like the blowing of a wind bringing dew, and the fire touched them not at all, nor troubled them, nor did them any harm.[26]

With this biblical verse in mind, one can see how the gilded figures of the three Hebrews and the angel in their midst are surrounded by billowing smoke from the charcoal in the censer, and how the sweet smell of incense ensures the beholder that the three young men are spared from the punishment. The slits in the angel reveal a loss of what would have been the angel's wings. They would have crowned the tip of the censer and contributed further to the dispersion of the smoke emanating from it. The three young men are sitting on a bench framing the censer's upper edge. The roundels decorating the upper half provide openings for the smoke and are filled by birds and beasts. A long inscription surrounds the middle of the censer, which is divided in two parts, and provides the name of Reiner of Huy:

> I, Reiner, give this sign so that you give your similar prayers when my death has been accomplished, and I ask that the prayers rise (like the smoke of incense) to the face of Christ.[27]

Heidi Gearhart has recently pointed our attention to the connection between this censer and the writings of Rupert of Deutz, a monk and exegete who taught in Liège in the twelfth century. According to Rupert, the different gestures and poses depicted on Reiner of Huys's censer represent "different aspects of the holy life: grace, action, and salvation." The three characters are described by Rupert: "Sidrach is my noble one, Misach the one who laughs, and Abdenago the one serving in silence." Gearhart convincingly argues that the censer functioned "as a gift for the sake of his soul when Reiner is gone, it is a sign and request for future spiritual benefits."[28] This inscription also emphasizes a strong connection between terrestrial and celestial spheres made through the smoke of incense. The smoke rising upwards from the censer accompanies the prayers, or leads towards a vision, and connects the earthly and the divine realms.

Around the turn of the fourteenth century, there are instances in which censers again became stationary objects, depicted within static media like sculpture, an artistic act that endowed such compositions with the transgressive properties of actual censers from the time. Such a shift is especially visible in a group of marble ensembles sculpted by the Pisano family (Figures 10 and 11). One is a tomb frieze from the circa-1289 tomb of Riccardo Annibaldi showing figures carrying censers in a funerary procession, where we can see in particular a male figure blowing into a carefully half-opened censer. Because he holds the censer within his hands, the carvers have emphasized its portability; the censer must have been the sort that had a suspended container holding coals within the larger body of the censer, thus preventing the heating of the exterior. The second example, attributed to the school of Nicola Pisano and now in the Bargello National Museum, probably served as an ornamental column supporting a pulpit. Again, we see three male figures, probably clerics or acolytes. One carries a tall bottle, and the other two censers of different types: one has a globular shape with long chains held in the figure's left hand; the other is a half-opened *navicula* held in the figure's right hand. Liturgical acts here are frozen into a columnar triad around which actual people would have moved and carried similar objects. In doubling the performance of censers and juxtaposing the static with the movable, spheres of time and space, of the terrestrial and celestial, seem to come together to produce a new set of order, neither here nor there, timely nor timeless. Smoke, blurred vision, and imagination is both frozen in time and leads the beholder to contemplate the relationship between the timeless and the ephemeral.

The blurring of such purported dichotomies brings us back to the fifteenth-century Northern European context that was our point of departure. Northern Europe in the fifteenth century provides a context in which paintings were conceived to embody a dialectic wherein close observation of the "natural" paradoxically belied painting's own reality and inherently signaled the temporal, divine, and performative expanses beyond it. Censers, we have seen, developed similarly, and their proliferation across paintings of the late Middle Ages suggests something of their status as an instrument able to communicate the blending of different spheres between which censers and painted alike are hinged. In one Death of the Virgin painted by the Master of Amsterdam, for example, we see two mourners activating a censer by pulling up the lid and adding new resin to the glowing charcoal, a specific moment that ushers in the contemplation of the mystery of Mary's death: where her body went, and the time(lessness) of her death and eternal life [Figure 12].

Figure 12

Yet as Allison Stielau has articulated around the famed engraving of a censer by Martin Schongauer, we should be wary about too easily ascribing a particular function to censers when depicted in other media, such as prints [Figure 3]. Schongauer, according to Stielau, displayed a "sensitivity to the way that objects can function as more than mere iconographical or anecdotal accessories."[29] That the censers in such late medieval paintings were not just pictorial motifs or conceits, but rather active agents in the performative logic both within and beyond the depicted scene, can be observed in another work from the same period [Figure 13]. Made in Bruges around 1490, the painting shows scenes from the life of St. Augustine. In the foreground of the central vignette, depicting him receiving the miter (the sign of his new office), we find three liturgical tools placed on the floor: a bucket, a censer, and a paten? These displaced, movable, and perhaps scattered objects stand in strong opposition to the stationary built environment around them. Unlike stained glass or the depicted altarpiece which remain in situ—much like the painted panel itself—objects like censers here are shown with the potential to move. Moreover, they can move outside of themselves. Smoke here is not depicted visually but implied, the empty space around the censer thus allowing the viewer to imagine through her or his

Figure 3

Figure 13

Figure 12
Master of the Amsterdam
Death of the Virgin, The
Death of the Virgin, ca. 1500,
oil on panel, 57.5 × 76.8 cm,
Amsterdam, Rijksmuseum.
Wikimedia Commons.

Figure 13
Master of Saint Augustine,
Scenes from the Life of
Saint Augustine of Hippo,
Bruges, ca. 1490, oil, gold,
and silver on wood,
137.8 × 149.9 cm. New York,
Metropolitan Museum of Art,
Cloisters Collection. Public
Domain / Creative Commons
Zero (CC0).

sense of sight, and with the mind's eye, how visual acuity is a fleeting tool much like smoke.

Returning to Rogier van der Weyden's painting at the beginning of this contribution, we begin to see the censer not as an iconographical tool, nor as an object in its own right necessarily, but rather an invitation to transgress thresholds [Figure 1]. One of these transgressions was temporal, for instance between the Roman and the medieval, as well as the Roman and Early Christian, as van der Weyden's altarpiece indicated. By staging a sensorial encounter of visual and olfactory impressions, van der Weyden invites the imagination of the beholders of this altar to reflect upon the thresholds between public and private, between profane and public, between here and elsewhere, and between the past, the present, and the future. The censer is the liturgical tool, the (depicted) smoke the visual and sensual hinge, bridging different periods, religions, the inner and the outer space for the beholder.

ENDNOTES

1   This chapter benefitted tremendously from the revisions, critique, and comments by Andrew Sears. Furthermore, the discussion with the members of the Global Horizons project, the current guests Ivan Foletti, Carlos Rojas Cocoma, and Aaron Hyman, the members of the Inheritance of Looting project, and the team of the ivory project lead by Manuela Studer was helpful for restructuring and rewriting a first draft. Elena Filliger was an important support for finding the images and completing the footnotes, for which I am very grateful.
This paragraph is based on the excellent description in Kemperdick 2012, 124–25.

2   Westermann-Angerhausen 2012, 24.

3   Tertullian, arguing in favor of prayers instead of incense, wine, or an animal as sacrifice, a position repeated by Augustine in his commentary on the psalms. See Westermann-Angerhausen 2012, 18. For an overview see Tonnochy 1937.

4   Brief X 96: C. Plinius to Emperor Trajan: "qui negabant esse se Christianos aut fuisse, cum praeeunte me deos appellarent et imagini tuae, quam propter hoc iusseram cum simulacris numinum adferri, ture ac uino supplicarent, praeterea male dicerent Christo, quorum nihil posse cogi dicuntur qui sunt re uera Christiani, dimittendos esse putaui. alii ab indice nominati esse se Christianos dixerunt et mox negauerunt."

5   The overview in Braun (1932) is still useful; Eder 2000 calls fourteen of the nearly one hundred censers she catalogues from the Late Antiquity and Early Christian periods silver censers.

6   See the discussion of Islamic censers with handles used in wealthy private contexts compared to Coptic and Byzantine precedents in Aga-Oglu 1954, 28–31.

7   E.g., the six-sided bowl with three chains and hanging hooks in Munich, Prähistorische Staatssammlung, Wamers 1983, figs. 11 and 12, 40; on typical chain-hangers see Wamers 1983, 39–42.

8   Pelka 1906, 16, no. 32, fig, 23; Witte 1910, including 140–44; Braun 1932, 609–61; Eder 2000, 3–4.

9   See Witte 1910, 105–6; Richter-Siebels 1990, 240–42.

10   Eder 2000. Eder's catalogue includes sixteen hexagonal thymateria, eleven made of bronze dating from the fifth to the sixth/seventh century and five made of silver dating from the fifth to the early seventh century, and one seven-sided bronze censer from the sixth/seventh century. The round censers include twenty metal censers made of copper, bronze, or brass dating from the fifth to the eleventh century with no figurative decoration, five round silver censers decorated with busts, and four figurative ornamented cylindrical bronze censers and six undecorated bronze censers of cylindrical shape dating from the fourth to the tenth century.

11   This conclusion and the following paragraph follows Westermann-Angerhausen 2014, 47–56.

12   Westermann-Angerhausen 2012, 7 and n. 6. Westermann-Angerhausen cites Pfeifer 1997, 65–66 and Jungmann 1958.

13   Ordo sec. Rom. N. (Andrieu II, 218 PL 78, 972): "Thuribula per altaria portantur et postea ad nares hominum feruntur et per manus fumus ad os trahitur." See also Jungmann 1958, 1:578 and n. 67.

14   See Ross 1962, no. 45–49; on a further example for many: the six-sided vessel with a hinged lid in Berlin, see Kat. Berlin 1983, no. 35, 56 (Victor H. Elbern).

15   The following information and paragraph are based on Westermann-Angerhausen 2014; Bischoff 1967; copper is more common than ore, thus in Kremsmünster we find "De aeno deaurata." This list was put together under Abbot Sigimar in the first half of the eleventh century (Bischoff 1967, 47), a censer from the Prüm treasury inventory of 1003 is listed as "Metallinum" (Bischoff 1967, 82).

16   On the material iconography, see Lein 1997, 67; 2001, 9–24 and n. 14. In Scandinavia, the particularly high number of objects with secure provenances convincingly demonstrates that preserved censers made of bronze were mainly from parish churches, see Westermann-Angerhausen 2014, 47–56.

17   Bischoff 1967, 91: "Invenimus ibi turabulum argenteum per loca deauratum I pensantum solidos XXX. Alium etiam tura bulum cuprinum antiquum 1."

18   I owe Hiltrud Westermann-Angerhausen suggestions and inspiration, for an excellent analysis of the censers in the Schedula. See Westermann-Angerhausen 2016.

19   Theophilus Presbyter 1986 [1961], prolog, 3rd book; see also Speer 2013 and Gearheart 2017.

20   Westermann-Angerhausen has repeatedly emphasized the evident analogies to surviving censers showing similar iconography with the juxtaposition of Evangelist symbols and the personifications of the rivers of paradise. Westermann-Angerhausen 2016. Most of the examples discussed by her are preserved at the Schnütgen Museum, originate from Westphalian or Rhenish churches, date to the twelfth century, and are made of bronze (with the exception of a circa-1200 silver censer preserved in Trebnice).

21   Theophilus Presbyter 1986, 112, referring to Apoc. 21.

22   Honorius Augustodunensis, Gemma Animae, PL 172, cap. 12, "De thuribulo. Thuribulum namque significat corpus Dominicum; incensum, eius divinitatem; ignis, Spiritum sanctum. Si est aureum, signat eius divinitatem omnia praecellentem; si argenteum, demonstrat ipsius humanitatem omnium sanctitate nitentem; si cupreum, declarat eius

carnem pro nobis fragilem; si ferreum, insinuat eius carnem mortuam in resurrectione mortem superantem. Si quatuor lineas habet thuribulum, significat quatuor elementis constare corpus Dominicum, quod quatuor virtutibus, prudentia, fortitudine, iustitia, temperantia fuit plenum. Quinta linea, quae thuribulum abinvicem separat, designat animam Christi, quae se morte a corpore sequestraverat. Si autem tribus lineis continetur, significat quod humana caro, et anima rationalis, et verbi divinitas una persona Christi efficitur, quarta quae partes dividit, est potestas quae animam pro ovibus in morte posuit. Si vero tantum una linea sustentatur, designat quod ipse solus absque sorde a virgine generatur, et solus liber inter mortuos praedicatur. Circulus, cui haec omnia innectuntur, est divinitas a qua haec omnia continentur, cuius maiestas nullo termino clauditur."

23   The twelve stones are the subject of several anonymous texts dating to the eleventh and twelfth centuries, including Bern, Burgerbibliothek A0091-11, A0092-26, and A0092-27; Cod. 410; Cod. 416. For a good overview, see Meier 1975.

24   Honorius Augustodunensis, Gemma Animae, PL 172, sp. 546. "Post haec thuribulum accipiens, altare thurificat in figura angeli qui in Apocalipsi cum aureo thuribulo altari astiterat, de quo fumus aromatum in conspectu Domini ascendebat. Quia Christus magni consilii angelus in ara crucis se pro nobis obtulit cujus corpus thuribulum Ecclesiae fuit. Ex quo Deus Pater suavitatem odoris accepit et propitius mundo exstitit. Fumus aromatum, orationes sanctorum sunt, quae super aram Christum per ~haritatis odorem, vel illuminationis Spiritus Sancti carbones incense ad Deum ascendunt."

25   Tonnochy (1937) has shown the importance of Durandus's *Rationale divinorum officiorum* for the medieval use of censers. Durandus, *Rationale divinorum officiorum*, lib. 4, ch. 10, 1: "diaconus postea thuribulum accipit, ut incenset Episcopum, vel sacerdotem moraliter instruit, quod si digne volumus incensum orationis offerre, turibulum Incarnationis debemus tenere ... per thuribulum enim Verbum accipitur incarnatum." Then follows the symbolism of the chains, copied almost word for word from the *De Sacra Altaris Sacrificio* of Innocent III, about I 190. "Per thuribulum autem cor humanum competenter notatur, quod debet esse apertum superius ad suspiciendum, et clausum inferius ad retinendum. ... Sicut enim thus in igne thuribuli suaviter redolet, et sursum ascendit; ita opus bonum, vel oratio ex charitate, ultra omnia thimiamata fragrat. Adhuc turibulum cum incenso corpus Christi suavitatis odore plenum, carbones Spiritum sanctum, thus boni operis odorem designant. ... Thuriferarius vero ceroferarios et alios

antecedit, ad notandum quod thuris significatio sanctis utriusque Testamenti communis est. Per thuribulum. autem cor humanum competenter notatur, quod debet esse apertum superius ad suspiciendum, et clausum inferius ad retinendum, habens ignem charitatis et thus devotionis, sive suavissimae orationis, seu bonorum exemplorum sursum tendentium, quod per fumum inde resultantem notatur. Sicut enim thus in igne thuribuli suaviter redolet, et sursum ascendit; ita opus bonum, vel oratio ex charitate, ultra omnia thimiamata fragrat. Adhuc turibulum cum incenso corpus Christi suavitatis odore plenum, carbones Spiritum sanctum, thus boni operis odorem designant." Durandus, *Rationale divinorum officiorum*, lib. 4, ch. 6, 6.

26 See Gearhart 2013.

27 "Hoc ego Reinerus do signu(m) quid michi vestris exequias similes debetis morte potito et reor esse preces veras (vras?) timiamata xp(ist)o." Translation by Heidi C. Gearhart, ibid., 106.

28 Ibid., 117.

29 Stielau 2014, 32.

BIBLIOGRAPHY

Aga-Oglu, Mehmet. 1954. "Remarks on the Character of Islamic Art." *The Art Bulletin* 36, no. 5: 175–202.

Bischoff, Bernhard. 1967. *Mittelalterliche Studien: Ausgewählte Aufsätze zur Schriftkunde und Literaturgeschichte*, 3 vols, vol. 2. Stuttgart: Hiersemann

Braun, Joseph. 1932. *Das christliche Altargerät in seinem Sein und in seiner Entwicklung*. Munich: Hueber.

Eder, Barbara. 2000. "Christliche Weihrauchgefässe des ersten Jahrtausends." PhD dissertation, University of Salzburg.

Gearhart, Heidi. 2013. "Work and Prayer in the Fiery Furnace: The Three Hebrews on the Censer of Reiner in Lille and a Case for Artistic Labor." *Studies in Iconography* 34: 103–32.

Gearhart, Heidi. 2017. *Theophilus and the Theory and Practice of Medieval Art*. Pennsylvania: Penn State University Press.

Jungmann, Andreas. 1958. *Missarum Sollemnia. Eine genetische Erklärung der römischen Messe*. 4th edn. Freiburg: Herder.

Kemperdick, Stephan. 2012. *Prestel Museum Guides—Gemäldegalerie, Berlin*. Munich: Prestel-Verlag.

Lein, Edgar. 1997. "Die Bedeutung der Materialien." In *Kunstchronik*, edited by Zentralinstitut für Kunstgeschichte, 65–69. Nürnberg: Zentralinstitut für Kunstgeschichte.

Lein, Edgar. 2001. "Die Kunst des Bronzegießens. Ihre Darstellung in Traktaten und die Bedeutung von Bronze." In *Bronze- und Galvanoplastik*, edited by Birgit Meißner, Anke Doktor, and Martin Mach, 9–24. Dresden: Landesamt für Denkmalpflege.

Meier, Christel. 1975. "Zur Quellenfrage des 'Himmlischen Jerusalem': Ein neuer Fund." *Zeitschrift für deutsches Altertum und deutsche Literatur* 104, no. 3: 204–43.

Pelka, Otto. 1906. "Ein syro-palästinensisches Räuchergefäss." In *Mitteilungen aus dem Germanischen Nationalmuseum Nürnberg*, edited by Otto Pelka, 85–92. Nürnberg: Germanisches Nationalmuseum.

Richter Siebels, Ilse. 1990. *Die palästinensischen Weihrauchgefässe mit Reliefszenen aus dem Leben Christi*. Berlin: Zentrale Universitätsdruckerei.

Ross, Marvin Chauncey. 1962. *Catalogue of the Byzantine and Early Mediaeval Antiquities in the Dumbarton Oaks Collection*, vol. 1, *Metalwork, Ceramics, Glass, Glyptics, Painting*. Washington, DC: Dumbarton Oaks.

Speer, Andreas. 2013. *Zwischen Kunsthandwerk und Kunst: Die Schedula diversarum artium*. Berlin: De Gruyter.

Stielau, Allison. 2014. "Intent and Independence: Late Fifteenth-Century Object Engravings." In *Visual Acuity and the Arts of Communication in Early Modern Germany*, edited by Jeffrey Chipps Smith, 21–42. Farnham, Surrey: Ashgate.

Theophilus Presbyter. "*De diversis artibus*, or *Schedula diversarum artium*." In *The Various Arts/De diversis artibus*, edited and translated by C. R. Dodwell. Oxford: Clarendon Press, 1986 (orig. [1961]).

Tonnochy, Alec Bain. 1937. "The Censer in the Middle Ages." *Journal of the British Archaeological Association*, 3rd series, 2: 47–62.

Wamers, Egon. 1983. "Ein Räuchergefäss aus dem Schnütgen-Museum. Karolingische Renovatio und byzantinische Kontinuität." In *Wallraf-Richartz-Jahrbuch*, edited by Friends of the Wallraff-Richartz-Museum, 29–56. Cologne: Freunde des Wallraf-Richartz-Museum und des Museum Ludwig.

Westermann-Angerhausen, Hiltrud. 2012. *Erlösung riechen*. Cologne: Sigurd-Greven-Stiftung.

Westermann-Angerhausen, Hiltrud. 2014. *Mittelalterliche Weihrauchfässer von 800–1500*. Petersberg: Michael Imhof.

Westermann-Angerhausen, Hiltrud. 2016. "The Two Censers in the Schedula Diversarum Atrium of Theophilus and Their Place in the Liturgy." In *Le cinq sens au moyen age*, edited by Eric Palazzo, 189–211. Paris: CERF.

Witte, Fritz. 1910. "Thuribulum und Navicula in ihrer geschichtlichen Entwicklung." *Zeitschrift für christliche Kunst* 23, cols. 57–62.

CENSER

THE CENSER IN AND AFTER THE REFORMATION: AUTHORITY, REBELLION, TRANSGRESSION

Allison Stielau

The revolution in Christian thought and practice now known as the Reformation would have a major impact on the existence and use of censers in Western Christendom. To consider these changes, we might begin in a somewhat unexpected space and time: at the heart of the papacy, in the final decades of the fifteenth century. Between 1480 and 1482, Sandro Botticelli painted a fresco in the Sistine Chapel that depicted censers as they had never quite been seen before [Figure 1]. The subject was the Punishment of Korah, the Israelite who attempted with his followers to wrest priestly authority from Moses and Aaron and conduct sacrifices on their own.[1] When these rebels take up censers and burn incense, God punishes their blasphemy with fire, and all 250 are swallowed by the earth. Botticelli carefully costumed the Old Testament scene in the forms of Renaissance visual culture, a mix itself of classical and medieval references, in order to underscore the fresco's primary message, which was the legitimacy of papal rule. Aaron's headgear takes the shape of the papal tiara, implying that the pope's unimpeachable authority is biblically sanctioned, and sending a warning to any who might attempt to test it.

While the hexagonal altar at center may be an imagined classical form, the censers exhibit both the basic shape and stylistic details of late Gothic microarchitectural thuribles, thus connecting biblical worship with contemporary liturgical practice. As Moses rebukes them with his rod, the rebels lose control of the censers they operate. The silver and gilt implements appear to attack their erstwhile handlers, becoming spiky, flame-filled grenades. This is not how censers ordinarily perform, either in practice or in Christian visual culture, where they appear as the often floating, celebratory instruments of angels, or the well-managed tools of acolytes performing the liturgy. Aaron and his son Eleazar, whose right to perform priestly ceremonies is divinely sanctioned, wield their implements with controlled energy.[2] The rebels' censers, on the other hand, have become untethered and move through the air with wild abandon, as if the pent-up potential energy from hundreds of swung censers across the span of Christian imagery has been released in a whirlwind of clattering metal.

Botticelli's fresco, along with its companions in the Sistine Chapel, was designed to defend a threatened papacy.[3] Papal authority became even more threatened in the next century as Martin Luther and other reformers took aim at the decadence of the Roman Church and its exploitative hierarchies of power. Their attempts to decenter ecclesiastical control, to pry from Rome its command over Christian worship, could be mapped directly on to the Israelite rebels, especially for those inclined to view the reformers as heretics. Due to its role in the Counter-Reformation and specifically the conceptualization of the Church's attitude to sacred images, the Sistine Chapel was a space in which the impact of reform was explicitly considered. The narrative reference to the unsanctioned use of censers and the portrayal of thuribles flying and in flames in Botticelli's *Korah* resonates in complicated

Figure 1
Sandro Botticelli,
The Punishment of Korah,
1480–1482, fresco,
Sistine Chapel, Vatican City.
Photo: © Scala, Florence.

ways with the fundamental changes reformers would bring to the physical expression of Christian liturgy and private devotion in the sixteenth century. For Protestants, wresting control of priestly authority meant eliminating the censer entirely from Christian worship. Some actually used the example of Korah to make a case against the liturgical use of incense.[4] The fate of the censers in Korah's story was to be transformed into plates to cover the altar as "a sign and a memorial" of the Israelites' rebellion. The reformers also found ways to reuse destroyed censers, though the melting down of precious metal church treasure (including reliquaries, monstrances, and excess chalices) in some communities in the sixteenth century was a means of destroying the memory of past ritual use as well as extracting value to serve new purposes.[5]

When read against these historical realities the *Punishment of Korah* may not offer a straightforward parallel between the rebel Israelites and Protestant reformers, but it remains an instructive starting point for this chapter's discussion of censers in and beyond the Reformation. Its diagramming of the power struggle pertaining to sanctioned and illegitimate devotional practice draws out some of the urgent debates about incense in this period. It also depicts the censer as a potentially unruly object, one that could resist control and even be weaponized, thus manifesting some of the danger that the censer held for reformers, which was not just physical but also moral and theological. Those perceived dangers informed both the elimination of the censer from Protestant contexts and its demonization in anti-Catholic propaganda.

The Reformation was not a monolithic event, which is why historians now often refer to it in the plural, as a set of related movements that unfolded over decades and even centuries.[6] Protestant theology, ritual, and private devotion developed in a variety of strands initiated by influential early modern reformers, such as Martin Luther, Huldrych Zwingli, and Jean Calvin and informed by specific national and local contexts. While significant, these distinctions are not addressed in detail here, where a broad overview of the fate of censers in the wake of reform also offers an orientation to some of the major issues surrounding the use of incense in Reformation and post-Reformation Protestant and Catholic Christianity. The historical frame includes not just the momentous ruptures of the sixteenth century, but also their reverberations through the early twentieth century, as the thurible remained controversial in Protestant environments. The nineteenth-century reintroduction of liturgical censing in the Anglican church is considered at length for the passionate arguments it engendered, which revealed the ongoing relevance of incense to the marking of confessional identity. This episode also prompted some of the seminal early historical work on incense and censers that continues to condition scholarship on these topics. The shift in focus toward the historiographic leads into a discussion of the display, photographic representation, and interpretation of Christian censers in modern museums. Particular attention is paid there, as throughout this chapter, to the thurible's chains, which were a foundational component of its visual interest as well as, I argue, its perceived danger and sensuality already before the end of the Middle Ages.

Sixteenth-century reform did not herald a "reformation" of the censer as it is understood to have done for Christian image-making.[7] It generally brought the end to thurifying, certainly in a liturgical context. Examining

"Reformation censers" then, or censers in and after the Reformation, means looking at the survival and destruction, and thus the presence or absence, of preexisting medieval examples. These took the form of the metal thuribles in Botticelli's fresco, a type that was commonly used in Western liturgy after the ninth century: a footed bowl covered with an openwork lid and manipulated by chains held together in an ornamented holder; often four to carry the vessel and a fifth to open the cover [Figure 2].[8] The thurifer lit and then placed incense on the coals in the base and lowered the lid, swinging the implement from the chain-holder's ring to disseminate the smoke. In addition to these concrete survivals from the immediate past, the field of analysis must include the many representations of censers deployed in discussion and critique of incense that were produced in the course of the Reformation and its aftermath. For the most part these maintain as their point of reference the late medieval swung thurible. Although conservative in their development from early modernity onwards, the form of censers employed in Catholic liturgical use was not entirely static. This chapter concludes with a brief glance toward the post-medieval global spread of Catholicism to witness the way incense traditions outside of Europe transformed Christian thurifying. Seeking to move beyond a narrowly Protestant view of the censer after the Reformation, and keeping to the volume's aim of examining censers cross-culturally, the conclusion is also included here to acknowledge that Protestant and Catholic identities are often produced in direct relation to one another.

Figure 2

PROTESTANT PERSPECTIVES ON
CENSING AND INCENSE

In the last two decades, scholarship across disciplines has focused greater attention on the Reformation's impact on both ritual practice and materializations of belief and confessional identity.[9] These studies consider the changes wrought not only to the possibilities for Christian images and the decoration of churches, but also the structure of landscape and urban space, the appointment of the home, as well as the attire and personal possessions of individual believers.[10] More recent investigations consider the effects of ritual change and material transformation on sensory experience, in church, in private devotional practice, and in daily life.[11] Censers have not yet been the subject of concentrated analysis within these frameworks, although recent studies on the "reformation of olfaction" in England and Germany offer a crucial foundation for any discussion of the fate of censing in the break with Catholicism.[12]

Typically, Protestant reform has been characterized as a rejection of sensual, material modes of worship in favor of the logocentric, whether reading, praying, or listening to sermons. The use of images, objects, sound and music, or multimedia performance was narrowed in order to limit the perceived dangers of deceit and material excess. This narrative had its origins in Protestant self-conceptualization and has been complicated more recently by historians of the Reformation, who have also worked to unpick different approaches to material religion among the various Protestant traditions.[13] The major question early reformers brought to the sensual aspects of Christian liturgy revolved around the Eucharist as the focal point of the Mass. According to Catholic doctrine, the bread and wine were fundamentally transformed into the body and blood, or real presence, of Christ. For Protestant reformers, the lack of perceptible change in these elements at the

Figure 2
Unknown English silversmith,
The Ramsay Abbey Censer,
ca. 1325, gilt silver with plain
silver chains, height (with chains):
64.3 cm, diameter 13.5 cm,
Victoria and
Albert Museum, London.

consecration was problematic, and they developed new theorizations of the Mass that, while differing across denominations, generally moved away from the doctrine of transubstantiation.[14] The nature of the central sacrament, which was entangled with profound questions about Christian materiality, divided not only Catholics from Protestants, but ultimately also Protestants among themselves.

As a multisensory spectacle—kinetic, olfactory, visually complex in the movement of metallic thurible and ephemeral smoke—censing would appear to be ripe for critique on the grounds of sensual exuberance. But because the liturgical use of incense, like other material aspects of traditional religion, did not directly impact reformers' questions about the status, nature, and meaning of the Eucharist, it was often not a topic of specific concern. In his *Formula missae* of 1523, which proposed a reformed Eucharistic liturgy, Martin Luther famously declined to weigh in on the matter of incense and candles, declaring "the matter is free," or open to interpretation.[15]

In fact, censing had always been an aspect of the liturgy that varied by location and was sometimes entirely absent. When it was employed, it was used to consecrate altars, to bless materials and objects over the course of the Christian calendar, and to accompany processions outside the church on special feast days. Censing sacralized and purified the space around individual bodies and identified and honored high-ranking members of the priesthood. During the Mass itself, incense could be employed at several different points, to mark the priest's entrance at the Introit, to cense the Gospel before it was read, or most commonly around the Offertory, when the Eucharistic wine and bread were prepared and placed on the altar.[16]

Part of the ambiguity surrounding the censer and its appropriateness for Protestant worship rested on the fraught and often changing position of incense in Christian history and particularly its overlap with other religious traditions.[17] Biblical sanction for the Christian use of incense was found throughout the Old Testament, in God's commandment that offerings be made in Exodus and Leviticus, and in the Psalms.[18] While Botticelli's fresco of the Korah story comes down to the assertion of papal authority, it too engages with the biblical justification for censing in Christian liturgy. Unlike the sacrifice of meat, with its greasy residues and association with human hunger and feasting, incense was a burnt offering that left nothing behind.[19] As an ephemeral medium moving from Earth to Heaven, the smoke of incense nicely symbolized prayer.

For Martin Luther and other reformers, however, the association of incense with Jewish sacrifice was problematic as they hoped to eliminate the sacrificial conceptualization of the Mass and the altar entirely: Christ's sacrifice rendered all other forms unnecessary. Luther's new version of the Mass excised the Offertory, which obviated the use of incense in that formerly sacrificial framework. Reformers could also turn to the Old Testament for passages that undermined the sacrificial use of incense, especially Isaiah 1:13: "Do not make vain offerings of food anymore. The incense is to me an abomination." Erasmus of Rotterdam drew attention to this text already in 1501, along with discussion of the Epistle to the Hebrews, a book that was a particular focus for reformers because it articulated the legacy of Jewish devotional practice for Christianity.[20] This critical view of incense as an "external ceremony of the Jews" required that later references to incense in the New Testament now be understood metaphorically, "as praise and glorification of God through good works and prayer."[21] Converting literal incense into an analogy for prayer became a common trope in Protestant texts.

Beyond the Bible's discussion of incense in sacrificial practice, other justifications for censing had been articulated over the centuries or come into popular belief. Incense was used to perfume and fumigate the church and to purify sacred space.[22] In other contexts it was thought to exorcise a person, space, or object of evil spirits.[23] The overdetermined nature of censing along with its somewhat marginal and inconsistent role in Christian liturgy accounts for the regulatory silence surrounding its use after the Reformation. But despite a relative lack of discussion about incense on a doctrinal level, it nevertheless proved a target for anti-Catholic polemic in popular vernacular texts.[24]

In addition to theological and cultural objections to incense, there were also practical concerns regarding cost, waste, and luxury that motivated some critiques. Imported by spice merchants, frankincense was an expensive commodity that would have been within the reach primarily of wealthy urban churches and monastic and royal institutions.[25] Censers could be brass or bronze, but church inventories often claimed their censers were silver, indicating a potentially meaningful store of value. Many rural churches simply did not own a censer, making the use of incense unlikely.[26] Because of their high financial value both incense and censer were vulnerable to reformers' concerns about the sensuousness and material ostentation of the Mass. Their olfactive role raised additional issues. The difficulty posed by scents, as Dugan has noted, is the ambiguous position they take between the spiritual and the worldly.[27] While pleasant smells had long been associated with holiness in the Christian tradition, the profane uses of perfumes, including their ability to mask putrid smells and their aphrodisiacal qualities, made them suspect. The potential association of incense with sex, sin, and luxury fit some Protestant reformers' characterization of the Mass as the Whore of Babylon, who seduced Christians with her sensuous exterior.[28]

Baum has argued that eliminating incense from the liturgy created "a desacralization of the sense of smell," as reformers "abandoned the manipulation of smells" both in the sanctuary and outside of it.[29] Part of this process involved the vilification of incense and its displacement onto Jews, Catholics, and Turks, the "Others" in Luther's social thought.[30] This rhetorical move operated not in the face of total erasure, but rather depended on a continued knowledge and memory of incense as it had operated in traditional worship and images of censers surviving in Protestant contexts may have provided the prompt, and perhaps a ghostly reminder, of the pre-Reformation sacred smellscape.[31] For Lutherans who worshipped in shared space with Catholics (*Simultankirche*), incense lingered more literally, in the air and in church furnishings, meaning it continued to inform the sensory experience of sacred space and complicated the marking of confessional difference.[32] The notion that the Reformation made "smell no longer theologically relevant" thus requires greater nuance.[33] As Luisa Coscarelli-Larkin has shown, Lutherans, like Roman Catholics in German-speaking Europe, used prayer-beads strung with pomanders in private devotion and also associated sweet smells with prayer and holiness.[34]

THE FATE OF CENSERS
IN THE WAKE OF REFORMATION

Shifts in liturgical practice and orientations to the accumulated treasure in churches and religious institutions as a result of the Protestant Reformations across Europe had significant consequences for the continued existence of censers, but these differed according to the local context and the valence of reform adopted. The practice of censing had varied widely, both geographically, and functionally within a given location.[35] It did not necessarily cease immediately, but sometimes became restricted to specific functions outside of Protestant comment and critique, as a preparatory, perfuming medium rather than a liturgical one. Even churches that had retired their censers and excised thurification from their rituals might continue to purchase incense for the purpose of fumigation, as there was widespread belief in the medical benefits of incense and other sweet-smelling substances.[36] Baum posits that the brass censers purchased in the 1580s for Nuremberg churches were meant to hold incense to counteract the plague.[37]

Reformers were keen to eliminate censing done outside the church and related to what they viewed as superstitious beliefs that had grown in the late Middle Ages. This included the tradition of censing and blessing the marriage bed and marriage chamber.[38] Protestants, according to Lyndal Roper, "affirmed their identity by rejecting such blessings."[39] Before the Reformation, post-partum women were sometimes censed during the ritual known as churching, which restored them to sexual and social intercourse after the period of their confinement.[40] In Protestant contexts, churching often remained a significant rite of passage, but without the incense and candles.[41] Incense and chrism were also excised from the inauguration rites of a new church, primarily as a way to differentiate from Catholic practice.[42]

The more urgent focus of reform when it came to incense, however, involved its use in the liturgy. As Susan Karant-Nunn has written, "Monstrances, pyxes and censers had their *raison d'etre* in the sacrificial theology of the Mass. When this theology was banned, its implements became superfluous. This alone was justification enough to sell or melt down the utensil."[43] But as *vasa non-sacra*, those implements that did not immediately touch and contain the Eucharistic elements of wine and bread, censers were not the urgent target for elimination in the way that monstrances and, for their involvement with the cult of saints and the system of indulgences, reliquaries were.[44] If there was no urgent need to extract their precious metal value, or indeed they were made of base metal, censers could remain stored away and eventually forgotten about, only to be sold off in later secularization campaigns when receptive audiences had developed who would acquire and save them as objects of historical and artistic interest.[45] What Johann Michael Fritz called the "preserving power of Lutheranism" describes the abiding presence in Lutheran churches of ostensibly "Catholic" implements, which were retained because it was simpler or cheaper to leave or repurpose them.[46] Lutheranism's doctrinal middle ground meant there was no pressing impetus to purge such artifacts.

In England, where King Henry VIII mined the stores of religious houses for valuable assets, very little medieval sacred metalwork, including censers, survives. A few examples, like the Ramsey Abbey censer, may have been deliberately hidden, either to protect a valuable treasure or in hopes of a return to future use [see Figure 2].[47] The abolition of rituals objectionable to reformers also sent censers into disuse. Until 1548 it had been the custom on Whitsun (Pentecost) at St. Paul's Cathedral in London, "for a great censer, emitting clouds of sweet smoke and sparks, to be swung from the roof [...] and for doves to be released, re-enacting the descent of the Holy Ghost on the Apostles."[48] Despite the cessation of its ritual, the monumental silver censer survived Henry's reign, for it is listed in an inventory of 1552.[49]

Thus, even in contexts that experienced radical reshaping of the Church's material landscape and forms of worship, like the Swiss cantons influenced by Huldrych Zwingli, the outright destruction of censers was not inevitable. In the years in which large collections of ecclesiastical plate, including censers, were gathered from Swiss churches for liquidation, the treasury of Basel cathedral remained intact.[50] During the iconoclasm of February 1529, which saw numerous altarpieces and other images destroyed, the treasure lay undisturbed in its sacristy cupboard ("whether by oversight or out of preternatural deference") and was subsequently secured behind window bars and an iron door, where it survived until it was sold off in the nineteenth century.[51] Through its inventories and now dispersed objects, this collection gives important insight into a major cathedral treasury effectively frozen in time in the late 1520s. It held multiple silver censers produced centuries apart that bear evidence of wear and repair and hint at practices of censing on the eve of the Reformation [see Figure 19].[52]

The functional specificity of censers made them difficult to convert to new ecclesiastical purposes, which was possible for other objects like pyxes and, sometimes, even monstrances.[53] Unlike vestments that could be cut up and repurposed or an altarpiece that might be broken down into its painted panels, the censer did not easily become an object of practical use or ornament.[54] This is likely because its ritual function was so specific and undisguisable. Its chains facilitating swinging made it particularly inappropriate for contemporary perfuming outside the church. Later in the sixteenth century, incense burners inspired by eastern forms began to enter elite German collections, but these were always static vessels, some large enough to exist almost as furniture, and they seem to have been owned primarily by Catholic princes, for whom incense even in the secular realm may have been more acceptable.[55]

Where censers and incense were banished from ecclesiastical use, they gained a new, or renewed, existence in metaphor.[56] Through this conversion process, the physical character of thuribles and sweet-smelling smoke came to signify abstract, non-physical concepts. Martin Luther himself evolved from a traditional understanding of incense as the material instantiation of prayer, to asserting prayer was superior to incense, and finally to the belief, articulated in 1544, that prayer is "the true incense of Christians": "take hold of the censer with me, that is, seize hold upon prayer," he wrote.[57] Puritan writers in seventeenth-century England continued in this vein, figuring the Gospel itself as incense, and the devotion rightly offered to God as exquisite perfume.[58] "[R]ather than disappearing entirely," as Sophie Reed explains, incense "took on a complex figurative life: this represented both [...] regret at the sensory depredations symbolized by its loss, and excitement at the opportunities for metaphorical expression thereby created."[59] She notes as well that the "rhetorical persistence" of incense in Protestant texts "hints also at the way in which its translation to the figurative realm keeps alive the possibility of its ritual reinstitution."[60] At the same time, non-metaphorical references to incense frequently appeared in English theatrical performances in this period, part of an ongoing debate about the legitimacy of its use in Christian devotional practice. In such pieces, incense was commonly displaced onto a pagan context, which could either serve to explain its appropriate use or cast it as idolatrous.[61]

Beyond its capabilities as a transcendent vehicle between Earth and Heaven, smoke also symbolized ephemerality. "For my days vanish like smoke" laments the sufferer in Psalm 102. Elsewhere in the Bible, the heretics who worship silver idols "will be like smoke escaping through a window."[62] As the censer and its perfumed smoke was excluded from its traditional liturgical role in Protestant frameworks, it found its way into the developing genre of vanitas images, where incense burners produced clouds of smoke whose perfume and visual presence symbolized the epitome of transience and also retained the vestige of association with rituals for the dead: a doubly effective *memento mori*. In these images, the incense vessel is usually an open-mouthed vase, vaguely but non-specifically ancient.[63] This distancing from the identifiably Christian form of the thurible deracinated the censer and allowed it to become a new symbol for contemplation in the still life imagery of Calvinist contexts like the Dutch Republic.

THE CENSER IN ANTI-CATHOLIC PROPAGANDA

As one of the most distinctive and easily identifiable components of Catholic material culture, the censer received special emphasis in Protestant propaganda. Other forms of ecclesiastical metalwork, like chalices, were still allowed to serve the modified form of Protestant ritual in many contexts.[64] More personal devotional objects, notably prayer beads, could also be confessionally ambiguous.[65] But the censer was associated most directly with forms of ritual practice that Protestants eliminated. Susan Juster has identified altars and incense as "two of the most recognizable 'papist' icons in the Protestant polemical arsenal."[66] But when it came to visual portrayals, incense usually needed a container to signify, and the censer was the preferred choice. Although never the most plentiful object type stored for ritual use, censers had a life and a visibility beyond the confines of the sanctuary because they were used in processions and benedictions and thus entered urban, rural, and even domestic spaces. They were also visually resonant, capable of assuming myriad shapes, with their chains and energetic movement, and the clouds of smoke that could be rendered as a small whisper of gray or a graphic billow. In visual representation they thus served as a "smoking gun" for Catholic practices, an easily recognizable sign that could allude to much more than what was pictured within a given scene.

Some anti-Catholic broadsheets criticized specific ritual uses of incense, like the censing of the dead in funeral processions.[67] But more commonly the censer's objectional liturgical uses were implied through its form alone. It appears prominently amongst collections of paraphernalia coded Catholic in Protestant propaganda across media throughout the sixteenth and seventeenth centuries, both in use and as a deactivated object amongst a catalogue of other items meant to be read as the superfluous and corrupting "stuff" of traditional worship. On a stoneware tankard lampooning the pope, for example, a tree is hung with a variety of Catholic objects—monstrances, a situla, a chalice—and, perhaps most naturally due to its chains, a censer. Christ digs at the base of this tree and a lettered tablet captures his destructive intention: The weeds I will root out and throw in the fire.[68] A tree similarly bearing the strange fruit of Catholic material culture had appeared in earlier propagandistic prints.[69]

Accreting these objects into piles or haphazard collections was meant to undermine the special status they held within enacted rituals. In Adriaen van de Venne's 1614 painted allegory *Fishing for Souls*, which dramatizes the competition between Catholic and Protestant churches in the divided Netherlands, austere Calvinists bait converts with texts while their more colorful Catholic counterparts net souls with help from a variety of captivating objects including floating crucifixes and papal bulls; the boat they steer is balanced on one end with a glittering monstrance and on the other with a smoking censer [Figures 3–4].[70]

Figures 3–4

The censer also appeared in scenes of iconoclasm, desacralization, and plunder. A condensed illustration of Edward VI's Protestant reforms in the virulently anti-Catholic *Acts and Monuments* (1570), shows "The Papistes packing away theyr Paltry," which includes candlesticks, croziers, and a large, ornate censer swung from one man's wrist, as if some sort of monstrous jewel [Figure 5].[71] The word "paltry" at this moment conveyed utmost disdain; before it gained the sense of trivialization it has today, it was a synonym for rubbish.[72] Still, a common strategy of Protestant critique was to reduce the significance of liturgical implements by equating them with superficial, insubstantial ornaments, rendering the resonant implements of Catholic devotion into simple "toys."[73]

Figure 5

The fragrant smoke emitted by the censer was often flipped satirically and instead associated with the repellent smells of excrement and filth. Lucas Cranach's image of the pope riding a sow, which plays on the antisemitic trope of the *Judensau*, places a steaming, odiferous pile of dung in the pontiff's hands [Figure 6]. According to a contemporary riddle, its scent entices the sow to run rather than attack the rider.[74] But the way the fumes are visualized recalls the curling plumes of incense smoke as they are portrayed in contemporary woodcuts. Here, it is as if the perfume that might ordinarily precede and envelope the pope while in procession has been replaced by the powerful fumes of pig shit.[75] A similar inversion appears in Peter Flötner's woodcut of a decade earlier, depicting a procession of friars and nuns [Figure 7].[76] The censer swung energetically by a corpulent priest at the head of the procession does not produce smoke as an honorific, cleansing the path for those that follow in its wake; instead it heralds the entry of a pig into the church that is meant to be consecrated [Figure 8].[77] The censer, along with the situla and asperger behind it, anchor the scene in Catholic ritual, allowing us to recognize the inversions it proposes. While the incense might serve to mask the procession's bad "pagan" smells—evoked by piles of cooked meat and tankards of alcohol—the telltale curls of smoke recall the bodily effluvia of snot and vomit emitted from other figures in the scene, thus completing the conversion of incense from enticing to repulsive. Such polemical images visualize the denigration of a social group by associating its members with foul odor, a rhetorical tool used by both Protestants and Catholics against each other.[78]

Figure 6

Figure 7

Figure 8

Another strategy for making the censer and its clouds of perfumed smoke alien to Christian devotion was to assert or reassert its association with other religious worship, including Muslim, Jewish, and pagan devotion,

Figure 3
Adriaen Pietersz van de Venne,
Fishing for Souls, 1614,
oil on panel, 98.5 cm × 187.8 cm,
Rijksmuseum, Amsterdam.

Figure 4
Detail of Figure 3.

Figure 5
Illustration of King Edward VI's
Protestant reforms (detail),
colored woodcut, in John Foxe,
Actes and Monuments
(London, 1570), fol. 1483 recto.
Reproduced by kind permission
of the Syndics of Cambridge
University Library.

Figure 6
Workshop of Lucas Cranach,
The Pope Riding a Sow,
woodcut illustration,
27.8 × 19.5 cm, in Martin Luther,
*Wider das Babstum zu
Rom vom Teufel gestifft*
(Nuremberg, 1545).
Photo: bpk / Herzog Anton
Ulrich-Museum.

Figure 7
Peter Flötner, Satirical Print
Showing Procession of Friars
and Nuns, ca. 1540,
woodcut, 11.9 × 57.1 cm.
Photo: Ashmolean Museum,
University of Oxford, UK.

Figure 8
Detail of Figure 7.

either in the idolatrous historical past or the exotic, geographically distant present.[79] The scene of Solomon worshiping the idol, which had been popular in Northern Europe in the sixteenth century, began in the seventeenth century to depict more elaborately the sacrifices surrounding Solomon's devotion, including both the burning of animal flesh and incense. The subject opened up a Protestant angle on the practice of censing, framing it as pagan and idolatrous. In some of these scenes painted by artists working in the Calvinist Dutch Republic, the king himself dramatically wields a censer [Figure 9]. This gesture highlights his active participation in image worship, and thus the extent of his rejection of God. As Solomon was understood to be led into idolatry by his wives and concubines, or more specifically the Queen of Sheba, layered into such portrayals is also the coding of perfumed veneration as dangerously Other, both feminine and foreign.

Protestant polemic often used representations of historical pagan or contemporary non-Christian worship as a "stand-in for Catholic idolatry," and censing could operate as a signifier for this replacement.[80] The rhetorical complexity of censing viewed cross-culturally is exemplified by the so-called "Idol of Calicut," an image of Hindu religious practice that derived from a sixteenth-century Italian travel narrative.[81] Illustrating this text in 1515, the German artist Jörg Breu translated its description of the venerated image into a European Christian visual language [Figure 10]. A metal sculpture that the text described as a monstrous devil consuming souls was wreathed in smoke dispensed by a medieval thurible swung from chains, while Breu gave the attendant the garb and crescent headplate of an ancient Jewish priest, a combination of dress and instrument deriving from contemporary illustrations of the Old Testament. While scholars have framed this woodcut as the artist's attempt to build "analogical bridges between Indian culture and his own," its potential to operate as a searing condemnation of non-European religions is undeniable.[82] The "Idol of Calicut" was also conducive to anti-Catholic satire, which explains its popularity in Northern Europe during the Reformation.[83] In the later sixteenth century the humanist Pierre Boaistuau revived Breu's pre-Reformation iconography for a manuscript with which he hoped to secure the Protestant Queen Elizabeth I's patronage [Figure 11].[84] Now the tiara worn by the Calicut "devil" is an overt satirical jab at the papacy and the thurifers wear European dress, thus conflating the Catholic practice of censing with idolatry. When Boaistuau later published his *Histoires prodigieuses* for a wider audience in his native France, the anti-Catholic messaging of this image was toned down in part by appointing the thurifers with turbans. The costume change allowed their censing, though it employed recognizably Christian thuribles, to be culturally distanced and displaced onto "the safer figure of the Ottomon Turk."[85]

Incense was also placed in scenes of magic and demonic ritual. In the sixteenth century, ancient pagan and demonic uses of perfumed smoke were more usually depicted in association with static, open vessels, as opposed to the closed vessel hung or swung from chains.[86] They appear set before idols and sometimes even held by them, an origin point for spectacular, billowing smoke.[87] In a 1523 letter to the dean of Zurich's Great Minster, Albrecht Dürer included a drawing of apes cavorting in a circle around a footed incense burner at its center and becoming intoxicated from the smoke.[88] This image played on contemporaneous portrayals of Morris dancers and female witches, whose attribute became the cauldron, another static, smoking vessel, in

Figure 9

Figure 10

Figure 11

Figure 9
Jacob Hogers,
The Idolatry of King Solomon
(detail), ca. 1635–1655,
oil on canvas, 124 × 197 cm,
Rijksmuseum, Amsterdam.

35

Der künig von Calicut mit allem seynem volck in seynem land
vnd künigreych ist ayn apgöttereyer/Vnd bettet den teyfel an
wie ir vernemen wert/Sy bekennen vnd veriechen das ain got sey d
beschaffen hab den hymel vnd dye erden vnd die gantzen welt/Vnd
sprechen wan got woltte richten vnd vrtaylen ainen vnd den andern
Vnd alle werck vnd übel der menschen rechen vnd straffen/Wer im
kain frewd so er das gethon mag durch seinen knecht/Vnd darumb
hab er vns disen gayst den teyfel gesant in dise welt vñ im den gwalt
gegeben zü richten vñ zü vrtaylen/wölcher wol thü dem thü er auch
wol/Vnd wer übel thü dem thü er auch übel/den selben nenen sy deu
mo/vnd got nenen sy tamerani/Zü wissen das der künig zü Calicut
die bildnuß des teyfels hält in seinem palast in ainem gepew wie ain
Capell die da weyt ist zwen schryt auff alle fyer ort vnd dreyer schryt
hoch mit ainer hültzen tür die alle durch schnite mit erhaben teyfele.

Vnd in mit
te diser capell
ist ayn sessel
darauff sytzt
ain teyfel ge
gossen vo glo
genspeyß vnd
mettrall/Hat
ain kron auff
dem kopff ge
leych wie ayn
bäbstliche ho
che kron myt
dreyen krone
Hat fyer hör
ner auff dem kopff/Vnd fyer groß zen mit ainem vngestalten weyt
ten offen maul/Die naß vnd augen greylichen an zü sehen/Seine
hend gemacht geleych wie die haggen/Vnd die füß wie aines hanen
füß/Alles so forchtsam gestalt das es erschrockenlich ist an zü sehen
vñ rings vmb dyse Capell ist das gemel alles teyfel/vñ auf alle fyer
ort sitzt ain teyfel auf ainem gestül der da gemacht ist in ainem flam
en feür/In den selben flamen ist ain große suma der seelen aines fin

i iij

Figure 10
Jörg Breu, The Idol of Calicut,
woodcut illustration to
Ludovico di Varthema, *Die
Ritterlich und lobwirdig rayß
des gestrengen und über all
ander weyt erfarnen ritters und
Lantfarers herren Ludowico
vartomans von Bolonia…*
(Augsburg, 1515), fol. i iij recto.
Photograph courtesy of the
Bayerische Staatsbibliothek
München, Rar 894.

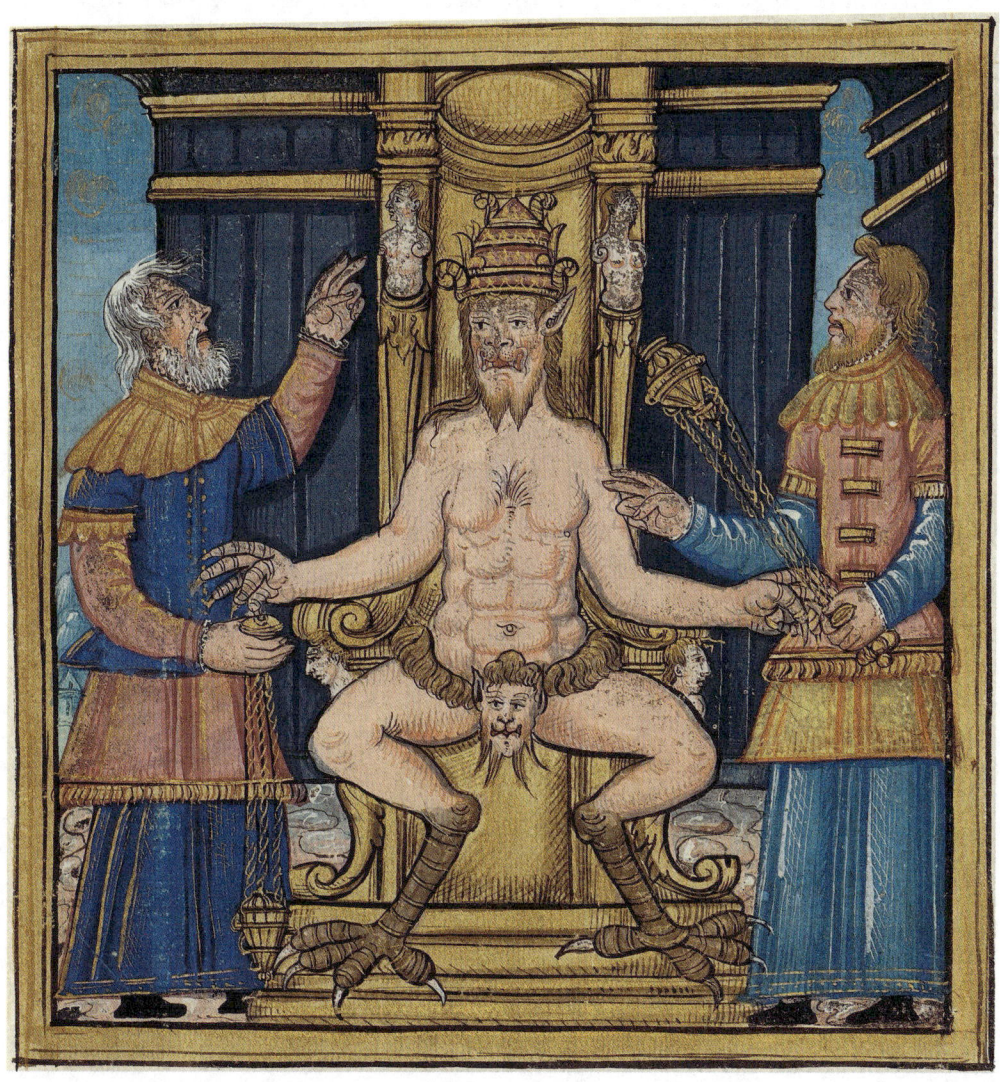

Figure 11
Unknown artist, Devil in
Calicut, manuscript
illumination in Pierre
Boaistuau, *Histoires
prodigieuses*, Western MS 136,
fol. 7 recto, The Wellcome
Library, London.

precisely this period.[89] In this same letter, Dürer sent his greetings to the reformer Huldrych Zwingli, by then a canon and preacher in the minster. In writings produced also in 1523, Zwingli forcefully rejected the use of incense because it lacked scriptural justification and was associated too closely with Jewish sacrificial practice.[90] He considered it idolatrous. Under his influence, incense would be eliminated from church services along with myriad other elements, including the use of music and precious metal plate.[91]

The standing open vessel was not definitively coded pagan, however. Woodcut illustrations to Martin Luther's translation of the New Testament give Apostles and angels large open smoking vessels, which visually relate to contemporary depictions of the incense altar from the Old Testament Books of Moses. In the early sixteenth century, such depictions were becoming increasingly antiquarian, attempting to capture the tabernacle and its altars and implements as the text described and with an imagination of the ancient past, rather than with reference to anachronistic Christian detail.[92] And yet, the forms that censers take in Old Testament and New Testament illustrations in reformed Bibles do not settle easily into coherent groupings. Korah and his rebels still swing "Catholic"-looking thuribles, while the ancient form of open vessel appears on the incense altar [Figure 12]. Matthias Gerung's Whore of Babylon, meanwhile, holds a smoking open cup in place of the more familiar covered vessel signifying luxury.[93] Here is a clever fusing of the witch's attribute with the Mother of Abominations, and perhaps a nod to the association of incense with the Whore of Babylon.[94] These Bible illustrations reflect the conflicted and changing status of incense in Christian history, which offered precedents both for those who found it central to liturgy and for those who wanted to eliminate it entirely. The goal of polemic on either side of the confessional divide was to simplify this complexity into the assertion of clear differences.

Figure 12

THE CENSER AS REBELLIOUS OBJECT

The Reformation's impact on the use of incense has primarily been treated through the sensory frame of olfaction.[95] The disappearance or downplaying of the censer in Protestant ritual is thus explained by its telos: the problem was not the object itself, but rather the function that it served. If the olfactory medium of incense was eliminated, then there was no need for the very functionally specific container that held and disseminated it, especially if that container might be liquidated to produce funds for other uses. But in their concentration on incense and smell, these analyses do not consider the censer itself as a particularly sensual object, one that had been at times a troubling presence in the century leading up to the Reformation. Part of the censer's sensual character was its connection to physical danger, as a container for hot coals, and as an object capable of powerful movement through its structural combination of heavy pendant attached to chains. The thurifer's handling of these inherent risks was an exercise in disciplined control. But late medieval visual and textual sources captured censers testing that control and highlighted the ways in which the thurible could be both physically and metaphorically rebellious.

Their function as fire-carriers made censers the origin point of violent destruction in biblical imagery and their role in sacrificial ritual made them an enticement to devotional error. In the Pentateuch, in addition to the story of Korah, there is the related episode involving Abihu and Nadab,

Figure 12
Erhard Altdorfer, woodcut
illustration of the incense
altar described in Exodus,
from *De Biblie vth der
vthlegginge Doctoris Martini
Luthers yn dyth düdesche
vlitich vthgesettet / mit
sundergen vnderrichtingen /
alse men seen mach*
(Lübeck, 1533).

Figure 13
Detail of Eleazar, Abihu and
Nadab, colored woodcut, from
the *Weltchronik* of Hartmann
Schedel (Nuremberg, 1493).

two of Aaron's sons who "each took a pan and put fire therein and put incense upon it and brought such a strange fire before the Lord, which he had not commanded them," and they are burned to death in punishment.[96] The passage has been notoriously difficult to interpret, turning precisely on why God punishes these ordained priests and why their sacrifice, and in particular their use of incense, was condemned.[97] Some reformers would find in this story a warning about improper devotional practice.[98] But even before the Reformation, the subject appealed to artists and reading audiences, appearing in illuminated Bibles.[99] Later, some of the major German artists of the sixteenth century, among them Hans Holbein, Hans Baldung, and Erhard Schön, included this subject in series of woodcut Bible illustrations. In these scenes, it is God who renders the censers dangerous, but there is also fascination and play here with the thurible's unique ability to be spectacularly weaponized, spurting flames, spewing great clouds of smoke, even knocking grown men flat. An illustration in Hartmann Schedel's *Weltchronik* of 1493 shows the four sons of Aaron connected to him through the twining tendrils of their family tree [Figure 13]. Eleazar swings a golden censer out horizontally towards Nadab and Abihu, who despair as flames stretch across the page to lick at the edges of their persons. This depiction entangles the Korah story's greater attention to incense burners, and the role played therein by Eleazar, with the anecdote of Nadab's and Abihu's transgression.[100] It implies that their destruction comes by means of the censer wielded by their brother, rather than the fire emanating from God. The angular lines emerging from the thurible's Gothic tracery have replaced the rounded whirls usually employed to indicate smoke and the wafting odor of incense. The substitution of flames for pleasant fumes exposes the censer's potential for danger.

Figure 13

The hazards posed by burning incense had shaped the formal development of censers in the medieval church. Early Christian censers were often open hanging vessels, suspended from chains; the move to cover the bowl and contain the coals acknowledged the threat inherent in live sparks.[101] But the cover also facilitated the increased energy and thus more damaging impact the thurible could make if it were swung. And it is the kinetic energy of the swinging censer, dependent on its lengthy chains, that rendered it more capable of damaging and being damaged.[102] Metalwork specialists have noted the particular vulnerability of censers to physical deterioration, as evidenced by the frequency with which they had to be repaired or replaced. They experienced greater daily strain than liturgical implements that stood on the altar or were passed by hand. As Margret Ribbert put it: "swung rhythmically on long chains, censers were predestined for minor damage."[103] Such minor but meaningful damage is evoked in this line from a 1517 English inventory, whose seven recorded censers each had some form of impairment: "Item a sencer of silver [...] Defectif in the cheyne / Item brused in the foote Lackyng vj [six] pynnacles and a greate rynge."[104] The specific locations of damage, in the chain and on the foot and pinnacles, reveal how the swinging of the thurible made it vulnerable to wear and breakage specifically at points most likely to experience tension and collision.

As an olfactory medium, incense is understood to constitute and transcend boundaries, but its container is also capable of transgressing physical confines.[105] It was their chains that rendered censers not just dangerous and endangered, but, by extending the thurifer's reach far beyond a human arm span, capable of crossing and even violating boundaries. The *Weltchronik*

Figure 14
Unknown English sculptor,
panel depicting the
Trinity (detail), second half
of the 15th century, carved,
painted and gilded alabaster,
58.9 × 24.4 cm, Victoria and
Albert Museum, London.

image makes this possibility clear, as Eleazar scorches his rebellious brothers from a distance. But there could be a sexual element to the extensional
capabilities of the censer as well. A literary fragment occasionally presented
as evidence of the association of sacred incense, already at the turn of the
fifteenth century, with the earthly and sexual is instructive.[106] In Geoffrey
Chaucer's *Canterbury Tales* the parish clerk Absolon, who courts the carpenter's wife Alison, is characterized as teasing and sexually eager:

> This Absolon, that jolly was and gay,
> Went with a censer on the holy days,
> Censing the wives of the parish eagerly,
> And many a lovely look on them he cast,
> And especially on this carpenter's wife:
> To look on her he thought a merry life.[107]

Matthew Milner uses this passage to discuss censing the congregation, a
practice that was not mentioned in prescriptive liturgical rubrics but may
have served to cover the human and associated animal smells that would
otherwise make church services unpleasant.[108] Chaucer's lines attend, however, not to scent, but rather to the specific movement of the thurifer. In
this memorable scene of flirtation Absolon pumps the censer into the physical space of the parish wives, extending by means of the chain his body to
theirs, so that "censing" takes on a distinctly sexual, perhaps even specifically phallic and coital, undertone. Absolon's enthusiastic censing is not an
extraneous detail of this ill-fated love affair, moreover, but something like
its fulcrum, for it is through this action that he comes to look more closely
at and desire Alison.

The superhuman reach of the swung censer received emphasis in
visual culture from the Middle Ages onward; it was often used to create ephemeral architectural framing in figural scenes. The angels' censers in fifteenth-century English alabaster panels depicting the Trinity, for example, often form
an arch around God the Father's crowned head [Figure 14]. At a larger scale
and in concrete, as opposed to fictive, architecture, angels with a thurible at Figure 14
the apex of its pendular arc perfectly fill the triangular space of a spandrel on
either side of an arch.[109] Some depictions of censers also registered the potential for more chaotic movement, which could highlight the emotive expression of the thurible as it fulfilled its celebratory function. But it could also hint
at the censer's potential resistance to human control. The slack and flying
chains in Botticelli's Sistine Chapel fresco elucidate the rebelliousness of censers that cannot be held in check by their illegitimate handlers.

Portrayals of the Mass of St. Gregory produced in Germany and the
Low Countries in the late fifteenth and early sixteenth centuries occasionally included a censer in the ritual scene whose unusual positioning suggested the object's potential instability.[110] A pronounced example of this iconographical detail appears in a panel now in Bruges [Figure 15]. As Christ Figure 15
manifests, flanked by the instruments of the Passion, above the chalice and
paten on the altar, an attendant swings a censer so that it is highlighted in
profile against the white altar cloth. In this tight space the censer does not
follow a graceful arc but is instead flipped up with slack chains, its cover
slightly open, as if it has just been jerked back and is about to experience
one of the events of stress or damage we know to have been quite common.

The significance of this gymnastic movement is difficult to pin down, but it is certainly more than just an anecdotal elaboration of the ritual event and its "ecclesiastical pomp."[111] It may be intended to punctuate the climactic moment of this subject, when the Man of Sorrows appears to assert the real presence of the Eucharist.[112] The narrative structure of the censer's pendular movement, which leads to and away from an apical point of stasis, could effectively emphasize the mystical change that occurred instantaneously within the miracle of transubstantiation. But in this case the censer calls attention to itself and to its movement because it behaves so strangely, as if defying the laws of physics that usually govern the practice of thurifying.[113] The "alternative physics" endorsed by the artist here makes the censer's floating position in the air feel even more fleeting and precarious.[114] It further highlights the potentially unruly, even anarchic, quality of the censer's movement at the end of its chains, suggesting how it might strain at and test the human subject's ability to control it.

The visual and aural effects created by the censer's vigorous movement were not the sensory basis for thurifying's rejection in the early Reformation. Nevertheless, a pervasive discomfort around censers' dynamic motion developed in England, which can be deduced from the way English Protestants attempted to avoid it. For example, when some pre-Reformation practices were revived during the so-called Anglican Counter-Reformation, the swinging and processing of censers was studiously avoided. Bishop Lancelot Andrewes's choice of a "static censer" for the table of his private chapel—what is referred to as the *still* use of incense—was likely designed to deflect any appearance of practicing "popish customs."[115] In addition to simply asserting a distinction from Catholic practice, abstaining from the swung censer also made it impossible to engage in the action of censing images and people, which was a point of particular concern for reformers because it putatively bordered so closely on idolatry.[116] In England an injunction in 1547 required all images that had been "censed" to be destroyed.[117]

Later, in the nineteenth century, when the use of the thurible again became a hotly debated issue within Anglicanism, the ecclesiologist Alexander Beresford Hope captured the threat that Roman Catholic thurifying posed to Anglican, for which we could read "English," identity: "the outward aspect of the unreformed rite of incense [...] is one which, with the perpetual unrest of its swinging censers, is peculiarly liable to irritate staid and undemonstrative English worshippers."[118] Censing was simply too emotive and disordered. Disputes about the traditional use of the thurible and its apparently tumultuous movement continued to shape Anglican worship. In 1917, a correspondent for *The Church Times* complained that a bishop in Australia required "the server to swing the censer *imperceptibly* with his back to the people," an instruction the writer found "ridiculous and impossible to follow."[119]

There is something suppressed in the anti-Ritualist objections to swinging that deserves further scrutiny, for it appears to come not just from a doctrinal position, but from a more deep-seated revulsion. What Dominic Janes has called the "voyeuristic Protestant gaze" in Victorian England transformed the imagined tools of public and private Catholic devotion into the equivalent of "kinky sex toys"—he notes the "perfumed rods" for sale in a well-known *Punch* cartoon mocking the use of incense by Ritualists.[120] But censers, the primary tool for perfuming Catholic worship, arguably already exhibited an element of kink for conservative Anglican observers, for they

Figure 15
Unknown Flemish painter,
The Mass of St Gregory the
Great, early 15th century,
Oil on panel. Photo: Alamy/
Groeningemuseum, Bruges.

share with scourges and cat-o'-nine-tails—those horrifying, and titillating, specters of the Protestant imagination—some of the same physical capabilities, notably the extensional swing and acceleration of the chain, with its threat of bodily violence.[121]

REFORMATION AND RITUALISM
IN NINETEENTH-CENTURY ENGLAND

Debates about incense in nineteenth-century England were more than a distant echo of the Reformation, for they constituted a meaningful working through of the Anglican Church's break with Rome in the sixteenth century and produced research foundational to the historical study of incense and of reformed liturgies.[122] They highlight the significance that censing continued to hold in the construction of confessional identity, whether it was considered a crucial aspect of worship or absolutely anathema. Because of the changing religious affiliations of its monarchs in the sixteenth and seventeenth centuries, England had a somewhat checkered history with respect to the use of incense in church. In addition to a brief period in the seventeenth century when, controversially, incense was reintroduced in a limited capacity, censers continued to be employed in the private chapels of recusants and the London embassies of Catholic nations.[123] But for the most part censers had been alienated from English worship, until the nineteenth century, when Catholicism was decriminalized and the Ritualism movement within Anglicanism began to revive some pre-Reformation church decorations and "ceremonies," including Eucharistic vestments, altar and processional lights, and the liturgical use of incense.[124]

The furor this revival caused permeated several spheres of public life. *Punch* published an "A.B.C. for Youthful Anglicans" that pointed directly to the censer's role in the Ritualist debates: "T is the Thurible, whose very smell / Incenses the people, and makes them rebel."[125] The pun turns ambiguously on two meanings of the verb *incense*: the rarer, early modern sense of kindling passion and the more familiar modern sense of enraging.[126] These lines frame censing once again as an act of rebellion and cast the seductive power of incense almost as a kind of illicit stimulant. At the same time, they capture the heated backlash against censing. Why was it considered so transgressive and why did it prompt such defensive anger? A number of anxieties were layered into the resistance to Ritualism, among them a xenophobic fear of Catholicism and of non-traditional sexual identities.[127]

Scholarship on Anglo-Catholicism has acknowledged the "emotional and aesthetic satisfactions" that made it "particularly attractive to members of a stigmatized sexual minority."[128] But the association of Ritualism with queer sub-cultures is also confounded by the vehement prejudices of nineteenth-century Anglicanism. Patrick O'Malley has identified "the deep cultural link in the evangelical imagination between religious 'absurdities' (including here all the physical motion of the Catholic liturgy) and the violation of gender and sexual norms."[129] The images of beautiful young men holding censers and other ecclesiastical implements that Simeon Solomon painted in the 1860s speak to this problematic convergence.[130] His watercolor *Two Acolytes, Censing, Pentecost* (1863) takes as its subject the sensual experience of the liturgy, including the church's neo-medieval furnishings, its stained glass, candlelight and lilies, and the smoking censer as it swings between the two splendidly dressed youths who lean their heads toward each other, focused on a point outside the picture [Figure 16].[131] Here was the multi-sensory, expressive mode of worship that Ritualists and others who shared an aesthetic appreciation for elements of religious ceremony craved. But the image's depiction of "High Church" elements, its absence of recognizable narrative content, and the undefined connection between the acolytes would make it a provocation to those who associated Ritualism with heresy and sexual deviance. Given England's pervasive history of antisemitism, Solomon's Orthodox Jewish background further complicated the reception of this portrayal of Christian thurifying. In 1873 and 1874 he was arrested and convicted for the criminal offense of sodomy. Read retrospectively, this ending to the artist's career risks narrowing the interpretation of his Ritualist-inspired scenes to modern notions of sexual orientation and identity and simplifying the physically and spiritually entangled transgressions they capture.[132]

Although only a small proportion of churches had reintroduced incense, it nevertheless prompted a crisis within English society more broadly as the question arose over who had the authority to regulate liturgical practice in the Anglican Church. A parliamentary inquiry in 1867 led in 1874 to the controversial Public Worship Regulation Act, which was explicitly designed to curb Ritualism and created a secular court to hear cases of "unlawful" rites and ceremonies. Trials proceeded and a few priests were even imprisoned as a result.[133] The matter was still not settled within the Church, however, and in 1899 the Anglican archbishops met at Lambeth Palace to hear evidence and make a final ruling "on the lawfulness of the liturgical use of incense and the carrying of lights in procession."[134]

It was this context of urgent debate, with legal, political, and material consequences, that spurred so much writing on incense in this period, including E. G. Cuthbert F. Atchley's *History of the Use of Incense in Divine Worship* (1909), which remains a foundational anglophone text.[135] Atchley's book was published with the support of the Alcuin Club, which aimed at restoring ecclesiastical ceremony according to correct historical precedent in the Church of England. It was the most comprehensive of a group of texts on incense written to inform the Ritualist debates. Henry Westall's *The Case for Incense*, which encompassed the set of legal arguments and documentary evidence he and other experts presented in 1899 at Lambeth Palace, had a decidedly pro-Ritualist bent.[136]

The legality of the ceremonial use of incense turned on the "Ornaments Rubric," a single line in the *Book of Common Prayer* that restricted church ornaments to those in use in the period between January 1548 and January 1549, during the reign of Edward VI. This line made the English Reformation newly present in the lives of Anglican worshipers and spurred intensive historical research and analysis that subjected primary texts from the Reformation to detailed, even sometimes philological, public discussion.[137] For anti-Ritualists, the matter was settled: the Reformation in England had eliminated the use of incense. But Westall and others believed there had never been an explicit prohibition. In particular they argued that the lack of discussion of incense in the *Book of Common Prayer* constituted tacit permission for its use rather than outright abolition.[138] They cited the survival of censers in church treasuries, including Elizabeth I's chapel, and the preservation of instructions for consecrating censers as further evidence for the continued acceptance of incense for liturgical use.[139]

Figure 16
Simeon Solomon, Two Acolytes
Censing, Pentecost, 1863,
Bodycolor on paper mounted on
canvas, 40.3 × 34.8 cm.
Photo: Ashmolean Museum,
University of Oxford, UK /
Bridgeman Images.

Westall had appeared at Lambeth Palace as the Vicar of St. Cuthbert's Philbeach Gardens, a Gothic Revival church in southwest London with definitively High Anglican practices and close association with the leaders of the liturgical revival movement.[140] Because of its use of candles, incense, and reservation of the sacrament, St. Cuthbert's was an explicit target of anti-Ritualist surveillance and protest, particularly by the radical campaigner John Kensit.[141] In April 1898 a nineteen-year-old follower of Kensit's attended Easter Sunday service there and, according to court testimony, "when the procession was close to the Defendant, he stepped out and caught hold of the thurifer who carried the incense, which might have been attended with danger if the charcoal had been scattered over the people. The Defendant called out, 'I can't stand this any longer. I must stop this Romanist nonsense.' He was removed from the church and handed over to the police."[142] In addition to explicitly highlighting the perceived danger of censing, including the precarity of the thurible and its hot coals, this anecdote demonstrates the passionate feeling on the anti-Ritualist side and the lengths to which some were willing to go to impede censing in Anglican churches.

The Lambeth Opinion of 1899 held that the use of incense was not legal in the Church of England and clergy were requested to discontinue its use outside of non-liturgical perfuming purposes.[143] Many priests and congregations found it difficult to come to terms with this guidance and relinquished unwillingly a practice that had in some churches been in place for decades. Some also chafed at having to submit to archiepiscopal authority, a feeling pithily captured by the Bishop of Chester: "We are thankful that the angels and archangels can still swing the censer, because they indeed are beyond the jurisdiction of the Archbishops of Canterbury and York."[144] The palpable disappointment displayed by congregations in response to the Lambeth Opinion testifies to the importance that incense had come to play in their conception of Anglican devotion. In one parish it was the blind congregants in particular who regretted the loss of incense, an anecdote that sheds light on the experience of disability in the Church and perhaps begs further consideration of the ways in which histories of sensory religion are framed around assumptions of able-bodiedness.[145] Did visually impaired worshipers experience the Reformation's elimination of incense in the sixteenth century similarly to those in this modern English parish?

In 1906 a Royal Commission on Ecclesiastical Discipline noted that incense was still being used ceremonially in about 20 percent of surveyed churches. Its report recommended loosening the regulation of public worship.[146] From this point forward, the ceremonial use of incense was less of a flashpoint issue. But installed in St. Cuthbert's is a prodigious testament to the passions surrounding the use of incense at the end of the nineteenth century. Though long planned, the towering carved *reredos* was not completed until 1913–1914.[147] Conceived by Ernest Geldart, a trained architect and Anglican priest who submitted historical evidence to the Lambeth Palace hearing, this altarpiece is a spectacular defense of incense in visual and material form [Figure 17].[148] Its iconographical program includes scenes capturing biblical justification for the ceremonial elements of both incense and processional lights, all framing the central panel of Christ in Glory surrounded by censing angels and a banner with a quotation from Malachi: "In every place shall incense be offered unto my name, and a pure offering."[149] Geldart later quipped that the real credit for the altarpiece went to the anti-Ritualist

Figure 17

Figure 17
Ernest Geldart (design),
Gilbert Boulton (execution),
Reredos depicting The Worship
of the Incarnate Son of God
with Incense and Lights (detail),
1913–1914, St Cuthbert's Church,
Philbeach Gardens, London.
Photo by Diliff via Wikipedia.

campaigner John Kensit and Archbishop Temple, whose judgment suppressed the ceremonial use of both incense and lights.[150] Given the immediate context of its conception around the Lambeth Palace hearing in 1899, the altarpiece stands as a bold rebuke to archiepiscopal authority and a subversive monument to Ritualist rebellion.

UNCHAINED:
CENSERS IN THE MODERN MUSEUM

Cuthbert Atchley was known as a "British Museum ritualist," a term that characterized an approach to modern Anglican devotion so rigorously antiquarian that it seemed fossilized to those who sought inspiration from the contemporary Roman Rite and the freedom to imagine what the English Church might have become "had it not been for the atrophying effect of Protestantism."[151] The association of Protestantism with the museum as a particular kind of institution is worth considering in more general terms, for it posits a shared project of deactivating and making strange the most animated forms of Catholic material culture, relegating them to the secular realm of historical inquiry and aesthetic analysis, rather than the sacred context of worship familiar through lived experience. In England in the mid-nineteenth century, the liturgical use of incense had fallen out to such a degree that one can find numerous examples of an inability, whether feigned or genuine, to recognize and understand the function of thuribles and their associated implements.[152] The fact that Anglicans were buying censers in Europe as "curiosities" in the nineteenth century shows just how alien, even ethnographic, these objects had become, with a destination more appropriate in the British Museum than in a Sunday service.[153]

As art historical research relies so heavily on the museum, and on media produced therein, it is important to ask what the censer became as a collected, musealized, and photographed object beginning in the nineteenth century.[154] A photograph from the early twentieth century suggests some of the methodological frames created by these contexts [Figure 18]. The medieval bronze censer has been placed into a white space, a setting that prompts formal analysis of the metalwork as object, as opposed to an implement performing its particular function. The image captures details of the censer's bronze, including patches of roughness and patina. It emphasizes the play of black and white as its voids open views into the dark interior and through to the indiscernible surface behind. The framing and positioning of the censer and the elimination of any further distractions in the background uncannily renders the perforations in the gable into a helmed face, with wide eyes and mouth and depressed round nose.

With all of the visual and material information that the photograph makes available to study, it is easy to overlook the absence of one feature central to medieval thuribles: the chains. What would ordinarily have been threaded through the apertures on the censer's four sides and attached to the loop on the pinnacle of the lid and taken up space in the rest of the image is missing. Of course, there are many explanations for missing chains, including their susceptibility to damage and loss over time. But the absence in this photograph allows us to reflect on the significance of the chain to the censer and to the censer's reception as artwork and artifact.

Removable, interchangeable, and formed of repetitive components, the thurible's chains are not usually the site of virtuosic metalworking skill,

Figure 18

Figure 18
Photograph of 14th-century
Rhenish bronze censer,
ca. 1916–1923. Photo:
Bildarchiv Foto Marburg.

which is why they rarely receive much detail in design drawings.[155] Alongside his detailed instructions for producing a raised and a cast censer in his twelfth-century treatise *De diversis artibus*, Theophilus did include a chapter on the censer's chains, though this section has received less scholarly attention because it is not rich in iconographical detail like the chapters that precede it.[156] He describes how the smith should draw wire for the links, ensure the resulting chain is of consistent thickness, and then attach five lengths of chain to the thurible's body and to the "lily" by which it will be swung from the ring, being careful to keep the censer well balanced.[157] Though the text does not mention the significance of the task, in determining the length of the chains, the smith was establishing the thurifer's embodied liturgical performance, including how far the censer would extend from the body and its physical manageability in pendular movement.

While unnecessary to depict for the purposes of metalwork design and execution, the censer's chains were what most interested artists tasked with capturing the practice of censing. They offered a means to diagram and make visceral the thurible's movement and its auditory and olfactory effects and to explore the thurifer's bodily relationship to the implement. Tim Ingold has written that chains are "articulated from rigid elements or links, and retain their connections even when tension is released. Yet they have no memory of their formation."[158] This means that their identical units have not been fundamentally changed by their interlinking and could be extricated with no impact on the remaining components. Nor, as they collapse together or extend, will the links bear any trace, or "memory," of the shapes the chain assumes. Formally dynamic and ever-changing, chains thus contrast with the body of the censer itself, whose profile and volume are firmly defined and permanent.

In their malleability and "memorylessness" chains present a particular challenge to the portrayal of the censer in repose. They can be trained into artful shapes or left in a confusing tangle that obscures the censer's form. Medieval and early modern artists of various media engaged with the potential for formal play in the thurible's chains.[159] In modern photographic representation and in museum display, the chains remain a problem that must be addressed, whether they are pulled away from or laid around the censer, or excised entirely.[160] The thurible's chains are determinative of the photograph's (as well as the vitrine's) format and dimensions, whether a squat rectangle [see Figure 2] or a long vertical [Figure 19]. There is also the issue of whether to show the mechanism by which the censer's chain is hung; museum photography from the nineteenth century to the present records a variety of solutions, from securing the ring with an invisible thread so it appears to float in space, to using a gloved crooked finger to hold the chain up.[161]

Figure 19

The challenge that the combination of solid thurible and flexible chain presents for display and photography is more than just an aesthetic museological issue. The treatment of the chain has implications for the interpretive framing of the censer. As we have seen, the chain provides the means by which the censer operates liturgically and in Christian visual culture, creating the swinging dispersal of perfumed smoke. In medieval theology, they also acquired symbolic resonances.[162] The chains are the component of the censer that renders it most unstable and, in Catholic-phobic contexts in and after the Reformation, most threatening. The removal or downplaying of the chain deprograms the object, distancing it from human physical and ritual use and allowing it to be consumed as a kind of relic of past devotional practice. This view of the censer may appear to be simply secular or—trained on typologies of the object—art historical, but we should recognize that it also shares something of the Protestant outlook familiar from anti-Catholic critique of sensual worship, what Baum has called "the sober, intellectual gaze of the Protestant subject."[163] More recent museum installations attempt to return a sense of dynamism to the censer by positioning the object as if it is in motion, tipping up its foot and allowing its chains to strain and slacken sympathetically.[164] Such positioning cannot convey the full ephemeral sensual experience of the censer, but even a slight disturbance to its static stance provides a visual cue to the missing auditory and olfactory expressions of the swung thurible.

CONCLUSION: CONTINUITY AND CHANGE IN THE GLOBAL SPREAD OF CATHOLICISM

Focusing on changes wrought by the Reformation can distort the broader view of Christian devotion by implying an end to certain practices that, quite to the contrary, maintain a vibrant role into the present.[165] Nor is it accurate to portray Catholic ritual, in contrast to the many shifts in Protestant theology and practice, as unchanging over the centuries. To avoid both such pitfalls, this chapter on the Reformation's impact on censing returns to where it began with Botticelli's *Korah*, to another group of eager thurifers in Rome. There, every October, a procession takes place that is dominated by incense smoke. The censers producing these fragrant clouds are not swung by acolytes accompanying richly dressed priests. Instead they are standing incense burners held by women of Italy's Peruvian community, who cleanse the path of a venerated image of Christ as it moves through the streets.[166]

For European Catholics, the form and basic function of the censer did not change radically over the ensuing centuries. Like other ecclesiastical plate, it evolved stylistically with current fashion, taking on Baroque linearity and Rococo swirls in turn, followed by historicist revival styles and eventually the Art Deco forms of the twentieth century.[167] With mass production and new industrial metalworking techniques, a wide variety of censers in bronze, brass, and even silver plate became available alongside the increasingly expensive prospect of a piece specially commissioned from an expert metalsmith.

The use and look of censers was nevertheless impacted by the global spread of Catholicism. In early modernity, they were part of the equipment that traveled with colonizing priests so that the Mass could be performed on missions abroad. Eventually the form of censing implements, and even the ingredients of incense, were influenced in certain parts of the world by existing local traditions. As Jeffrey Collins and Meredith Martin have shown, *naviculae* (boat-shaped incense containers) took on the style and resonances of these new contexts, and because of their ship-shape, played up associations with the trade routes that made people and goods mobile in this period.[168]

In what Collins and Martin call the "global republic of sacred goods," censers too took on local styles and modified functions. In the Viceroyalty of Peru, for example, new vessel-shapes combined the functional requirements of incense-burning with the forms of indigenous flora and fauna. Produced by local silversmiths, such *sahumadores* or *incensarios* were likely based on

Figure 19
Unknown Basel silversmith,
censer, before 1477, silver, raised
and cast, height (with chains):
89.4 cm, diameter 14.6 cm.
New York: Metropolitan Museum
of Art, Gift of J. Pierpont
Morgan, 1917.

Figure 20
Women thurifers *(sahumadoras)*
of Lima censing the procession
of the Lord of Miracles,
October 18, 1982. Photo by
Darío Médico / El Comercio.

Asian precedents, but took specifically Andean forms, such as fruit, or local animals like armadillo, deer, turkeys, or the Peruvian gray dove.[169] Unlike typical Roman Catholic censers, these vessels were not designed to be swung by chains, but were instead stabilized on a tray. While many were employed in purifying and perfuming domestic space, their use was not only secular; they can be seen in the hands of elegantly attired *sahumadoras* in paintings of nineteenth-century processions and church interiors.[170]

To this day a charitable sorority of women in Lima shares the task of censing during the procession of an image that miraculously survived early modern earthquakes [Figure 20].[171] The fragrant mixture burned includes *palo santo* and *copal*, the native tree resin that had been employed by Indigenous peoples of the Americas, as well as conventional gum incense.[172] This longstanding devotional tradition subverts some of the expectations around the use of incense in European Catholic practice, not least through the non-typical form of the hand-held, static censer. Whereas the labor of formal liturgical and processional censing is ordinarily performed by male deacons, acolytes, and priests, here in the lay context of a popular Christian festival, the role is exclusively female. This mode of censing ritual, now enacted by the Peruvian diaspora in Italy, weaves together Afro-Peruvian image devotion, elements of Catholic liturgical practice, indigenous olfactory materials, and a specifically Andean form of censer, thus witnessing the complex legacies of the colonial past.[173] It is yet another instance in which censing becomes a site of, if not exactly transgression, than at least a pushing of the boundary around what constitutes the accepted form of material worship.

Figure 20

* *
*

The story of censers after the Reformation is multi-stranded. Rendered superfluous by new conceptualizations of the liturgy, in Protestant communities censers were pointedly destroyed, sold, or preserved and simply forgotten about. Or they remained to serve non-ceremonial purposes. They also came to metonymize what Protestants considered to be the most decadent and doctrinally unacceptable aspects of Catholic worship, and thereby featured prominently in textual and visual propaganda. For Catholics and other Christians, the censer continues to play an important role in liturgy to this day and, while it may have changed stylistically over the centuries, the basic form facilitating its ceremonial functions remained the same. Nevertheless, as the Christian censer moved across the globe during the colonial period, it was sometimes shaped anew by local traditions. Nor were reformed views of incense permanent. Even where it had been entirely discontinued, incense could still be reexamined and even reintroduced, as the case of Ritualism in the Anglican Church demonstrates. The ensuing debates in nineteenth-century England indicate that incense and the tools used to facilitate its use were burdened by many layers of associations, as indeed they had been in the sixteenth century. Censers were not simply objects made, discarded, and musealized, but also powerful symbols and metaphors that operated as well in the immaterial worlds of imaginaries across the confessional spectrum.

ENDNOTES

1   I thank Beate Fricke, Joanne Luginbühl, and Zumrad Ilyasova in Bern for encouraging this essay into being. The text has benefitted from several generous readers, including Emily Floyd, Caitlin Miller, and Róisín Watson. I owe a particular debt to Rev. Dr. Ayla Lepine for sharing both her ecclesiastical expertise and her art historical knowledge of nineteenth-century England at an early stage. The extensive comments and suggestions offered by three anonymous reviewers helped improve the text significantly, saving me from more than a few errors and infelicities. Those that remain are my own. Num 16:1–40.

2   Lewine 1990, 16.

3   Smith 2014.

4   Baum 2013, 338 n. 94.

5   Stielau 2014a.

6   Lindberg 2020.

7   Koerner 2008.

8   Westermann-Angerhausen 2011. For overviews of medieval censers, see Westermann-Angerhausen 2014; Braun 1932, 598–631; and essays in the current volume.

9   Building on the early work of Robert Scribner (2001). See Karant-Nunn 1997; Heal 2016.

10   Morrall 2002; Spicer 2005; Walsham 2011; Coscarelli-Larkin 2020.

11   Hahn 2014; 2017; Milner 2011.

12   Milner 2011; Dugan 2011; Baum 2013; Hahn 2017; Baum 2019.

13   Hahn 2017, 92–94; Baum 2019, 2–11.

14   These are succinctly summarized in Wandel 2006. See also Karant-Nunn 2016.

15   Baum 2013, 337.

16   Baum 2019, 31. The functions mentioned in this paragraph and their historical origins are covered extensively in Atchley 1909.

17   Reinarz 2013, 26–27. On the developing use of incense in early Christianity, see Harvey 2006, 75–83; Caseau 2007.

18   Exod 30:7–8; Psalms 141:2.

19   Reinarz 2013, 29.

20   Fisher 2016.

21   Baum 2013, 338–39.

22   Karant-Nunn 1997, location 254.

23   Milner 2011, location 3044.

24   Pickett 2016, 22–24.

25   On the expense of incense and its inaccessibility, see Baum 2013, 336. On the early trade in frankincense and myrrh, see Groom 1981.

26   Baum 2019, 35.

27   See the chapter "Censing God" in Dugan 2011, 24–41.

28   Milner 2011, location 7311.

29   Baum 2013, 336–37.

30   Ibid., 341; Dugan 2011, 29.

31   Hahn 2014, 64.

32   Christ 2021, 202–3.

33   Hahn 2017, 108, 111; Baum 2013, 336–37.

34   Though with a new orientation to Christ as opposed to the Marian focus of the rosary. Coscarelli-Larkin 2020, 31–32. See also Christ 2021, 172–73.

35   Baum 2013, 332–33.

36   This emphasis on the practical uses of incense signals a return to the functions of purification and health that had made incense popular in Christian ritual from the beginning, as Béatrice Caseau (2007) has argued.

37   Baum 2019, 163–65.

38   Roper 1985, 90–92; Karant-Nunn 1997, location 315.

39   Roper 1985, 99.

40   Karant-Nunn 1997, location 1770.

41   See the section entitled "Reformation Churching" in ibid., location 1784 and following.

42   Hahn 2014, 84.

43   Karant-Nunn 1999, 78.

44   On *vasa sacra et non sacra*, see Braun 1932.

45   Baum 2013, 343; Hahn 2017, 107; Husband 2001a; 2001b.

46   Fritz 1997.

47   Stielau 2014b.

48   Duffy 2005, 459–60.

49   Oman 1957, 90.

50   On the Reformation in Switzerland, see Gordon 2002. On iconoclasm in the Swiss Reformation, see Dupeux, Jezler, and Wirth 2000.

51   Husband 2001a, 26.

52   Ribbert 2001; Husband 2001b.

53   Seyderhelm 2001, 235; Oman 1957, pl. 60.

54   On the secular reuse of ecclesiastical objects, see Yeoman 2018; Walsham 2017.

55   Grosse 1997.

56   Christ 2021, 172–73. The metaphorical substitution of prayer and incense was articulated by early Christian theologians like Origen. Read 2018, 180.

57   Quoted in Baum 2013, 340.

58   On incense in English literature in the seventeenth century, see Robertson 2009; Read 2018, 179–89.

59   Read 2018, 181.

60   Ibid., 182.

61   Pickett 2016, 20; Gurnis-Farrell 2011, 102–3; Milner 2011, location 7337.

62   Hosea 13:3.

63   For example, Hendrick Goltzius's *Homo bulla* (1594) adds to the familiar tropes of the skull and the infant blowing bubbles, an open incense burner on what appears to be a stone altar in the distance. Amsterdam, Rijksmuseum RP-P-OB-10.227.

64   Fritz 2000; 2004.

65   Nevertheless, in its typical mode of simplified binary juxtaposition, early Protestant visual propaganda utilized prayer-beads as legible signifiers of Catholic devotional practice that contrasted with the Lutheran emphasis on the Word. Coscarelli-Larkin 2020, 15–18.

66   Juster 2016, 18.

67   Janssens 2013–2014, 178.

68   "Das unkraut wil ich aus roten und werfen es ins feur." Stoneware tankard with pewter lid from Siegburg, ca. 1552–1575. Museum für Kunst und Gewerbe, Hamburg, inv. no. 1876.104.

69   See the print by Erhard Schön, discussed in Baum 2019, 2–3.

70   Viewable in high resolution via artsandculture.google.com/asset/de-zielenvisserij. Accessed January 14, 2022.

71   King 2006, 164–66.

72   Oxford English Dictionary, "paltry."

73   Moshenska 2019.

74   Scribner 1994, 82–83.

75   Lewine 1990, 17.

76   Dodgson 1935, 93.

77   Reinarz 2013, 33.

78   Wauters 2021, 23.

79   Baum 2013, 341.

80   Gurnis-Farrell 2011, 102.

81   Leitch 2010, 131–37; Spinks 2014.

82   Leitch 2010, 135.

83   Spinks 2014, 16–17.

84   This section on Boaistuau is indebted to Spinks 2014, 27–29.

85   Spinks 2014, 29.

86   For the association of open braziers with witchcraft and the demonic manipulation of air and smoke, see Wood 2006, 165; Cole 2002; Zika 2007. On the occult use of incense in the sixteenth century, including libanomancy, see "Weihrauch" 1987, 285.

87   See the drawing by Niklaus Manuel of *Death Embracing a Woman*, 1517. Historisches Museum, Basel, Inv. Nr. 419; and the woodcut by Lucas van Leyden, "Solomon's Idolatry," 1516–1519. Cleveland Museum of Art, 1960.156.

88   Albrecht Dürer, *Apes Dancing around a Brazier*, 1523. Pen on paper. Basel: Öffentliche Kunstsammlung. Müller 1992, 21.

89   Zika 2007.

90   Baum 2013, 339–40.

91   On Zwingli, see Gordon 2002 and Dupeux, Jezler, and Wirth 2000.

92   On the tabernacle and its service, see Childs 2004, 512–52.

93   See the preparatory sketch in the British Museum from ca. 1546–1548. 1949,0411.112. https://www.britishmuseum.org/collection/object/P_1949-0411-112.

94   Milner 2011, location 7311.

95   Dugan 2011; Milner 2011; Baum 2013; 2019; Pickett 2016, 19.

96   Lev 10:1–2.

97   Wiesel 1997.

98   Karlstadt 1522, 8; Knox 1854, 38–39; Calvin 1854, 430–37; Baum 2013, 338 n. 94.

99   For example, see the fifteenth-century illustration by Diebold Lauber in Bayerische Staatsbibliothek Cgm. 1101, fol. 122r. Available online at https://www.digitale-sammlungen.de/en/view/bsb00092281?page=251.

100   Eleazar is tasked with rescuing the censers from the fire that destroyed the rebels. Num 16:36–40.

101   Ribbert 2001, 147; Westermann-Angerhausen 2011.

102   Oman 1957, 90.

103   Ribbert 2001, 148.

104   Hope 1908, 72.

105   Baum 2013, 325–26. On the movement of angels and incense across the frontier between Heaven and Earth, see Caseau 1996, 340–41.

106   Dugan 2011, 29.

107   Chaucer, lines 3339–44.

108   Atchley reads this passage as a document of late medieval practice. Atchley 1909, 263–64; Milner 2011, location 3273.

109   See for example the censing angel on the wall of the south transept in Westminster Abbey, sculpted in the 1250s.

110   This topic awaits more comprehensive analysis, but examples include Adrian Isenbrandt's Mass of St. Gregory (ca. 1510–1550) on panel (69.PB.11) and a manuscript illumination from the workshop of Gerard Horenbout from around 1500, Ms Ludwig IX 17 (83.ML.113), fol. 102v, both at the J. Paul Getty Museum in Los Angeles.

111   Bynum 2006, 220.

112   On the theology of the Mass of St. Gregory, see Bynum, 2006; Lentes and Gormans, 2006; Meier 2006.

113   Sanmartín 1984.

114   Casati and Cavanagh 2019, 299.

115   Oman 1957, 249.

116   Baum 2019, 264; Dugan 2011, 28.

117   Atchley 1909, 329–30.

118   Beresford Hope 1874, 241.

119   My emphasis. "The Church Abroad" 1917, 529. According to Ayla Lepine, this complaint concerns a particular technique of Ritualist censing, in which the thurifer faces east and allows the censer to "move by its own force" without the interference of the arm or wrist (personal communication, January 27, 2023). Still, the existence of this display of ritual skillfulness highlights the significance of swung movement, whether exuberant or rigorously controlled, to the discourse on censing in the Anglican Church.

120   Janes 2013, 687.

121   On the post-Reformation reframing of flagellant practices, see Largier 2007, 175–218. The physical similarity of the scourge's flexible thongs to the censer's chains and the related forms of gesture and movement both objects afford are observable in medieval representations of the Passion and the *arma Christi*.

122   Thus Janes's phrase, "Victorian Reformation," Janes 2009.

123   Parry 2008; Murdoch 2008, 79. I thank Tessa Murdoch for kindly sharing materials about recusant plate when libraries were inaccessible during the pandemic.

124   Anson 1966, 207. I use "Ritualism" broadly here to encompass the groups advocating a return to pre-Reformation devotional practices in the long nineteenth century, though other terms are often used. For more on Ritualism in the Anglican Church, see Reed 1996; Janes 2009.

125   "Mr. Punch's A.B.C." 1871; On Punch's campaign against Ritualism, including further commentary on incense, see Horrocks 2013.

126   Oxford English Dictionary, s.v. "incense, v. 2."

127   O'Malley 2006; Hilliard 1982.

128   Hilliard 1982, 181.

129   My quotation marks. O'Malley 2006, 87.

130 On Solomon's religious paintings, see Janes 1996 and Cruise 2005.
131 On Solomon's portrayal of censing, see Bradstreet 2022, 157–65. Unfortunately I was not able to engage fully with Bradstreet's text before this chapter went to press.
132 On the collapsing of the era's "fascinating play of religious and sexual deviance" into "mere homosexuality," see O'Malley 2006, 193.
133 Anson 1966, 209.
134 *Archbishops on the Lawfulness of the Liturgical Use of Divine Incense* 1899.
135 Wauters 2021, 34.
136 Westall 1899.
137 Mickelthwaite 1897; on Mickelthwaite, see Anson 1966, 303–5.
138 Westall 1899, 37; Atchley 1909, 328–69.
139 Westall 1899.
140 Findlay 1991, 4.
141 *Roman Mass in the English Church* 1899, 6–10.
142 *The Church Times*, April 15, 1898, 415.
143 *Archbishops on the Lawfulness of the Liturgical Use of Divine Incense* 1899.
144 "Angels and Archbishops" 1899.
145 "Lambeth Opinion" 1899, 328. On disability studies of Reformation sensual experience, see Hahn 2017, 93.
146 *Report of the Royal Commission on Ecclesiastical Discipline* 1906.
147 On St. Cuthbert's see Findlay 1991; Lepine 2017; Anson 1966, 252.
148 Westall 1899, 103–36.
149 Malachi 1:11.
150 Geldart 1935.

151 "Review of A History of Incense in Divine Worship" 1910; Anson 1966, 316.
152 Law and Law 1925, 170–171.
153 Ibid., 171.
154 On the musealization of medieval sacred artifacts, see the essays in Brückle, Mariaux, and Mondini 2015.
155 Stielau 2014c, 29–30.
156 Westermann-Angerhausen 2016, 200.
157 Theophilus 1979, 138–39. On the liturgically specific iconography of Theophilus's censers, see Westermann-Angerhausen 2016.
158 Ingold 2015, 15.
159 Stielau 2014c.
160 To keep the objects compact for photography in the 1893 sale catalogue of the Spitzer Collection, the chains of two medieval censers were, unusually, wrapped tightly around their lids. Spitzer 1893, plate V, lots 347 and 385.
161 For example, see the photograph associated with a Coptic censer in the British Museum (OA.853), https://www.britishmuseum.org/collection/object/H_OA-853. This surprising incursion of human anatomy highlights the powerful conventions of museum photography, which rarely incorporates the body, even for functional objects like the censer, which is designed to be held and swung.
162 Westermann-Angerhausen 2011. The twelfth-century theologian Honorius of Autun interpreted the censer's number of chains in relation to the nature of Christ. Quoted in Beate Fricke's chapter in this volume, 183.

163 Baum 2019, 3. On the typological framing of Christian sacred art in the modern museum, see Beer 2015.
164 See the medieval censers displayed at the Museum für Kunst und Gewerbe, Hamburg.
165 Such tendencies are arguably connected historiographically to the noted Protestant bias of the discipline of art history. See the early chapters on this topic in Squire 2009.
166 Cruzzolin 2018.
167 Braun 1932, 624–26.
168 Collins and Martin 2017, 513–46.
169 Phipps, Martín, and Hecht 2004, 255–56, 360–61; Briceño 2011, 54. These forms in turn inspired European secular incense burners, like the late sixteenth-century German example in the form of a turkey. Schütte 2003, 154–57.
170 Watercolors by Francisco Javier Cortés and Francisco Fierro Palas, known as Pancho Fierro, in particular feature the *sahumadoras*. On these mixed-race descendants of African and Indigenous Peruvians, see Melling 2017, 302–3.
171 Pinilla et al. 2016; I thank Daen Palma Huse for his swift and diligent efforts to acquire this image for publication.
172 RPP Noticias 2019; Briceño 2011, 70. On copal, see Brittenham, this volume, 25.
173 Barrantes and Aguilar 2015, 158–59.

BIBLIOGRAPHY

"Angels and Archbishops." 1899. *The Church Times*.

Anson, Peter F. 1966. *Fashions in Church Furnishings, 1840–1940*. New York: London House & Maxwell.

The Archbishops on the Lawfulness of the Liturgical Use of Divine Incense and the Carrying of Processional Lights, Lambeth Palace, July 31, 1899. 1899. London: Macmillan and Co.

Atchley, Edward Godfrey Cuthbert Frederic. 1909. *A History of the Use of Incense in Divine Worship*. London: Longmans, Green.

Barrantes, Maribel Arrelucea, and Jesús A. Cosamalón Aguilar. 2015. *La Presencia Afrodescendiente en el Perú, Siglos XVI–XX*. Lima: Ministry of Culture.

Baum, Jacob M. 2013. "From Incense to Idolatry: The Reformation of Olfaction in Late Medieval German Ritual." *Sixteenth-Century Journal* 44, no. 2 (2013): 323–44.

Baum, Jacob M. 2019. *Reformation of the Senses: The Paradox of Religious Belief and Practice in Germany*. Urbana: University of Illinois Press.

Beer, Manuela. 2015. "Typenreihen und Museumsweihen für die mittelalterliche Kunst. Alexander Schnütgens Kölner Sammlung als kuratorische Herausforderung." In *Musealisierung mittelalterlicher Kunst. Anlässe, Ansätze, Ansprüche*, edited by Wolfgang Brückle, Pierre Alain Mariaux, and Daniela Mondini, 127–48. Berlin: Deutscher Kunstverlag.

Beresford Hope, Alexander. 1874. *Worship in the Church of England*. London: John Murray.

Bradstreet, Christina. 2022. *Scented Visions: Smell in Art, 1850–1914*. State College: Pennsylvania State University Press.

Braun, Joseph. 1932. *Das christliche Altargerät in seinem Sein und in seiner Entwicklung*. Munich: Max Hueber.

Briceño, Ximena Natanya. 2011. "Filigree: A Migrant Metal Practice." PhD diss., Australian National University.

Brückle, Wolfgang, Pierre Alain Mariaux, and Daniela Mondini, eds. 2015. *Musealisierung mittelalterlicher Kunst. Anlässe, Ansätze, Ansprüche*. Berlin: Deutscher Kunstverlag.

Bynum, Caroline Walker. 2006. "Seeing and Seeing Beyond: The Mass of St. Gregory in the Fifteenth Century." In *The Mind's Eye: Art and Theological Argument in the Middle Ages*, edited by Jeffrey F. Hamburger and Anne-Marie Bouché, 208–40. Princeton, NJ: Princeton University Press.

Calvin, John. 1854. *Commentaries on the Four Last Books of Moses Arranged in the Form of a Harmony*, vol. 3. Edited by Charles William Bingham. Edinburgh: Calvin Translation Society.

Casati, Roberto, and Patrick Cavanagh. 2019. *The Visual World of Shadows*. Cambridge, MA: The MIT Press.

Caseau, Béatrice. 1996. "Crossing the Impenetrable Frontier between Earth and Heaven." In *Shifting Frontiers in Late Antiquity*, edited by Ralph W. Mathisen and Hagith S. Sivan, 333–43. Aldershot: Variorum.

Caseau, Béatrice. 2007. "Incense and Fragrances from House to Church." In *Material Culture and Well-Being in Byzantium (400–1453)*, edited by M. Grünbart, E. Kislinger, A. Muthesius, and D. Stathakopoulos, 75–92. Vienna: Verlag der Österreichischen Akademie der Wissenschaften.

Chaucer, Geoffrey. *The Canterbury Tales*. Harvard University. Accessed February 1, 2022. https://chaucer.fas.harvard.edu/pages/millers-prologue-and-tale.

Childs, Brevard S. 2004 *The Book of Exodus: A Critical, Theological Commentary*. Louisville, KY: Westminster John Knox Press.

Christ, Martin. 2021. *Biographies of a Reformation: Religious Change and Confessional Coexistence in Upper Lusatia, c. 1520–1635*. Kindle edition. Oxford: Oxford University Press.

"The Church Abroad: Australian Notes, April 17." 1917. *The Church Times*, June 22, 529.

Cole, Michael. 2002. "The Demonic Arts and the Origin of the Medium." *The Art Bulletin* 84, no. 4 (2002): 621–40.

Collins, Jeffrey L., and Meredith Martin. 2017. "Early Modern Incense Boats: Commerce, Christianity, and Culture Exchange." In *The Nomadic Object: The Challenge of World for Early Modern Religious Art*, edited by Christine Göttler and Mia Mochizuki, 513–46. Leiden: Brill.

Coscarelli-Larkin, Luisa. 2020. *Der lutherische Rosenkranz: Konfessionelle und sinnliche Aspekte von Gebetszählgeräten in Porträts der Frühen Neuzeit*. Bern: Peter Lang.

Cruise, Colin. 2005. "'Pressing All Religions into His Service': Solomon's Ritual Paintings and Their Contexts." In *Love Revealed: Simeon Solomon and the Pre-Raphaelites*, 57–63. London and New York: Merrell.

Cruzzolin, Riccardo. 2018. "The Cult of Señor de Los Milagros of Peruvians in Italy." In *Local Identities and Transnational Cults within Europe*, edited by Fiorella Giacalone and Kevin Griffin, 69–76. Wallingford: CABI.

Dodgson, Campbell. 1935. "Rare Woodcuts in the Ashmolean Museum: IV. Other Nuremberg Artists (Continued)." *Burlington Magazine* 66, no. 383: 88–91, 93.

Duffy, Eamon. 2005. *The Stripping of the Altars: Traditional Religion in England, 1400–1580*. New Haven, CT: Yale University Press.

Dugan, Holly. 2011. *The Ephemeral History of Perfume: Scent and Sense in Early Modern England*. Baltimore, MD: Johns Hopkins University Press.

Dupeux, Cécile, Peter Jezler, and Jean Wirth, eds. 2000. *Bildersturm. Wahnsinn oder Gottes Wille?* Munich: Fink.

Findlay, Donald. 1991. "All Glorious Within: An Appreciation of St Cuthbert's Philbeach Gardens." *Victorian Society Annual*, 4–21.

Fisher, Jeff. 2016. *A Christoscopic Reading of Scripture: Johannes Oecolampadius on Hebrews*. Göttingen: Vandenhoeck & Ruprecht.

Fritz, Johann Michael. 1997. *Die bewahrende Kraft des Luthertums, Mittelalterliche Kunstwerke in Evangelischen Kirchen*. Regensburg: Schnell & Steiner.

Fritz, Johann Michael. 2000. "Vasa sacra et non sacra: Stiefkinder der Theologie und Kunstgeschichte." *Das Münster* 53, no. 4: 350–56.

Fritz, Johann Michael. 2004. *Das evangelische Abendmahlsgerät in Deutschland: Vom Mittelalter bis zum Ende des Alten Reiches.* Leipzig: Evangelische Verlagsanstalt.

Geldart, Ernest. 1935. "The Reredos." *St Cuthbert's Parish Magazine*, February. Accessed February 10, 2022. saintcuthbert.org/the-reredos.

Gordon, Bruce. 2002. *The Swiss Reformation.* Manchester: Manchester University Press.

Groom, Nigel. 1981. *Frankincense and Myrrh: A Study of the Arabian Incense Trade.* London: Longman.

Grosse, Fritz. 1997. "Anmerkungen zur 'Jamnitzerburg.'" In *Kunst und Denkmalpflege: Hiltrud Kier zum 60. Geburtstag, Festgabe der Schülerinnen und Schüler*, edited by Ulrich Hermanns and Gabriele Wiesemann, 43–62. Weimar: VDG.

Gurnis-Farrell, Musa. 2011. "Heterodox Drama: Theater in Post-Reformation London." PhD diss., Columbia University.

Hahn, Philip. 2014. "Sensing Sacred Space: Ulm Minster, the Reformation, and Parishioners' Sensory Perception, c. 1470 to 1640." *Archiv für Reformationsgeschichte* 105, no. 1: 55–91.

Hahn, Philip. 2017. "Lutheran Sensory Culture in Context." *Past & Perfect* 234, no. 1, Supplement 12: 90–113.

Harvey, Susan Ashbrook. 2006. *Scenting Salvation: Ancient Christianity and the Olfactory Imagination.* Berkeley: University of California Press.

Heal, Bridget. 2016. "Visual and Material Culture." In *The Oxford Handbook of the Protestant Reformations*, ed. Ulinka Rublack, 601–20. Oxford: Oxford University Press.

Hilliard, David. 1982. "Unenglish and Unmanly: Anglo-Catholicism and Homosexuality." *Victorian Studies* 25, no. 2 (Winter): 181–210.

Hope, W. H. St. John. 1908. "On an Inventory of the Goods of the Collegiate Church of the Holy Trinity, Arundel, taken 1st October, 9 Henry VIII. (1517)." *Archaeologia* 61, no. 1: 61–96.

Horrocks, Jamie. 2013. "Asses and Aesthetes: Ritualism and Aestheticism in Victorian Periodical Illustration." *Victorian Periodicals Review* 46, no. 1 (Spring): 1–36.

Husband, Timothy. 2001a. "Dormant then Divided, Dispersed and Reunited." In *The Treasury of Basel Cathedral*, 25–33. New York: Metropolitan Museum of Art.

Husband, Timothy. 2001b. "Rauchfass." In *Der Basler Münsterschatz*, edited by. Historisches Museum Basel, 149–52. Basel: Christoph Merian.

Ingold, Tim. 2015. *The Life of Lines.* London; New York: Routledge.

Janes, Dominic. 1996. "Seeing and Tasting the Divine: Simeon Solomon's Homoerotic Sacrament." In *Art, History and the Senses, 1830 to the Present*, edited by Patrizia Di Bello and Gabriel Koureas, 35–50. Farnham: Ashgate.

Janes, Dominic. 2009. *Victorian Reformation: The Fight over Idolatry in the Church of England, 1840–1860.* Oxford: Oxford University Press.

Janes, Dominic. 2013. "*The Confessional Unmasked*: Religious Merchandise and Obscenity in Victorian England." *Victorian Literature and Culture* 41: 677–90.

Janssens, Eva L. E. 2013–2014. "World of Wickedness: A Remarkable Sixteenth-Century Print of the Parable of the Good Shepherd." *Simiolus* 37, no. 3/4: 170–86.

Juster, Susan. 2016. *Sacred Violence in Early America.* Philadelphia: University of Pennsylvania Press.

Karant-Nunn, Susan. 1997. *The Reformation of Ritual: An Interpretation of Early Modern Germany.* Kindle edition. London; New York: Routledge.

Karant-Nunn, Susan. 1999. "Die Unterdrückung der religiösen Emotionen." In *Kulterelle Reformation: Sinnformation im Umbruch, 1400–1600*, edited by Bernhard Jussen and Craig Koslofsky, 61–96. Göttingen: Vandenhoeck und Ruprecht.

Karant-Nunn, Susan. 2016. "The Reformation of Liturgy." In *The Oxford Handbook of the Protestant Reformations*, edited by Ulinka Rublack, 409–30. Oxford: Oxford University Press.

Karlstadt, Andreas von. 1522. "On the Removal of Idols." *German History in Documents and Images.* Accessed February 5, 2022. https://ghdi.ghi-dc.org/docpage.cfm?docpage_id=5207.

King, John N. 2006. *Foxe's "Book of Martyrs" and Early Modern Print Culture.* Cambridge: Cambridge University Press.

Knox, John. 1854. *A Vindication of the Doctrine that the Sacrifice of the Mass Is Idolatry* (1550). In *The Works of John Knox*, edited by David Laing, vol. 3, 33–70. Edinburgh: Johnstone and Hunter.

Koerner, Joseph Leo. 2008. *The Reformation of the Image.* Chicago: University of Chicago Press.

"The Lambeth Opinion: The Position of the Clergy." 1899. *The Church Times*, September 29, 328.

Largier, Niklaus. 2007. *In Praise of the Whip: A Cultural History of Arousal.* Translated by Graham Harman. Princeton, NJ: Zone Books.

Law, Henry William, and Irene Law. 1925. *The Book of the Beresford Hopes.* London: Heath Cranton.

Leitch, Stephanie. 2010. *Mapping Ethnography in Early Modern Germany: New Worlds in Print Culture.* Basingstoke: Palgrave Macmillan.

Lentes, Thomas, and Andreas Gormans, eds. 2006. *Das Bild der Erscheinung: Die Gregorsmesse im Mittelalter.* Berlin: Reimer.

Lepine, Ayla. 2017. "'There Is No Wealth but Life': London's Gothic Revival and Urban Resurrection." In *Visualising a Sacred City: London, Art and Religion*, edited by Ben Quash, Aaron Rosen, and Chloë Reddaway, 143–57. London: I. B. Tauris.

Lewine, Carol F. 1990. "Botticelli's *Punishment of Korah* and the 'Sede Vacante.'" *Source* 9, no. 2: 14–18.

Lindberg, Carter. 2020. *The European Reformations.* 3rd edn. Hoboken, NJ: Wiley-Blackwell.

Meier, Esther. 2006. *Die Gregorsmesse: Funktionen eines spätmittelalterlichen Bildtypus.* Cologne: Böhlau Verlag.

Melling, Helen. 2017. "Escondidos en plena vista: Afrodescendientes en la cultura visual del Perú decimonónico." *Estudios Afrolatinoamericanos* 3: 295–308.

Micklethwaite, John T. 1897. *The Ornaments of the Rubric.* London: Longmans, Green.

Milner, Matthew. 2011. *The Senses and the English Reformation.* Kindle edition. Farnham: Ashgate.

Morrall, Andrew. 2002. "Protestant Pots: Morality and Social Ritual in the Early Modern Home." *Journal of Design History* 15, no. 4: 263–73.

Moshenska, Joe. 2019. *Iconoclasm as Child's Play.* Stanford, CA: Stanford University Press.

"Mr. Punch's A.B.C. for Youthful Anglicans." 1871. *Punch*, April 8, 145.

Müller, Christian, ed. 1992. *Das Amerbach-Kabinett. Zeichnungen Alter Meister.* Basel: Kupferstichkabinett der Öffentlichen Sammlung.

Murdoch, Tessa. 2008. "Recusant Plate in England." In *Treasures of the English Church: A Thousand Years of Sacred Gold and Silver*, edited by Timothy Schroder, 78–85. London: Goldsmiths' Company.

O'Malley, Patrick. 2006. *Catholicism, Sexual Deviance, and Victorian Gothic Culture.* Cambridge: Cambridge University Press.

Oman, Charles. 1957. *English Church Plate, 597–1830.* London; Oxford: Oxford University Press.

The Oxford English Dictionary. s.v. "incense, v. 2." Accessed February 22, 2022. oed.com.

The Oxford English Dictionary. s.v. "paltry." Accessed July 15, 2023. oed.com.

Parry, Graham. 2008. *The Arts of the Anglican Counter-Reformation: Glory, Laud and Honour.* Woodbridge: Boydell & Brewer.

Phipps, Elena, Cristina Esteras Martín, and Johanna Hecht. 2004. *The Colonial Andes: Tapestry and Silverwork, 1530–1830.* New York: Metropolitan Museum of Art.

Pickett, Holly Crawford. 2016. "The Idolatrous Nose: Incense on the Early Modern Stage." In *Religion and Drama in Early Modern England: The Performance of Religion on the Renaissance Stage*, edited by Jane Hwang Degenhardt and Elizabeth Williamson, 19–38. Farnham: Ashgate.

Pinilla, Ramón Mujica, et al. 2016. *El Señor de los Milagros: historia, devocion e identidad.* Lima: Banco de Crédito.

Read, Sophie. 2018. "What the Nose Knew: Renaissance Theologies of Smell." In *Literature, Belief and Knowledge in Early Modern England*, edited by Subha Mukherji and Tim Stuart-Battle, 175–93. London: Palgrave Macmillan.

Reed, John Shelton. 1996. *Glorious Battle: The Cultural Politics of Victorian Anglo-Catholicism.* Chapel Hill, NC: Bozart Books, 2017; 1st edn. Vanderbilt University Press, 1996.

Reinarz, Jonathan. 2013. *Past Scents: Historical Perspectives on Smell.* Champaign: University of Illinois Press.

Report of the Royal Commission on Ecclesiastical Discipline. 1906. Section IV: Present Breaches and Neglects of the Law. Online via the Canterbury Project. Accessed February 10, 2022. http://anglicanhistory.org/pwra/rced4/section4.html.

"Review of *A History of Incense in Divine Worship* by E. G. Cuthbert H. Atchley." 1910. *The Church Times*, February 4, 153.

Ribbert, Margret. 2001. "Zwei Weihrauchfässer." In *Der Basler Münsterschatz*, edited by Historisches Museum Basel, 147–48. Basel: Christoph Merian.

Robertson, David. 2009. "Incensed over Incense: Incense and Community in Seventeenth-Century Literature." In *Writing and Religion in England, 1558–1689, Studies in Community-Making and Cultural Memory*, edited by Roger D. Sell and Anthony W. Johnson, 389–411. Farnham: Ashgate.

The Roman Mass in the English Church: Illegal Services Described by Eye Witnesses. 1899. London: Chas. J. Thynne.

Roper, Lyndal. 1985. "'Going to Church and Street': Weddings in Reformation Augsburg." *Past & Present* 106: 62–101.

RPP Noticias. 2019. "Sahumadoras abren paso al Señor de los Milagros." October 29. Accessed December 29, 2020. https://www.youtube.com/watch?v=RBF50tQdh50.

Sanmartín, Juan R. 1984. "O Botafumeiro: Parametric Pumping in the Middle Ages." *American Journal of Physics* 52, no. 10: 937–45.

Schütte, Rudolf-Alexander. 2003. *Die Silberkammer der Landgrafen von Hessen-Kassel.* Kassel: Staatliche Museen.

Scribner, R. W. 1994. *For the Sake of Simple Folk: Popular Propaganda for the German Reformation.* Oxford: Clarendon Press.

Scribner, R. W. 2001. *Religion and Culture in Germany (1400–1800).* Edited by Lyndal Roper. Leiden: Brill.

Seyderhelm, Bettina, ed. 2001. *Goldschmiedekunst des Mittelalters: Im Gebrauch der Gemeinden über Jahrhunderte bewahrt.* Dresden: Sandstein.

Smith, Shirley. 2014. "The Fresco Decoration in the Sistine Chapel: Biblical Authority and the Church of Rome." In *The Edinburgh Companion to the Bible and the Arts*, edited by Stephen Prickett, 254–71. Edinburgh: University of Edinburgh Press.

Spicer, Andrew, ed. 2005. *Lutheran Churches in Early Modern Europe*. Farnham: Ashgate.

Spinks, Jennifer. 2014. "The Southern Indian 'Devil in Calicut' in Early Modern Northern Europe: Images, Texts and Objects in Motion." *Journal of Early Modern History* 18, no. 1–2: 15–48.

Spitzer. 1893. *Catalogue des objets d'art et de haute curiosite antiques, du moyen-age & de le renaissance, composant l'importante et précieuse Collection Spitzer*. Paris: Ménard.

Squire, Michael. 2009. *Image and Text in Graeco-Roman Antiquity*. Cambridge: Cambridge University Press.

Stielau, Allison. 2014a. "The Weight of Plate in Early Modern Inventories and Secularization Lists." *Journal of Art Historiography* 11: 1–29.

Stielau, Allison. 2014b. "The Dolgellau Chalice and Paten." Object Narrative. *Conversations: An Online Journal of the Center for the Study of Material and Visual Cultures of Religion*. doi:10.22332/con.obj.2014.21.

Stielau, Allison. 2014c. "Intent and Independence: Late Fifteenth-Century Object Engravings." In *Visual Acuity and the Arts of Communication in Early Modern Germany*, edited by Jeffrey Chipps Smith, 21–42. Farnham: Ashgate.

Theophilus. 1979. *On Divers Arts: The Foremost Medieval Treatise on Painting, Glassmaking and Metalwork*. Translated and introduced by John G. Hawthorne and Cyril Stanley Smith. New York: Dover.

Walsham, Alexandra. 2011. *The Reformation of the Landscape: Religion, Identity and Memory in Early Modern Britain and Ireland*. Oxford: Oxford University Press.

Walsham, Alexandra. 2017. "Recycling the Sacred: Material Culture and Cultural Memory after the English Reformation." *Church History* 86, no. 4: 1121–54.

Wandel, Lee Palmer. 2006. *The Eucharist in the Reformation: Incarnation and Liturgy*. Cambridge: Cambridge University Press.

Wauters, Wendy. 2021. "Smelling Disease and Death in the Antwerp Church of Our Lady, c. 1450–1559." *Early Modern Low Countries* 5: 17–39.

"Weihrauch." 1987. In *Handwörterbuch des deutschen Aberglaubens*, edited by Hanns Bächtold-Stäubli, vol. 9, 283–85. Berlin: Walter de Gruyter.

Westall, Henry. 1899. *The Case for Incense Submitted to His Grace the Archbishop of Canterbury on Behalf of the Rev. H. Westall on Monday, May 8, 1899*. London: Longmans, Green.

Westermann-Angerhausen, Hiltrud. 2011. "Incense in the Space between Heaven and Earth: The Inscriptions and Images on the Gozbert Censer in the Cathedral Treasury of Trier." *Acta ad archaeologiam et artium historiam pertinentia* 24, no. 10: 227–42.

Westermann-Angerhausen, Hiltrud. 2014. *Mittelalterliche Weihrauchfässer von 800 bis 1500*. Petersberg: Michael Imhof.

Westermann-Angerhausen, Hiltrud. 2016. "The Two Censers in the *Schedula diversarum atrium* of Theophilus and Their Place in the Liturgy." In *Les cinq sens au Moyen Âge*, edited by Éric Palazzo, 189–201. Paris: Les Éditions du Cerf.

Wiesel, Elie. 1997. "Nadab and Abihu." *European Judaism* 30, no. 2 (Autumn): 18–28.

Wood, Christopher S. 2006. "Countermagical Combinations by Dosso Dossi." *RES* 49/50: 151–70.

Yeoman, Victoria. 2018. "Reformation as Continuity: Objects of Dining and Devotion in Early Modern England." *West 86th* 25, no. 2: 176–98.

Zika, Charles. 2007. "Witches' Cauldrons and Women's Bodies." In *The Appearance of Witchcraft: Print and Visual Culture in Sixteenth-Century Europe*, 70–98. London and New York: Routledge.

VISUALIZING THE INCENSE SMOKE: THE PORTRAIT OF THE MING EMPEROR XIZONG (1605–1627)

Yao Ning

When smoke rises from a stick of incense, it dissipates as it is carried away by the wind. We may smell it as it circulates around our nose, but it is most visible and tangible in the moment it emanates from an incense burner. In contrast to its pervasive and ephemeral character in a real space, however, its visual presence can be restrained and permanently captured through a physical medium like a painting. In seventeenth-century China, images of incense smoke that take on specific patterns and figurative forms flourished in representations found in various media, such as paintings, woodblock prints, and porcelains.[1]

The Portrait of the Ming Emperor Xizong, Zhu Youjiao 明熹宗朱由校朝服像 (1605–27, r. 1620–27) is a well-known example.[2] In the portrait, the young emperor Xizong is presented in a frontal pose looking out at the beholder [Figure 1]. An incense burner with elephant-head legs is depicted on the right [Figure 2]. A pipe entwined by a long, serpentine dragon has been placed behind the censer. The pipe culminates in a slender tube dangling from the dragon's mouth; smoke exits from this tube—as if emerging from the dragon's maw itself. The slender ribbon of smoke forms the Chinese character s*hou* 壽—for longevity. This portrait was produced for funeral and ancestor worship. Why does the painting call attention to incense smoke, which is normally conceived as invisible, in an image designed to commemorate? Why is it important for this normally invisible entity to take a specific character form? And why did this particular motif enjoy such popularity in the seventeenth century?

This essay attempts to answer these questions by using the Xizong portrait as a case study. Before doing this, however, I begin by discussing the implications of incense smoke by taking into consideration the relationship between *qi* 氣 (vital force), clouds, and incense smoke. I then analyze some representative images of incense smoke and take a closer look at the representation of the character *shou*. I will argue that the reason behind the popularity of visualized incense smoke in seventeenth-century China was the revival of Daoism, accompanied by specific ideas and practices connected to auspiciousness and divination. Moreover, in the late sixteenth century, the highly developed printing industry of the late Ming period (1368–1644) played an important role in the transmission of these ideas and practices.

The Xizong portrait deserves a lengthy study. This essay will only touch its surface by focusing on two goals. It will suggest some new ways of studying (1) Chinese portrait painting for ancestor worship, and (2) the representation of ephemeral material or immaterial elements such as incense smoke. In this study, the Xizong portrait is treated as a portrait-object or portrait-thing. Relying on the concept of "hierotopy" (Alexei Lidov) and the study of the senses, I will argue that the use of a Chinese portrait for ancestor worship must be understood in its ritual context and examine the inter-

Figure 1
Unidentified court painter,
The Portrait of the Ming
Emperor Xizong, Zhu Youjiao
明熹宗朱由校朝服像,
1620–1627, ink and colours on
silk, 111.2 × 75.7 cm, The Palace
Museum, Beijing, GU 6209,
in *Faces of China. Portrait
Painting of the Ming and
Qing Dynasties (1368–1912)*,
ed. Klaas Ruitenbeek
(Berlin: Michael Imhof Verlag,
2017), 99.

Figure 2
Detail of Portrait of the
Ming Emperor Xizong

action between humans (viewers or participants), non-humans (images, objects, or the network of things), and the multisensorial environment as a whole. Drawing on the concepts of "divine nearness" (Martin Heidegger) and "material flux" (Bissera Pentcheva), I take incense smoke to be among the triggers to be experienced in the process of this interaction.

QI (VITAL FORCE), CLOUDS, AND INCENSE SMOKE

In the West, incense is often called "food of the gods." It seems that deities from many cultures have "longstanding relations to burning substances, as smoke and smell are offerings that connect the here below to that up above."[3] In China, the belief that incense smoke has the capacity to connect the celestial realm with the earthly world has persisted through the centuries to the present. However, exactly what the belief entails is complex. In Chinese culture, incense smoke is easily associated with clouds and *qi* (vital force). Below, I discuss how its close relationship with *qi* and clouds may provide a way to understand the multilayered implications of incense smoke.

In the treatise "Tianxiang zhuan 天香傳 (The Records of Heavenly Fragrance, around 1022–25)" by Ding Wei 丁謂 (966–1037) the close connection between incense smoke and clouds is apparent:

> The scent of incense burned by the true immortals can reach a hundred *li*. The accumulated smoke transforms into clouds. The accumulated clouds then transform into rain. Two valuable types of incense that they used can be found in the earthly realm as well. These two are agarwood and frankincense.

> 真仙所焚之香, 皆聞百里, 有積煙成雲, 積雲成雨, 然則與人間所共貴者, 沉水, 熏陸也.[4]

In this text, (auspicious) clouds are created when the incense smoke used by the immortals accumulates. *Qi* can also become clouds. According to Guo Pu 郭璞 (276–324), "the *qi* of *yin* 陰 and *yang* 陽 forces becomes wind when it blows, becomes clouds when it ascends, becomes rain when it descends ..." (夫陰陽之氣, 噫而為風, 升而為雲, 降而為雨).[5] "*Qi* can be described as a form of subtle energy, a vital flow that forms things, animates beings, and causes the changes and developments of all."[6] Atmospheric phenomena such as moving clouds and ephemeral substances such as smoke can all be seen as *qi*. In other words, the implied associations between incense smoke and clouds are shared with those of *qi*. Indeed, the whole world can be understood as one integrated whole that shares the same underlying force of *qi*.[7]

Since the Han dynasty (206 BCE–220 CE) at the latest, an increasing belief has taken hold that claims both auspicious omens, *xiangrui* 祥瑞, and inauspicious omens are Heaven's responses—either as blessings or warnings—to the behavior of reigning emperors and humans.[8] This idea is embedded in the fundamental concept of *tianming* 天命, the mandate of Heaven stated by Dong Zhongshu 董仲舒 (179–104 BCE) who claimed, "When a King is about to rise to power, beautiful signs of good omen will appear first" (帝王之將興也, 其美祥亦先見).[9] Auspicious clouds, *xiang yun* 祥雲, belonged to one of the categories of auspicious omens. The emperor Wudi 武帝 (156–87 BCE, r. 140–87 BCE) had *fang shi* 方士, masters of recipes and techniques, at his court. These masters were in charge of *wang qi* 望氣, *qi* observation, including cloud-pattern analysis.[10] Although cosmic *qi* is fundamentally unchangeable, it is predictable in some senses. Human beings have to adapt their attitudes and behaviors to cope with the flow of the cosmic *qi*.[11] This explains why the masters in charge of observing *qi* at the court of emperor Wudi not only searched for auspicious signs but also had expertise in divination. For centuries, the idea that clouds could be observed, visualized, and used as a means of prediction has been deeply embedded in Chinese traditions. Also, from the very early periods of Chinese history, the concepts of divination and auspiciousness have been intertwined and entangled; in particular, the goal of divination concerns determining the most auspicious moment or spot for a certain activity to be undertaken by a particular person.[12]

Bearing this key concept in mind will enable a better understanding of the following analysis of visualized incense smoke. The woodblock print representing the character *ji* 吉 for luckiness in the divinatory booklet entitled *Tianzhu lingqian* 天竺靈籤 (Efficacious Lots of Tianzhu) is dated to the first half of the thirteenth century [Figure 3].[13] The character *ji* is evident in the incense smoke that emanates from an incense burner set on an incense table on the left. The text below the image on the lot starts with a four-line verse (on the right) followed by a prose explanation, *jie* 解 (on the left). The prose begins with a warning that something inauspicious has occurred in the household. This danger can only be defeated when the signs *shi* 十, *yi* 一, and *kou* 口 appear. It goes on to explain: "In this lot *shi*, *yi*, and *kou* have been written on the upper part of the incense burner. This forms the character *ji* 吉. This should be understood as good fortune. However, you should pray, only then the auspiciousness can arrive" (卦中香炉上有十一口，乃吉字也。須作福，祈之必有其吉。).[14] The dissection of *ji* 吉 into three parts—*shi* 十, *yi* 一, and *kou* 口—is a typical example of a divinatory technique termed *chai zi* 拆字 (dissecting graphs).[15] In this case the auspiciousness indicated by the visualized incense smoke is reinforced by the appearance of the character *ji* for luckiness. Beginning in the fifteenth century, China witnessed a renewed interest in divination and a flourishing of divinatory techniques and books. A significant number of the predictions were concerned with *qi* and cloud observations.

Figure 3

The *Guiding (or Yinlu) Bodhisattva* is one of the earliest extant examples to represent visualized incense smoke with specific patterns [Figure 4]. In the hanging scroll, the bodhisattva is leading a deceased soul—a woman in a red robe depicted in a reduced scale—along the route to the Pure Land paradise. Standing on auspicious red clouds, the bodhisattva's right hand holds an incense burner. The incense smoke is depicted curling up into an S-shaped flower scroll line; the end of this billowing form blooms in the direction of paradise—a three-floored building that emerges among *lingzhi* 靈芝 (fungus)—formed clouds. The smoke thus functions as a signpost showing the direction of paradise and indicates its strong connection with the celestial. The representation of auspicious clouds in the form of *lingzhi*-fungus has a long tradition. *Shizhou ji* 十洲記 (Record of the Ten Islands, attributed to Dongfang shuo 東方朔, 160–93 BCE) provides a literal description of Mt. Kunlun 崑崙, where the immortals lived, as "middle thin, upper wide" (*zhong xia shang guang* 中狹上广)—resembling a *lingzhi*-fungus.[16] During the Han dynasty, the *lingzhi*-fungus emerged as a symbol of immortality.[17] Thus, to suggest immortality and longevity, the visualized incense smoke in

Figure 4

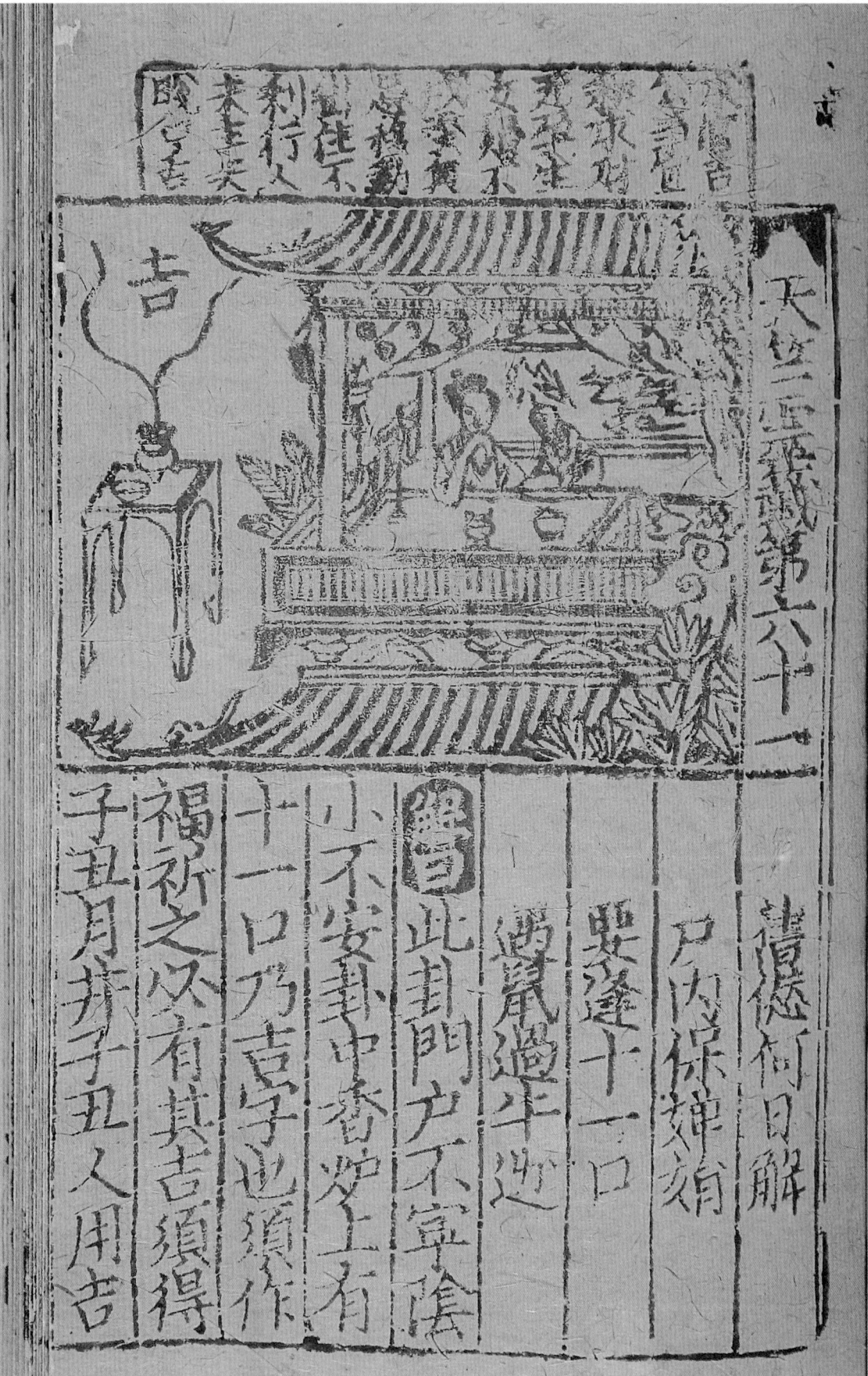

Figure 4
Guiding (or Yinlu)
Bodhisattva, ca. 901–950,
hanging scroll,
ink and colour on silk,
84.8 × 54.7 cm,
The British Museum,
1919,0101,0.46

Figure 5
Portrait of Buddhamitra
伏馱蜜多尊者像, woodblock print,
in *San cai tu hui* 三才圖會
(Pictorial Compendium of the
Three Power), reprinted
during 1735–1795,
Bayerische Staatsbibliothek.

Figure 6
Portrait of Buddhamitra
伏馱蜜多尊者像, woodblock print,
in *Hua fa da cheng* 畫法大成
(Manual of Painting Techniques),
reprinted in *Zhonguo gu
huapu jicheng* 中國古畫譜集成
(Collections of Chinese
Old Manuals of Painting
Techniques), vol. 3, 221.

the *Portrait of Buddhamitra* 伏馱蜜多尊者 in *San cai tu hui* 三才圖會 (Pictorial Compendium of the Three Powers) curls into the form of a *lingzhi*-fungus [Figure 5]. *San cai tu hui*, with its 106 volumes, is an encyclopedia published in 1609 (preface dated in 1607). Just six years later, in 1615, a copy of this illustration of Buddhamitra appeared in *Hua fa da cheng* 畫法大成 (Manual of Painting Techniques), a painting manual compiled by two Ming princes, Zhu Shouyong 朱壽鏞 (?–1639) and Zhu Yiya 朱頤厓 (active in the late sixteenth and early seventeenth centuries) [Figure 6]. The lines in *San cai tu hui* are more finely engraved than those in the copy; the eyes, in particular, are represented in a more naturalistic manner.

Figure 5

Figure 6

THE REVIVAL OF DAOISM

The woodblock-print album leaf currently in the British Museum, presents a landscape scene with visualized incense smoke emanating from an incense burner [Figure 7]. The smoke shapes the image of a pagoda—an architectural form that originated from Buddhism. A figure in the image's center facing the censer may be a Daoist priest. On the left, a man riding a deer is crossing a river. Two Confucian scholars inside a rocky cave on the right are discussing a book. The deer, crane, and pine tree are all present as symbols of longevity. The images in this print reflect not only the popular motif of longevity but also religious syncretism in Ming China.[18] Moral excellence, health, and longevity are aspects of the concept of self-cultivation *xiuji* 脩己 central to Neo-Confucianism promoted by the influential Wang Yangming 王陽明 (1472–1529). In Ming China, it is often impossible to discern the boundaries between Daoism, popular religion, and Buddhism. A man in the Ming period could be a Confucian official by day, a Daoist when searching for longevity techniques in his spare time, a practitioner of popular religions when he consults a fortune-teller before making an important decision, and a Buddhist hoping to be brought to a Pure Land paradise at his death.

Figure 7

Daoism during the Ming compared with the Han period is not only less studied, but is regarded as having declined by many scholars.[19] Some new movements and ideas of Daoism that appeared or were revived in the Ming—such as local Daoism and Daoist internal alchemy, *nei dan* 內丹—have been overlooked in the scholarship. Daoist internal alchemy documented from the eighth century aims at compounding an elixir within the practitioner's own body, while *waidan* 外丹, external alchemy, documented from the second century BCE, aims at compounding the elixir through the manipulation of minerals and metals.[20] Numerous writings on *yangsheng* 養生 —nurturing life and longevity techniques—a core aspiration of Daoist internal alchemy—became omnipresent in the Ming society. Regarding internal alchemy, the Jesuit Nicolas Trigault (1577–1628), who arrived in Beijing around 1620, wrote: "Here in the province of Peking, in which we are living, there are few if any of the magistrates, of the eunuchs, or of others of high station, who are not addicted to this foolish pursuit."[21]

In recent years, rather than focusing on purely conventional historical documents, new research has attended to vernacular literature, archaeological reports, and artwork produced in the Ming period.[22] During the Han period, people created auspicious signs as well, but on a more limited scale. The practice was called *fa rui* 發瑞—invoking an auspicious omen—since people "believed that the portrayal of *xiangrui* [auspicious] images on cloths and objects of daily use would invoke the appearance of real *xiangrui*."[23]

Figure 7
Woodcut, printed in
colour on paper, ca. 1690–1720,
28.8 × 26.1 cm (image),
39 × 36 cm (paper),
The British Museum, 1906,
1128,0.32.8.

Under the Ming, people from all social groups participated in the practice of creating or inventing good omens to bring themselves good luck and health. Ming artworks with auspicious signs and symbols were mass-produced.

After the middle of the sixteenth century, with the expansion of the printing industry, the availability of books, and the spread of practices and ideas such as auspiciousness and divination proliferated to a new extent.[24] Divinatory books, encyclopedias, daily-use almanacs, vernacular texts such as *shanshu* 善書, morality books—were highly popular and ubiquitous in Ming culture.[25] Two of the most popular divinatory books in Chinese history are *Mayi xiangfa* 麻衣相法 (Mayi's Physiognomy, first published between 1481 and 1482) and *Shenxiang quanbian* 神相全編 (Complete Compilation of the Magical Physiognomy, first published ca. 1622). They were purported to have been written earlier, under the Song dynasty; in reality, they were Ming publications.[26] Almost all the books, concepts, and movements related to determining fate and creating auspicious signs in the hope of attracting good luck had appeared and had already been developed in the Song and Yuan dynasties. However, the number and types of books in publication in the late Ming was beyond anything China had previously experienced.[27] Thus, vernacular literature and popular religion entered print culture and became available in the privacy of one's home.

A comprehensive discussion about the revival of Daoism is beyond the scope of the current essay. Here, I will mention only three aspects that provide a glimpse of the state of Daoism in the Ming period. First, the majority of the Ming emperors patronized Daoism. In fact, the pattern of Ming imperial patronage of Daoist temples and rituals was repeated in virtually every reign. This reached its apogee during the reign of Emperor Jiajing 嘉靖 (1507–67, r. 1521–67), when Daoism was elevated to a state orthodoxy.[28] Second, Ming China witnessed highly developed local forms of Daoism in which the Ming princes took an active interest.[29] Third, the role of vernacular literature, discussed above, has been largely overlooked by many scholars. Both Anna Seidel and Daniel L. Overmyer noticed the significant role of vernacular literature in the development of Daoism in the Ming.[30] As Anna Seidel claimed, "It is mainly through this vernacular literature that Daoist beliefs, myths and values reached the growing educated middle section of Chinese society situated between the scholar-official class and the illiterate people."[31] Thus, to sum up the last two sections very briefly, the revival of Daoism and the emergence of the printing industry can be said to have fueled the flourishing of visualized incense smoke.

REPRESENTING LONGEVITY

Two exemplary representations of the character *shou* produced during the Jiajing reign are prototypes for the Xizong portrait. The first one is found on a lacquer box. In the middle of the box cover, the smoke emanating from an incense burner on an incense table forms the character *shou* as it wafts upward [Figure 8]. A pine tree is depicted on each side. The pine tree to the left has the character *fu* 福 for luckiness, while the one to the right features the character *lu* 禄 for wealth. Both of the characters are twisted as branches of the trees. Nineteen immortals are represented on the box cover, since nineteen, *shijiu* 十九, is a homophone for the phrase *shi jiu* 是久 "to be eternal." The second representation of *shou* is displayed on a blue-and-white porcelain. Here, the character *shou* between two five-clawed dragons emerg-

Figure 8

Figure 8
Carved red lacquer box of
immortals celebrating
birthday, Jiajing reign
(1521–1567), 39,5 × 10 cm,
The Palace Museum, Beijing,
from Yuan Ming Qiqi 元明漆器
(Lacquer Wares of the Yuan
and Ming Dynasties),
in 故宫博物院藏文物珍品全集
(The Complete Collection of
Treasures of the Palace
Museum), ed. Xia Gengqi 夏更起
(Hong Kong, 2006), 158.

es from a fungus [Figure 9]. The fungus grows out of a mountain that, in turn, emerges from the waves of the sea. The upper end of the slightly curvy stroke of *shou* can be associated with smoke. This detail resembles the ascending smoke of the *shou* in the Xizong portrait [Figure 2]. Both cases indicate that *shou* is not simply a character; rather, it is also a message from Heaven—god's will conveyed through incense smoke.

The Jiajing emperor was a devoted Daoist. He retreated from the Forbidden City to the West Park, Xiyuan 西苑, for twenty-five years. There, he spent the rest of his life in the hope of becoming an immortal.[32] A poem describes the frequency of Daoist rituals and the quantity of incense burned at the Jiajing court as follows: "Agarwood and ambergris were burned throughout the night. At Cassia Palace and Fungus Hall auspicious clouds were formed" (沈水龍涎徹夜焚，桂宮芝館結祥雲).[33] Thus, the visualized-smoke *shou* in the Xizong portrait can be understood as an auspicious sign wishing the emperor a long life. This, however, is surprisingly complex. For another detail of the portrait hints at a related wish. The elephant-head incense burner in the Xizong portrait is quite rare. This is not only due to the visualized incense smoke that billows from it, but also because of its surface design. Its surface is divided into two parts by a ribbon featuring a red gemstone [Figure 2]. It is highly unusual for the design of these two parts to be asymmetrical. The strokes are unreadable except for a sign on the left corner resembling the character *sheng* 生, which means birth or giving birth. According to the tenets of Daoist internal alchemy, practitioners take part in an active journey involving their search for true form (*zhenxing* 真形). This entails a series of metamorphoses (*hua* 化). The practitioners invest themselves with the task of "re-generating" their own persons. "One gives birth to 'a person outside one's person'" or "a self outside oneself" (*shen zhi wai shen* 身之外身).[34] This is a process of conception, gestation, or birth of an embryo (*tai* 胎). The final result occurs when the embryo exits through the top of the head of the practitioner—a so-called celestial rebirth. The embryo then transforms into the pure spirit body of the immortals, a body of primordial *qi*.[35] Livia Kohn describes the rebirth scene as follows: "[It] is accompanied by the perception of a deep inner rumbling, like a clap of thunder. After passing into the celestial spheres, the spirit communicates with the gods, thus transcending the limitations of the body."[36]

The practically unreadable strokes on the surface of the incense burner can be associated with *fuji* 扶乩, planchette writing or spirit writing. During the sixteenth and seventeenth centuries, this was a divinatory practice that was widely performed in funeral and memorial services or in situations such as predicting the future, curing people, or calling back the soul. During a séance, the medium—a literatus or a Daoist priest or Buddhist monk—usually enters a trance and incarnates a deity, who speaks through the medium or depicts a picture, or writes in calligraphy that requires deciphering by the medium.[37] It was believed that the picture or calligraphy expressed the will of the gods or celestial beings.[38] In her fascinating article "Jiajing Emperor and His Auspicious Words," Maggie Wan has pointed out the connections between spirit writing and the character *shou* represented on the porcelains and lacquerwares produced during the Jiajing reign. According to Wan, the Jiajing emperor was enthusiastic about practicing spirit writing.[39]

According to Daoist thinking, longevity can be achieved in this life as well as in the afterlife, after death. The character for longevity in the

Xizong portrait could represent a wish for this-life longevity as well as longevity after the Xizong emperor's death. A helpful explanation is found in a commentary to Laozi's 老子 (sixth-century BCE) *Daode jing* 道德經 entitled *Laozi xianger zhu* 老子想爾注, one of the earliest Daoist canonical texts. The commentary was written in the second to third century. It describes another means of achieving longevity: "When he retires from the world, he *simulates* death and passes over into the realm of the Extreme Yin (T'ai Yin). There he revives, goes forth anew and thus does not perish. This is what is meant by 'longevity'" (original emphasis).[40] The concept of longevity here refers to a belief in post-mortem longevity—a Daoist resurrection of the body.[41] It is belief in a feigned death. The method of achieving it is called *shijie* 尸解, liberation from the corpse, a discourse first found in the writings by Wang Chong 王充 (27–97 CE).[42] Significant ways to achieve *shijie* include taking drugs, doing meditation, and macrobiotic exercises.[43]

Thus, the smoke that visually forms *shou* and the character *sheng* on the censer in the portrait can be understood as auspicious signs with divinatory features designed for the emperor. Both signs indicate the emperor's desire to become immortal. The frontality of the emperor Xizong's body and face lend the portrait a certain flatness, functioning like a curtain or a mask. The implication is that behind this bodily "curtain," an "embryo" has been reborn; the dynamics of this alternative body are indicated by the smoke. The portrait itself is a medium for the body. In particular, the portrait wishes the sitter auspiciousness for longevity, and it announces the sitter's rebirth to the viewer. At the same time, the portrait invites the beholder to participate in ancestral worship. Traditional Chinese beliefs understood the spirit of the dead to be present in their image in the moment the incense was burned; at this time, music would be performed and offerings would be made. In this ritual, the image—including all of the depicted objects surrounding the portrayed person—interacted with viewers. In other words, in the multisensorial sacred space of an ancestor hall or temple, the ritual creates an enlivened environment that facilitates an exchange between the living and the dead. The concept "hierotopy"—the creation of sacred spaces—proposed by Alexei Lidov in 2001 refers to the spatial dynamics of sacred ritual unfolding in architectural interiors, urban spaces, and liturgical objects. Following this concept, the portrait in Chinese ancestor worship is perceived as animated; that is, it becomes an inseparable part of the spatial milieu just as in a Byzantine liturgical performance during which the deceased soul actively participates and interacts with beholders or worshipers.[44] In this sense, the images are not just there, but "arrive with a predetermined *mise-en-scène* that also includes a predetermined site for their perception, which they guide by way of performance."[45] Livia Kohn's description of the sensorial environment of the scene of rebirth quoted above is pertinent for understanding Xizong's portrait. Clearly, attention was paid not only to the careful design of the setting. Importantly, the Xizong portrait features movement, liveliness, and sensory stimulation. These enlivening factors contrast with the stillness of the seated figure. In particular, emphasis has been given to the liberal ornamentation of the scene, which includes precious stones that mirror and reflect light as well as the presence of fragrant blossoms that are associated with Buddhist and Daoist paradise.[46] Also, on the central screen, a pair of heraldic dragons are playing with a pearl. This screen features the character *shou*, which is centrally located above the sitter's head.

Figure 9
Blue-and-white porcelain jar
with dragons and the character
shou, height: 71 cm,
mouth 25 cm, base 29 cm,
The Huaihaitang collection.

The visualized-smoke *shou* that emerges from the pipe can be understood as a material echo—a tangible response to the character from Heaven. Two pendants richly decorated with gemstones hang on each side of the screen. Their tassels seem to be blown by the wind. This vitality is reinforced by the reiterated appearance of the character *shou* for longevity. In all probability, the whole setting is deliberately arranged and animated to engage the senses: the sense of vision, the sense of smell, the sense of movement, and the sense of the sound of wind. The sensorial dimension suffuses this portrait with a level of liveliness and richness rarely encountered in any other imperial ancestor portrait from any period of Chinese history.

It may be useful, here, to introduce the term "intersensoriality" in order to describe an environment within which the network of senses work together to enhance sensory experience.[47] The term does not necessarily imply "a state of equality,"[48] however, in the context of visualized incense smoke especially, as scent and sight may head the list of the senses invoked. Incense transforms from material substance into smoke. Visually and olfactorily, this intangible smoke conveys the descent of the divine or a deity. Smell pushes beyond the borders of the visible; in other words, smell becomes a means through which to experience the divine and the presence of a deity. This process of transformation can be better understood by calling on Heidegger's "divine nearness" together with Bissera Pentcheva's concept of "material flux." Pentcheva terms an idea that Heidegger discusses in his article "The Thing" as "divine nearness." Pentcheva explains this as referring to the moment when the "nearness of the celestial in the terrestrial emerges in what is fleeting, phenomenal, and ungraspable."[49] Heidegger famously discusses the earthen jug filled with water or wine in which the jug "presents the conditions that can ingather the celestial in the liquid's reflective surface." Heidegger's essay "offers a platform for understanding the interaction between matter and Spirit," in which "the 'thing' mediates the appearance of the metaphysical in the sensorial."[50] Based on Heidegger's "divine nearness," "material flux" refers to "a series of changing appearances unfolding in time," explored in Pentcheva's monumental study on Hagia Sophia.[51] In terms of the concept of "material flux," the process of visualizing the incense smoke unfolding in a realm of continuity leads to interaction, entanglement, and the transcendence of smoke, scent, and sight.[52] The smoke and fragrance provide visual and olfactory bridges between the human and divine spheres. As such, they convey the descent of a deity and elicit supernatural visions. In this sense, the smoke and its scent are both the trigger and the index of transformation. The experience of the viewer is activated as they become transformed into a participant within the environment where ancestor worship is performed and incense burned. Both the visualized smoke and the fragrance of the burning incense in the worship provide a means through which to experience the deities, the interactions between subjects, things, and environment. Succinctly put, one experiences their "intersensorial" "material flux."

Although no extant sources specifically discuss the production process behind the Xizong portrait, it is quite possible that the emperor himself designed this arrangement for his afterlife.[53] The emperor was a passionate carpenter, sculptor, and fabricator of toys and objects with mechanical functions, according to *Zhuozhong zhi* 酌中志 (A Record of Consideration), written by one of his eunuchs, Liu Ruoyu 劉若愚 (1584–ca. 1642).[54] No historical writings specifically address Xizong's Daoist thinking and practices, except for the fact that a portable edition of the Daoist Canon (*Daozang* 道藏) was published in 1626 during his reign.[55] The Xizong emperor ascended to the throne at the age of fifteen, following the death of emperor Taichang 泰昌 (1582–1620, r. 1620), his father, who ruled for twenty-eight days and died after consuming *hong wan* 紅丸, literally the red drug, a divine elixir. The Xizong emperor reigned for seven years and died at the age of twenty-two in the same manner.[56]

Many Chinese historical sources can be found with descriptions about specific incense used to produce certain images. In *Xiang sheng* 香乘 (The Book on Incense) by Zhou Jiazhou 周嘉冑 (1582–1658), compiled between 1617 and 1618, a recipe for making longevity incense, *shou xiang* 壽香, has fourteen ingredients; among these are *ruxiang* 乳香 (frankincense), *chenxiang* 沉香 (agarwood), *longnao* 龍腦 (ambergris), *hanliancao* 旱蓮草 (herba ecliptae), and a single hair of a new-born baby boy (男孩胎髮一個). The smoke has to be guided (*yin*, 引) in order to create Chinese characters or to "paint" a figure. Zhou describes this:

> When the incense is ready to be used, mix the pulverized black ginseng with honey onto the top of chopsticks, [use the chopsticks] to guide the smoke in order to write Chinese characters or to draw a human figure. Both the characters and human figures will stay and not dissipate. If you want these to dissipate, you have to scatter some pulverized *semen plantaginis* onto the smoke.

> 燒香時, 以玄參末蜜調箸梢上, 引煙寫字畫人物, 皆能不散. 從其散時, 以車前子末彈於煙上, 即散.[57]

The reason for naming the incense "longevity incense" is possibly because it lasts longer before being dissipated. It is quite possible that the visualized smoke in the Xizong portrait is based on such a recipe.

EPILOGUE AND CONCLUSION

The Xizong portrait is indicative of a remarkable shift that occurred in seventeenth-century China. At this time, Chinese artists took an interest in reconsidering the art and aesthetics of the past. Realistic representation and the aesthetics of representing transitory and poetic moments had been favored in the court of the Northern Song dynasty 北宋 (960–1127), especially during the Huizong 徽宗 reign (1082–1135, r. 1100–26). Later, they were disdained and forgotten in the Yuan (1279–1368) and during nearly all of the Ming period. Beginning in the seventeenth century, a renewed interest took hold in Song aesthetics and naturalistic representation, especially in portrait paintings. This interest was stimulated by exposure to Western art that was introduced with the arrival of Jesuits in the late sixteenth century.[58] Many artworks were made in this period that captured a sense of holding a moment in eternal poise—a process that features using art to stop time. In the Xizong portrait, *bewegtes Beiwerk*—accessories of movement—are evident in the animation carried out through the emanating smoke, the wind-swept tassels, and the mirroring of gemstones.[59] *Bewegtes Beiwerk* is a term that was coined by Aby Warburg to describe details such as the wind-swept hair and garments of the human figures that give Botticelli's painting *Primavera* its dynamism.[60] Many scholars have interpreted and enriched Warburg's concept in the last few decades. For Horst Bredekamp, *bewegtes Beiwerk* can be interpreted as a type of *Spielform* (play form) or *Dingbeseelung* (thing animation), or it should be understood as *psychodynamisch* (psychodynamic), expressing inner energy.[61]

The manipulation of incense smoke to depict certain specific patterns is a process enchanted with humans, things, and environments. All elements—material as well as ideas, actions, and processes involved—can be experienced and have influence on the outcome. In this sense all these elements, as depicted in images, are not a set of visual codes to be deciphered, but "a series of triggers and presences to be viscerally experienced."[62] In the case of the Xizong portrait, the image would become three-dimensional as it emanates into the environment and comes alive. All of the factors—the participation of the beholders in the spatial environment, the transformation from viewer to participant, the activation or animation of the dead soul and sacred space, as well as sensations and effects created by the visualized incense smoke with its vison and scent—allow the Chinese ancestor rite to come alive, to be vivid as it unfolds in the ancestor hall. The input of incense smoke leads to changes in the relationship between material and depiction. Like all things, the materials of incense smoke are themselves actors possessing agencies. This understanding of incense smoke frees it from a static position by seeing it as an active agent in the process of visualized image-making or seeing its sensitivity in the process of art-making. The flourishing of visualized incense smoke is one of the many phenomena reflecting the turbulent yet innovative changes experienced in seventeenth-century China. In this period, many aspects of the Confucian ideal could no longer maintain their dominance; rather, popular culture and Daoism became highly developed.

ENDNOTES

1   My heartfelt thanks first go to the international workshop "The Censer: A Comparative Approach" organized by Beate Fricke and Ittai Weinryb where I received valuable comments, inspiration, and ideas. I would also like to thank Gerhard Wolf and the "Bilderfahrzeuge" project for the generous support and opportunity of object studies in museums worldwide. Without the study on the original painting and the invaluable support from the formal CAHIM fellowship directed by Hannah Baader, I would not have been able to complete this article. More heartfelt thanks go to the following scholars who inspired and helped me in various ways: Horst Bredekamp, Shihhwa Chiu, Sabiha Göloğlu, Lothar Ledderose, Luk Yu-ping, Maggie Wan, and Weiqiang Zhou. Luk Yu-ping and Maggie Wan provided some of the images and gathered extremely valuable information for me. Finally, I would like to thank the Huaihaitang collection for allowing me to use the images.

2   The era name for his reign is Tianqi 天啟. His personal name is Zhu Youjiao 朱由校.

3   Plate 2014, 62.

4   A *li* is approximately 0.5 km (Ding 1641, no. 1, no pagination, my translation).

5   Translated by Maggie Wan. Cited in Wan 2007, 106.

6   Sakade Yoshinobu 2000, 559.

7   Ibid.

8   The concept of auspiciousness already existed during periods before Han, especially in the Eastern Zhou dynasty (771–256 BCE) according to Wu Hung. However, inauspicious omens were more frequently mentioned at that time. Wu Hung 1984, 39.

9   Ibid., 42.

10 Sakade 2000, 545.

11 Ibid., 559.

12 Ibid., 561.

13 Tianzhu refers to the Tianzhu Buddhist Temple in today's Hangzhou, which was famous for the magical and divinatory powers of the monks in the Song period. This booklet of a Buddhist oracle with

eighty-five extant prints is from an original set of one hundred. See Huang 2007, 243.

14 Ibid.

15 Führer 2006, 25, 47, 62, 63. *Kou* not only functions as a graphic element; at the same time, it means "mouth."

16 Wu Hung 2005a, 465; 2005b, 247.

17 Wu Hung 2005a, 461, 465.

18 I am aware of the critical views expressed by scholars such as Michel Strickmann and Anna Seidel regarding syncretism; moreover, syncretism in China is not the same as in the West. Michel Strickmann, for example, has pointed out that Islam and popular religion were two other relevant religions in the Ming period, too. For Strickmann and some other scholars, syncretism should only refer to *sanjiao* 三 教 (the Three Teachings), namely Buddhism, Daoism, and Confucianism. Strickmann has also pointed out that an earlier syncretism had already had an effect in fifth-century China (Seidel 1989, 245–46).

19 De Bruyn 2000, 594. Anna Seidel has pointed out that the focus of religious Daoist life shifted away from the established Daoist institutions in the Ming period (Seidel 1989, 245–46). Regarding study on Daoism in the Ming period, Isabelle Robinet has criticized that "most historians of Daoism tend to pass it by quickly after discussing the Yuan, or even stop in the fourteenth century" (in ibid.).

20 In Daoist internal alchemy, it is claimed that longevity can be achieved by taking an elixir and by accessing, guiding, and sublimating the *qi* in the body; in other words, to use breath techniques to guide the *qi* (Kohn 2009, 135).

21 Needham 1976, 227. Regarding the involvement in Daoist alchemy of the Ming royal family, see Wang 2012; Yuan Wenqing 2016, 163–69.

22 Clunas 2013; Clunas, Harrison-Hall, and Luk 2016. John Lagerwey has pointed out that the Ming dynasty founder emperor Zhu Yuanzhang was a devoted Daoist and

engaged in divination as well (Lagerwey 2016, 113–30).

23 Wu Hung 1984, 45.

24 Park 2016, 74.

25 The *shanshu* movement was a sectarian movement led by laymen who adopted various mixtures of Daoist, Buddhist, or Confucian beliefs (Seidel 1989, 245–46). Its idea is that one can control one's own destiny by striving for virtue or one can judge the value of one's own actions and be thus assured of an appropriate reward (Sakai Tadao 2010, 14–15). The movement started in the Southern Song period and reached its peak in the seventeenth and eighteenth centuries (Brokaw 1991, 61).

26 Leong Wei Hean 2016, 160.

27 Brook 1998, 637.

28 Little 2000, 28.

29 Wang 2009, 105–6.

30 Seidel 1989, 245–46.

31 Ibid.

32 A large part of it is today's Zhongnan hai and Beihai Park. A map and an explanation of the exact location can be found in Wan (2009, 65–99).

33 Based on Maggie Wan's translation with slight changes of my own. Wan 2007, 107.

34 Translated by Fabrizio Pregadio 2021, 118.

35 Kohn 2009, 172.

36 Ibid.

37 Teiser 1996, 22.

38 Wan 2007, 112.

39 Ibid., 111.

40 Seidel 1987, 230.

41 Ibid.; Seidel 1989, 261–62.

42 Seidel, 1987, 230.

43 Ibid., 232.

44 Lidov 2012, 77–78.

45 Belting 2005, 51.

46 Up to the time of this portrait, the mirroring and glittering of precious stones had rarely been represented before in Chinese painting. Yu-ping Luk has discussed this new "three-dimensional" way of depicting gemstones in Ming courtly portraits. She claims that it was likely to have been a consequence of the seven voyages led by the eunuch admiral

Zheng He 鄭和 (1371–1433) during the reign of emperor Yongle (1360–1424, r. 1403–24) (Luk 2016, 71). Between 1405 and 1433, Zheng He journeyed south through Vietnam, Thailand, and Indonesia as well as west to India, Sri Lanka, the Persian Gulf, the Red Sea, and the east coast of Africa. On voyages to South Asian countries such as Sri Lanka he collected hoards of precious gems and brought them back to China.

47 Howes, 2006, 164; see also McHugh 2011, 162.

48 Howes, 2006, 164.

49 Pentcheva 2017, 10.

50 Ibid., 10 and 20.

51 Ibid., 10.

52 Ibid., 10.

53 Wang Cheng-hua has pointed out that two Ming emperors—Taizu 太祖 (1328–98) and Chengzu 成祖 (1360–1424)—controlled their paintings (Wang Cheng-hua 1998, 172).

54 This book is considered as one of the most reliable documents on the Xizong emperor as well as on the administration and daily life of the late Ming court. A reliable reprint was published in 1994 by Beijing Guji Chubanshe (Ancient Book Publishing House). Regarding its different historical prints and editions, see Chen Tianhao 2015: 271–314.

55 Kang Fen and Hu Changchun 2003, 84.

56 There is another almost identical version of the portrait preserved at the National

Palace Museum in Taiwan. By comparing the two versions, the Beijing one discussed in this essay seems to indicate the emperor's premature and sudden death—though this would have to be explored further.

57 *Xiang sheng* 20: 5–6. Harvard Yenching Library, Rare Book, T 8580 7245, accessed 22 December 2020, https://iiif.lib.harvard. edu/manifests/view/drs:54074990$1i (my translation).

58 Yao Ning 2017, 41.

59 Translated by Bissera Pentcheva (2017, 184).

60 Warburg [1893] [1932] 1998.

61 Bredekamp 2010, 299–301.

62 Morgan 2020.

BIBLIOGRAPHY

Primary Literature

Ding Wei 丁謂. 1641. "Tian xiang zhuan" 天香傳. In *Xiang sheng* 香乘. Zhou Jiazhou 周嘉冑. Harvard Yenching Library Rare Book (T 8580 7245), vol. 28, 1–6.

Zhou Jiazhou 周嘉冑. 1641. *Xiang sheng* 香乘. Harvard Yenching Library Rare Book (T 8580 7245).

Secondary Literature

Belting, Hans. 2005. "Toward an Anthropology of the Image." In *Anthropology of Art*, edited by Mariet Westermann, 41–58. New Haven, CT: Yale University Press.

Bredekamp, Horst. 2010. *Theorie des Bildakts.* Berlin: Suhrkamp.

Brokaw, Cynthia J. 1991. *The Ledgers of Merit and Demerit: Social Change and Moral Order in Late Imperial China.* Princeton, NJ: Princeton University Press.

Brook, Timothy. 1998. "Communications and Commerce." In *The Cambridge History of China*, vol. 8, *The Ming Dynasty, 1368–1644, Part 2*, edited by Denis Twitchett and Frederick W. Mote, 579–707. Cambridge: Cambridge University Press.

Chen Tianhao陳天浩. 2015. 劉若愚《酌中志》版本詳考. *Ming Qing shi jikan* 11, no. 3: 271–314.

Clunas, Craig. 2013. *Screen of Kings: Royal Art and Power in Ming China.* London: Reaktion Books.

De Bruyn, Pierre-Henry. 2000. "Daoism in the Ming (1368–1644)." In *Daoism Handbook*, edited by Livia Kohn, 594–622. Leiden; Boston; Cologne: Brill.

Führer, Bernhard. 2006. "Seers and Jesters: Predicting the Future and Punning by Graphic Analysis." *East Asian Science, Technology and Medicine* 25: 47–68.

Howes, David. 2006. "Scent, Sound and Synaesthesia: Intersensoriality and Material Culture Theory." In *Handbook of Material Culture*, edited by Christopher Tilley, Webb Keane, Susanne Küchler, Michael Rowlands, and Patricia Spyer, 161–72. London; Thousand Oaks, CA; New Delhi: Sage.

Huang, Shih-Shan Susan. 2007. "Tianzhu Lingqian: Divination Prints from a Buddhist Temple in Song Hangzhou." *Artibus Asiae* 67, no. 2: 243–96.

Kang Fen 康芬 and Hu Changchun 胡長春. 2003. "Mingdai daojiao cangshu kaolue 明代道教藏書考略 (A Brief Survey on the Daoist Book Collection in the Ming Dynasty)." *Jiangxi tushuguan xuekan* 江西圖書工學刊 33, no. 4: 83–85.

Kohn, Livia. 2009. *Introducing Daoism.* JBE Online Books.

Lagerwey, John. 2016. "The Ming Dynasty Double Orthodoxy: Daoxue and Daojiao." *Cahiers d'Extrême-Asie* 25: 113–30.

Leong Wei Hean 梁偉賢. 2016. "'Mayi xiangfa' banben chutan《麻衣相法》版本初探 (A Preliminary Study on the Editions of 'Mayi Xiangfa')." *Hanxue yanjiu* 34 juan 4: 131–64.

Lidov, Alexei. 2012. "Creating the Sacred Space: Hierotopy as a New Field of Cultural History." *Spazi i percoprsi sacri*: 61–89. Accessed November 28, 2019. http://hierotopy.ru/contents/LIDOV_Hierotopy_Spazi_%20sacri_2015.pdf.

Little, Stephen. 2000. "Taoism and the Arts of China." In *Taoism and the Arts of China*, edited by Stephen Little and Shawn Eichman, 13–32. Chicago: The Art Institute of Chicago.

Luk, Yu-ping. 2016. "The Empress' Dragon Crown: Establishing Symbols of Imperial Authority in the Early Ming." In *Ming China: Courts and Contacts 1400–1450*, edited by Craig Clunas, Jessica Harrison-Hall, and Luk Yu-ping, 68–76. London: The British Museum.

McHugh, James. 2011. "Seeing Scents: Methodological Reflections on the Intersensory Perception of Aromatics in South Asian Religions." *History of Religion* 51, no. 2: 156–77.

Morgan, David. 2020. "The Sensory Web of Vision: Enchantment and Agency in Religious Material Culture." In *The Oxford Handbook of History and Material Culture*, edited by Ivan Gaskell and Sarah Anne Carter, 255–75. New York: Oxford University Press.

Needham, Joseph, with Ho Ping-Yu and Lu Gwei-djen, collabs. 1976. *Science and Civilisation in China*, vol. 5, part 3, *Chemistry and Chemical Technology. Spagyrical Discovery and Invention: Historical Survey, from Cinnabar Elixirs to Synthetic Insulin.* Cambridge: Cambridge University Press.

Park, J. P. 2016. "Art, Print, and Culture Discourse in Early Modern China." In *A Companion to Chinese Art*, edited by Martin J. Powers and Katherine R. Tsiang, 73–90. Malden, MA: Wiley Blackwell.

Pentcheva, Bissera V. 2017. *Hagia Sophia: Sound, Space, and Spirit in Byzantium.* University Park: Pennsylvania State University Press.

Plate, S. Brent. 2014. *A History of Religion in 5 ½ Objects: Bringing the Spiritual to Its Senses.* Boston: Beacon Press.

Pregadio, Fabrizio. 2021. "The Alchemical Body in Daoism." *Journal of Daoist Studies* 14: 99–127.

Sakade Yoshinobu 坂出祥伸. 2000. "Divination as Daoist Practice," trans. by Livia Kohn. In *Daoism Handbook*, edited by Livia Kohn, 541–66. Leiden; Boston; Cologne: Brill.

Sakai Tadao 酒井忠夫. 2010. *Zhongguo shanshu yanjiu* 中國善書研究 (Research on Chinese Morality Books). Translated by Liu Yuebing and He Yingying. Nanjing: Jiangsu renmin chubanshe.

Seidel, Anna. 1987. "Post-Mortem Immortality or the Taoist Resurrection of the Body." In *Gilgul: Essays on Transformation, Revolution and Permanence in the History of Religions*, edited by S. Shaked, D. Shulman, and G. G. Stroumsa, 223–37. Leiden: Brill.

Seidel, Anna. 1989. "Chronicle of Taoist Studies in the West 1950–1990." *Cahiers d'Extrême-Asie* 5: 223–347.

Teiser, Stephen F. 1996. "Introduction." In *Religions of China in Practice*, edited by Donald Lopez Jr., 3–37. Princeton, NJ: Princeton University Press.

Wan, Maggie C. K. 2007. "Jiajing Emperor and His Auspicious Words." *Archives of Asian Art* 57: 95–120.

Wan, Maggie C. K. 2009. "Building an Immortal Land: The Ming Jiajing Emperor's West Park." *Asia Major*, 3rd series, 22, no. 2: 65–99.

Wang Cheng-hua. 1998. "Material Culture and Emperorship: The Shaping of Imperial Roles at the Court of Xuanzong (r. 1426–35)." PhD thesis, Yale University.

Wang, Richard. 2009. "Ming Princes and Daoist Ritual." *T'oung Pao*, 2nd series, 95, fasc. 1/3: 51–119.

Wang, Richard. 2012. *The Ming Prince and Daoism: Institutional Patronage of an Elite.* Oxford; New York: Oxford University Press.

Warburg, Aby. [1932] 1998. "Sandro Botticellis 'Geburt der Venus' und 'Frühling'. Eine Untersuchung über die Vorstellungen von der Antike in der italienischen Frührenaissance, (1893)." In *A. Warburg. Gesammelte Schriften*, vol. 1, edited by Bibliothek Warburg, 6–59. Leipzig; Berlin: B. G. Teubner.

Wu Hung. 1984. "A Sanpan Shan Chariot Ornament and the Xiangrui Design in Western Han Art." *Archives of Asian Art* 37: 38–59.

Wu Hung. 2005a. "Handai daojiao meishu shitan漢代道教美術試探 (On the Daoist Art in the Han Dynasty)." In *Liyi zhong de meishu. Wu Hong Zhongguo gudai meishushi wenbian* 禮儀中的美術. 巫鴻中國古代美術史文編 (Art in Its Ritual Context: Essays on Ancient Chinese Art by Wu Hung), translated by Zheng Yan and others, 455–84. Beijing: Sanlian shudian.

Wu Hung. 2005b. "Handai yishu zhong de 'Tiantang' tuxiang he 'Tiantang' guannian 漢代藝術中的 "天堂" 圖像和 "天堂" 觀念 (The Image and Concept of 'Paradise' in the Art of the Han Period)." In *Liyi zhong de meishu. Wu Hong Zhongguo gudai meishushi wenbian* 禮儀中的美術. 巫鴻中國古代美術史文編 (Art in Its Ritual Context: Essays on Ancient Chinese Art by Wu Hung), translated by Zheng Yan and others, 243–59. Beijing: Sanlian shudian.

Yao Ning. 2017. "Reshaping Portraiture: The Emergence of Chinese Literati Portraiture." In *Faces of China: Portrait Painting of the Ming and Qing Dynasties (1368–1912)*, edited by Klaas Ruitenbeek, 35–46. Berlin: Michael Imhof Verlag.

Yuan Wenqing. 2016. "Religious Consciousness and Beliefs in the Ming Tombs of Princes and Royal Family Members in Hubei Province." In *Ming China: Courts and Contacts 1400–1450*, edited by Craig Clunas, Jessica Harrison-Hall, and Luk Yu-ping, 163–69. London: The British Museum.

THE SUBSTANCE OF INCENSE FROM ROMAN ANTIQUITY TO THE MIDDLE AGES

Béatrice Caseau & Claire-Marie Caseau

This article studies sources mentioning substances used to create incense in Greek and Roman Antiquity and then in the Middle Ages, including the Islamic world.[1] Ancient Egypt before the Roman conquest is not discussed in this article. The aim is to show the complexity of incense and the evolution in the substances used to create fragrant smoke. Recent analysis of incense residues helps us understand this complexity and evolution in taste. Chemical analysis of ancient and medieval incense residues also changes the perception we obtain from written sources and allows us to better understand the complexity of incense use from the fourth century BCE to the sixteenth century CE.

Studies on the subject of incense used during Antiquity and the Middle Ages are rare in the field of history, although they have recently increased, thanks to a renewed interest in perfumes in Antiquity.[2] Incense was widely used in the ancient and medieval worlds, in everyday life as an air purifier and health protector, but also in religious or political rituals as well as for medicinal and magical purposes. Contemporary medicine recently became interested in incense as its smoke has been seen as a possible trigger for lung cancer, while research was also done to prove the potentially beneficial properties of oleo-gum resins and spices.[3] We know that resins were commonly used as a substance capable of producing perfumed smoke. But what kinds of resins? Archaeobotany and pharmaceutical studies can help us find the proper words to use even before tracing the presence of frankincense and other resins in archaeological discoveries. Parimal Kotkar and two colleagues clearly explain the distinction between different sorts of resins: "Resins and oils in homogenous mixtures are called as oleoresins. Oleo-gum resins are the homogenous mixtures of volatile oil, gum and resin. If the resin contains benzoic acid and/or cinnamic acid, it is called as a balsam."[4] With ancient incense, we are dealing with these diverse sorts of resins and it is not easy to reconcile modern identifications with ancient sources, which deploy their own words to name or describe the substance of incense.

Historical research on incense in Antiquity and the Middle Ages often focused on frankincense and myrrh—resins produced by trees growing in Arabia Felix, South Arabia, and the coast of Somalia in East Africa—because scholars were interested in showing how Asia was connected to the Mediterranean world through trade.[5] Scholars also aimed to establish the different land and maritime commercial routes taken to reach the Mediterranean world from the Far East or from Africa and South Arabia.[6] Along with spices coming from India and the Asian lands of the Far East, frankincense was of great interest in the ancient world as a high value trade commodity. Yet, incense cannot be reduced to frankincense and myrrh. It is often a compound product that mixes different sorts of resins, scented woods, roots, and seeds in order to produce a fragrant smoke. This is still the case in present-day Yemen, where frankincense is produced and available. There, it is polite, when visiting friends or family, to bring incense, and while the wealthiest bring the frankincense of choice, the poorest bring seeds, bark, and twigs that contribute to the smell emanating from the *brasero*.[7]

Similarly in the past, as frankincense and myrrh were expensive products, they were often either adulterated or mixed with other resins and fragrant woods. Indeed, in the Mediterranean region incense was produced using local matter such as the resin of trees, for example pine resin, styrax, or mastic, which were well appreciated and often included in the composition of compound incense.[8]

Let us retrace the story of the substances used to create incense and study recent chemical analyses of incense residues.

WRITTEN SOURCES:
BOTANICAL, PHARMACOLOGICAL,
AND MEDICAL LITERATURE

Hebrew, Greek, and Latin use generic words to describe the burning of matter to produce a perfumed smoke. Greek and Latin deploy words such as *thymiama* or *incensum*,[9] referring to the burning of the matter rather than to the matter being burned. The verb *thumiao* points to the smoke produced as well as to the perfume created while burning resins or other fragrant substances. So, when sources only mention words created from the roots of *incendo* and *thumiao*, they indicate that matter is burned, and smoke is produced but they do not inform us about what, in fact, was burning in the incense burner to perfume a space. The same is true in Hebrew with the root *q-ṭ-r*, meaning to burn and transform into smoke, which is used to refer to incense in the word *qĕtōret*.[10]

Even if references to incense and perfumes can also be found in poetry and other sources,[11] we need to turn to botany, pharmacology, and medicine to discover more about the substance of incense. Three major literary authors from Antiquity reveal the different plants and ingredients used in incense production: Theophrastus (372–287 BCE), Dioscorides (first century CE), and Pliny the Elder (first century CE). Theophrastus was one of the first authors to gather systematic information on plants and plant exudates. In Book IX of his *Enquiry into Plants*, he devotes an entire section to plants from Arabia that provide resins to burn as incense and for use in perfumes.[12] He had not traveled to Arabia himself, so he therefore reports what he has heard from sailors or traders about the trees. Theophrastus's focus is on describing plants; even though he mentions the use of resins in incense, he is not interested in incense recipes. He explains the process used to extract incense by incising the tree and harvesting the tears (*to dakruon*). He knows the difference between the frankincense tree and the myrrh tree, and the color of the exudates based on the age of the trees. He also explains how its trade is organized locally in Arabia.[13] After the chapter on frankincense and myrrh, he describes *kasia* (*cinnamomum*) and kinamômos (*cinnamomum zeylanicum*), thinking they grow in Arabia because traders brought them along with incense. He then describes trees that provide fragrant exudates, which were used as incense and in perfumery: balsamon (*commiphora opobalsamum ou gileadensis*) growing in Syria (which includes Palestine), which provides a small harvest and is a very expensive product for a highly appreciated perfume; *chalbanè* (*ferula galbaniflua*) from Syria (in fact from Central Asia and Iran); and styrax (*styrax officinalis*) from Phoenicia,[14] to which one should add herbaceous plants such as the aromatic *kalamos* (*acorus calamus L.*) from Lebanon, which is fragrant when dried, and other plants potentially used in an incense recipe. Theophrastus considers as "aromata," fragrant plants or plant parts, roots, bark, twigs and wood, seeds, resin, and flowers.[15] Not all fragrant plants or aromata were *thumiamata* —that is, suitable to burn as incense—but many could potentially enter into the composition of an incense compound.

The second important author is Pliny. In his *Natural History* he too describes plants and, in particular, frankincense trees. He did not travel to South Arabia and his description also derives from hearsay and from the texts of previous authors he has read. He explains how the trees are exploited for their precious "tears" of resin. He is especially interested in trade and prices and provides the information that, because of all the intermediaries, the best frankincense in his time cost 6 denarii per pound, the second best 5, and the third best 3. He adds: "It is tested by its whiteness and stickiness, its fragility and its readiness to catch fire from a hot coal."[16] He mentions how precious it is and the surveillance in Alexandria of workers preparing incense drops to be sold.[17] Finally, he reveals that it is often adulterated with white resin.[18]

While Pliny lived in Italy until Vesuvius erupted in 79 CE, Dioscorides, born in Anazarbus, was a doctor and pharmacologist from Cilicia in the same period. His treatise, *De materia medica*, is like an encyclopedia of some 600 plants and provides references to different plant parts used as incense—not only exudates (resin, gum, sap) but also leaves or bark.[19] His work is not only about plant description, but is also concerned with "the preparation, properties and testing of drugs," evaluating a plant's medicinal usefulness. Staub and colleagues have made a list of health issues (gynecological, urological, dermatological, and more) and the plant families recommended by Dioscorides to address each issue.[20] They also mention what part of the plants (leaves, bark, sap, roots …) are used. Exudates, for example, can be used in fumigations, potions, and pastes for ointments. Indeed flexibility in the use of the same plant or parts of the same plant is noticeable. Dioscorides's focus is not, however, on incense per se, but he mentions the use of some plant parts in incense simply in passing. This is the case, for instance, for the *Juniperus sabina*, whose leaves, which resemble those of the cypress, are used for incense.[21] Although frankincense (*libanos*; from *Bowellia sp.* trees) is a particularly renowned incense, he only notes its qualities and medical usefulness in drinks or ointments. And although *De materia medica* has a section on burning frankincense, it is for the purpose of using its soot in medicine.[22] Dioscorides's work was widely admired during the Middle Ages and it was copied and transmitted in Greek in the Byzantine world as well as translated into Latin, Arabic, and Armenian, so we can surmise that learned people in the Middle Ages knew about the medical properties of resins.

Ancient and medieval Greek medicine widely recommends the use of resins, spices, and aromatics, which were granted power to heal[23] and considered very beneficial to possess, thus stimulating trade.[24] This positive opinion stemmed from their perfume: while stench was considered dangerous, a good odor was deemed health protective.[25] Resins, spices, and aromatics were often incorporated in the composition of medicine to cure illnesses. They could be used in fumigations, in gynecology for example,[26] but more often they were reduced into a powder to form a potion to drink or a paste. One open question, beyond the scope of this paper, concerns the correspondence between their medical uses in potions, ointments, and fumigations. Still, medical literature is the first type of source to consider when searching for compound incense recipes because it provides a list of resins, spices, and fragrant woods used together for beneficial health effects.

If it is not possible to provide a complete overview of all oleo-resins and fragrant woods cited in Greek medical treatises by authors such as Galen, Rufus of Ephesus, Alexander of Tralles, and Aetius of Amida, to cite a few, it is possible to concentrate on the variations of the most famous incense compound of Antiquity: *kyphi*. This substance served as incense in Egyptian temples, and recipes to compose it are recorded on temple walls at Edfu and Philae as well as in numerous medical treatises.[27]

The Edfu and Philae recipes date back to the second century BCE. They record similar ingredients but differ on the quantities. Following Manniche, for Philae, these ingredients are:

> Raisins
> Wine
> Fresh "Horus eye" (oasis wine)
> Sweet "Horus eye" (honey)
> Frankincense (around 1.2 kg)
> Myrrh (around 1.1 kg, slightly less than frankincense)
> Mastic (273 g)
> Pine resin (273 g)
> Sweet flag (227 g)
> Aspalathos (273 g)
> Camel grass (273 g)
> Cyperus (1.5 l)
> Juniper (1.5 l)
> Pine kernels (1.5 l)
> *Peker* (1.5 l: an unidentified plant)

Kyphi is also recorded in Greek medical texts.[28] In the *De materia medica*, Dioscorides writes:

> Kyphi is an incense preparation that pleases the gods; the priests in Egypt use it lavishly. It is also mixed with antidotes and it is given to asthmatics in drinks. Many are the accounts proffered for preparing it and among them there is also this one: one-half *xestes* galingale, and an equal amount of ripe juniper berries, 12 *mnai* shiny seedless raisins, five *mnai* purified pine resin, one *mna* each of sweet fleg, camel's thorn, and camel hay, 12 *drachmai* myrrh, nine *xestes* old wine, and *mnai* honey. After removing the seeds from the raisins, cut and pound them in a mortar with wine and myrrh, and after pounding and sifting the other ingredients, mix them with the raisins and let them steep together for a day. Then boiling the honey until it reaches a viscous consistency, mix carefully the melted pine resin; then rubbing in together the remaining ingredients, stow in an earthenware vessel.[29]

Following Dioscorides, ten ingredients are necessary for *kyphi*:

Galingale
Juniper berries
Raisins
Pine resin
Sweet flag
Camelthorn
Camel hay
Myrrh
Wine
Honey

In this recipe, resins from distant lands only play a small role. Manniche, converting ancient measures, has provided estimates that one needs 42 g of myrrh but 2.2 kg of pure resin (the most commonly accessible being pine resin).[30]

It is revealing to note that ancient Egyptian recipes reversed the proportion of frankincense to pine resin given by Dioscorides; there are few trees in Egypt, while caravans brought the precious resins from the famous Punt region of Arabia or East Africa. This flexibility to adapt to available resources is an essential element to keep in mind when dealing with the matter of incense. We can see it in the different recipes for *kyphi*.

The second century CE also provides recipes for *kyphi*. When Plutarch (d. ca. 119 CE) describes the cult of Isis and Osiris, he mentions incense used in their temples, especially myrrh, but also the fragrant woods of cypress, juniper, and pine. *Kyphi*, he tells us, is offered at nightfall and is a compound incense made of sixteen ingredients:[31]

Honey
Wine
Raisins
Cyperus
Resin
Myrrh
Aspalathus
Seselis
Mastic
Bitumen
Rush
Sorrel
Juniper (large and small)
Cardamom
Calamus

Plutarch explains that these ingredients have aromatic properties, which bring relaxation and are conducive to sleep. The recipe mixes plants and minerals. Among ancient authors, Plutarch seems to be the only one to mention bitumen or asphalt, but the ingredient is present in more recent recipes such as the 1574 "tiryac of Farouq," where it comes from Judea.[32] Plutarch also explains that *kyphi*'s potency comes from careful preparation (compounding) while sacred writings are read to the perfumers as they mix the ingredients. This is a religious ceremony. The medical tradition also mentions the potency of this incense, but claims it comes from the mixing of powerful ingredients and not from the magical combination of words with perfume.

In his treatise *De antidotis*, Galen, who lived in the second century CE, explains how the mixing of ingredients changes the potency (*dynamis*) of individual ingredients to create a unity in the medicine.[33] His treatise also reveals the flexibility of recipes, which can be adapted to one use or another and go from potion to incense and vice versa. In *De antidotis*, Book I, he records many ways to help recover from serpent's venom. In book II, he provides a *kyphi* recipe already known by Rufus of Ephesus and attributed to Damocrates. It includes different plants such as saffron, cardamom, cassia, spikenard, and bdellium.[34]

Byzantine medicine inherited the antique traditions concerning *kyphi*. Alexander of Tralles, who lived in the sixth century CE, prescribes solar *kyphi*.[35] Paul of Egina, who lived in the seventh century CE, provides yet another recipe for *kyphi*, mixing spices, fragrant woods, and resins, with two variants of more than thirty ingredients.[36] The Latin world benefited from the translation of Greek medical texts into Latin. For example, the anonymous *Alphabet of Galen*, a handbook of ancient Greek pharmacy translated into Latin that probably dates to Late Antiquity, describes around 300 natural products for medicinal use. Despite employing the prestigious name Galen, it has no link to the doctor and survives in early medieval manuscripts from the seventh century CE onward. The *Alphabet of Galen* was popular and circulated in the Latin world until the thirteenth century.[37] It includes a recipe for *kyphi*:

> Kyphi is a type of incense which is made from these ingredients: a pound each of sweet flag and ashes of camelthorn, a pound of myrrh, young galingale, ripe juniper berries and crushed grapes, all of which can then be pulverized together, pulped, sifted, and then that which remains is marinated in wine for a day. Camelthorn is then burned, crushed, and sprinkled on top, then this is mixed with honey that has been reduced by cooking. All of this is carefully and thoroughly blended together then stored in an earthenware vessel. The ancients used to burn it for their gods. Doctors place it in other compound medicines also. It can sharply and effectively loosen.[38]

Under its different forms, this incense recipe invented in ancient Egypt was still renowned in medieval times. Its dual function as incense and medical remedy is attested in Antiquity, but the Middle Ages preserved it for pharmaceutical and medical purposes. It is clear in medical literature that one can find incense recipes in the Middle Ages because the medieval medical texts inherited this long tradition of mixing resins and spices to create medicines that could be burned as incense or used in other fashions. In Codex Sangallensis 761, from an insular script dated ca. 800, Claire Burridge has noted an interesting incense compound, entitled simply "thimiama," which simply refers to matter to burn as incense.[39] This "Thimiama is made of: cozumber – 3, aloeswood, ambergris – 3 denarii, confita, camphor – 1 denarius, musk – 1 denarius."[40]

Compared to other recipes, we have here a list of ingredients that is original. Burridge notes the presence of camphor, which is hypothetically identified here.[41] The seventh-century expansion of the Umayyad Islamic empire into the Sassanian world created a very large empire extending from Spain to the border of India. This led to increased trade in spices and substances to burn as incense during the High Middle Ages. Among the substances reaching Europe was camphor, which came from the *Cinnamomum camphora*, the fragrant camphor tree, which grows in Southeast Asia. Camphor has long been used in Chinese and Japanese medicine and was introduced in the Islamic world before reaching Western Europe.[42]

In the Islamic word, incense was commonly burned in prophylactic medicine and belonged to traditions of hospitality. Incense filled the spaces where festive events took place. It surrounded caliphs in much the same way it was present in Byzantine imperial processions. Yet incense was not reserved for the political elite. In polite well-to-do Abbasid society, it was customary to light an incense burner at the end of a meal. Clothes and linen were also perfumed by fumigation. Vessels holding water could also be fumigated, as noted in Ibn Ridwan,[43] as were cooking-pots, following, among others, Al-Warraq.[44]

Jean-Charles Ducène points to the evolution in the substances used as incense in the Islamic world, with the addition of products coming from Asia such as musk, sandalwood, the wood of agarwood, and camphor.[45] As in the earlier Roman world, one substance or a combination of resins and fragrant woods could be burned. One finds perfume recipes in medical treatises but also in cookbooks.[46] Products came from Arabia (frankincense and myrrh, acacia gum from *Acacia arabica*) but also from the Mediterranean world: mastic from Chios called Greek resin (from the *Pistacia lentiscus*), balsam from Judea, *ladanum* from Crete (*cistus ladanifer* or *cistus creticus*). Different fragrant woods could be added, such as sandalwood or agallochum, also known as eaglewood (*Aquilaria malacensis*). Finally, animal products used in perfumery could also be a component of incense: musk, amber, and marine shells known as *unguis odoratus* or sweet hoofs and "blattes de Byzance."[47] Some incense compositions were more popular than others, for example "nadd," which mixed ambergris, Indian agarwood, and musk, as well as perhaps frankincense.[48] A thirteenth-century Aleppo cookbook includes a whole section on incense recipes for different occasions—for health during the change of seasons, for perfuming those who have been to the rest room, for use on furs—and different "nadd" incense recipes. One includes the following substances: "camphor, sweet and bitter costus, ambergris, labdanum, tree moss, saffron, fragrant shell, agarwood. Pound everything, sift it, and knead with ben oil ... and make into tablets."[49] "Nadd" incense was recommended for use in a room where the air is cold by Ibn Ridwan, who wrote in the eleventh century a treatise on the *Prevention of Bodily Ills in Egypt*.[50]

Zohar and Lev even point to a changing trend in incense and perfumes following the Arabic conquest, with certain substances in decline (myrrh, Judean balsam) and others in higher demand, such as new fragrant substances from India: camphor, ambergris, and sandalwood.[51] They use the documents found in the Cairo Genizah to show that these commodities were imported by Jewish merchants from China or India to Egypt in the eleventh century. Judean balsam was highly praised in Roman times and was recommended to create holy chrism, the perfumed oil used to consecrate persons during baptism and churches or altars. Zohar and Lev explain that camphor replaced Judean balsam because it was cheaper and could be moved in much larger quantities than balsam, whose production depended on a few trees from a small region. It is also possible that its production was bought by Christians for Christian ceremonies. Legends around the miraculous origin of the balsam tree perfume at Matarieh amplified its importance for Christians, and perhaps dissuaded Muslim traders or perfume producers from including it in their practices.[52]

It is not easy to follow religious lines when dealing with incense recipes because the main source of information concerning these substances was medical literature, which was largely shared by Jews, Christians, and Muslims in the Middle Ages, all drawing on ancient Greek medicine.[53] The Nestorian Christian author Ibn Masawayh (777–857) wrote a treatise on simple aromatic substances. He considered the main aromatic substances to be musk, ambergris, *agallochum* wood, camphor, and saffron. He obviously shared the new interest in these substances.[54]

Scholars today have debated the use of incense in mediaeval mosques. It was used as an air-freshener to make the space pleasing very early on and is mentioned in a few sources, but its deployment was far from systematic.[55] According to some scholars, mosques seldom used incense in the early Middle Ages, except when a caliph visited or, as already noted, to create a pleasant atmosphere.[56] Its use seems to have become more frequent after the twelfth century and was common in Ottoman mosques.[57] In this context incense was not deployed in cultic or sacrificial rites, as it had been in the traditional cults of the Greek and Roman world, but as a mark of honor or simply to achieve pleasing effects. Yet, incense nonetheless found its place among Sufis in the Muslim world. In Jewish and Christian texts, incense served as the bearer of prayers, which ascended to heaven on its fragrant billows of smoke. Sufis introduced a similar use for incense and claimed that it eased the movement of prayers and pleased angels.[58]

In Ottoman times, incense appears in the expense registers of mosques' endowments. Musk, *aggalochum*, and ambergris seem to have been favorites. Nina Ergin, who has published on Ottoman incense burners but also on incense recipes, details one called "Prophet's incense," produced in the Topkapi palace's pharmacy. It contains:

> Ambergris 1 dirhem
> Gum benzoin 15 dirhems
> Agallochum 5 d
> Mastic 4 d
> Saffron 5 d
> C. opobalsamum 4 d
> Hyacinth 5 d
> Myrtle leaf 5 d
> Labdanum 6 d
> Camphor 1 d
> Bitter orange peel 3 d
> Storax 3 d
> Tragacanth gum 3 d
> Musk 3 d
> Sugar 8 d

All of these ingredients are reduced into a fine powder, then kneaded with rose water and molded into pastilles. They will burn on willow charcoal.

We would love to have such a recipe for the Byzantine and Latin Christian worlds, instead of a simple reference to *thymiama* or *incensum*, but medieval Greek and Latin liturgical sources are silent on the type of incense used during liturgies.

In the Greek sources, besides those of the medical tradition, incense recipes are mentioned in the so-called magical papyri. These refer to fumigations as part of spells and are precise on what resins or plants should be used.[59] They combine references to different religious traditions of the Greco-Roman world and provide us with a list of ingredients to burn for offerings. For example, PGM I, 262–347, which contains an Apollonian invocation, lists the following ingredients: "the burnt offering is a wolf's eye, storax gum, cassia, balsam gum and whatever is valued among the spices, and pour a libation of wine and honey and milk and rainwater, and [make] 7 flat cakes and 7 round cakes."[60] Except for animal parts, the substances listed are those known to ancient medicine, more particularly frankincense, myrrh, and storax. They are succeeded by Coptic and Islamic magical recipes.[61] However, these documents do not provide further detail about incense in Christian churches of Late Antiquity and the Middle Ages. Incense recipes in the Islamic world continued to be connected to ancient polytheism.[62] It is perhaps precisely because the magical tradition insisted on utilizing the proper substances to burn for each occasion that the mainstream Christian churches refrained from providing such details.

In their article, Hedrick and Ergin state that three substances (frankincense, myrrh, and storax) were Christians' favorite ingredients for incense.[63] Where does this idea come from? Did the authors draw this notion from Hippolytus? The latter mentions that candidates to the Sethian community were required to be able to distinguish the components in the smoke of a given piece of incense. He cites styrax, myrrh, and frankincense as possible ingredients.[64] But it would be rather odd to draw conclusions for churches belonging to the majority branch of Christianity from a marginal branch that had been condemned along with other forms of Gnosticism.[65]

We have analyzed the reasons why frankincense and myrrh could be considered the choice substances, yet their citation in the New Testament is not enough to make them *mandatory* substances. Moreover, myrrh was usually mixed with oil and connected to funerals and embalming rather than used as incense. As for styrax, some late antique and medieval sources reveal its importance for Christian communities of Late Antiquity. In the *Syriac Life of Symeon Stylite the Elder*, little Symeon as a boy would gather styrax and burn it while the animals he kept were grazing.[66] The text explains that he did not know the Bible, nor the Christian faith, living a pastoral life in the mountains. He accompanied villagers to church and decided to offer to God the styrax he continued to collect. This is a rare and precious testimony of incense offering in a village church of the Nicopolis region of northern Asia Minor in the late fourth or the early fifth century, if it is not an invented early sign of his monastic vocation. Styrax trees grow more commonly in South Anatolia. In the *Life of Symeon the Younger*, another stylite, whose hagiographer copies in many ways the earlier *Saint's Life* of the first stylite,

Symeon the Elder, his mother prays for a child and spends days and nights
in the church of Saint John the Baptist in Antioch, who eventually appears
to her in a dream. When she wakes up, she holds a lump of styrax in her
hand, and throws it in a censer to fill the church with perfume.[67] Styrax had
the great advantage of being accessible in the eastern part of the Mediterranean and it certainly cost less than spices and resins coming from Southeast Asia or Arabia. We should not be surprised to see it mentioned in
Christian sources. Yet, even if styrax is referenced in hagiography and in
other sources such as the *Geoponica,* where it is used to chase away pests,
this is not proof that it was the resin present in Christian censers everywhere,
even if the introduction of incense in churches began in Syria/Palestine, as
noted by Susan Ashbrook Harvey and Bissera Pentcheva.[68] There are no
particular prescriptions in canon law or liturgical regulations concerning
which substances to burn or avoid burning in liturgical incense. Christian
sources use generic terms to refer to incense and I tend to think that this
was part of a deliberate strategy to avoid confusion with magical incense or
medical recipes strongly connected with ancient polytheism. For Christians
of Late Antiquity, having the church smell like a temple of Isis was certainly not acceptable, considering anti-pagan propaganda and the wish to make
a clear cut with sacrificial practices of the religious past. The second reason
not to provide a list of ingredients, as was done for the liturgical Myron, is
that the preparation of Myron was in the hands of bishops and in the Byzantine church: it was the privilege of the patriarch. The eighth-century Bar-
berini *Euchologium* provides a list of thirteen ingredients for the preparation
of the liturgical *myron.* The number of ingredients increased in the following centuries and the recipe became so complex that no ordinary bishop
would be able to get hold of all the necessary substances. It continued to be
a patriarchal privilege. Incense, on the other hand, was never under patriarchal control; bishops and priests could prepare their own.

The final reason not to provide a list of ingredients is an economic
one. All substances were not available everywhere, depending on the period
and the region. When they were available, price remained an obstacle. Incense
was therefore made with available substances and largely depended on the
financial resources of a particular church. Burning local resins or fragrant
woods was not as costly as importing exotic spices and Arabian frankincense.
Imperially funded churches could afford such expenses but ordinary churches could not. In the *Vita Silvestri,* the *Liber pontificalis ecclesiae Romanae*
states that emperor Constantine secured the importation of incense, spices,
and perfumes for the Roman basilicas that he founded. Each basilica received
a donation recorded under his name. For the basilica dedicated to St. Peter,
the donation included a censer of the finest gold, decorated with sixty jew-
els and properties to provide the church with aromatic substances that could
be used in incense in censers or to create the perfumed liturgical oil:

> [I]n the suburbs of Antioch: the property Sybilles, presented
> to the emperor, revenue 322 *solidi,* 150 decads of paper, 200
> lb. spices, 200 lb. nard-oil, 35 lb. balsam;
> [I]n the suburbs of Alexandria: the property Trimalca, given
> to the emperor Constantine by Ambronius, revenue 620 *sol-
> idi,* 300 decads of paper, 300 lb. nard-oil, 60 lb. balsam, 150
> lb. spices, 50 lb. Isaurian storax; ...

> In Egypt, in the suburbs of Armenia: ... the property Passin-
> opolimse, revenue 800 *solidi*, 400 decads of paper, 50 *med-*
> *imni* of pepper, 100 lb. saffron, 150 lb. storax, 200 lb. cassia
> spices, 300 lb. nard-oil, 100 lb. balsam, 100 sacks of linen, 150
> lb. cloves, 100 lb. cyprus-oil, 1000 ..."[69]

We shall not discuss here the original date of these documents, but they are present in the sixth-century compilation of the *Liber pontificalis* and make reference to the types of resins and perfumes that one would expect to find in a wealthy church. Note the number of products which could be mixed to create a delicious incense for the church: styrax, cassia, balsam, perhaps cloves, saffron, and pepper.[70] The absence of frankincense is surprising, though it was perhaps included in the word "*aromata*," which is a generic, inclusive word. Nonetheless, the lack of specific reference to frankincense is remarkable given that details regarding other fragrant oils, resins, and spices are so detailed. In any case, what this list implies is that liturgical incense was clearly a composite product and not restricted to just one sub-stance. If in the Latin world for a long time, the holy chrism was made of olive oil mixed with the perfume of Judean balsam—for incense many dif-ferent resins could be mixed—and if we follow the *kyphi* recipes, we cannot exclude the possibility that perfumed oils were sometimes mixed with dried resins to create new pastilles of incense.

The only way to know what was really used in Christian ceremonies is, therefore, to analyze residues. Unfortunately, we do not yet have a com-plete repository of examples for different centuries and regions. Nonetheless, the few examples that we do have are significant. The analytical techniques used to characterize molecules in complex mixtures of resins and other organic material include: gas chromatography-mass spectrometry (GC-MS), which separates the organic components based on their molecular weight and then looks for individual fingerprints produced by the fragmentation ions of the molecules; Fourier transform infrared spectroscopy (FTIR), which can be used to identify molecules based on their functional groups; Fourier transform Raman spectroscopy, which can identify molecules based on their structural fingerprint; attenuated total reflection (ATR), to investigate coat-ings on metal; and thin layer chromatography (TLC) to analyze mixtures.

In the case of incense, the durability of resins over centuries provides an analytical advantage, while vegetable oils used in lighting, perfumes, some incense recipes, and medications are highly susceptible to oxidative degra-dation.[71] The last thirty years have witnessed the development of new meth-odologies to characterize resins and other organic materials.[72] Nonetheless, many difficulties persist. The identification of ancient plant remains becomes more and more precise as the database of modern plant molecules grows. In 1997, resin found in a cellar dating to 400–500 CE was identified as frank-incense because analysis revealed pentacyclic triterpenoids, components characteristic of modern frankincense.[73] Studies on the chemical composi-tion of resins help us to make distinctions between the trees they come from. A comparative study of frankincense from various species helped to better determine accurate species-specific biomarkers.[74] Such a study was also done for styrax, a resin from the *Liquidambar spp.*, which grows in Turkey, to distinguish it from benzoin balsam coming from South Asian trees of the *Styracaceae* family.[75] Plants have evolved over time, and some have disappeared, so it is sometimes difficult to find the genus. *Boswellia papyrifera* and *Boswellia sacra* were incised for their resin in Antiquity and are now in danger of extinction, while contemporary frankincense resins are mostly produced by *Boswellia carteri* and *Boswellia frereana*, which grow in East Africa, Sudan, and Ethiopia, or *Boswellia serrata* from India.[76] The same is true for myrrh: different sorts of *Commiphora* trees were exploited, some providing "common myrrh" from *Commiphora myrrha* while other genera, such as *Commiphora erythraea* provided perfumed myrrh or bdellium.[77]

Another difficulty appears when incense that has been burned is found in a vessel, as its residues are often carbonized, which leads to both the disappearance of expected biomarkers and the appearance of novel compounds indicative of the degradation processes undergone.[78] In the ancient Yemeni harbor of Qâni, founded in the first century BCE and active until the fifth century CE, thirty-nine samples of resins from an antique religious complex and a burned down warehouse were analyzed.[79] The analysis was performed on preserved frankincense, thermally altered (hypothesis of mild thermal degradation and/or aging), and carbonized frankincense. Several samples were identified as pure as well as burnt frankincense via GC-MS. Analysis of the biomarkers excluded *Boswellia frereana* (endemic to North Somalia) as the source of the frankincense.

Two important pieces of information can be noted: (1) bitumen was used, probably to light fires in the incense burners, and it came from a region of Iran; (2) incense used in fumigation was made of different sorts of frankincense, not myrrh. Incense was, therefore, a blended mixture of this precious resin, flowers, wood, and oils, as revealed by the presence of fatty acids of animal or vegetal origins. These origins could not be traced specifically.

Because of embalming protocols and fumigations, many analyses concerning ancient Egypt will not be addressed in this article. Furthermore, few analyses have been performed on residues from the Middle Ages. Some residue analyses have nevertheless been published for different late antique and medieval sites, and their results are an indicator that more research is needed to write a new history of aromatic resins.

Let us start with Egypt and Nubia, where we understand that it was possible to find incense (*libanos*). Incense and spices traveled along trade routes that crossed Egypt to reach Alexandria, from where they were shipped to the rest of the Mediterranean world. One assumes that it was possible to buy frankincense and other resins in Egyptian and Nubian cities. The choice of another resin is therefore highly significant, probably revealing a preference for a cheaper ingredient. Let us examine some case studies of archaeological discoveries providing different ingredients used as incense.

MASTIC RESIN
FOUND IN A LATE ANTIQUE CENSER

A fifth-to-seventh-century CE ceramic censer discovered in the necropolis of Antinoe revealed that the resin used was mostly mastic, mixed with *Pinaceae* resin and *Brassicaceae* seeds (that is, mustard seeds).[80] Mastic resin comes from trees of the genus *Pistacia*, such as: *Pistacia terebinthus*, widely found in the Middle East but also in Greece and Turkey; *Pistacia lentiscus*, growing on the island of Chios; or *Pistacia atlantica*, present in Cyprus, to name only three. It was probably not difficult and quite cheap to find mastic resin in late antique Egypt.

COPTIC INCENSE
MADE OF FRANKINCENSE AND PINE

Chemical analysis was performed on incense during the excavation of a cellar in a house, located in Nubia at Qasr Ibrîm, that was lived in from the fourth to the eighth century. The result revealed that pine resin was present as well as frankincense.[81] Both had to be imported. Considering that frankincense was probably quite readily available—either from Egypt where caravans brought South Arabian resins, or from East Africa—the presence of pine resin is interesting. Frankincense traveled long distances and was often adulterated to maximize profit. There is no way of knowing if the mixture was bought for pure frankincense (and had been adulterated by the merchant) or if the mixture was the choice of the owner. Clearly pine resins should not be considered as a cheaper ingredient, because in Nubia, it was an imported product. If price had been a consideration in the decision to burn blended substances as incense, we should take into account a taste for perfume which could also have played a role. This mixture of frankincense with pine was already used during the reign of ancient pharaohs, such as Amenemhat II, who reigned from 1929 to 1892 BCE.[82] This was not a new recipe.

LADANUM INCENSE

In Faras, in lower Nubia, not far from Qasr Ibrîm, a specimen of seventh-century Coptic incense was discovered. It was analyzed and revealed to be probably *ladanum*, a black resin exuded from various species of *Cistus*, growing around the Mediterranean.[83] Chemical analysis cannot always identify the matter discovered, especially when it has been carbonized. Such was the case regarding another fragrant resinous specimen from the same Faras, which could not be precisely identified: "On analysis, it proved to be a true resin, as distinguished from a gum-resin, and therefore could not be frankincense, myrrh, galbanum or storax, and its color was not that of *ladanum*."[84]

COPAL INCENSE

Turning to later centuries, we see a surprising decline in the presence of frankincense and the rise of new imported ingredients. This is revealed by archaeological excavations. For example, in Sharma, a medieval trading port active between 980 and 1140,[85] eleventh-century resins were revealed to be copal, coming mainly from Hymenaea trees growing in Madagascar and East Africa. Very little frankincense was discovered, which was surprising for this Hadramawt harbor, although samples were taken from many different houses.[86] This is, however, consistent with changing tastes in incense substances already recorded in Islamic sources. Copal, coming from distant Zanzibar, was perhaps more exotic and desirable than local frankincense. By the eleventh century, East African copal had become an important part of the medieval incense trade, along with camphor.[87]

If new substances from far-off locations changed incense in the Mediterranean Islamic world, what was the place of frankincense in the late antique and medieval West? Frankincense remained highly valued in the West, and was imported not only to the shores of the Mediterranean but also to Northern Europe, where it was used during the liturgies and accompanied the dead to their graves. Three medieval examples prove this last use. Fourteen Late Roman inhumations from Britain (from a total study of forty-nine graves) have provided evidence of exudates from pine resin, mastic

(*Pistacia spp.* resins), and frankincense from *Boswellia spp.* trees. The resins were used as embalming agents, sprinkled on textile wrappings, and placed inside the coffin as offerings. They were a marker of high status, and were found in the graves of males and females of all ages. They were not a clear religious marker, however: pagans and Christians alike would desire the presence of incense at their funeral. It was, on the other hand, a marker of Romanization, through the adoption of Roman mores in funerary practices.[88]

INCENSE COMBINING JUNIPER
MIXED WITH FRANKINCENSE

In the southern region of Belgium called Wallonia, perforated funerary pots were discovered in four burial sites belonging to men or women from between the twelfth and fourteenth centuries. These pots had served as incense burners. Analysis of the residues proved the presence of frankincense with small amounts of juniper. Pine tar was also identified, but this may have been residue on the vessels from a previous use other than as a funerary incense burner. The pots were recycled. This clearly establishes a strong preference for frankincense to accompany the dead in the other world. Jan Baeten and his colleagues have concluded that "the dominance of serratol in the archaeological samples corresponds to *B. sacra* or *B. serrata* and thus excludes *B. papyrifera* and *B. carterii*."[89] Identifying the particular species of *Boswellia* is interesting but given that these genera may grow in different regions, it does not reveal the resin's precise point of origin.[90]

The same funerary practice is recorded in Denmark. In Roskilde and Lund, and to a lesser extent in Jutland, funerary pots were sometimes deposited in graves of the thirteenth and fourteenth centuries. Some contained charcoal residues and one in Smørum was an actual censer. This practice, perhaps stemming from French influence,[91] follows the advice of John Beleth (twelfth century) and Durand de Mende (thirteenth century) to place incense on glowing charcoals at different places in the grave.[92] Incense was placed in pots but also around the body during inhumation.

CONCLUSION

The list of substances used as incense matter is long. It increased from Antiquity into the Middle Ages as trade with Arabia and then India and the Far East developed. Incense could be quite cheap and easy to procure in the Mediterranean where many different trees and plants provided resins which gave a pleasing smell when burned. Incense was also a luxury product, providing its owner with social status. Incense matter from far-away lands was in demand. Oleo-resins from Arabia and further south in Africa were highly praised for their ability to create a perfumed white smoke, with visual, acoustic, and olfactory effects. Resins and spices were combined to create specific perfumes for different uses. Incense was present in domestic settings, in association with health benefits and cosmetics, as well as for religious or magical purposes. Religious use was particularly important during Antiquity and the Middle Ages. While medical and religious antique texts provide recipes for incense, as do Islamic cookbooks, Christians carefully avoided detailing recipes for blended incense to use in a liturgical context. This raises numerous questions and suggests a Christian wish to create distance from earlier magical or medico-magical practices. To know more about the substances actually burned as incense requires more analyses of incense residues. Further scientific information will allow us to put together a clearer picture of the specific substances associated with the religious use of incense by the different cults during this long period running from Antiquity to the end of the Middle Ages.

ENDNOTES

1   My heartfelt thanks first go to the international workshop "The Censer: A Comparative Approach" organized by Beate Fricke and Ittai Weinryb, where I received valuable comments, inspiration, and ideas.

2   Miller 1969; Groom 1981; Dayagi-Mendels 1989; Gyselen 1998; Manniche 1999; Grasse 2003; Bodiou, Frère, and Mehl 2008; Verbanck-Piérard, Massar, and Frère 2008; Frère and Hugot 2012; Brun and Fernandez 2015.

3   A search in the database of Sorbonne university library provides a number of articles on the subject. Articles mostly originating in China to warn against the use of incense in domestic contexts. For example: Li et al. 2022; On health benefits: Rashan et al. 2019.

4   Kotkar, Khale, and Pramod 2011, 1078.

5   Pirenne 1937; McCormick 2001; Groom 1981; Casson 1974 and *Periplus Maris Erythraei*, ed. Casson 1989; Miller 1969; Crone 1987; Vallet 2011; Peacock and Williams 2007; Raschke 1978; Regert et al. 2008.

6   Sidebotham 2011; Miller 1969; Champault 1996; Avanzini 1997.

7   Champault 1996, 168. Seeds, bark, twigs contribute to the smell emanating from the brasero but they are added only after the precious resins have given their perfume; Bel 2001.

8   Amigues 2007; Hovaneissian et al. 2008.

9   Isidore of Seville, *Etymologies* IV, XII: "Incense is so called because it is consumed by fire when it is offered." Barney et al. 2006.

10   Nielsen 1986, 51–67.

11   Lilja 1972; Patzelt 2021.

12   Amigues 2006; 2010; Hort 1980.

13   Theophrastus IX, 4, in Amigues 2006, 10–14.

14   Amigues (2006, 112) warns not to confuse it with liquid styrax from a tree growing in Greece, Crete, and South Anatolia (*Liquidambar orientalis*).

15   Theophrastus IX, 7, 3, in Amigues 2006, 18.

16   Rackham 1955: Pliny, *Natural History*, bk XII, chap. XXXII, 46–47; on different qualities of frankincense, Assefa et al. 2012.

17   Rackham 1955: Pliny, *Natural History*, bk XII, chap. XXXII, 42–43.

18   Ibid., 46–47.

19   Dioscorides in Wellman 1958; transl. Beck 2011; Riddle 1985; Staub, Casu, and Leonti 2016.

20   Staub, Casu, and Leonti 2016, 1047–51.

21   Dioscorides, *De materia medica*, I, 76, transl. Beck 2011, 59.

22   Dioscorides, *De materia medica*, I, 68, transl. Beck 2011, 48–51.

23   Scarborough 1991; Stannard 1982. On contemporary evaluation of plants' power to heal and on their danger, see Harborne, Baxter, and Moss 1999.

24   Nutton 1985.

25   Caseau 2001; 2005; 2007.

26   Byl 1989.

27   Attempts to recreate it cited in Brun and Fernandez 2015, 231–33.

28   Manniche 1999, 47–59.

29   Dioscorides, *De materia medica*, I, 25, transl. Beck 2011, 22–23.

30   Manniche 1999, 49.

31   Plutarch, *Isis and Osiris*, 80, transl. Babbitt 186–87.

32   Chouliara-Raïos 2018, 36; Manniche 1999, 58.

33   Galen, *De antidotis*, I, 10, ed. Kühn.

34   Galen, *De antidotis*, II, 2, ed. Kühn.

35   Alexander of Tralles, ed. Puschmann 1878, 573.

36   Paulus Aegineta, *Epitomae medicae*, VII, 22, 4, ed. Heiberg, 393–94; Miller 1969, 26.

37   Everett 2012, 3–35.

38   *Alphabet of Galen*, 76, transl. Everett 2012, 205.

39   Burridge 2020, 219.

40   "cozumbar III aloa arbor denarius III confitum cafora denarius I musico denarius I."

41   Burridge, *Crossroads*, https://www.earlymedievalmedicine.com/.

42   Ducène 2016; Chen, Vermaak, and Viljoen 2013; Donkin 1998.

43   Dols and Gamal 1984.

44   Nasrallah 2007; Marín 1998, 161–62; Yungman 2020.

45   Ducène 2016.

46   Yungman 2020.

47   McHugh 2013.

48   Ducène (2016) includes frankincense in the recipe; Zohar and Lev (2013) exclude frankincense.

49   Perry 2020, 6–7 (I wish to thank Limor Yungman for this reference).

50   Dols and Gamal 1984.

51   Zohar and Lev 2013.

52   Zanetti 1993; Caseau 2015.

53   Strohmaier 1998; Bouras-Vallianatos 2021.

54   Le Maguer 2015.

55   Le Maguer-Guillon 2021.

56   Bonneric 2016.

57   Ergin 2014 and Hedrick and Ergin 2015.

58   Ducène 2016, 172–73.

59   LiDonnici 2001.

60   Betz 1986, 10.

61   Frankfurter 2019; Meyer and Smith 1994; Coulon 2016.

62   Coulon 2016.

63   Hedrick and Ergin 2015

64   Hippolytus, *The Refutation of all Heresies*, 5, 21, 3, ed. M. Marcovich, 196.

65   Brankaer 2017.

66   *Syriac Life of Simeon Stylite the Elder*, 1–2, transl. Doran 1992, 103–5.

67   *Life of Symeon Stylite the Younger*, 2, ll. 18–19, ed. Van den Ven 1962, 4.

68   Ashbrook Harvey 2006; Pentcheva 2010, 22.

69   *Le Liber pontificalis*, ed. Duchesne 1955, vol 1: 177–78: "sub civitatem Antiochiam: possessio Sybilles, donata Augusto, praest. sol. CCCXXII, charta decadas CL, aromata lib. CC, oleum nardinum lib. CC, balsamum lib. XXXV. Sub civitatem Alexandriam: possessio Trimalica, donata Augusto Constantino ab Ambrosio, praest. sol. DCXX, charta decadas CCC, oleum nardinum lib. CCC, balsamum lib. LX, aromata lib. CL, storace Isaurica lib L; ... Per Aegyptum, sub civitatem Armenia, ... possessio Passinopolimse, praest. sol. DCCC, charta decadas CCCC, piper medemnos L, crocum lib. C, storace lib CL, aromata cassia lib CC, oleu nardinu lib. CCC, balsamu lib. C, linu saccus C, cariophylu lib. CL, oleu Cypriu lib. C ...."; transl. in Davis 1989, 19–20.

70   Caseau 2012.

71   Koupadi et al. 2021, 3611

72   Ibid.

73   Evershed et al. 1997, 667.

74   Archier and Vieillescazes 2000; Evershed 2008.

75   Hovaneissian et al. 2008.

76   Tucker 1986, 426–27; Assefa et al. 2012.

77   Tucker 1986, 429.

78   Baeten et al. 2014, 16.

79   Connan, Joliot, and Mathe 2018.

80   Modugno, Ribechini, and Colombini 2006.

81   Van Bergen et al. 1997, 8409–12.

82   Mathe et al. 2003.

83   Lucas 1962, 94–95; 1911, 31–32.

84   Lucas 1962, 95.

85   Rougeulle 2015.

86   Regert et al. 2008.

87   Crowther et al. 2015; Le Maguer 2016, 142.

88   Brettell et al. 2015, 639–48.

89   Baeten et al. 2014, 10.

90   Le Maguer 2016, 143.

91   Prigent 1996.

92   Christensen and Bjerregaard 2021.

BIBLIOGRAPHY

Primary Sources

Alexander of Tralles. 1878. *Ein Beitrag Zur Geschichte der medicin. Original-text und übersetzung.* Edited by Th. Puschmann. Vienna.

Betz, H. D. (ed.). 1986. *The Greek Magical Papyri in Translation, Including the Demotic Spells.* Chicago: University of Chicago Press.

Davis, R. 1989. *The Book of Pontiffs (Liber Pontificalis): The Ancient Biographies of the First Ninety Roman Bishops to AD 715.* Liverpool: Liverpool University Press.

Dioscorides. 1958. *De materia medica.* Edited by Max Wellman. Pedanii Dioscuridis Anazarbei de materia medica libri quinque, 3 vols. Berlin: Weidmann, vol. 1, 1907; vol. 2, 1906; vol. 3, 1914; repr. 1958.

Dioscorides. 2011. *De materia medica.* Translated by Lily Y. Beck. Hildesheim: Olms – Weidmann.

Galen. 1821–83 [1964–65]. *De antidotis*, ed. C. G. Kühn, *Claudi Galeni opera*, vol. 14: 1–209. Leipzig: Knobloch; repr. Hildesheim: Olms.

Hippolytus. 1986. *Refutatio Omnium Haeresium.* Edited by Miroslaw Marcovich. Berlin; New York: De Gruyter.

Liber Pontificalis ecclesiae romanae. 1886–92 [1955]. Edited by L. Duchesne. Paris. E. Thorin.

Life of Symeon Stylite the Younger: Paul Van den Ven, ed. 1962. *La vie ancienne de S. Syméon Stylite le jeune (521–592).* Brussels: Société des Bollandistes.

Paulus Aegineta. 1921 and 1924. *Epitomae medicae libri septem*, ed. J. L. Heiberg, *Paulus Aegineta*, 2 vols. Corpus medicorum Graecorum 9.1 and 9.2. Leipzig: Teubner.

Periplus Maris Erythraei: Lionel Casson, ed. 1989. *The Periplus Maris Erythraei. Text with Introduction, Translation and Commentary.* Princeton, NJ: Princeton University Press.

Plutarch. 1936. "Isis and Osiris." In *Moralia*, translated by Frank Cole Babbitt, 306. Cambridge, MA: Harvard University Press.

Syriac Life of Symeon Stylite the Elder: Robert Doran, transl. 1992. *The Lives of Symeon Stylites.* Spencer, MA: Cistercian Publications.

Secondary Sources

Amigues, Suzanne. 2006. *Théophraste. Recherches sur les plantes*, vol. V, book IX. Paris: Les Belles Lettres (collection des universités de France).

Amigues, Suzanne. 2007. "Le styrax et ses usages antiques." *Journal des savants* 2, no. 1: 261–318.

Amigues, Suzanne. 2010. *Théophraste. Recherches sur les plantes. À l'origine de la botanique.* Paris: Belin.

Archier, P., and C. Vieillescazes. 2000. "Characterisation of Various Geographical Origin Incense Based on Chemical Criteria." *Analusis* 28: 233–37.

Ashbrook Harvey, Susan. 2006. *Scenting Salvation.* Berkeley: University of California Press.

Assefa, M., A. Dekebo, H. Kassa, A. Habtu, G. Fitwi, and M. Redi-Abshiro. 2012. "Biophysical and Chemical Investigations of Frankincense of *Boswellia papyrifera* from North and Northwestern Ethiopia." *Journal of Chemical and Pharmaceutical Research* 4: 1074–89.

Avanzini, A. (ed.). 1997. *Profumi d'Arabia: Atti del Convegno.* Rome: L'Erma di Bretschneider.

Baeten, Jan, Koen Deforce, Sophie Challe, Dirk De Vos, and Patrick Degryse. 2014. "Holy Smoke in Medieval Funerary Rites: Chemical Fingerprints of Frankincense in Southern Belgian Incense Burners." *PLoS ONE* 9, no. 11: e113142. doi:10.1371/journal.pone.0113142.

Barney, Stephen A., et al. 2006. *The Etymologies of Isidore of Seville*, translated with introduction and notes. Cambridge: Cambridge University Press.

Bel, Jean-Marie, en compagnie de Théodore Monod. 2001. *Botanique au Pays de l'Encens. Exploration naturaliste au Yémen.* Brussels: Éditions Amyris.

Bodiou, Lydie, Dominique Frère, and Véronique Mehl. 2008. *Parfums et odeurs dans l'Antiquité.* Rennes: Presses universitaires de Rennes.

Bonneric, Julie. 2016. "Reflexions sur l'usage des produits odoriférants dans les mosquées au Proche-Orient (Ier–VIIe / VIe–XIIe s.)." *Bulletin d'études orientales* 1, no. 64, *Histoire et anthropologie des odeurs en terre d'Islam à l'époque médiévale*: 293–317.

Bouras-Vallianatos, Petros. 2021. "Cross-cultural Transfer of Medical Knowledge in the Medieval Mediterranean: The Introduction and Dissemination of Sugar-Based Potions from the Islamic World to Byzantium." *Speculum* 96, no. 4: 963–1008.

Brankaer, Johanna. 2017. "Revisiting those Elusive Sethians." In *Shadowy Characters and Fragmentary Evidence: The Search for Early Christian Groups and Movements*, edited by Joseph Verheyden, Tobias Niklas, and Elisabeth Hermitscheck, 159–76. Tübingen: Möhr Siebeck.

Bretell, Rhea C., Eline M. J Schotsmans, Penelope Walton Rogers, Nicole Reifarth, and Rebecca C. Redfern. 2015. "'Choicest Unguents': Molecular Evidence for the Use of Resinous Plant Exudates in Late Roman Mortuary Rites in Britain." *Journal of Archaeological Science* 53: 639–48.

Brun, Jean-Pierre, and Xavier Fernandez. 2015. *Parfums antiques. De l'archéologie au chimiste.* Grasse; Milan: Musée International de la Parfumerie; Silvana Editoriale.

Burridge, Claire. 2020. "Incense in Medicine: An Early Medieval Perspective." *Early Medieval Europe* 28, no. 2: 219–55.

Burridge, Claire. n.d. *Crossroads: The Evolution of Early Medieval Medicine in Global and Local Contexts.* A Leverhulme Trust Early Career Fellowship project based at the University of Sheffield. https://www.earlymedievalmedicine.com/.

Byl, Simon. 1989. "L'odeur végétale dans la thérapeutique gynécologique du Corpus hippocratique." *Revue belge de philologie et d'histoire* 67, no. 1: 53–64.

Caseau, Béatrice. 2001. "Les usages médicaux de l'encens et des parfums. Un aspect de la médecine populaire antique et de sa christianisation." In *Air, Miasmes et Contagion. Les épidémies dans l'Antiquité et au Moyen Age*, edited by Sylvie Bazin-Tacchella, Danielle Quéruel, and Evelyne Samama, 75–85. Langres: Dominique Gueniot.

Caseau, Béatrice. 2005. "Parfum et guérison dans le christianisme ancien et byzantin: Des huiles parfumées au *myron* des saints byzantins." In *Les Pères de l'Eglise face à la science médicale de leur temps*, edited by V. Boudon-Millot, B. Pouderon, and Y.-M. Blanchard, 141–91. Paris: Beauchesne.

Caseau, Béatrice. 2007. "Incense and Fragrances from House to Church." In *Material Culture and Well-Being in Byzantium (400–1453)*, edited by M. Grünbart, E. Kislinger, A. Muthesius, and D. Stathako-poulos, 75–92. Vienna: Verlages der Österreichischen Akademie der Wissenschaften.

Caseau, Béatrice. 2012. "Constantin et l'encens. Constantin a-t-il procédé à une révolution liturgique?" In *Costantino prima e dopo Costantino. Constantine Before and After Constantine*, edited by G. Bonamente, N. Lenski, and R. Lizzi, 535–48. Bari: Edipuglia.

Caseau, Béatrice. 2015. "Le parfum de Dieu." In *Parfums et odeurs au Moyen Âge. Science, usage, symboles*, edited by A. Paravicini Bagliani, 3–22. Micrologus' Library 67. Florence: SISMEL Edizioni del Galluzzo.

Casson, L. 1974. *Travel in the Ancient World.* London: Allen and Unwin.

Champault, Dominique. 1996. *La route de l'encens.* Paris: Imprimerie nationale.

Chen, Weiyang, Ilze Vermaak, and Alvaro Viljoen. 2013. "Camphor: A Fumigant during the Black Death and a Coveted Fragrant Wood in Ancient Egypt and Babylon—A Review." *Molecules* 18: 5434–54.

Chouliara-Raïos, Hélène. 2018. "A propos du κῦφι de la lettre fragmentaire P. Warr 13. Le kyphi dans les papyrus grecs." *Pallas. Revue d'études antiques* 108, *Babis Polypragmôn. Mélanges en mémoire de Charalampos Orfanos*: 225–40. https://doi.org/10.4000/pallas.10389.

Christensen, Jakob Tue, and Mikael Manøe Bjerregaard. 2021. "Materiality in Medieval Burials." In *Materiality and Religious Practice in Medieval Denmark*, edited by Sarah Croix and Mads Heilskov, 239–68. Turnhout: Brepols.

Connan, Jacques, Céline Joliot, and Carole Mathe. 2018. "Frankincense and Bitume of the Middle Period (1st Century–5th Century AD) from the Ancient Harbour of Qâni (Yemen)." *Journal of Historical Archaeology and Anthropological Sciences* 3, no. 5: 696–722.

Coulon, JeanCharles. 2016. "Fumigations et rituels magiques. Le rôle des encens et fumigations dans la magie arabe médiévale." *Bulletin d'études orientales* 64, no. 1, *Histoire et anthropologie des odeurs en terre d'Islam à l'époque médiévale*: 179–248.

Crone, Patricia. 1987. *Meccan Trade and the Rise of Islam.* Princeton, NJ: Princeton University Press.

Crowther, Alison et al. 2015. "Use of Zanzibar Copal (Hymenaea verrucose Gaertn.) as Incense at Unguja Ukuu, Tanzania in the 7th–8th Century CE: Chemical Insights into Trade and Indian Ocean Interactions." *Journal of Archaeological Science* 52: 374–90.

Dayagi-Mendels, Michal. 1989. *Perfumes and Cosmetics in the Ancient World.* Jerusalem: Israel Museum.

Dols, Michael, and Adil Gamal. 1984. *Medieval Islamic Medicine: Ibn Ridwân's Treatise "On the Prevention of Bodily Ills in Egypt."* Berkeley: University of California Press.

Donkin, Robin A. 1998. *Dragon's Brain Perfume: A Historical Geography of Camphor.* Leiden: Brill 1998.

Ducène, Jean-Charles. 2016. "Des parfums et des fumées: Les parfums à brûler en Islam médiéval." *Bulletin d'études orientales* 64, *Histoire et anthropologie des odeurs en terre d'Islam à l'époque médiévale*: 159–78.

Ergin, Nina. 2014. "The Fragrance of the Divine: Ottoman Incense Burners and their Context." *The Art Bulletin* 96, no. 1: 70–97.

Everett, Nicholas. 2012. *Pharmacy from Antiquity to the Middle Ages: The Alphabet of Galen.* A critical edition of the Latin text with English translation and commentary. Toronto: University of Toronto Press, 2012.

Evershed, Richard P. 2008. "Organic Residue Analysis in Archaeology: The Archaeological Biomarker Revolution." *Archaeometry* 50, no. 6: 895–924.

Evershed, Richard P., P. F. Van Bergen, T. M. Peakman, E. C. Leigh-Firbank, M. C. Horton, D. Edwards, M. Biddle, B. Jjolbye-Biddle, and P. A. Rowley-Conwy. 1997. "Archaeological Frankincense." *Nature* 390: 667–68.

Frankfurter, David. 2019. *Guide to the Study of Ancient Magic.* Leiden: Brill.

Frère, Dominique, and Laurent Hugot. 2012. *Les huiles parfumées en Méditerranée occidentale et en Gaule (VIIIe siècle AV. – VIIIe s. apr. J.-C.).* Rennes: Presses universitaires de Rennes.

Grasse, Marie-Christine. 2003. *L'Égypte. Parfums d'histoire.* Grasse: Musée international de la Parfumerie.

Groom, Nigel. 1981. *Frankincense and Myrrh: A Study of the Arabian Incense Trade.* London: Longman.

Gyselen, Ryka. 1998. *Parfums d'Orient*. Res orientales XI. Bures-sur-Yvette: Groupe pour l'Etude de la Civilisation du Moyen-Orient.

Harborne, Jeffrey B., Herbert Baxter, and Gerald P. Moss, eds. 1999. *Phytochemical Dictionary: A Handbook of Bioactive Compounds from Plants*. 2nd edn. London: Taylor & Francis.

Hedrick, Tera Lee, and Nina Ergin. 2015. "A Shared Culture of Heavenly Fragrance: A Comparison of Late Byzantine and Ottoman Incense Burners and Censing Practices in Religious Contexts." *Dumbarton Oaks Papers* 69: 331–54.

Hort, Arthur. 1980. *Theophrastus: Enquiry into Plants*, vol. 2. Cambridge, MA: Harvard University Press.

Hovaneissian, Michael, et al. 2008. "Analytical Investigations of Styrax and Benzoin Balsams by HPLC-PAD-Fluorimetry and GC-MS." *Phytochemical Analysis* 19: 301–10.

Kotkar, Parimal, Anubha Khale, and Kadu Pramod. 2011. "Resins from Herbal Origin and a Focus on Their Applications." *International Journal of Pharmaceutical Sciences and Research* 2, no. 5: 1077–85.

Koupadi, Kyriaki, Stamatis C. Boyatzis, Maria Roumpou, Nick Kalogeropoulos, and Despoina Kotzamani. 2021. "Organic Remains in Early Christian Egyptian Metal Vessels: Investigation with Fourier Transform Infrared Spectroscopy and Gas Chromatography – Mass Spectrometry." *Heritage* 4: 3611–29.

Le Maguer, Sterenn. 2015. "The Incense Trade during the Islamic Period." *Proceedings of the Seminar for Arabian Studies* 45: 175–84.

Le Maguer, Sterenn. 2016. "Une archéologie des odeurs: Identifier les encens et leurs usages au Proche et Moyen-Orient (VIIIe–XIIe siècles)." *Bulletin d'études orientales* 64, no. 1, *Histoire et anthropologie des odeurs en terre d'Islam à l'époque médiévale*: 136–58.

Le Maguer-Guillon, Sterenn. 2021. "L'encens dans le monde islamique médiéval (VIIe–XVe siècles): Usages sacrés, usages profanes." In *Rituels religieux et sensorialité (Antiquité et Moyen âge). Parcours de recherche*, edited by Béatrice Caseau, and Elisabetta Neri, 463–74. Milan: Silvana Editoriale.

Li, Jie et al. "Emission Characteristics and Assessment of Potential Health Risks on PM2.5-Bound Organics from Incense Burning." *Atmospheric Pollution Research* 13, no. 3: 101326.

LiDonnici, Lynn. 2001. "Single-Stemmed Wormwood, Pinecones and Myrrh: Expense and Availability of Recipe Ingredients in the Greek Magical Papyri." *Kernos. Revue international et pluridisciplinaire de religion grecque antique* 14: 61–91.

Lilja, S. 1972. *The Treatment of Odours in the Poetry of Antiquity*. Helsinki: Societas Scientiarum Fennica.

Lucas, Alfred. 1911. *Preservative Materials Used by the Ancient Egyptians in Embalming*. Cairo: National Printing Department.

Lucas, Alfred. 1962. *Ancient Egyptian Materials and Industries*. London: Edward Arnold & Co.

Manniche, Lise. 1999. *Sacred Luxuries: Fragrances, Aromatherapy and Cosmetics in Ancient Egypt*. Ithaca, NY: Cornell University Press.

Marín, Manuela. 1998. "The Perfumed Kitchen: Arab Cookbooks from the Islamic East." In *Parfums d'Orient*, edited by Ryka Gyselen, 159–66. Res orientales XI. Bures-sur-Yvette: Groupe pour l'Etude de la Civilisation du Moyen-Orient.

Mathe, Carole, Paul Archier, Gérald Culioli, and Catherine Vieillescazes. 2003. "Caractérisation chimique d'une résine naturelle en Égypte ancienne: Application à un exemple de la collection Victor Loret." *Revue d'Archéométrie* 27: 43–47.

McCormick, Michael. 2001. *Origins of the European Economy: Communications and Commerce AD 300–900*. Cambridge: Cambridge University Press.

McHugh, James. 2013. "Blattes de Byzance in India: Mollusk opercula and the History of Perfumery." *Journal of the Royal Asiatic Society* 23, no. 3: 53–67.

Meyer, Marvin, and Richard Smith, eds. 1994. *Ancient Christian Magic: Coptic Texts of Ritual Power*. San Francisco: Harper.

Miller, James Innes. 1969. *The Spice Trade of the Roman Empire, 29 B.C. to 641 A.D.* Oxford: Clarendon Press.

Modugno, Francesca, Erika Ribechini, and Maria Perla Colombini. 2006. "Chemical Study of Triterpenoid Resinous Materials in Archaeological Findings by Means of Direct Exposure Electron Ionisation Mass Spectrometry and Gas Chromatography." *Rapid Communications in Mass Spectrometry* 20: 1787–800.

Nasrallah, Nawal. 2007. *Annals of the Caliphs' Kitchens: Ibn Sayyār al-Warrāq's Tenth-Century Baghdadi Cookbook*. Leiden: Brill.

Nielsen, Kjeld. 1986. *Incense in Ancient Israel*. Leiden: Brill.

Nutton, Vivian. 1985. "The Drug Trade in Antiquity." *Journal of the Royal Society of Medicine* 78: 138–45.

Patzelt, Maik. 2021. "Favete linguis and the Experience of the Divine: A Cognitively Grounded Approach to Sensory Perception in Roman Religion." In *Sensorium: The Senses in Roman Polytheism*, edited by A. Alvar Nuño, J. Alvar Ezquerra, and G. Woolf, 102–24. Leiden: Brill.

Peacock, David P. S., and David Williams, eds. 2007. *Food for the Gods: New Light on the Ancient Incense Trade*. Oxford: Oxbow.

Pentcheva, Bissera. 2010. *The Sensual Icon: Space, Ritual and the Senses in Byzantium*. University Park: Pennsylvania State University Press.

Perry, Charles, transl. 2020. *Scents and Flavors: A Syrian Cookbook*. New York: New York University Press.

Pirenne, Henri. 1937. *Mahomet et Charlemagne*. Brussels; repr. Paris: Presses universitaires de France, 1992.

Prigent, Daniel. 1996. "Les céramiques unéraires (XIe–XVIIe siècle)." In *Archéologie du cimetière chrétien*, edited by Henri Galinié, and Elisabeth Zadora-Rio, 215–24. Tours: FERACF/La Simarre.

Rackham, Harris, transl. 1955. *Pliny. Natural History*, with an English translation, vol. IV, bk. XII–XVI. Cambridge, MA: Harvard University Press.

Raschke, Manfred G. 1978. "New Studies in Roman Commerce with the East." In *Aufstieg und Niedergang der römischen Welt*, vol. 2, bk. 9/2, edited by Hildegard Temporini, 604–1378. Berlin; New York: De Gruyter.

Rashan, Luay, et al. 2019. "Boswellia Gum Resin and Essential Oils: Potential Health Benefits – An Evidence Based Review." *International Journal of Nutrition, Pharmacology, Neurological Diseases* 9, no. 2: 53–71.

Regert, Martine, Thibault Deviese, Ann-Solenn Le Hô, and Axelle Rougeulle. 2008. "Reconstructing Ancient Yemeni Commercial Routes during the Middle Ages Using Structural Characterization of Terpenoid Resins." *Archaeometry* 50, no. 4: 668–95.

Riddle, John M. 1985. *Dioscorides on Pharmacy and Medicine*. Austin: University of Texas Press.

Rougeulle, Axelle, ed. 2015. *Sharma: Un entrepôt de commerce médiéval sur la côte du Hadramawt (Yemen, c. 980–1180)*. British Foundation for the Study of Arabia Monographs 17. Oxford: Archaeopress.

Scarborough, John. 1991. "The Pharmacology of Sacred Plants, Herbs, and Roots." In *Magika Hiera: Ancient Greek Magic and Religion*, edited by Ch. A. Faraone and D. Obbink, 138–74. New York: Oxford University Press.

Sidebotham, Steven E. 2011. *Berenike and the Ancient Maritime Spice Route*. Berkeley: University of California Press.

Stannard, Jerry. 1982. "Medicinal Plants and Folk Remedies in Pliny, Historia Naturalis." *History and Philosophy of the Life Sciences* 4: 3–23.

Staub, Peter O., Laura Casu, and Mario Leonti. 2016. "Back to the Roots: A Quantitative Survey of Herbal Drugs in Dioscorides' De Materia Medica (ex Matthioli, 1568)." *Phytomedicine* 23: 1043–52.

Strohmaier, Gotthard. 1998. "Reception and Tradition: Medicine in the Byzantine and Arab World." In *Western Medical Thought from Antiquity to the Middle Age*s, edited by Mirko D. Grmek, coordinated by Bernardino Fantini, and translated by Antony Shugaar, 139–69. Cambridge, MA, Harvard University Press.

Tucker, Arthur O. 1986. "Frankincense and Myrrh." *Economic Botany* 40, no. 4: 425–33.

Vallet, Eric. 2011. "Le marché des épices d'Alexandrie et les mutations du grand commerce de la mer Rouge (XIVe–XVe siècle)." In *Alexandrie médiévale*, vol. 4, edited by Christian Décobert, Jean-Yves Empereur, and Christophe Picard, 213–28. Alexandria: Centre d'Etudes Alexandrines.

Van Bergen, P. F., T. M. Peakman, E. C. Leigh-Firbank, and R. E. Evershed. 1997. "Chemical Evidence for Archaeological Frankincense: Boswellic Acids and Their Derivatives in Solvent Soluble and Insoluble Fractions of Resin-Like Materials." *Tetrahedron Letters* 38, no. 48: 8409–12.

Verbanck-Piérard, Annie, Natacha Massar, and Dominique Frère. 2008. *Parfums de l'Antiquité. La rose et l'encens en Méditerranée*. Mariemont: Musée royal de Mariemont.

Yungman, Limor. 2020. "Les livres de cuisine du Moyen-Orient médiéval (IVe–Xe/Xe–XVIe s.)." PhD thesis, EHESS.

Zanetti, Ugo. 1993. "Matarieh, la sainte Famille et les Baumiers." *Analecta Bollandiana* 111: 21–68.

Zohar, Amar, and Ephraim Lev. 2013. "Trends in the Use of Perfumes and Incense in the Near East after the Muslim Conquests." *Journal of the Royal Asiatic Society* 23, no. 1: 11–30.

Incense burner in shape
of cicada, Japan,
late 19th century, 5.1 × 7 cm,
red lacquer (negoro),
The Metropolitan Museum
of Art, New York, Gift of
Reverend and Mrs. Henry
V. E. Stegeman, 1979.

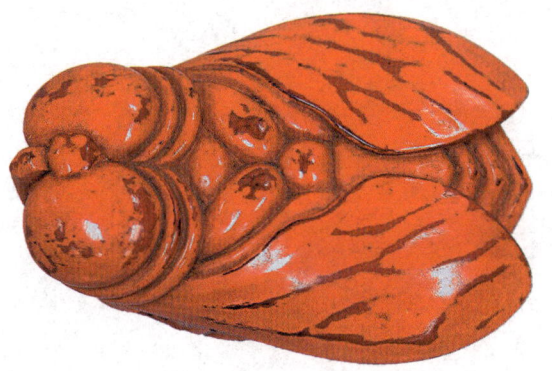

AFTERWORD:
CENSERS AND SENSATION
Jaś Elsner

CENSING AND SENSIBILITY ACROSS
RELIGIOUS CULTURES

The essays collected in this volume, concerned with artifacts that enable olfaction, are a testament to the diverse empirical world of the synesthesia of religion.[1] The big questions to which the specific material evidence of censers give empirical elaboration involve the importance of smell and the senses generally in social life and historical sociology.[2] More precisely, given that the objects discussed in this book are almost entirely ones used in sacred contexts, they address how scent and smell matter in religion, how they define religious experience and phenomenology by pervading space in given pockets of time or across certain liturgical patterns, and how they affect the rhythms of ritual action.[3] While this book is not about scent or incense as such, but rather about the material mechanisms that afford their possibility, censers cannot and should not be separated from these bigger questions. For they are the engines of a sensual ecology of religion which has been insufficiently understood by scholarship but is becoming highly significant.

Let me give one example. The major anthropological literature on pilgrimage in the 1960s and 1970s posited an idealized model of "communitas" as a space of antistructure (that is, unlike the normal social structures of society) in the collective experiences of pilgrims along the journey or at the sacred center.[4] In the following decade this model was taken apart on the entirely correct grounds that no ethnographic data from pilgrims reporting their experiences, ideologies, ideas, subjective responses, or personal views could be shown to fulfill this ideal, and that "contestation" was much more the norm.[5] But if one shifts the focus to the ways the scent-scape, sound-scape and light-scape in any given site are infused to create a powerful sacral atmosphere at particular moments of ritual enactment through collective embodied experience (for instance in the combination of candles, chanting, and incense at dusk in a church or temple or shrine room), then one can potentially reclaim aspects of the concept of communitas as a collectively experienced sensual series of effects engineered by material means and shared physically by the group of people present, whatever their views or accounts. The question becomes to what extent does a shared series of sensual effects on the body within a collective space constitute some element of shared subjectivity. Censers are a fundamental cross-cultural engine for creating such effects—powerful as objects of art within sacred space in their own right and powerful instrumentally as generators of incense.

This book explores how the sense of smell in the embodied ritual participant is engaged through material culture in the form of censers affording olfaction. But its essays show evidence of how multiple senses and their objects are evoked through and by each other. In the case of censers, the materials that generate olfactory experience and, when pictorially represented, evoke the sense of smell, work through visual and haptic means, as well as being attested through textual documentation. In a significant development of the last few decades, scholarship on religion has moved decisively beyond a scripturally founded textuality, bequeathed to us by centuries of Protestant-dominated scholarship, to an understanding of its extremely rich material underpinnings and constructions.[6] As demonstrated by the spread of the censers discussed here—across four continents—it is important that the sensual materiality of religion is a matter of cross-cultural indigenous exploitation and effect. The book might certainly have included discussions of the uses of incense and smell in the Indian religions,[7] which are evidenced by the same kinds of textual, artistic, and archaeological means as the religious cultures discussed here; and might also have explored the place of scent in the anthropologically attested religious worlds of sub-Saharan Africa and Australasia.[8] But the point is that there is a universality about the uses of scent, grounded in the universal human possession of the sense of smell, which—for all the multiple specific cultural and historical variations—has a powerful place in the social, cultural, and religious life of human beings.[9]

The volume's rich discussions give in-depth access to particular instances, modulated by different given cultures, for how religious space and religious practice were constructed in part through scent and its ritualized dissemination within specific liturgies or contexts. Censers appear here as surviving archaeological artifacts, as representations in works of art that allude to religious activity, as accoutrements of architectural settings, and above all in relation to bodies. They may be used by the body (as in the classic Christian swinging censer or the incense stick of East Asia), they may determine a space around which the body moves (as in the standing incense burner—thymiaterion, from the Greek θυμιάειν *thymiaein*, "to smoke"—of the kind used in Mesopotamian and Mediterranean antiquity). But in all cases they have an active purpose in generating a mediating or equalizing medium between bodies (for example, to modulate foul smells in large crowds), something like the use of loud music to accompany the screams of sacrificed animals as represented in ancient Roman marble reliefs,[10] and they relate beyond the individuals who collectively smell the scents they create to the space or wind or air around the body.

Censers as represented in art objects that were themselves accoutrements of, or decorations within, the spaces of material religion offer a visual self-reflection on religious practice through representation. One might cite the many flaming censers hanging from chains alongside lamps in what purports to be a church interior, in the sixth-century fresco from the north apse of the Church of St. Pshoi at the Red Monastery in the Nile valley (illustrated by Nathan Dennis as Figure 2). These determine the space represented as sacred as well as its specific celebration of the Mother of God. Strikingly both lamps and censers use heat in parallel ways to generate the light and odors of a Christian holy place. The human-sized thymiateria represented in such Athenian pots as the crater and cylix illustrated by Milette Gaifman (her Figures 5 and 7) or the Mesopotamian examples shown by Kiersten Neumann (see her Figures 1A–E) evoke the sanctity of the envisaged site, often alongside other imagery such as altars. The fantastical rise of incense smoke into the forms of fungi symbolizing immortality or pagodas in Ming Chinese Buddhist art (in Figures 6, 7 and 8 of Yao Ning's chapter) or the similar rising incense smoke from the great brazen censer atop a white marble column placed between the Virgin and the angel in the encaustic Annunciation, perhaps painted as early as the eighth century, from Deir al-Surian in Egypt (Dennis's Figure 4) imply the potential supernatural effects of the subjects evoked. The censer (and its flame or smoke) in these different religious contexts from very different times and parts of Afro-Eurasia as a visual object—evoking smell, evoking the generation of scent, evoking the technologies and economies that enabled the uses of incense within and as part of religion—is a powerful symbolic, and we may say ideological, device in such images.

The technology of incense—the human production of beautiful aromatics to appease the gods and to define sacred contexts or charged moments of ritual activity—is at the heart of the censer's purpose. The censer is the engine for both these functions, the means by which a particular olfactory transformation comes about, and at the same time an essential element of the sacral furniture of material religion across cultures. The censer's act of transformation is a votive offering—arguably a miniature sacrifice in a miniature flaming altar—transmuting valuable materials from across the world (the range of these from antiquity is well captured in Beatrice Caseau's chapter in this book). The censer thus offers the site of a final ritual repurposing of the complex logistics and economics of long-distance trade (that is to say, the social and commercial lives of those involved in worship) into an exchange with the divine world. The fine smells and (as in the cultural systems of Mesoamerica described by Claudia Brittenham) the clouds of smoke it produces are an appeasement of the gods and a plea for their mercy.[11] In this sense, the system of liturgical energization offered by the use of censers marks space in two directions. On the one hand, it is about collective human relationships within a defined space temporarily marked and fumigated by a particular perfume, which effectively constructs a scented sensual liminality of sacred boundaries,[12] and by this means suggests a collective subjectivity for those present through the shared bodily experience of the pervasive scent. On the other, as a destructive sacrificial offering of precious, expensively traded, and specially collected materials, it is directly about communicating with the divine.

INCENSE, CENSERS, AND HISTORICAL CHANGE

The most momentous transformation in the history of Afro-Eurasia, especially and above all in the practices, beliefs, and materiality of religion, took place with incredible rapidity in the course of the fourth century CE. Between 312, when the Roman emperor Constantine legalized Christianity, and the 380s, when his successors instituted bans on all forms of pagan religion, on pain of death,[13] millennia of polytheistic practices and convictions were eliminated from the social, cultural, and political landscape. Their final extirpation—especially in rural pockets where traditional practices were hard to eliminate and among philosophically committed intellectual pagans in some urban centers—took a while longer, but frankly there are no competing examples of such all-pervasive and universal cultural change in the history of the West. That instantiation of Abrahamic monotheism in all the lands of the Roman world west of Sasanian Persia would itself be followed in the seventh century by the extraordinarily rapid conquest of the Asian mainland up to the borders of India, all of North Africa, and Spain by Arab armies fighting beneath the banner of the Prophet Mohammed, whose opposition to paganism was at least as stringent as that of the least tolerant Christians.

What this meant for the practices of religion is so immense it can hardly be grasped. Swiftly, the making of three-dimensional statuary and the use of figurines in ritual action and social life vanished in the lands taken over by Christianity and later by Islam.[14] In the arena of sacrificial action, three kinds of offerings were normal in polytheism—both at the private level of individual practice and domestic lived religion,[15] and at the official level of the public rituals of the state.[16] Here is how the great orator and novelist Apuleius puts it, in relation to his personal devotions, in his *Apology*, composed in the middle years of the second century CE in North Africa:

> I usually carry with me, wherever I go, a statuette of some god, keeping it among my books. On feasts I offer up incense (*ture*) and wine to it, and sometimes an animal victim. (*Pro se de magia* 63)

> Nam morem mihi habeo, quoquo eam, simulacrum alicuius dei inter libellos conditum gestare eique diebus festis ture et mero et aliquando uictima supplicare.

That is, his worship consists of offerings that may be of incense, of liquid (in this case a wine libation), and of animal sacrifice (effectively a blood libation). The pattern is confirmed in the anti-Pagan legislation of the fourth century. For example, in a law promulgated by the emperors Theodosius, Arcadius, and Honorius in Constantinople on November 8, 392, we find the following (*Codex Theodosianus* 16.10.12. proem):

> No person at all, of any class or order whatsoever of men or of dignities, whether he occupies a position of power or has completed such honors, whether he is powerful by the lot of his birth or humble in lineage, legal status, and fortune, shall sacrifice an innocent victim to senseless images in any place at all or in any city. He shall not, by more secret wickedness, venerate his *lar* with fire, his *genius* with wine, his *penates* with fragrant odors; he shall not burn lights to them, place incense before them, or suspend wreaths for them.

> Nullus omnino ex quolibet genere ordine hominum dignitatum vel in potestate positus vel honore perfunctus, sive potens sorte nascendi seu humilis genere condicione ortuna in nullo penitus loco, in nulla urbe sensu carentibus simulacris vel insontem victimam caedat vel secretiore piaculo larem igne, mero genium, penates odore veneratus accendat lumina, imponat tura, serta suspendat.

The prohibition—on both public religious activity and private worship ("more secret wickedness," *secretiore piaculo*)—again covers offerings of animal sacrifice and of wine, adds the offering of flowers ("suspend wreaths"), and above all repeats its objection to the use of fire and incense for the "senseless images" of pagan gods, including the multitude of household deities (*lares, penates,* and *genii*).

In the visual culture we find all three kinds of sacrifice richly represented.[17] In the interior of the east pier of the Arch of the Argentarii in the Forum Boarium in Rome—famous for the iconoclasm of the emperor Geta by his brother Caracalla conducted after his fratricide—we see a fine large-scale panel of the emperor Septimius Severus, his wife Julia Domna, and the now destroyed figure of their son Geta to the right, with the emperor conducting a libation over an altar laden with fruit [Figure 1].[18] Above them is a panel of victories carrying a wreath, while immediately below is a frieze of implements used in the ritual culture of Roman religion and especially sacrifice. Beneath this is a frieze showing the act of killing a bull. Together, the reliefs of this pier constitute a *Gesamptkunstwerk* of pagan sacrificial offerings, to which we must add, on the outer side of the west pier in the same place as the panel with victories (and perhaps originally repeated in the now lost outer side of the east pier), a panel of four figures flanking a flaming thymiaterion [Figure 2]. The sprinkling of incense on an altar is a significant aspect of the sacrificial imagery of the Roman Empire—for instance in the famous later fourth-century ivory plaque from Rome commissioned by the Symmachi in visual defiance of the anti-pagan legislation [Figure 3],[19] or in the many painted and relief images of sacrificial action that were excavated from the city of Dura Europos on the western bank of the Euphrates which was destroyed in the wars with the Sasanians in the 250s CE [Figures 4 and 5],[20] or equally in Roman North Africa [Figure 6].[21] Strikingly, the tall flaming altars represented in the images from Roman Syria (by contrast with the lower more compact altars of Rome) resemble thymiateria in shape and form—combining the function of censer with that of central sacrificial focus (notably Figure 4).

However, my point in all this is that when the Christians disestablished pagan religions and replaced them with their own monotheism, with a vast range of newly invented ritual practices to energize huge new churches, the aspects of the ancient votive paraphernalia that survived were the use of incense and lights—as the Christian chapters of this volume so well attest. The end of blood sacrifice and the abolition of libation did not mean the elimination of olfaction or scented offerings, although incense could no longer be offered to what the Christians classed as idols. Sacred scent and the censer—whether hand-held and movable or monumental and fixed—slid under the hard line that changed so much in social and religious attitudes between the pagan world and Christianity. Ultimately this non-change—in many ways a very surprising continuity between ancient polytheistic and Abrahamic religions—depends on the key role of incense in biblical scripture, especially the ancient accounts and practices recorded in the Hebrew Bible (discussed in this volume by Karen Stern). These were accorded a complex translation into Greek in the remarkable project of the Septuagint, when the Jewish scriptures were translated not only into the Hellenic language but into a series of non-Semitic concepts and categories.[22] Most importantly in the Christian context, the Septuagint would serve as the Old Testament for the Christian Bible, whose first evangelist famously uses incense to announce and venerate the Epiphany, as one of the gifts of the Magi:

Figure 1

Figure 2

Figure 3

Figures 4–6

Figure 1
Arch of the Argentarii, Rome,
inner face of the east pier,
marble relief veneer with
figural imagery between two
Corinthian pilasters with
acanthus decoration showing a
wreath carried by Victories
at the top, the emperor
Septimius Severus with his
wife Julia Domna pouring a
libation over an altar with the
excised space to the right that
once included their son Geta
(large central panel), a frieze of
sacrificial implements below
them and a relief of bull
sacrifice at the bottom.
Completed 204 CE, iconoclasm
conducted in 212 CE. Photo:
after Elsner 2012, figure 6.3.

Figure 2
Arch of the Argentarii, Rome,
upper part of the outer face of
the west pier, marble relief
veneer with thymiaterion flanked
by four figures, about 204 CE.
Photo: J. Elsner.

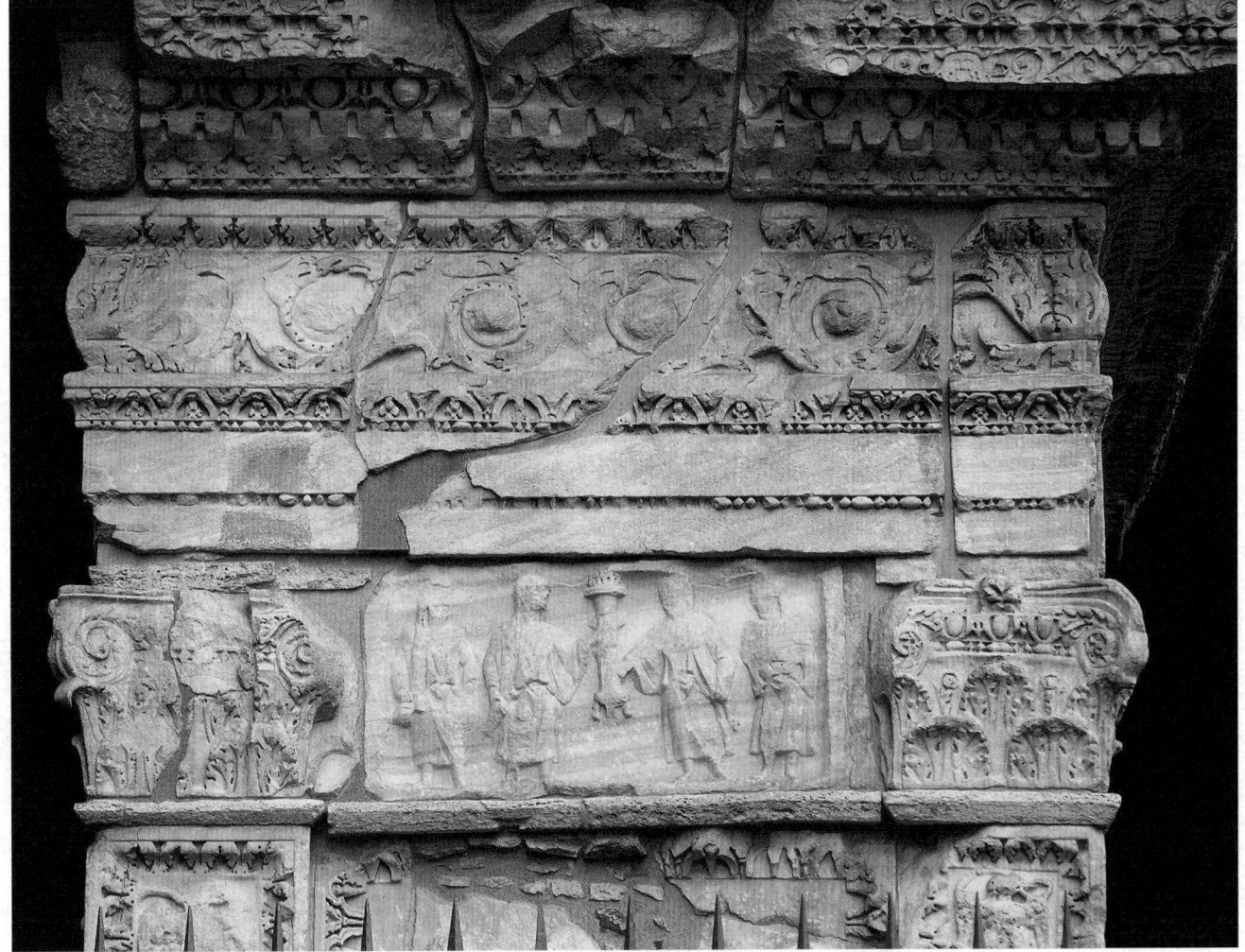

Figure 3
Symmachorum ivory leaf from the right side of a diptych made in Rome, a female figure with a girl acolyte sprinkles incense over a flaming altar beneath an oak tree, end of the 5th century, Victoria and Albert Museum. Photo: after Elsner 2012, figure 6.10.

Figure 4
Temple known as "of the Palmyrene gods" or "of Bel," south
wall of the "naos," fresco
showing Conon and his family
making sacrifice, with three
priests in white conical hats
sprinkling incense on tall
thymiaterion-like altars, now
largely destroyed, Dura Europos
in Syria, late second or early
3rd century CE, fragments in the
Damascus Museum, tinted
print of J. Breasted's on site
photograph of 1925.
Photo: after Cumont 1926.

Figure 5
Vicinity of the Palmyrene Gate,
limestone relief of Julius
Aurelius Malochas sprinkling
incense on a tall altar in
the presence of Nemesis and
beneath a bust of Helios,
Dura Europos in Syria, 245 CE,
Yale University Art Gallery.
Photo: after Elsner 2012,
figure 6.22.

Figure 6
Neo-Punic votive stele, marking
a grave, with a girl sprinkling
incense on an altar in the centre,
Saturn between the Dioscuri
at the top and an image of bull
sacrifice below, Central Tunisia
(Roman North Africa), 2nd
or 3rd century CE, British
Museum. Photo (by M. MacCarty)
after Elsner 2012, figure 6.15.

And when they were come into the house, they saw the young
child with Mary his mother, and fell down, and worshiped
him: and when they had opened their treasures, they presented unto him gifts; gold, and frankincense (λίβανον),[23] and
myrrh. (Matthew 2.11)

καὶ ἐλθόντες εἰς τὴν οἰκίαν εἶδον τὸ παιδίον μετὰ Μαρίας τῆς
μητρὸς αὐτοῦ, καὶ πεσόντες προσεκύνησαν αὐτῷ, καὶ ἀνοίξαντες
τοὺς θησαυροὺς αὐτῶν προσήνεγκαν αὐτῷ δῶρα, χρυσὸν καὶ
λίβανον καὶ σμύρναν.

Similarly, despite the many changes in cultural and devotional attitudes that
accompanied the Islamic conquest, as Margaret Graves shows in her chapter of this volume, Islamic censers, like the remarkable example from about
800 CE found in Gävle in Sweden, where it had come as Viking booty (her
Figures 2–6), owe their forms, functions, and techniques of working (perhaps
their very workshops and artisans) to traditions of Christian censer-making
in the late antique Mediterranean (see the examples in her Figures 7 and 8).
Again, despite extraordinary cultural and doctrinal change, initially conducted at great speed and then bedded in as lasting transformation over
centuries, the uses of sacred scent in sensual religion and the instruments
carefully created for their affordance show significant continuity. The case
of Islam is striking because, however comfortable it may have been with
tracing an ancestry in religions of the book promulgated by earlier prophets
than Mohammed (notably Judaism and Christianity), the culture of sacral
olfaction was shared with the "pagan idolatries" of the east—Jainism, Buddhism, the Hindu cults of India—against which Muslim dominion abutted
from the end of the seventh century and much of which Islam would venture
to conquer in the succeeding centuries.

In other words, the censer and its product—scented smoke pervading
an environment to intimate a non-normative space of access to the divine—
were not only ubiquitous across world cultures, geographies, and social ecol-
ogies but extraordinarily unassailable by historical change. The exception
to this, as well demonstrated in Alison Stielau's chapter on the censer after
the Reformation, is the complex of self-consciousness and indeed explicit
disagreement about incense among varieties of Protestants. While Martin
Luther—in many ways an orthodox Roman Catholic except in his refusal to
accept Papal authority (he was a firm upholder of the Eucharistic transubstantiation of the Host into the Body of Christ)[24]—was happy with the material accoutrements of ritual, including paintings and incense, many of his
more stringent associates and Calvinist successors were not. The battle over
materiality and sensuality in religion has raged in Protestant circles (as well
as in Protestant disputes with Catholics) for five centuries, with incense as
one of the items of debate.[25] As in the disagreements between "Low Church"
Evangelicals and the "Smells and Bells" High Anglicans of the Church of
England, the issue is one of continuing and fundamental dispute about theological stakes much bigger than incense itself—it is, in Christian language,
about the place of materiality and embodiment in religion, the relation of
the body and the senses to the possibility of salvation, the place of material
things and the created world in relation to the spirit. As Stielau shows, the

humble censer becomes a kind of material focus, what Freud once called a "cathexis" (*Besetzung*),[26] for the intense beliefs and passions generated by the great religious divides inaugurated in the early modern period.

THE CENSER AS GADGET:
TOWARDS A MATERIAL SEMIOTICS

The cathectic focalization on material objects within culture and especially religion (one may think also of iconoclastic attacks on images and statues) always gives pause for thought. The object comes to carry greater ideological and polemical weight than its simple materiality can bear. In the case of censers, across cultures and millennia, they offer a dual material ontology. On the one hand they are objects in their own right—sometimes very simple containers and sometimes, as we have repeatedly seen in this book, really fine works of human ingenuity and manufacture, works of art. On the other hand, they are always instruments, objects with an active purpose whose effects in producing olfactory sensations are of a different sensory order (that of smell) from their own normally available sensible materiality in sight and touch. In this sense they belong to a very rich category of material objects that have never been adequately theorized in art history or archaeology. They belong to the world of lamps, candle-sticks, drinking cups, musical instruments, cooking vessels, bronze cauldrons, toiletry caskets, and many other such items whose functional uses engage different senses from the ones of their primary access and whose simplicity of function may nonetheless belie the lavish workmanship in expensive materials that they are sometimes afforded. I am arguing that censers belong in a class of objects, let us call them "gadgets," for the instrumental transformation of natural materials into something else,[27] in this case a scenting of the air and a casting of a sensuous infusion across the immateriality of space. Like lamps, they enable a constrained material container to use fire to create a transformative intervention in space and in the sensory appreciation of space by embodied human beings.[28] In the case of censers (as Claudia Brittenham's paper cogently argues, that instrumental function is to take solids with aromatic potential but little impact in themselves and transform them into gases with a large pervasive force that is both olfactory and visible in the movement of smoke.

The Oxford English Dictionary defines "gadget" as "a (small) mechanical or electronic device, especially one regarded as ingenious or novel; an ingenious or practical device or tool" and also as "an ingenious or novel procedure; an ingenious trick or scheme; a gimmick." Most contemporary theory of the gadget as a material object is focused on the digital age—notably the computer and the cell phone. One can see how the latter—a small artifact capable of being carried in one pocket, intimate to the body and so responsive to touch, which affords such a range of (virtual) sensual experience from speaking by phone to watching movies, to listening to music, and offering satnav directional guidance—is an instrument that couples extraordinary power with intense personal closeness for its possessor. My point is that such devices are far from new and certainly pre-digital, although their effects (both embodied and formless) did not depend on wifi or data.

In understanding the prehistory and material psychology of the gadget as a device that links the body and an embodied subjectivity through material objects to a vast virtuality of fantasy and desire, ancient and historical kinds of object—like the censers in this book—are key items. Issues of substantive import include the materials in which they are made, that in the case of censers need to be capable of withstanding the high heat of burning charcoal that enables the scent to diffuse. This means the employment of clay, stone, and metal, but not (for example) wood, wax, or bone. At the same time, the ways these materials need to be susceptible to cleaning (given the inevitable blackening caused by smoke and soot) and potentially to mending given that censers sustain high-risk levels of treatment (especially when swung on chains or participant in ritual movement). These kinds of gadget may be figural in form and realization (as in Figures 2–4 from Mesoamerica in Claudia Brittenham's chapter) but are more often forms of furniture or miniature architecture whose piercings or openings have functional value in diffusing scent (one thinks of Brittenham's Figure 1, Kirsten Neumann's Figures 4B and 5A, Milette Gaifman's Figure 1, the censers both Byzantine and Islamic illustrated in Margaret Graves's chapter or the wonderful example of miniature gothic architecture from Ramsay Abbey, now in the V&A, illustrated by Alison Steilau as her Figure 2). Their surface decoration may include iconography, whether flat-painted, incised, inlaid, or in relief. For instance, one might cite Brittenham's Figures 8 and 9 (painted), or Margaret Graves's Figures 2–4 and 6–8 (pierced, incised, and engraved), or the large corpus of Syrian censers of late antiquity and the early middle ages of which examples are illustrated by Nathan Dennis in his Figures 9 and 10 (decorated with reliefs).[29] How essential are such decorative aspects to the function of a given object in its cultural and historical context? To what extent is ornament or figural form largely tangential to a censer's prime purpose as an artifact designed to give an olfactory affordance, to have an effect in space and time?

A full exploration of the immense conceptual complexity of the censer as a category of this kind, let alone the totality of pre-modern gadgets, is beyond a brief Afterword to this volume. But the substantive point is that this conceptual work needs to be done, and the rich, historically embedded case studies of this book represent a significant starting point in the study of at least one class of such gadgets.

ENDNOTES

1 For some scholarly work in this arena, one might suggest Meyer 2008; Keane 2008; Lidke 2011; Promey 2014; Harvey and Hughes 2018; Daelemans 2020; Gunderson 2021.

2 On the senses in historical sociology one might suggest the journal *The Senses and Society* established in 2006.

3 On the senses in religion and ritual, see e.g. Bull and Mitchell 2015; Watts 2018 and 2019.

4 The classic studies, focused on Christianity, are by Victor (and Edith) Turner: Turner 1973 and 1974; Turner and Turner 1978, 240–45.

5 See esp. Sallnow 1981; Eade and Sallnow 1991; Coleman and Elsner 1991; Coleman 2021, 57–135.

6 Notably one might cite the journal *Material Religion* established in 2005 with e.g. McDannell 1995; Morgan 2009; Houtman and Meyer 2011; Hazard 2013; Plate 2015; Chidester 2018; Hutchings and McKenzie 2018; Morgan 2021.

7 E.g. McHugh 2012 (generally); McHugh 2011 and Schopen 2015 (on Buddhism); McHugh 2014 (on Hinduism).

8 E.g. Low 2005 or Moeran 2007 (generally on anthropology of scent); Diaz 2012 for an "olfactory history of Oceania"; Rasmussen 1999 for West Africa.

9 For scent in Christian religious practice, see e.g. Harvey 2006; Brazinski and Frixell 2013; for Islam see Evans 2002; Bursi 2020.

10 On music in Greek and Roman sacrifice, see e.g. Goulaki-Voutira 2004; Vendries and Péché 2004, 405–9; Sfyroeras 2020. For the power of soundscapes (of which this is one example), see e.g. Pentcheva 2018; Calvert 2019; Della Dora 2021; Kühtz and Rizzi 2021; Pentcheva 2021.

11 The literature on votive exchange is very rich. See on reciprocity in the votive system e.g. Mauss 1923–24; Osborne 2004; Wood 2011; Peels 2016; Elsner 2018, 4–6.

12 The classic literature on liminality includes Van Gennep 1960 and Turner 1969.

13 For the legislative assault on paganism in the fourth century, see the Codex Theodosianus 16.10.1–25 with Curran 2000, 161–217 and Leone 2013, 40–46.

14 On statues, see Smith and Ward-Perkins 2016; on figurines, see Elsner 2020.

15 On "lived religion," see e.g. Rüpke 2016; Albrecht et al. 2018; Gasparini et al. 2020.

16 The literature on sacrifice in antiquity is extremely rich. See e.g. Scheid 2005; Prescendi 2007; Petropoulou 2008; Knust and Varhelyi 2011; Faraone and Naiden 2012; Naiden 2013.

17 The classic and comprehensive account of imperial Roman sacrificial reliefs is Scott Ryberg 1955. On the use of incense in Greek and Roman ritual, see e.g. Simon and Sarian 2004 with bibliography and references.

18 See e.g. Elsner 2005. On the iconoclasm see Elsner 2003, 212–16 and Varner 2004, 156–99.

19 See e.g. Kinney 1994.

20 On the sacrificial images of Dura, see Elsner 2001.

21 Elsner 2012, 139–41.

22 For just one aspect of the complexities of biblical plant hermeneutics regarding the word we translate as "cedar" (itself also a fragrance derived from a kind of wood), see e.g. Naude and Miller-Naude 2018.

23 The same word is used for frankincense in the Septuagint's version of Exodus 30.34 and Song of Songs 3.6 and 4.14.

24 E.g. Burnett 2017; Trigg 2017.

25 On the Reformation and sensual religion, see Milner 2011; de Boer and Göttler 2013; Baum 2019. Specifically on olfaction, Baum 2013.

26 E.g. Nagera 2014, 77–96.

27 By "gadget" here I mean a device that is used instrumentally to transform what it contains into something else and acquires particular material forms through which it is articulated. For a theorized account of televisions and computers as gadgets, see e.g. Adler 2016, 176–212; for a general account, mainly concerned with the digital, see Hands 2019, with discussion of complexity e.g. at 14–15, definition as "a device that mediates between the user and the world, other users and other devices" at 20, on materialism at 33–57.

28 For lamps, light, and the wonder they elicit, see e.g. Bielfeldt 2016; Neer 2018, 480–88; Bielfeldt et al. 2022.

29 Fricke and Flood forthcoming.

BIBLIOGRAPHY

Adler, C. A. 2016. *Celebricities: Media Culture and the Phenomenology of Gadget Commodity Life*. New York: Fordham University Press.

Albrecht, J. et al. 2018. "Remaking Religion: The Lived Ancient Religion Approach." *Religion* 48: 1–26.

Baum, J. 2013. "From Incense to Idolatry: The Reformation of Olfaction in Late Medieval German Ritual." *The Sixteenth Century Journal* 44: 323–44.

Baum, J. 2019. *Reformation of the Senses: The Paradox of Religious Belief and Practice in Germany*. Urbana: University of Illinois Press.

Bielfeldt, R. 2016. "Sight and Light: Reified Gazes and Looking Artefacts in the Greek Cultural Imagination." In *Sight and the Ancient Senses*, edited by M. Squire, 123–42. London: Routledge.

Bielfeldt, R. et al., eds. 2022. *Neues Licht aus Pompeji*. Exhibition catalogue. Munich. Oppenheim: Nünnerich-Asmus.

Brazinski, P., and A. Frixell. 2013. "The Smell of Relics: Authenticating Saintly Bones and the Role of Scent in the Sensory Experience of Medieval Christian Veneration." *Papers from the Institute of Archaeology* 23: 1–15.

Bull, M., and J. Mitchell, eds. 2015. *Ritual, Performance and the Senses*. London: Bloomsbury Academic.

Burnett, A. 2017. "Luther and the Eucharistic Controversy." *Dialog* 56: 145–50.

Bursi, A. 2020. "Scents of Space: Early Islamic Pilgrimage, Perfume, and Paradise." *Arabica* 67: 200–234.

Calvert, A. 2019. "Singing with Durham Cathedral: Exploring the Relationship between Architecture and Singing." *The Senses and Society* 14: 271–83.

Chidester, D. 2018. *Religion: Material Dynamics*. Oakland: University of California Press.

Coleman, S. 2021. *Powers of Pilgrimage: Religion in a World of Movement*. New York: New York University Press.

Coleman, S., and J. Elsner. 1991. "Contesting Pilgrimage: Current Views and Future Directions." *Cambridge Anthropology* 15: 63–73.

Cumont, Franz. 1926. *Fouilles de Doura-Europos (1922–1923). Bibliothèque archéologique et historique 11*, 2 vols. Paris.

Curran, J. 2000. *Pagan City and Christian Capital*. Oxford: Clarendon Press.

Daelemans, B. 2020. "Healing Space: The Synaesthetic Quality of Church Architecture." *Religions* 11: 635. doi:10.3390/rel11120635.

De Boer, W., and C. Göttler, eds. 2013. *Religion and the Senses in Early Modern Europe*. Leiden: Brill.

Della Dora, V. 2021. "Listening to the Archive: Historical Geographies of Sound." *Geography Compass* 15: e12599. doi:10.1111/gec3.12599.

Diaz, V. 2012. "Sniffing Oceania's Behind." *The Contemporary Pacific* 24: 324–44.

Eade, J., and M. J. Sallnow, eds. 1991. *Contesting the Sacred: The Anthropology of Christian Pilgrimage*. London: Routledge.

Elsner, J. 2001. "Cultural Resistance and the Visual Image: The Case of Dura Europos." *Classical Philology* 96: 269–304.

Elsner, J. 2003. "Iconoclasm and the Preservation of Memory." In *Monuments and Memory, Made and Unmade*, edited by R. Nelson and M. Olin, 209–31. Chicago: University of Chicago Press.

Elsner, J. 2005. "Sacrifice and Narrative in the Arch of the Argentarii in Rome." *Journal of Roman Archaeology* 18: 83–98.

Elsner, J. 2012. "Sacrifice in Late Roman Art." In *Greek and Roman Animal Sacrifice: Ancient Victims, Modern Observers*, edited by C. Faraone and F. Naiden, 120–66. Cambridge: Cambridge University Press.

Elsner, J. 2018. "Place, Shrine, Miracle." In *Agents of Faith: Votive Objects in Time and Place*, edited by I. Weinryb, 3–25. New Haven, CT: Yale University Press.

Elsner, J. 2020. "The Death of the Figurine: Reflections on an Abrahamic Abstention." In *Figurines: Figuration and the Sense of Scale*, edited by J. Elsner, 130–81. Oxford: Oxford University Press.

Evans, S. 2002. "The Scent of a Martyr." *Numen* 49: 193–311.

Faraone, C., and F. Naiden, eds. 2012. *Greek and Roman Animal Sacrifice*. Cambridge: Cambridge University Press.

Flood, F. B., and B. Fricke. forthcoming 2023. *Tales Things Tell: Material Histories of Early Globalisms*. Princeton, NJ: Princeton University Press.

Gasparini, V. et al., eds. 2020. *Lived Religion in the Ancient Mediterranean World*. Berlin: De Gruyter.

Goulaki-Voutira, A. 2004. "Musik bei öffentlichen und privaten Opfern." In *Thesaurus Cultus und Rituum Antiquorum*, vol. 2, edited by V. Lambrinoudakis and J. Balty, 371–75. Los Angeles: Getty Publications.

Gunderson, J. 2021. "Feeling Apollo: Sensory Engagement in the Sanctuary of Apollo at Klaros." *Material Religion* 17: 405–28.

Hands, J. 2019. *Gadget Consciousness: Collective Thought, Will and Action in the Age of Social Media*. London: Pluto Press.

Harvey, G., and J. Hughes, eds. 2018. *Sensual Religion: Religion and the Five Senses*. Sheffield: Equinox Publishing.

Harvey, S. A. 2006. *Scenting Salvation: Ancient Christianity and the Olfactory Imagination*. Berkeley: University of California Press.

Hazard, S. 2013. "The Material Turn in the Study of Religion." *Religion and Society: Advances in Research* 4: 58–78.

Houtman, D., and B. Meyer, eds. 2011. *Things: Religion and the Question of Materiality*. New York: Fordham University Press.

Hutchings, T., and J. McKenzie, eds. 2018. *Materiality and the Study of Religion: The Stuff of the Sacred*. London: Routledge.

Keane, W. 2008. "The Evidence of the Senses and the Materiality of Religion." *Journal of the Royal Anthropological Institute* 14: 110–27.

Kinney, D. 1994. "The Iconography of the Ivory Diptych Nicomachorum-Symmachorum." *Jahrbuch für Antike und Christentum* 37: 64–96.

Knust, J., and Z. Varhelyi, eds. 2011. *Ancient Mediterranean Sacrifice*. Oxford: Oxford University Press.

Kühtz, S., and C. Rizzi. 2021. "Sound Atmospheres in Architecture: A Case Study in the South of Italy." *The Senses and Society* 16: 278–91.

Leone, A. 2013. *The End of the Pagan City*. Oxford: Oxford University Press.

Lidke, J. 2011. "The Resounding Field of Visualised Self-Awareness: The Generation of Synesthetic Consciousness in the Sri Yantra Rituals of Nity ṣoḍa ik ṛnava Tantra." *Journal of Hindu Studies* 4: 248–57.

Low, K. 2005. "Ruminations on Smell as a Sociocultural Phenomenon." *Current Sociology* 53: 397–417.

Mauss, M. 1923–24. "Essai sur le don. Forme et raison de l'échange dans les sociétés archaïques." *L'année sociologique* 1: 30–186.

McDannell, C. 1995. *Material Christianity: Religion and Popular Culture in America*. New Haven, CT: Yale University Press.

McHugh, J. 2011. "The Incense Trees of the Land of Emeralds: The Exotic Material Culture of 'Kāmaśāstra'." *Journal of Indian Philosophy* 39: 63–100.

McHugh, J. 2012. *Sandalwood and Carrion: Smell in Indian Religion and Culture*. Oxford: Oxford University Press.

McHugh, J. 2014. "From Precious to Polluting: Tracing the History of Camphor in Hinduism." *Material Religion* 10: 30–53.

Meyer, B. 2008. "Media and the Senses in the Making of Religious Experience: An Introduction." *Material Religion* 4: 124–34.

Milner, M. 2011. *The Senses and the English Reformation*. Farnham: Ashgate.

Moeran, B. 2007. "Marketing Scents and the Anthropology of Smell." *Social Anthropology* 15: 153–68.

Morgan, D. 2009. *Religion and Material Culture: The Matter of Belief*. London: Routledge.

Morgan, D. 2021. *The Thing About Religion: An Introduction to the Material Study of Religions*. Chapel Hill: University of North Carolina Press.

Nagera, H., ed. 2014. *Basic Psychoanalytic Concepts on the Libido Theory*. London: Routledge.

Naiden, F. 2013. *Smoke Signals for the Gods*. Oxford: Oxford University Press.

Naude, J., and C. Miller-Naude. 2018. "Lexicography and the Translation of 'Cedars of Lebanon' in the Septuagint." *Hervormde Teologiese Studies* 74, no. 3: 1–13.

Neer, R. 2018. "Amber, Oil and Fire: Greek Sculpture beyond Bodies." *Art History* 41, no. 3: 466–91.

Osborne, R. 2004. "Hoards, Votives, Offerings: The Archaeology of the Dedicated Object." *World Archaeology* 36: 1–10.

Peels, S. 2016. "Thwarted Expectations of Divine Reciprocity." *Mnemosyne* 69: 551–71.

Pentcheva, B. V., ed. 2018. *Aural Architecture in Byzantium: Music, Acoustics, and Ritual*. Abingdon: Routledge.

Pentcheva, B. V., ed. 2021. *Icons of Sound: Voice, Architecture, and Imagination in Medieval Art*. New York: Routledge.

Petropoulou, M.-Z. 2008. *Animal Sacrifice in Ancient Greek Religion, Judaism and Christianity 100 BC to AD 200*. Oxford: Oxford University Press.

Plate, S. 2015. *Key Terms in Material Religion*. London: Bloomsbury.

Prescendi, F. 2007. *Décrire et comprendre le sacrifice: Les réflexions des Romains sur leur propre religion à partir de la littérature antiquaire*. Stuttgart: Franz Steiner Verlag.

Promey, S. 2014. *Sensational Religion: Sensory Cultures in Material Practice*. New Haven, CT: Yale University Press.

Rasmussen, S. 1999. "Making Better 'Scents' in Anthropology: Aroma in Tuareg Sociocultural Systems and the Shaping of Ethnography." *Anthropological Quarterly* 72: 55–73.

Rüpke, J. 2016. *On Roman Religion: Lived Religion and the Individual in Ancient Rome*. Ithaca, NY: Cornell University Press.

Sallnow, M. 1981. "Communitas Reconsidered: The Sociology of Andean Pilgrimage." *Man* 16: 163–82.

Scheid, J. 2005. *Quand faire, c'est croire: Les rites sacrificiels des Romains*. Paris: Aubier.

Schopen, G. 2015. "The Fragrance of the Buddha, the Scent of Monuments, and the Odor of Images in Early India." *Bulletin de l'École française d'Extrême-Orient* 101: 11–30.

Scott Ryberg, I. 1955. *Rites of the State Religion in Roman Art (MAAR 22)*. Rome: American Academy in Rome.

Sfyroeras, P. 2020. "The Music of Sacrifice." *Greek and Roman Musical Studies* 8: 97–110.

Simon, E., and H. Sarian. 2004. "Rauchopfer."
In *Thesaurus Cultus und Rituum Antiquorum*,
vol. 1, edited by V. Lambrinoudakis and J. Balty,
255–68. Los Angeles: Getty Publications.

Smith, R. R. R., and B. Ward-Perkins, eds. 2016.
The Last Statues of Antiquity. Oxford: Oxford
University Press.

Trigg, J. 2017. "Disputes on Baptism and the
Eucharist, 1521–1532." In *Martin Luther:
A Christian between Reforms and Modernity
(1517–2017)*, edited by A. Melloni, 295–311.
Berlin: De Gruyter.

Turner, V. 1969. *The Ritual Process: Structure
and Antistructure*. London: Aldine Transaction.

Turner, V. 1973. "The Center Out There:
Pilgrim's Goal." *History of Religions* 12: 191–230.

Turner, V. 1974. "Pilgrimage and Communitas."
Studia Missionalia 23: 305–27.

Turner, V., and E. Turner. 1978. *Image and
Pilgrimage in Christian Culture*. Oxford:
Blackwell.

Van Gennep, A. 1960. *The Rites of Passage*.
Chicago: University of Chicago Press.

Varner, E. 2004. *Mutilation and Transformation*. Leiden: Brill.

Vendries, C., and V. Péché. 2004. "Musique
romaine." In *Thesaurus Cultus und Rituum
Antiquorum*, vol. 2, edited by V. Lambrinoudakis and J. Balty, 397–415. Los Angeles: Getty
Publications.

Watts, J. 2018. *Sensing Sacred Texts*. Sheffield:
Equinox Publishing.

Watts, J. 2019. "Sensation and Metaphor in
Ritual Performance: The Example of Sacred
Texts." *Entangled Religions* 10. doi:10.13154/
er.10.2019.8365.

Wood, C. 2011. "The Votive Scenario." *RES:
Anthropology and Aesthetics* 59/60: 207–27.

Incense burner, Etruscan,
Faliscan, Hellenistic Period,
bronze, 18.4 × 36.2 cm,
The Metropolitan Museum
of Art, New York, Gift of
Alexander and
Helene Abraham, 2000.

Cover of a Censer, South
Netherlands, mid-12th century,
copper alloy, cast, engraved,
chased, punched, and gilded,
10.5 × 10.5 cm, The Metropolitan
Museum of Art, New York,
The Cloisters Collection, 1979

Censer with Pierced Geometric
Motifs, Germany, 12th century CE,
Copper alloy, 15 × 11.7 cm,
The Metropolitan Museum of Art,
New York, Rogers Fund, 1909.

Incense burners in the form
of a group of women seated
around a well head,
Greece, Tarentine,
2nd half of 4th century BCE,
height: 21cm, Terrakotta,
The Metropolitan Museum
of Art, New York,
Gift of Mary Jaharis, in honor
of Thomas P. Campbell, 2012.

BIOGRAPHIES

Claudia Brittenham is Professor of Art History at the University of Chicago. Her research focuses on the art of Mesoamerica, with interests in the materiality of art and the politics of style. She is the author of *Unseen Art: Making, Vision, and Power in Ancient Mesoamerica*, as well as *The Murals of Cacaxtla: The Power of Painting in Ancient Central Mexico; The Spectacle of the Late Maya Court: Reflections on the Murals of Bonampak* (with Mary Miller); and *Veiled Brightness: A History of Ancient Maya Color* (with Stephen Houston and colleagues). Her next book examines the interconnected Mesoamerican world.

Béatrice Caseau, born Chevallier, senior member at the Institut Universitaire de France, is professor of Byzantine history at Sorbonne University and former director of a research cluster Religions and society in the Mediterranean (2015–2021). Her research focuses on the religious and social history of the Byzantine world. Her recent publications include a book of collected essays on the senses, *Rituels religieux et sensorialité (Antiquité et Moyen âge)*, Milan, Silvana Editoriale, 2021, co-edited with E. Neri; a monograph on Byzantine food culture, entitled *Nourritures terrestres, nourritures célestes : la culture alimentaire à Byzance*, published in 2015.

Nathan S. Dennis is Associate Professor of Art History and Museum Studies at the University of San Francisco. He specializes in late antique and medieval art and theology, particularly of the Mediterranean and Middle East, including the material and visual traditions of Western Christian, Byzantine, Jewish, and Islamic cultures. He has published a number of articles and book chapters on the art, architecture, archaeology, and theology of early Christianity, especially baptisteries and the ritual of baptism, as well as cross-cultural interactions in late antique and Byzantine Africa. He is currently completing two book projects on early Christian baptismal space, an archaeological report on early Christian Carthage, and a themed journal volume on the arts of medieval northern Africa.

Jaś Elsner is Professor of Late Antique Art at Oxford and Humfry Payne Senior Research Fellow at Corpus Christi College. He is also Visiting Professor of Art and Religion at the University of Chicago and External Scientific Member at the Kunsthistorisches Institut in Florence. He has long worked on the visual, sensual and material culture of embodied religion, pilgrimage and the gaze in the European tradition from antiquity to modernity as well as on comparative issues in art and religion across Eurasia. His next book will be *Amaravati: Art and Buddhism in Ancient India*, London: Reaktion Books, 2024.

Beate Fricke was Professor for Medieval Art at the University of California, Berkeley, before joining the University of Bern (Switzerland) in 2017. Her research focuses on the history of sculpture, image theory and the objects as archives of a history of applied arts, materiality, knowledge transfer, and trade in the global "Middle Ages." Together with Finbarr Barry Flood she was awarded a collaborative research grant *Object Histories: Early Modern Flotsam* (ACLS), leading to the co-authored monograph *Tales Things Tell: Material Histories of Early Globalisms*, 2023. She is leading the research projects *Global Horizons in Pre-Modern Art* (ERC) and *The Inheritance of Looting: Medieval Trophies to Modern Museums* (SNF). She is founder and editor-in-chief of the journal *21: Inquiries into Art, History, and the Visual. Beiträge zur Kunstgeschichte und Visuellen Kultur*.

Milette Gaifman is the Andrew Downey Orrick Professor of Classics and History of Art at Yale University. A scholar of ancient art and archaeology, her work focuses primarily on Greek art of the Archaic and Classical periods. She is the author of *Aniconism in Greek Antiquity* (Oxford University Press, 2012); *The Art of Libation in Classical Athens* (Yale University Press, 2018); and co-editor of *Exploring Aniconism*, thematic issue of *Religion* 47, (2017); and *The Embodied Object in Classical Antiquity*, special issue of *Art History* (June 2018). Her current book project, *Classification and the History of Greek Art and Architecture* (forthcoming with Chicago University Press), is the revised and expanded version of the Louise Smith Bross Lectures she delivered at the Art Institute of Chicago and the Department of Art History at the University of Chicago in 2018. Additionally, she was the co-editor-in-chief of the *The Art Bulletin*, in 2020–2022. Her honors include the Samuel and Ronnie Heyman Prize for Outstanding Scholarly Publication from Yale College (2009), and the Gaddis Smith International Book Prize from the MacMillan Center at Yale (2013). She was a visiting scholar at Corpus Christi College, Oxford in 2008–2009, an invited professor at the University of Paris Diderot – Paris 7 in 2015, and the 2023 Geddes-Harrower Chair of Greek Art and Archaeology, a visiting professorship at the University of Aberdeen.

Margaret S. Graves is Adrienne Minassian Associate Professor of Islamic Art and Architecture at Brown University, specializing in the plastic arts and histories of craftsmanship in the Islamic world. Her 2018 monograph, *Arts of Allusion: Object, Ornament, and Architecture in Medieval Islam* (OUP), won the 2019 book prize of the International Center of Medieval Studies and the 2021 Karen Gould prize from the Medieval Academy of America. She is also editor, co-editor, and co-author of books on the art and material culture of the Islamic world and beyond, most recently *Making Modernity in the Islamic Mediterranean* (Indiana University Press, 2022), and *Ceramic Art* (Princeton University Press, 2023). Her research has been supported by, amongst others, the Institute for Advanced Study, Princeton, the Clark Art Institute, and the British Academy.

Kiersten Neumann is Curator at the Institute for the Study of Ancient Cultures Museum, as well as an Institute for the Study of Ancient Cultures Research Associate and Lecturer on Near Eastern Art and Archaeology in the Department of Art History, University of Chicago. She received her PhD from the University of California, Berkeley, and was awarded The American Academic Research Institute in Iraq Donny George Youkhana Dissertation Prize for the best U.S. doctoral dissertation on ancient Iraq. She is co-editor of *The Routledge Handbook of the Senses in the Ancient Near East* (2022) and has published numerous articles on sensory experience, ritualized practice, and material culture of the first millennium BCE, as well as museum practice, collecting histories, and the reception of Assyrian and Achaemenid art. Kiersten has held teaching appointments for courses on the art and archaeology of the ancient Near East, Egypt, and the Mediterranean, and has conducted archaeological fieldwork in Turkey and Greece. At the ISAC Museum, Kiersten has curated such exhibitions as "Persepolis: Images of an Empire" (2015), "Joseph Lindon Smith: The Persepolis Paintings" (2022), and "Making Sense of Marbles: Roman Sculpture at the OI" (2022–2023), and "Artifacts Also Die" (2023).

Yao Ning is currently Wissenschaftliche Mitarbeiterin in the department Gerhard Wolf at Kunsthistorisches Institut in Florenz, Max-Planck-Institut. She is working on her book project *Cylindrical Incense Burners (xiang tong 香筒) in Late Imperial China, 1500–1900* (working title) under the international research project "Bilderfahrzeuge: Aby Warburg's Legacy and the Future of Iconology." She earned a doctorate in East Asian Art History from Heidelberg University in 2013. From 2013 to 2014, she had a postdoctoral position at the Internationales Kolleg für Geisteswissenschaftliche Forschung "Fate, Freedom and Prognostication: Strategies for Coping with the Future in East Asia and Europe" at Erlangen-Nürnberg University; from 2016 to 2018, she was a CAHIM (Connecting Art Histories in the Museum, Staatliche Museen zu Berlin, Kunsthistorisches Institut in Florenz, Max-Planck Institut) postdoctoral fellow and was the curatorial assistant for the Berlin exhibition "Faces of China: Portrait Painting of the Ming and Qing Dynasties."

Karen B. Stern is Professor of History at Brooklyn College of the City University of New York. Her research deploys methods from fields of archaeology, anthropology, epigraphy, history, and religion to investigate the daily lives of Jews in antiquity, who inhabited areas around the Mediterranean through Arabia and Mesopotamia. She is author of *Inscribing Devotion and Death: Archaeological Evidence for Jewish Populations of North Africa* (Brill 2007); and *Writing on the Wall: Graffiti and the Forgotten Jews of Antiquity* (2018; paperback edn. 2020), winner of a 2020 Jordan Schnitzer Book Award through the Association for Jewish Studies (category: Jews and the Arts); and co-editor of *With the Loyal You Show Yourself Loyal: Essays on Relationships in the Hebrew Bible in Honor of Saul M. Olyan* (Atlanta: SBL Press, 2021). Her next book considers Jewish history through the senses.

Allison Stielau is Lecturer in Early Modern Art at University College London. Her research and teaching cover the art and material culture of Northern Europe and its contact zones between 1400 and 1700, and the afterlife of that period and its artifacts in later centuries. A particular focus has been precious metal and its ability to be melted down and transformed. Her studies on emergency currency, on the affective function of coins in fifteenth-century Germany, and on ingots made from Aztec metalwork during the conquest of Tenochtitlan have appeared in journals and edited volumes. More recent articles examine German silver cups and civic rituals of toasting, Renaissance mounts for ancient pottery, and early modern treasure hoards. Her in-progress book manuscript traces the fates of silver plate in the Thirty Years' War.

Incense Burner in the shape
of a sourtier's hat with scrolling
peonies, Edo period (1615–
1868), porcelain with celadon
glaze (Hizen ware, Nabeshima
type), 15.2 × 24.1 cm,
The Metropolitan Museum
of Art, New York, Gift of
Charles Stewart Smith, 1893.

Incense burner, Japan, 1650,
height: 22.9cm, clay with
a thin glaze (Bizen ware),
The Metropolitan Museum
of Art, New York, Gift of
Charles Stewart Smith, 1893.

GLOSSARY

THE ART OF SMOKE AND FIRE:
BRAZIERS AND CENSERS IN MESOAMERICAN TRADITION
Claudia Brittenham

Brasero	Spanish term for brazier.
Chahk	Maya rain deity.
Chicle	Latex produced by sapodilla trees (*Manilkara sp.*), used as incense, also an ingredient in chewing gum (Nahuatl *tzictli*).
Copal	Resins produced by *Bursera* and *Protium spp.*, used as incense (Nahuatl *copalli*).
Incensario	Spanish term for a fixed incense burner.
Hule	Rubber, a latex produced by *Castilla elastica* trees (Nahuatl *olli*).
Palygorskite	A kind of fine white clay used in the production of Maya blue pigment.
Pom	Mayan term for copal.
Quetzalcoatl	Central Mexican deity, literally "feathered serpent".
Sahumador	Spanish term for a censer.
Tlaloc	Central Mexican rain deity.
Tlapalnamacac	Vendor of colors, who sold copal in the Aztec marketplace
Tlemaitl	Literally "fire-hand," the Nahuatl term for a long-handled ladle censer.
Totiotzin	Literally "our honored divinity or divine forces," the contemporary Nahuatl term for the numinous surrounding us.
Xanitl	Zapotec term for a cylindrical censer in the form of a deity, common ca. 1200–1500 CE.
Yauhtli	Nahuatl term for a pungent herb burned as incense (*Tagetes lucida*).

CENSERS REAL AND IMAGINED:
JEWS AND INCENSE FROM ANTIQUITY THROUGH THE PRESENT
Karen Stern

Baraita	A tradition of oral interpretation, handed down through sources outside of the *Mishnah*. Teachings compiled in the Tosefta and other interpretive texts (Mekhilta, Sifre and Sifra) comprise this category.
Cairo Geniza	A geniza is a trove of texts, in Jewish traditions, which are too significant to discard (for instance, if they include the transcription of the divine name, or include binding legal agreements). The term Cairo Geniza specifically refers to collections of hundreds of thousands of texts, of multiple genres (letters, marriage documents, magical texts), compiled over hundreds of years, that were secreted into a space within the wall of the Ibn Ezra synagogue in Fustat (Coptic) Cairo. Discovery of the trove at the end of the nineteenth century transformed the study of ancient, medieval, and early modern Jewish history and traditions.
Kaf	Term from the Hebrew Bible that designates a ladle, sometimes used as an instrument of sacrificial cult in the Jerusalem Temple.
Karaites	Populations of Jews originating in the Levant in late antiquity, who followed the teachings of the Torah, but did not embrace the same interpretive traditions as did Jews who participated in rabbinic cultures. Animosity flared between rabbinic and Karaite Jews in antiquity through the Middle Ages, even if marriage contracts (*ketubot*) from the Cairo Geniza document marriages between Karaite and other Jews.

Lulab and Ethrog	Two distinct objects connected to the historical celebration of the festival of Sukkot (*Tabernacles*), including a palm branch (*lulab*), clustered with branches of other plant species, and a citron (*ethrog*). Epitaphs and synagogues from late antiquity frequently include representations of these objects.
Maḥtah	Shovel or similar multi-purpose implement described in biblical texts, which served to carry coals, ashes, or incense, or to clean the lamps of the menorah in the Jerusalem Temple.
Menorah	Lampstand with seven branches on a monumental base, which once stood in the Jerusalem Temple. Its image became emblematic of Jewish presence and identification throughout the ancient Mediterranean, particularly after the destruction of Herod's Temple. Scholars consider this to be a Jewish symbol par excellence in antiquity.
Mishnah	The *Mishnah* constitutes an early corpus of texts documenting oral traditions of rabbinic teachings, redacted by Rabbi Judah the Prince in Roman Palestine in the third century CE. The collection includes six orders (Zeraim-Seeds; Mo'ed-Seasons; Nashim-Women; Nezikim-Damages; Qodoshim-Holy Things—which is mostly, though not exclusively about Temple offerings; and Tohorot-Purities), which are themselves subdivided by tractates and chapters. Traditionally designated as the "Oral Torah," this written and redacted form constitutes the foundation of subsequent traditions of rabbinic interpretation, including the *Gemara* (Talmud).
Rabbinic culture	Rabbinic culture emerged in earlier centuries of Roman Judea and Palestine, also flourishing in Sassanian period Babylonia. In this culture, the study hall (*beit midrash*) acquired pride of place and rabbis served as authoritative figures; study and interpretation of the Torah and its real-life applications remained paramount. Only men were eligible to participate in these activities and associated hierarchies. While not all ancient Jews participated in rabbinic culture, those who did (today retroactively called rabbinic Jews) adhered to common modes of religious and scholarly discourse and participated in common cultures of learning.
Shofar	Horn of a ram or a wild goat, repurposed as a trumpet in Israelite, Judahite and Jewish traditions. Blasts from the shofar were used for ritual purposes, including announcement of sabbaths and the new moon. It was used in the Temple and in Jewish contexts through to the present day.
Talmud(s)	The Talmud, as it is commonly called, is one of two corpora of texts classified as such. One of these, developed and circulated in Mesopotamia and other regions of the Sassanian Persian Empire (the *Bavli*) was redacted between the fifth and seventh centuries CE; the Talmud from Roman Palestine (the *Yerushalmi*) dates to slightly earlier periods (fourth through sixth centuries CE). The *Bavli's* commentaries on the *Mishnah* are classified as *Gemara* and are surrounded by later commentaries of Rashi and other medieval scholars. Each Talmud offers commentary on the Mishnah, but the *Bavli* became more authoritative and central to subsequent Jewish learning traditions.

THE INCENSE BURNER IN GREEK ART
OF THE FIFTH CENTURY BCE
Milette Gaifman

Kanephoros	Basket bearer in ancient Greek procession.
Kanoun	Ancient Greek ritual basket.
Lekythos	Ancient Greek oil flask.
Omphalos	The navel of the world at Delphi.
Thymiaterion	Greek term for incense burner.

VESSELS OF HOLY FIRE:
THE CENSER AND THE WOMB OF THE MOTHER OF GOD
IN EARLY BYZANTINE AND COPTIC DEVOTION
Nathan Dennis

Apa	From the Coptic ⲁⲡⲁ ("father"); a reverential title given to saints, martyrs, and clergy in the Coptic tradition.
Cenobitic / Coenobitic	From the Greek κοινόβιος (κοινός, "common" + βίος, "life"); a term applied to monks living in community, as opposed to eremitic monasticism for solitary hermits. Although the term predates early Christian monasticism, it became widely associated with early monastic communities in Egypt, where St. Pachomius is thought to have created the first cenobitic community of monks at Tabennese, Egypt, in the early-fourth century.
Council of Ephesus	The third general (or ecumenical) council of the early Christian church, which convened at Ephesus on June 22, 431, under the authority of Emperor Theodosius II and with the support of Memnon, bishop of Ephesus, and Cyril, patriarch of Alexandria. The council sought to address the teachings of Nestorius, patriarch of Constantinople, who rejected the term *Theotokos* (Θεοτόκος, "God-Bearer") for the Virgin Mary and preached instead the term Christotokos (Χριστοτόκος, "Christ-Bearer"). Nestorius's accusers claimed that he also rejected the idea of Christ's hypostatic union (fully human and fully divine in one person) and asserted that two separate persons resided in Christ. The council branded Nestorius a heretic and excommunicated him, reasserted the Nicene Creed from the First Council of Nicaea in 325, and officially endorsed the term *Theotokos* for the Virgin Mary.
Galaktotrophousa	From the Greek Γαλακτοτροφούσα ("Milk-Giver"); a Byzantine/Orthodox iconographical type of the Virgin Mary nursing the infant Christ, similar to the *Virgo* or *Madonna Lactans* iconographical tradition in the Latin West.
Jacobite	From Jacob Baradaeus, bishop of Edessa in the mid- to late-sixth century; the term is loosely synonymous with the Syrian Orthodox Church. The term also generally alludes to a rejection of the canons of the Council of Chalcedon in 451, which declared that the personhood of the Incarnate Christ consisted of two natures (human and divine). Non-Chalcedonian Jacobites were branded "Monophysites" for asserting one unified nature for the personhood of Christ.
Lares (singular Lar)	Roman household protector gods, originally associated with the crossroads of cultivated fields but later incorporated into household worship to promote prosperity. They were often associated with the Penates, who were also household gods of protection and provision, and Vesta, goddess of the hearth.

Penates	From the Latin *penus* ("storehouse"), Penates were Roman household deities worshiped for their ability to protect and provide for the family, as well as for prosperity. They were sometimes used interchangeably with the Lares as gods of the hearth, alongside other household deities such as Vesta.
Pseudepigrapha	From the Greek ψευδεπίγραφα (ψευδής, "false" + ἐπιγραφή, "inscription"); writings falsely attributed to known authors or historical figures, often for the purpose of bolstering authority through name recognition and reputation. The term is often applied to the body of ancient Jewish texts written in Greek that were not included in the Hebrew Bible or the Septuagint.
Septuagint	From the Latin *Septuaginta* ("seventy") and sometimes abbreviated as LXX, the Septuagint is one of the earliest and most influential Greek translations of the Hebrew Bible (Old Testament). According to Jewish tradition, which is preserved in the *Letter of Aristeas*, Pharaoh Ptolemy II Philadelphus authorized a translation of the Hebrew Bible into Greek for the Library of Alexandria in the third century BCE, and he commissioned 72 translators for the project. The translation was likely completed by the mid- to late-second century BCE and would come to be one of the most widely used biblical translations in antiquity.
Theotokos	From the Greek Θεοτόκος (Θεός, "God" + τόκος, "child-birth"), the term is generally translated as "God-Bearer" or "Mother of God." The title was applied to the Virgin Mary by early Christian theologians and officially endorsed as an honorific for Mary at the Council of Ephesus in 431. Since Christ was considered both God and man in early Christology, the term *Theotokos* was adopted for the Virgin to reflect the divine nature of the Incarnation.
Typikon	From the Greek Τυπικόν ("following the order"); a manual in the Orthodox Christian tradition that establishes the order of liturgical services throughout the year. It can also include rules for monastic communities.
Vulgate	From the Latin *vulgata* ("common" or "popular"), the Vulgate was a Latin translation of the Hebrew and Greek scriptures of the Bible. The project was managed primarily by St. Jerome under the authority of Pope Damasus I at the end of the fourth century, with other translators and redactors completing the text by the early-fifth century.

BETWEEN MATTER AND MAGIC, OVER LAND AND SEA:
A MIDDLE EASTERN CENSER IN SWEDEN
Margaret Graves

Bakhūr or bukhūr	Incense, sometimes referring specifically to frankincense (Arabic).
Bismillah	The titular name of the phrase *bi-ismillāh al-raḥmān al-raḥīm*, "In the name of God, the compassionate, the merciful." One of the most important phrases in Islam, it prefaces all but one of the suras (chapters) of the Qur'an and is traditionally invoked at the start of many prayers and actions.
Buhurdan	Incense burner (Turkish).
Cold working	Incised ornamentation and/or inscriptions made directly into cast and cooled bronze (as opposed to being made into the mold before casting).
Geomancy	Divination from tossed handfuls of soil or rocks, or from marks on the ground.

Greater Syria	Historical region of the eastern Mediterranean littoral, corresponding to the lands known in Arabic as *al-shām* and largely synonymous with the Levant.
Hadith	The collected traditions of the Prophet Muhammad. These are reports of the things the Prophet said and did in his lifetime, as transmitted through chains of verified narrators.
Khurasan	Historical region comprising much of what is now north-western Iran and northern Afghanistan.
Kīmiyā'	Alchemy (Arabic).
Kufic	An angular form of the Arabic script, used primarily in the early Islamic period for architectural inscriptions and Qur'an manuscripts.
Libanomancy	Divination from incense smoke.
Linear Kufic	An angular form of the Arabic script that disregards the normal conventions of ligature and letter separation. Used for magical inscriptions, especially on seals, in the early to medieval Islamic periods.
Lost-wax casting	Complex, multistage technique for producing cast objects in copper-alloy.
Mabkhara or mibkhara	Incense burner (Arabic).
Majmar or mijmara	Lit. "place of burning," i.e. incense burner (Arabic).
Mesopotamia	Historical region of the Tigris-Euphrates river system, corresponding to modern-day Iraq plus parts of Syria, Turkey, and Kuwait.
Nīranjāt	Rituals and incantations performed as part of the occult sciences (Arabic).
Rūs	Norsemen, Vikings (Arabic).
Sabians	A term used in Arabic sources to denote pagan cultures that practiced astral worship and natural philosophy, often associated with astral cults in what is now northern Syria.
Siḥr	Magic (Arabic).
Ṭilasm	Talismans (Arabic).
Ūd	Aloeswood or agarwood. Aromatic resin of the Aquilaria, one of the most common substances used for censing in the Islamic world (Arabic and Persian).
Ūd-sūz	Lit. "aloes burner," i.e. incense burner (Persian).
Ulūm al-ghayb	Occult sciences (Arabic).

VISUALIZING THE INCENSE SMOKE:
THE PORTRAIT OF THE MING EMPEROR XIZONG (1605–1627)
Yao Ning

Nei dan 內丹	Internal alchemy, and *waidan* 外丹, the external alchemy: two main practices in Chinese Daoist alchemy. *Neidan*, literally internal elixir, emerging later than *waidan* in the Song dynasty (960–1279), addresses the way that one can produce an elixir within the human body. *Waidan*, literally external elixir, is concerned with laboratory practice, where drugs made of natural substances are mostly used.
Pure Land paradise	A term derived from Pure Land Buddhism, whose goal is to achieve rebirth in a Buddha's Pure Land or a Pure Land paradise. Practices such as meditation, Buddha recitation (*nianfo* 念佛) are some of the relevant tools for achieving the rebirth.
Qi 氣	Steam, breath, vital force or vital energy, which makes up and binds together all things in the cosmos.

AFTERWORD: CENSERS AND SENSATION
Jaś Elsner

Antistructure	A sociocultural structure that intentionally counteracts the mainstream.
Communitas	As understood by anthropologists (especially in the wake of Victor Turner, 1920–1983), an unstructured state in which all members of a community are equal allowing them to share a common experience, usually through a rite of passage.
Thymiaterion	A static standing incense burner, used across the Mediterranean and Western Asia since antiquity.

Censer, Swiss or German, before 1842, silver, 24.6 × 14.6 cm, The Metropolitan Museum of Art, New York, Gift of J. Pierpont Morgan, 1917.

Tripod censer, China, glass, 7.3 × 10.8 cm, The Metropolitan Museum of Art, New York, Purchase, The Vincent Astor Foundation and Barbara and William Karatz Gifts, 2020.

Censer in form of a rooster perched on a rooftop, Japan, 1700, stoneware covered with a thin glaze showing lustre (Bizen ware), 13.3 × 24.4 cm, The Metropolitan Museum of Art, New York, Gift of Mrs. V. Everit Macy, 1923.

INDEX

Incense burner, China, pottery
(Jun ware),11.4 × 17.5cm,
The Metropolitan Museum
of Art, New York, Gift of
Mrs. Samuel T. Peters, 1926.

Ritual incense burner,
6th century, Pakistan
(ancient region of Gandhara),
The Metropolitan Museum
of Art, New York,
Samuel Eilenberg Collection,
Ex Coll.: Columbia University,
Purchase, Mrs. Arthur
Hays Sulzberger Gift, 1987.

IMPRINT

Published by:
Hirmer Publishers
Bayerstrasse 57-59
80335 Munich
Germany
www.hirmerpublishers.com

Edited by: Beate Fricke
Authors and Contributors: Claudia Brittenhan, Béatrice Caseau &
Claire-Marie Caseau, Nathan Dennis, Jaś Elsner, Beate Fricke,
Milette Gaifman, Margaret Graves, Kiersten Neumann, Yao Ning,
Karen Stern, Allison Stielau

Senior Editor Hirmer Publishers: Elisabeth Rochau-Shalem
Project Manager Hirmer Publishers: Rainer Arnold

Line-editing: Sasha Rossmann
Production coordination: Zumrad Ilyasova
Image coordination: Joanne Luginbühl
Copy-editing: Jonathan Hoare
Design and visual editing: Kaj Lehmann
Pre-press: Reproline Mediateam, Munich
Printing & binding: Druckerei Vogl, Zorneding
Printed in Germany

Paper: Munken Print White 1,5 Vol. 80 g/m2
Typeface: Cigars, Jan Horčík & Filip Matějíček

The production of this publication has been supported by the
European Research Council.

erc

The Deutsche Nationalbibliothek lists this publication in the
Deutsche Nationalbibliografie; detailed bibliographic data is available on
the Internet at http://www.dnb.de.

ISBN: 978-3-7774-3948-8

Yuan porcelain incense burner,
Inner Mongolia Museum, Hohhot,
China.